THE SENTENCE

THE PARAGRAPH

THE COMPOSITION

THE SPECIAL COMPOSITION

LANGUAGE RESOURCES

FOURTH EDITION

McGraw-Hill

HANDBOOK
of
ENGLISH

HARRY SHAW

formerly Director, Workshops in
Composition, New York University,
and Lecturer in English,
Columbia University

McGraw-Hill Book Company

New York St. Louis San Francisco
Auckland Bogotá Düsseldorf Johannesburg
London Madrid Mexico Montreal
New Delhi Panama Paris São Paulo
Singapore Sydney Tokyo Toronto

Acknowledgments

We wish to thank the following for permission to reprint copyrighted materials:

The excerpt from "The Pretensions of Science" by Hugh Stevenson Tigner, copyright 1938 by Christian Century Foundation, reprinted by permission from the September 14, 1938 issue of *The Christian Century*. The excerpt from *Looking Back* by Joyce Maynard; copyright © 1972, 1973 by Joyce Maynard, reprinted by permission of Doubleday & Company, Inc. The excerpt from *My Sister Eileen* by Ruth McKenney, reprinted by permission of Harcourt Brace Jovanovich, Inc. The excerpt from *This I Remember* by Eleanor Roosevelt, reprinted by permission of Harper & Row, Publishers, Inc. The excerpt from *The Mind in the Making* by James Harvey Robinson, copyright 1921 by Harper & Row, Publishers, Inc., reprinted by permission of the publisher. The excerpt from *A Mencken Chrestomathy* by H. L. Mencken, copyright 1949, reprinted by permission of Alfred A. Knopf, Inc. The excerpt from *Education for Freedom* by Robert Hutchins, copyright 1943, reprinted by permission of Louisiana State University Press. The excerpt from *Love and Liberation* by Lisa Hobbs, copyright © 1971, used with permission of McGraw-Hill Book Company. The excerpt from *Blackberry Winter* by Margaret Mead, copyright © 1972 by Margaret Mead, reprinted by permission of William Morrow & Company, Inc. The excerpts from "Life and Birth in New Guinea" by Joyce S. Mitchell and "What It Would Be Like If Women Win" by Gloria Steinem, copyright © Ms. Magazine Corporation, reprinted with permission. The excerpt from "Topics," copyright © 1960 by The New York Times Company. Reprinted by permission. The excerpt from *The Sea Around Us*, Revised Edition, by Rachel L. Carson, copyright © 1961 by Rachel L. Carson, reprinted by permission of Oxford University Press, Inc. The excerpt from *A Remarkable and Marvelous Sex* by Estelle Ramey, reprinted by permission of Estelle Ramey. The excerpts from *How to Read a Book* by Mortimer J. Adler, *The Secret of Santa Vittoria* by Robert Crichton, and *The Organization Man* by William Whyte (copyright © 1956), reprinted by permission of Simon & Schuster, a division of Gulf & Western Corporation. The excerpt from *The Grapes of Wrath* by John Steinbeck, copyright 1939, reprinted by permission of The Viking Press, Inc.

2345678910 MUMU 98

Library of Congress Cataloging in Publication Data

Shaw, Harry, date
  McGraw-Hill handbook of English.

  Includes index.
  SUMMARY: A comprehensive handbook of English grammar, usage, diction, and composition with general review exercises.
  1. English language—Grammar—1950– 2. English language—Composition and exercises. [1. English language—Grammar. 2. English language—Composition and exercises] I. Title. II. Title: Handbook of English.
PE1112.S5 1977   808'.042   77-10794
ISBN 0-07-056506-6

Foreword

The *McGraw-Hill Handbook of English*, Fourth Edition, is designed to help you discover, develop, and refine the skills you need to meet the speaking and writing demands of a lifetime. Its fundamental objective is to provide training in correct, clear, effective, and appropriate writing and rewriting. To this end, the book now in your hands describes American English as it is employed by careful, accurate speakers and writers—and by others not always either careful or accurate. It states the facts about American usage of the English language that educated people should know, whether or not they wish to adopt and follow them in part or in whole.

Throughout, the *McGraw-Hill Handbook of English* tries to make clear distinctions between *grammar* and *usage*, that is, between (1) a systematic description of words and their structures, patterns, and relationships in, say, a sentence, and (2) the ways in which Americans actually use their language in various situations. The handbook takes the position that the writing of students is normally and rightly expected to be different from informal speech, but it also recognizes that the style of one's writing and speech should be appropriate to each occasion and modified as needed by differing purposes.

This handbook is not rigid and inflexible in its prescriptive rules concerning usage, but neither does it advocate a laissez-faire, or "anything goes," attitude. Such a "middle of the road" approach may appear reactionary to some and overly liberal to others. Staying in the middle of the road is indeed fatal on a highway, but not, perhaps, on the highway to better speech and composition.

The author believes that the writing needs of most students are best served by genuinely solid work, under teacher supervision, in thinking, planning, writing, and rewriting. Learning to think clearly and to write correctly and appropriately are worthwhile intellectual pursuits that are valuable not only in composition classes but in all intellectual endeavors.

This new edition offers a thorough reworking of previous editions. Addition, deletion, emendation, reorganization, and expansion are evident throughout.

The principal changes in the fourth edition occur in five major areas: (1) Reorganization to achieve a more logical presentation of material, visible especially in the Diction unit. Regrouping is also evident in the combining of, for example, diagraming with sentences, semantics with diction, and thinking with writing. (2) Expansion of the composition unit, especially sections on revision. (3) A refining and general tightening of the text to simplify basic definitions and to achieve greater clarity throughout. (4) Many new exercises, including chapter review exercises. (5) A completely new and more functional design that makes the handbook even easier to use as a reference tool.

In short, this edition of the *McGraw-Hill Handbook of English* has been thoroughly revised and updated. Yet it would be far less helpful than I hope it is without the thoughts, suggestions, and contributions of others. My indebtedness is greatest to Brian McLaughlin, editor of the third edition, and to Laura Mongello, editor of the present one. These two capable and dedicated professionals, both with previous classroom experience, have added immeasurably to the content and style of the current edition. The roll call of others who have aided along the line is too lengthy for listing here, including, as it does, former students, teachers who have used previous editions, and colleagues in various schools and colleges. Among these, mention must be made at least of Philip Burnham, St. Paul's School, Concord, New Hampshire; Dr. Hans J. Gottlieb, of Upper Black Eddy, Pennsylvania, formerly of New York University; Robert Morris, St. George's School, Newport, Rhode Island; Margaret Casey, formerly of the Bethesda-Chevy Chase High School, Maryland; Dudley C. Enos, George Washington High School, Denver, Colorado; Mary Ellen Bridges, Central High School, Tulsa, Oklahoma; George S. Wykoff, formerly of Purdue University. Special thanks are due to Roderic Botts, Idaho State University, for his guidance on this revision and his contribution to the Teacher's Manual. I wish to express my gratitude to Winnie Leo and Nancy Gage, who have performed many secretarial and typing chores with loyalty and capability.

HARRY SHAW

Contents

THE SENTENCE 279

THE PARAGRAPH 341

THE COMPOSITION 381

THE SPECIAL COMPOSITION 443

LANGUAGE RESOURCES 481

Grammar

A **grammar** is a series of statements about the way a particular language works. English grammar is "the English way of saying things." Grammar is concerned with the structure of a language—with the forms of words and the ways they are used and arranged. Thus defined, grammar is the scientific *description* of a language.

It is true that *what* we have to say is more interesting than a study of the language itself. But grammar is worth studying because an understanding of it can help us to express our ideas clearly and effectively. Unclear writing and sloppy sentence structure can often be traced to an inadequate understanding of grammar.

The grammar section of this book is designed to give you a clear and working understanding of how to write effective sentences. You simply cannot put pen to paper with confidence if you do not have a sure sense of the sentence.

When you begin to write sentences, you become impressed with a basic difference between speaking and writing. Writing is a more formal way to communicate than speaking. In ordinary conversation you can rely on tone of voice, surrounding circumstances, what the hearer knows of you and the subject, and the opportunity to explain if your meaning is not clear.

However, a written text is usually read at another time, in another place, by a reader who is alone. You cannot rely on the easygoing give-and-take that makes talking a pleasant pastime. Instead, all information that you want to be communicated must come from the words on the page. To be sure your reader will understand you and respond to what you are saying, you must know *how to* write. The words *how to* involve the mastery of practical guidelines that have been evolving since our alphabet was invented.

That everyone should be able to read and write is now one of the central assumptions of our economic, political, and social system. Try to get a decent job, cast an intelligent vote, or run for public office and you will see how essential it is to read and write well.

You *must* be literate. You will be judged by the literate character of your speaking and your writing. And literate writing, among many other things, is grammatical. This book attempts to present an approach to English grammar that will give you a clear sense of how English sentences are written.

Sentences are composed of words. Grammar classifies words as parts of speech. They are grouped according to the purpose they serve, or how they convey meaning *as words:*

Naming words	nouns and pronouns
Asserting words	verbs
Modifying words	adjectives and adverbs
Joining words	conjunctions and prepositions
Exclamatory words	interjections

But words work together to convey meaning. Grammar is also concerned with explaining how the parts of speech can be grouped together in sentences. Structures involving groups of words, that is, *phrases* and *clauses*, are essential to mature sentence construction, and so we must see how parts of speech are placed with one another to produce these structures.

Finally, words take on basic functions in the sentence, which is the central unit of meaning in all writing. How the parts of speech function in the sentence as a whole is what grammar is all about.

G1. Nouns

G1a. A NOUN NAMES A PERSON, PLACE, THING, OR IDEA.

Notice how the italicized nouns in these sentences perform their function of naming:

> *Albert* met his *sister*'s best *friend*, a superb *swimmer*. (persons)
> They were standing at the *corner* of *Maple* and *Third* in the downtown *section* of *Crystal City*. (places)

Alice was carrying her *coat, gloves,* and *scarf.* (things)
They were on their way to the *Homecoming Dance,* which was held every *fall,* usually in *November* before the *game* with Central. (events and points in time)
His *pride* suffered because of his *forgetfulness.* (qualities)
The family *honor* had been preserved. (general idea)

The markers, or characteristics, of nouns can be summarized as follows:

1. Nouns are usually preceded by such words as *the, a, an, my, your, his, her, some, each, every, their, this,* and *that.*

2. Certain nouns have characteristic endings— *–al, –tion, –ness, –ment, –ure, –dom, –ism, –ance,* for example—which distinguish them from corresponding verbs or adjectives: *arrive, arrival; refine, refinement; depart, departure; soft, softness; real, realism; rely, reliance; wise, wisdom; create, creation.*

3. Nouns and identically spelled verbs may sometimes be differentiated by accent. The first member in each of these pairs of words is a noun, the second a verb: *per' mit, per mit'; rec' ord, re cord'; sur' vey, sur vey'; sub' ject, sub ject'.*

4. Nouns are found in set positions, such as before a verb (a *lion* roars), after a verb (wash the *car*), or after a preposition (working for *money*).

5. Nouns may be singular or plural in *number.* The plural of most English nouns is obtained by adding *–s* or *–es* to the singular form: *girls, boys, trees, fields, beaches, peaches.* Some nouns have only one form for both the singular and the plural: *deer, sheep, moose.* Some nouns have irregular plurals: *ox, oxen; mouse, mice; wife, wives.*

6. Nouns have four *genders.* They may be *masculine* (*man, boy*), *feminine* (*girl, woman*), or *neuter* (*chalk, dirt*). Also, when a noun may be either masculine or feminine, it is said to have a *common* gender (*teacher, companion, friend*).

7. Nouns have three *cases: subject* case, *object* case, and *possessive* case. In English, nouns have a common form for both the subject and the object case. An apostrophe is used to designate a noun in the possessive case: *Joe's, ship's, neighbor's, students'.*

G1b. KINDS OF NOUNS

Nouns are classified in several ways: *common* or *proper; abstract* or *concrete;* and *collective.*

A **common noun** is a name given to the members of a class, that is, to words designating types of persons, things, or places. All common nouns can be recognized as such because they do not begin with capital letters: *dozen, child, girls, road, farm, town, city, box, structure.*

A **proper noun** names a particular member of a class; it *does* begin with a capital: *Rover, Michele, Sunny Acres, Kennedy Freeway, Chicago, Jack Dempsey, Eiffel Tower.*

An **abstract noun** is the name of a quality or general idea that cannot be felt by the senses: *faith, intelligence, grace, happiness, courage, fear.*

A **concrete noun** names a material (tangible) thing that can be perceived by one or more of the senses: *fire, aroma, book, hamburger, stone, rose, record, candy.*

A **collective noun** names a group of individuals or items. Although it refers to more than one, it is singular in form: *pair, committee, squad, team, congress, species, crowd, army, crew, assembly.* ~~takes singular verbs~~

Can you name a noun that can fit in three or more classes or compose a sentence using all five classes?

EXERCISE 1

Write down all the nouns in the following sentences. Be prepared to discuss in class the classification (common, proper, concrete, abstract, or collective) of each noun.

1. They saw a marvelous performance at the theater.
2. That is a delightful perfume that you are wearing.
3. All generalizations are false.
4. Your daughter told me that she wants to be a chemist someday.
5. Which lawn mower do you prefer?
6. Snoopy has become a national hero; Linus is also popular.
7. The police officer opened up the hydrant, and we then had a good time splashing around in the water.
8. I shall never forget what's his name; he was quite a fellow.

9. Tessie was born with sparkling eyes that reflected the merriment in her soul.
10. Autumn is my favorite season, although I am also very fond of summer; spring and winter have never appealed to me.

2 sent. joined by a semi colon = Compound Sent.

G2. Pronouns

G2a. A PRONOUN ACTS IN THE PLACE OF ONE OR MORE NOUNS.

It is difficult to define the pronoun because this part of speech includes groups of quite different words. In general, though, a **pronoun** is a word that can be replaced by a noun in most sentences. Both nouns and pronouns can act as the subjects and objects of verbs. Many pronouns are like nouns in having plural forms and a possessive case formed with –*s*.

G2b. KINDS OF PRONOUNS

Pronouns are classified as:

personal	reflexive
relative	intensive
demonstrative	indefinite
interrogative	reciprocal

Personal Pronouns

A **personal pronoun** refers to an individual or individuals. Of all pronouns, this group causes the greatest difficulty. Personal pronouns have thirty case forms, some of which include all genders and some with special forms for feminine, masculine, and neuter.

Personal pronouns also bear the labels of first person, second person, third person. First person pronouns indicate the speaker or writer, either singular or plural. Second person pronouns indicate the person or persons spoken to, with identical forms for singular and plural. Gender (or sex) is the same for all first and second person pronouns. Third person pronouns indicate the person or persons spoken of or written about. Third person pronouns involve considerations of number and gender, as shown in this table:

Singular			
	Nominative (Subject Case)	*Possessive (or Genitive)*	*Objective (Object Case)*
1st person	I	my, mine	me
2nd person	you	your, yours	you
masculine	he	his	him
feminine	she	her, hers	her
neuter	it	its	it
Plural			
1st person	we	our, ours	us
2nd person	you	your, yours	you
3rd person (all genders)	they	their, theirs	them

Relative Pronouns

A **relative pronoun** relates or connects the clause it introduces to an independent clause (see Section G8). Specifically, a relative pronoun connects an adjective clause to an antecedent (the noun or pronoun to which a pronoun refers or for which it is substituted).

> The candidate *who* wants to become President must campaign vigorously.
> The used car *which* was badly in need of repair, broke down yesterday.
> The novel *that* I read has since become a best seller.

Each of these relative pronouns has an antecedent (*candidate, car,* and *novel*), and each introduces a subordinate clause.

The relative pronoun forms—*who, whose, whom, which, that*—have no specific gender or number. Their having gender or

being singular or plural depends, instead, upon their antecedents. The choice of a relative pronoun is also largely determined
by its antecedent. *Who, whose,* and *whom* are used to refer to
persons. *Which* is used to refer to inanimate objects, animals, and
groups of persons. *That* may refer to either things or persons.

Who, *which,* and *that* are frequently used relative pronouns;
whoever, whenever, whichever, and *whatever* are less often used.

Demonstrative Pronouns

A **demonstrative pronoun** points out and identifies a noun or
another pronoun. The important demonstrative pronouns are
this and *that* (singular), *these* and *those* (plural), and *such* (singular or plural).

> *This* is the woman I told you about in my letter.
> *That* is the school I attended for six years.
> *These* are the missing articles.
> *Those* are the ideals we all admire.
> *Such* a newspaper and *such* magazines are worth reading.

Interrogative Pronouns

An **interrogative pronoun** introduces a question. The important
interrogative pronouns are *who, whom, whose, which, what,* and
occasionally *whoever, whichever,* and *whatever.*

> *Who* has asked you to go hiking?
> *Whom* did they expect to play in the finals?
> *Which* of the crabgrass experts did they recommend?
> *What* can I say, dear, after I say I'm sorry?
> *Whose* Corvette has the best chance of winning the race?
> *Whatever* do you mean by that remark?

Reflexive Pronouns

A **reflexive pronoun** is used to refer to the subject of a sentence or
clause. It is a compound of one of the personal pronouns plus *–self*
or *–selves: myself, yourself, herself, himself, itself, ourselves, your-
selves, themselves.*

> Did you burn *yourself?*
> He gave *himself* a present for his birthday.
> They appointed *themselves* to the committee.

Intensive Pronouns

An **intensive pronoun** is used to draw particular attention to a noun. Intensives take the same forms as reflexives.

> We must give the same rights to the workers *themselves.*
> The doctor *herself* examined the X rays.

Indefinite Pronouns

An **indefinite pronoun** is less specific in reference and less exact in meaning than other pronouns. It is often difficult or impossible to pin down a precise antecedent for an indefinite pronoun. Among the more frequently used are *all, another, any, anyone, anything, everybody, everyone, everything, few, many, nobody, none, one, several, some,* and *each.* The pronoun *one,* its compound forms, and the compound forms built on the element *–body* form the possessive in the same way as nouns (*anybody's, everyone's*).

Reciprocal Pronouns

A **reciprocal pronoun** completes an interchange of action. *Each other* and *one another* are the only reciprocal pronouns:

> The two teams complimented *each other.*
> The opposing lines scowled at *one another.*

EXERCISE 2

Certain pronouns are italicized in the sentences below. On a separate sheet, classify each as one of the eight kinds of pronouns.

1. That battered chemistry book is *yours.*
2. *Which* of the sailboats crossed the finish line first?
3. *All* the sea gulls hovered above the pier, waiting for scraps of fish.
4. *Whom* did you vote for, Mr. Peepers?
5. Mother, I want to do it *myself!*
6. Do you know what *it* means to be down and out?
7. As for the flamingos, *theirs* is not to reason why; *theirs* is but to do or fly.
8. *Few* of us remember streetcars on State Street.
9. The passengers on the flight were friendly to *one another.*
10. *This* is a gross error of judgment, Colonel Arnold.

EXERCISE 3

On a separate sheet of paper substitute a noun for each of the pronouns in these sentences:

1. Please give the hamburger patties to him.
2. That is the building referred to in the catalog.
3. Be kind to one another.
4. Edgar Blossom himself attended the concert.
5. Elena Gumbody asked them to roll back the carpet.
6. Those in the top balcony can listen to the music on the radio.
7. Anybody can see that the game is lost.
8. For whom are you preparing the dessert?
9. My friend and she have had a violent argument.
10. Nearly everybody left the theater before the play was finished.
11. Denise waited for her brother to arrive.

G3. Verbs and Verbals

G3a. A VERB EXPRESSES ACTION OR MAKES A STATEMENT.

Through internal changes or the addition of various endings, verbs specify actions or events that take place in time. Again, a **verb** may be defined as a word that expresses action, state of being, or relation between two things. It functions as the main element of a predicate (what is said about the subject). When altered in form, it can indicate tense, tone, voice, mood, and agreement with its subject or object.

> By next week, the Johnsons *will have moved* away.
> I *was* ready before you *arrived.*
> Sue *will work* this summer at a new job.
> The Johnsons *moved* to their new home last week.
> I *shall be* ready when you *arrive.*
> Sue *worked* all summer for the community newspaper.

G3b. KINDS OF VERBS

Verbs are classified as *transitive, intransitive,* and *linking.*

Transitive Verbs

A **transitive verb** takes an object—a noun or pronoun that tells *who* or *what* completes the action of the verb.

> Janice *hit the ball*.
> Linda *has a part-time job* on weekends.
> The farmer *planted three rows* of corn near the barn.

A transitive verb shows the relationship between the subject and the object—the noun that follows the verb. In a sentence such as *Juan hit the ball*, *hit* expresses the nature of the relationship between *Juan* and *ball*.

Intransitive Verbs

An **intransitive verb** does not take an object.

> The fullback *ran* directly through the center of the line.
> Adelaide *walked* slowly down the street.

Many verbs can be used in either a transitive or intransitive sense.

> We *read* the *news* with great care. (transitive)
> We *read* until late at night. (intransitive)
> I *won* the first *set*. (transitive)
> I *won* easily. (intransitive)

Linking Verbs

A **linking verb** (such as *become, seem,* or *appear*) shows the relationship between the subject and the noun that follows it. The noun that follows is called a *predicate noun*. Frequently, a linking verb expresses the relationship between the subject and an adjective following it. The adjective that follows it is sometimes called the *predicate adjective*. (Linking verbs are discussed more fully in Section U6.)

G3c. CHARACTERISTICS OF VERBS

Verbs have certain characteristics, as described below:

1. English verbs have a base form. The base form of a verb is

called the *infinitive* form. It is sometimes preceded by the word *to*.

> to run, to walk, to cook, to evaporate

2. Verbs in English have four *forms*. These forms have certain inflectional endings. (See Section U5.)

Present Tense—The present tense of English verbs is the same as the base form.

> to run, *run;* to walk, *walk;* to hide, *hide*

Past Tense—The past tense of English verbs varies, depending upon whether the verb is *regular* or *irregular*. In regular verbs, the past tense is formed by adding the ending *–ed* to the base form.

> walk, *walked;* invent, *invented;* originate, *originated*

The past tense of irregular verbs differs from word to word and must be learned individually. Most past tense forms of irregular verbs are familiar to native speakers of English.

> throw, *threw;* tear, *tore;* say, *said;* go, *went*

Past Participle—The past participle of regular verbs is identical to the past tense.

> organize, organized, *organized;* arrange, arranged, *arranged;* conduct, conducted, *conducted;* solve, solved, *solved*

The past participle of irregular verbs differs from word to word and must be learned individually. It is always the form that makes sense with the verb *have:* have *gone,* have *written,* have *torn.*

> run, (have) *run;* sing, (have) *sung;* draw, (have) *drawn;* do, (have) *done*

Present Participle—English verbs also have a present participle form that is obtained by adding *–ing* to the base form.

> have, *having;* go, *going;* rain, *raining;* speak, *speaking*

3. Verbs in English have one other characteristic inflectional ending. When a verb in the present tense follows either the words *he, she,* or *it* or a noun that may be substituted for *he,*

she, or *it*, the letter *–s* (or *–es* with some verbs) is added to the base form.

sing, sing*s;* run, run*s;* go, go*es;* laugh, laugh*s*

4. In the present tense, an English verb changes its inflectional ending when the subject changes from singular to plural.

A bird *sings.* Birds *sing.* Joe *goes.* Bill and Joe *go.*
Sara *plays* the piano. The girls *play* the piano.

5. Certain *prefixes* and *suffixes* are used with verbs. The prefixes *en–* and *be–* are often used with verbs.

*en*force, *en*able, *en*title, *en*tangle, *en*tail
*be*come, *be*friend, *be*head, *be*stir, *be*moan

The suffixes *–(i)fy*, *–ate*, and *–ize* commonly signal verbs.

test*ify*, ver*ify*, clar*ify*, cod*ify*
segreg*ate*, supplic*ate*, oper*ate*, domestic*ate*
civil*ize*, colon*ize*, urban*ize*, symbol*ize*

6. *Verb markers*, or *auxiliaries*, frequently signal verbs. The most common auxiliaries in English are *be* (and all its forms), *have, do, can, could, shall, should, will, would, may, might, must,* and *ought.* (See Section U7.)

G3d. VOICE

The voice of a verb indicates whether the grammatical subject of the verb *acts* or is *acted upon.*

A verb is in the **active voice** when the subject of the verb *actually performs* the action indicated by the verb.

We *built* a large house in the country.

The engineers *have developed* new types of electric refrigerators.

The Marshall Plan *helped* reconstruct Europe.

A verb is in the **passive voice** when it expresses an action *performed upon* its subject. When a verb appears in the passive voice, the actual performer of the action appears either in a prepositional phrase at the end of the sentence or is not specifically named at all. The actual performer of the action of passive verbs can always be determined by converting the verb to the active voice.

> The criminal *was apprehended* by the police. (passive)
> The police *apprehended* the criminal. (active)
> The firm *was run* by one woman. (passive)
> One woman *ran* the firm. (active)
> The money *was found* in the subway. (passive)
> (The man) *found* the money in the subway. (active)

NOTE: The passive voice always consists of some form of the verb *be* followed by the past participle form of the verb.

G3e. MOOD

Mood is a characteristic of verbs that reveals the attitude of the speaker or writer to what she or he is expressing. This attitude may be one of certainty or uncertainty, emphasis, hesitancy, wish, or command. The three moods of English verbs—*indicative, subjunctive,* and *imperative*—are discussed in Section U9.

G3f. TENSE

The **tense** of a verb indicates the time of the action or the state of being expressed by the verb—past, present, or future. Tense can be thought of as *simple* or *progressive*. The simple tenses (*past, present,* and *future*) designate actions or states of being that have occurred or existed in the past, that are occurring or existing now, or that will occur or exist in the future. The progressive tenses (*present perfect, past perfect,* and *future perfect*) indicate continuing action in either present, past, or future time. (See Section U8.)

G3g. VERBALS

Verbals are verb forms that are not used as verbs but as nouns, adjectives, or adverbs. Verbals are classified as *participles, gerunds,* and *infinitives.*

Participles

A **participle** is a verb form that is used as an *adjective*. A *present participle* (referring to present time) always ends in *–ing*: *Laughing*, Rona picked up the plate. A *past participle* (referring to past time) ends in *–ed* when the verb is regular: *Delighted*, Berta and Luis accepted the invitation.

NOTE: The present and past participle forms are usually used as part of a verb phrase: Hazel *was going* to the convention. Randy *had talked* to the coach. It is when they stand alone, without a helping verb, that they function as verbals.

Gerunds

A **gerund** is a verbal noun. Gerunds have the same form as present or perfect participles but are used as nouns instead of adjectives.

> *Studying* is hard work.
> *Saying* that studying is hard work is easy.
> Do you call this *living?*

A gerund may take an object and may be modified by an adverb or adjective.

> *Completing* the *project* was the goal of the committee.
> *Ending* the *famine* was *difficult.*
> *Eating well* is *desirable.*
> *Running* the *marathon* was a great *accomplishment.*

Infinitives

An **infinitive** is the form of the verb usually preceded by *to*. An infinitive may be used as a noun, an adjective, or an adverb.

> His greatest fear is *to forget* his lines in the play. (noun)
> Luisa had three weeks *to spend* on her vacation. (adjective)
> Nancy was pleased *to have passed* the examination. (adverb)

Sometimes the word *to* is omitted from the infinitive.

> Let her *sail* with you.
> Will they make him *resign?*
> Help me *decorate* the gymnasium.

The infinitive may take an object and be modified by an adverb or an adverbial phrase or clause.

To find the missing lens, we searched for 20 minutes.
Daisy and Tanya struggled *to swim faster.*
The debris began *to accumulate along the highway.*
Pedro plans *to wait until we call him.*

EXERCISE 4

On a separate sheet of paper write a complete sentence for each of the following verbs. Each must be *transitive.* Use any tense form that you prefer.

expedite	deter
harass	allow
rattle	pursue
throw	slap
submerge	congratulate

EXERCISE 5

On a separate sheet of paper write a complete sentence for each of the following verbs. Each must be *intransitive.* Use any tense form that you prefer.

incorporate	publicize
read	hike
laugh	cough
write	insinuate
race	bounce

EXERCISE 6

The italicized verbs in these sentences are active. On a separate sheet, rewrite the sentences to make each of them passive. (Slight changes of wording may be necessary to make the revised sentences read smoothly.)

1. Eileen *read* the newspaper.
2. The musicians *carried* their instruments to the theater.
3. The arrow *split* the apple.
4. Mickey Mantle *hit* his 500th home run on May 14, 1967.
5. Dolores *took* the St. Bernard for a walk on Fifth Avenue.
6. The Apaches *captured* Fort Davis.
7. Gloria *drove* the diesel truck through the restaurant window.

8. Charlie Johnson *wrote* five poems last week.
9. Carol *drank* the cough syrup reluctantly.
10. The airline strike *inconvenienced* thousands of travelers.

EXERCISE 7

The italicized verbs in these sentences are passive. On a separate sheet, rewrite the sentences to make each of them active.

1. The picture window was *shattered* by the softball.
2. The robins were *blown* all the way to Idaho by the hurricane.
3. "Muffin the Mule" is *loved* by millions of young television viewers.
4. The groundhog was *chased* by Taffy across the field.
5. We were *seen* by the spectators who then cheered us wildly.
6. The Maverleys' crops were *consumed* by locusts.
7. I was *given* complete directions by the state trooper.
8. Esmerelda is *considered* to be a hard worker by her parents.
9. The weather report was hastily *revised* by the bureau after the tidal wave.
10. Were you *asked* to participate by the officials?

EXERCISE 8

On a separate sheet of paper, make a list of verbals from the following sentences. After each verbal, write an identifying letter: *P*—participle; *G*—gerund; *I*—infinitive.

1. A smiling face is better than a discontented one; to smile is one way to win friends.
2. Sean liked to swim and dance with me, but I always felt that he would rather read than do either.
3. The woman buying her ticket is a local merchant going to New York.
4. Having written with more than usual care, I was surprised when the teacher said that my writing was illegible.
5. As it flowed down the gray rock wall, the swiftly falling water seemed to have lost its liquid quality; it looked like a smooth and solidified pillar of green.
6. Jim's volleying and serving are excellent, but I don't believe that he will ever learn to lob or hit dropshots.
7. To know more about a subject than other people know is a

worthy ambition; not to make a parade of one's learning is an even worthier ambition.

8. Waking, bathing, and dressing are necessary preliminaries to eating breakfast.
9. The game already having been won, we decided to leave soon after the intermission.
10. Spoken words are naturally kept in mind with much more difficulty than those one reads, but a well-trained person can retain amazing amounts of conversation.

EXERCISE 9

Follow the directions for Exercise 8.

1. Courage is the tempering of passion with purpose.
2. My ambition is to be head of the photography club next year.
3. Josie, seated to the rear of the auditorium, heard every word clearly.
4. Does your uncle still work in the Bureau of Missing Persons?
5. It seems that everyone is getting ready to leave on vacation.
6. The ringing of the alarm attracted the attention of the guard.
7. To keep your emotions under control is not always easy.
8. A great deal of learning is not necessarily a dangerous thing.
9. Shrinking from the scene, the guilty person quickly left the room.
10. Their aim in life seems to be spending money.

G4. Adjectives and Adverbs

An **adjective** is a word used to *modify* a noun or a pronoun. An **adverb** is a word used to *modify* a verb, an adjective, or another adverb.

What does the word *modify* mean? To **modify** is to specify the exact meaning of another word. A modifier such as an adjective or adverb does not change the basic meaning of the word it modifies. A *black* dog is still a dog, and sleeping *soundly* is still sleeping. The modifier (*black, soundly*) merely tells us something more specific about the word it modifies.

Adjectives and adverbs are the only parts of speech whose

primary function is to modify. Complete definitions of these two parts of speech are given in Section U10.

EXERCISE 10

In one column on your paper, list each word (including verbals) used as an adjective in this paragraph. In another column, list the noun that each adjective modifies. (Do not list the articles *the, a,* or *an.*) If necessary, check Section U10 before completing this exercise.

> Across a sea that was now turquoise, now emerald, we could watch the Venezuelan coastline with the purple Andes in the background. Flying fish stood a moment on their tails, flew a little distance, and dived back into the sea. The air was still. The fresh odor of the sea mingled with the heavy smell of sweat from the stevedores' bodies. In a few moments a dozen small boats had reached the side of our ship, and their occupants were slipping into the clear water to find the money that the passengers had thrown down for them.

EXERCISE 11

In one column on your paper, list each word (including verbals) used as an adverb in the following paragraph. In another column, list the word that each adverb modifies. If necessary, check Section U10 before completing this exercise.

> Have you read *The Rime of the Ancient Mariner?* Many very interesting stories are told about the author of the poem, Samuel Taylor Coleridge. Among them are some particularly good tales of the poet's love for talking. One day Coleridge met Charles Lamb walking rapidly to work and stopped to talk to him. Lamb, who was hurrying to reach his job on time, moved away; but Coleridge quickly grabbed the button of his listener's coat and insisted upon finishing his story. For a few minutes Lamb waited patiently, but Coleridge was apparently preparing for a long talk. Presently Lamb took a knife from his pocket and carefully cut off the button that Coleridge was holding. That evening Lamb, returning from work, saw Coleridge still holding the button and still talking vigorously.

G5. Conjunctions

A **conjunction** is a word that joins words or groups of words. Conjunctions have several uses. They join both words and series of words, and they introduce and tie together clauses and phrases. The principal kinds of conjunctions are (1) *coordinating*, which join words and word groups of equal grammatical rank (*and, but, for*); (2) *subordinating*, which introduce subordinate (adverbial) clauses (*because, since, unless*); and (3) *correlative*, which always appear in pairs (*both . . . and; either . . . or; neither . . . nor*).

> Renee *and* George are in the library.
> Manuel is in the yard, *but* Beulah is in the chemistry lab.
> We cannot leave *because* we still have work to finish.
> *Either* she *or* I will go with you to the store.

A full definition of the conjunction and a detailed list of the meanings and purposes of all commonly used conjunctions appear in Section U11.

EXERCISE 12

On your paper, identify each of the conjunctions in the sentences below according to its classification (coordinating, subordinating, or correlative). If necessary, check Section U11 before completing this exercise.

1. *After* we lit the fire, we sat back and waited for the steaks.
2. *Neither* time *nor* energy was wasted at Valley Forge.
3. We danced *and* laughed until sunrise.
4. Priscilla cannot decide *whether or* not to study chemistry.
5. *Unless* you season the hamburgers properly, they will taste awful.
6. Harvard and Yale are excellent colleges, *although* I prefer Princeton.
7. *Inasmuch as* Santa Fe and Taos both plan to celebrate authentic Southwestern art, Carlotta plans to visit New Mexico soon.
8. Jan will let you know *when* the tide goes out.
9. *Not only* Taffy *but* Tasha chases woodchucks all over the meadow.
10. Harry Philbin seldom loses a debate *unless* an opponent has the sense to challenge his source material.

G6. Prepositions

G6a. A PREPOSITION IS A WORD USED TO SHOW THE RELATIONSHIP OF A NOUN OR PRONOUN TO SOME OTHER WORD IN THE SENTENCE.

The following list contains all the prepositions commonly used in English:

about	beside	in	since
above	besides	inside	through
across	between	into	throughout
after	beyond	like	till
against	but	near	to
along	by	notwithstanding	toward
alongside	concerning	of	under
amid	despite	off	underneath
among	down	on	until
around	during	onto	unto
at	ere	outside	up
before	except	over	upon
behind	excepting	per	with
below	for	regarding	within
beneath	from	save	without

For further information about prepositions, especially their use in phrases and clauses, see Sections G7 and G8.

G6b. USES OF THE PREPOSITION

All prepositions (1) require an object and (2) relate to other words by modifying (modification).

Nouns, pronouns, gerund and prepositional phrases, and noun clauses can serve as the objects of prepositions placed before them.

> The deer ran *into* the *forest*. (noun)
> I did it *for him*. (pronoun)
> She took great interest *in running the contest*. (gerund phrase)
> The column advanced *to within a mile* of town. (prepositional phrase)

You can quote *from whatever source serves your case.* (noun clause)

The preposition and its object are called a *prepositional phrase.* When such a phrase modifies a noun, it acts like an adjective and thus is called *adjectival.* When it modifies a verb, it acts like an adverb and thus is called *adverbial.*

Adjectival Prepositional Phrases:

> The road *to the left* leads nowhere. (modifies *road*)
> She bought the horse *with the brown spots.* (modifies *horse*)

Adverbial Prepositional Phrases:

> He left *for the airport.* (modifies *left*)
> *In the morning* I will ask for a raise. (modifies *will ask*)

G6c. SIMPLE AND COMPOUND PREPOSITIONS

There are two kinds of prepositions, *simple* and *compound.* Note these examples of simple prepositions:

> the knock *at* the door (knock–door)
> the house *by* the river (house–river)
> presents *for* children (presents–children)
> a letter *from* home (letter–home)
> a cat *in* the hat (cat–hat)
> a handful *of* dust (handful–dust)
> the face *on* the floor (face–floor)
> going *to* Kansas City (going–Kansas City)

Now consider these examples of compound prepositions:

> the room *across from* the library (room–library)
> places *apart from* the commonwealth (places–commonwealth)
> results *due to* circumstances (results–circumstances)

Many of the problems involved in using prepositions correctly concern idiomatic usage. (See Section D7.)

EXERCISE 13

On your paper, copy the following sentences, inserting prepositions in the blank spaces. You may use simple or compound prepositions, but do not use the same one twice. Indicate the function (use) of each prepositional phrase.

1. ____ the discovery, Maria went out and celebrated.
2. We plan to borrow the power mower ____ Dick and Karen.
3. Willie made his way ____ the wind, rain, and hail.
4. Chichi sat ____ her favorite uncle.
5. The professor sought the answer ____ the pages of her notes.
6. ____ you and me, I prefer drawing to writing.
7. The leaflets were distributed ____ the student demonstrators.
8. We always walk in the forest ____ sunset.
9. ____ our late start, we had a successful trip.
10. For many reasons, he was a man ____ a country.

EXERCISE 14

Identify all the prepositions in the following sentences. Be sure to include both parts of compound prepositions.

1. The desk across from mine has been empty for a month.
2. Everyone went downtown except Millie and Josh.
3. She found the hubcap beneath the car.
4. Most people slept throughout the entire lecture.
5. Apart from a slight cold, I am feeling very fit.
6. We saw the sun setting beyond a low ridge of hills.
7. I am determined to go despite what you say.
8. The proceedings were late in starting last night.
9. Tom bought a suit exactly like one he already has.
10. Myra chose a seat near the entrance.
11. Let's walk in the rain through the park.
12. Please come with me to the store after dinner.

G7. Phrases

G7a. A PHRASE IS A GROUP OF WORDS WITHOUT SUBJECT AND PREDICATE USED AS A PART OF SPEECH.

There are five kinds of phrases: *prepositional, participial, gerund, infinitive,* and *absolute.* They are used as *nouns, adjectives,* and *adverbs.*

G7b. FORMS OF THE PHRASE

Prepositional Phrase

A **prepositional phrase** is a group of words that begins with a preposition and ends with a noun or pronoun. For example:

on the table	*by* the chair
at the corner	*for* me
from you	*in* the morning newspaper
of interest	*to* the lighthouse

Participial Phrase

A **participial phrase** includes a participle together with its modifiers:

> *Straightening his tie,* Pierre welcomed his guests.
> *Leaving before sunrise,* we reached Denver that night.
> The village, *ravaged by the tornado,* was like a ghost town.

Note that each participle (*straightening, leaving, ravaged*) introduces a phrase and that each phrase, as a unit, then modifies a noun or pronoun (*Pierre, we, village*). These are participial phrases functioning as adjectives.

Gerund Phrase

A **gerund phrase** contains a gerund and may also include one or more modifiers and other closely related words. Gerund phrases function as nouns.

> We lost the game by *failing to score enough points.* (gerund phrase as object of preposition *by*)
> *Lying to your friend* is a serious mistake. (gerund phrase as subject of sentence)
> My teacher urges *sending in applications on time.* (gerund phrase as object of verb *urges*)
> My ultimate goal is *winning the history prize.* (gerund phrase as predicate nominative)

A gerund phrase can be introduced by a preposition. Such constructions are sometimes referred to as *prepositional–gerund* phrases: *After graduating from high school,* I hope to go to college.

Infinitive Phrase

An **infinitive phrase** contains an infinitive. The unit can serve as a noun or as a modifier:

> The soldiers plan *to attack soon*. (*Soon* modifies *to attack*. The phrase serves as the object of *plan*.)
>
> We intended *to call them*. (*Them* is the object of *to call*. The phrase serves as the object of *intended*.)
>
> *To attend Mugwump College* is Donna's great desire. (An infinitive phrase is used as the subject of the sentence.)
>
> The plumber insists there is a method *to solve the leak*. (An infinitive phrase modifies *method*.)
>
> Hazel claims that she is too busy *to attend the dance*. (An infinitive phrase modifies *busy*.)
>
> Michael Cassio's decision is *to visit his employment office*. (An infinitive phrase acts as a predicate nominative.)

Absolute Phrase

The **absolute phrase,** an odd construction, usually consists of a noun followed and modified by a participle or participial phrase. The unit is a phrase because it cannot stand alone as a sentence (it is without a subject and predicate). It is absolute because it modifies no single word in the sentence of which it is a part, but the absolute phrase does have a thought relationship to the sentence or some word or phrase in it.

> *My work completed*, I left for home.
> Sue left the party, *her foot hurting badly*.
> *Nightfall coming*, many of the birds in the forest began to sing.
> *The storm threatening*, we moved the party indoors.

G7c. USES OF THE PHRASE

A phrase normally fulfills the function of a noun, adjective, or adverb. Phrases containing adjectives modifying nouns or containing adverbs modifying verbs are labeled according to what are considered their more important, or stronger, words.

Noun Phrase

A phrase used as a noun (as subject, object, etc.) is called a **noun phrase.**

After tomorrow will be too late.
In the garage is where the bicycle should be.
Playing in the school orchestra was her main ambition.
Over the bridge was the best route to their house.

Adjective and Adverb Phrases

Prepositional phrases usually serve as adjectives or adverbs. We can use the examples in Section G7b within complete sentences:

> The book sits *on the table*. (adv.)
> We met them *at the corner*. (adv.)
> The gift *from you* meant the most to him. (adj.)
> The teacher's strike is *of interest*. (adj.)
> Taffy slept *by the chair*. (adv.)
> The spectators cheered *for me*. (adv.)
> She replied *in the morning newspaper*. (adv.)

When a phrase modifies a noun or pronoun, we call it an **adjective phrase.** Consider these examples:

> Many *of the strikers* went back to work. (*many*)
> Relatives *from Chicago* visited us for a week. (*relatives*)
> Dozens of magazines *in the waiting room* are ten years old.
>   (*magazines*)
> The calm *after the storm* renewed our hope. (*calm*)

But when a phrase modifies a verb, an adjective, or another adverb, it is an **adverb phrase.** For example:

> Shirley sings *with enthusiasm*. (how)
> We prefer to study the problem *before trying to solve it*. (when)
> Al collects butterflies *for his biology class*. (why)
> Dr. O'Leary searched *for years* before finding the cure. (to what
>   extent)

In the above sentences, adverb phrases modify verbs.
In the sentences which follow, adverb phrases modify adjectives:

> Nathan Hale was true *to his promise*. (true)
> That coffee is good *to the last drop*. (good)
> Alicia claims that children are unpredictable *in the extreme*.
>   (unpredictable)

Adverb phrases also modify other adverbs. For example:

Governor Fuzzle smiled coyly *for a reason*. (coyly)
My friend Judy parked the car far *in back*. (far)
We dropped the ice cream slowly *into the punch*. (slowly)

NOTE: A construction known as a **verb phrase** is treated in Section U7.

EXERCISE 15

Pick out the phrases in the following sentences. Indicate the *form* of each phrase: *Prep*—prepositional; *Par*—participial; *Ger*—gerund; *Inf*—infinitive. Then show the *function* of each phrase: *N*—noun; *Adj*—adjective; *Adv*—adverb.

1. Many students have to work during school vacations.
2. All of us hoped to remain calm during the test.
3. Having finished the work, the agent sent for a heavy meal.
4. At last a heavy rain fell on the parched ground.
5. He played several of the games with his legs taped heavily.
6. An attitude of anxiety does not appeal to anyone.
7. Teaching a small puppy is a good way to develop patience.
8. To get an A is the goal of many students.
9. The thing Brenda liked most about sports was playing them.
10. Putting all her strength into the effort, Ann did her level best.

EXERCISE 16

On your paper copy each of the italicized phrases in the following sentences. After each phrase, (1) list the word (or words) it modifies, (2) state what kind of phrase it is, (3) indicate its use as what part of speech.

1. *Enjoying myself fully* is what I plan to do next summer.
2. We plan to meet you in St. Louis *at the fair*.
3. My grandfather, *crippled by arthritis*, was still able to smile good-naturedly whenever we entered the room.
4. *To be with you an hour a day*, that is why I took the course.
5. The legionnaires fought the invaders *to the last rebel*.
6. Mallard dropped the litter *into the basket*.
7. Most *of the swallows* have returned to Capistrano.
8. Marcia plays tennis *with a passion*.

9. The student remained in the library *for two hours*.
10. Louise walked calmly *into the interview*.

EXERCISE 17

On a sheet of paper write down all the phrases in the following sentences. Opposite each phrase, supply the three items of information called for in Exercise 16.

1. Having been unanimously elected president, I expressed my gratitude for the honor bestowed upon me.
2. To get experience and not to make money was her goal in seeking a summer job.
3. Through the night the huge four-engined jet roared on to its destination.
4. Your teacher has no objection to your turning in well-written themes.
5. Having reached the age of eighteen, I have no desire ever to fall in love again.
6. A motion was made to close the nominations, no other names being proposed.
7. To get along well with people, you must learn to share their interests.
8. Smith being pretty well exhausted, the coach sent in Olivetti to replace him as center.
9. In the summer, Carlos loves to read under a shady tree in the park.
10. Seen from a distance, the night train, creeping up the mountain grade, looked like an animated glowworm.

G8. Clauses

G8a. A CLAUSE IS A GROUP OF WORDS HAVING A SUBJECT AND PREDICATE AND FORMING PART OF A SENTENCE.

Through the use of a conjunction or an implied connection, a clause is related to the remainder of the sentence in which it appears. "The girl and boy danced slowly around the room to increasing applause" is a *sentence,* not a *clause.* It consists of one main statement and is not a *part* of a sentence.

Clauses are of two kinds: *independent* (also called *main* and *principal*) and *dependent* (also called *subordinate*).

G8b. KINDS OF CLAUSES

Independent clauses assert the central act of predication (that is, action or state of being) in a sentence. The subject and especially the predicate in such a clause are the sentence elements to which everything else in the sentence is related.

When two or more clauses in the same sentence are not subordinated in any way, they must be coordinated. This structure results in a *compound* sentence, which has more than one main clause. The unsubordinated clauses in a compound sentence are called *coordinate clauses* and are usually joined by a coordinate or correlative conjunction. (See Section G5.)

> *Tom went to the movies,* but *Janice went to the circus.*
> Not only *will she make a contribution herself,* but *she will also ask her friends.*

Dependent Clauses

Dependent clauses contain a predicate. They are different from independent clauses because they are introduced by a subordinating conjunction, a relative pronoun, or a similar subordinating construction (see Section G8c.). Each of these subordinators specifies the relationship of the dependent clause to the main clause.

> *That Einstein formulated the theory of relativity* is a commonly known fact. (This is a noun clause acting as the subject and is introduced by the subordinating word *that.*)
> The elephant, *which had a long ivory tusk,* thundered toward us. (A relative clause, introduced by a subordinating relative pronoun, includes the predicate *had.*)
> *When Terry drives,* traffic scatters. (An adverbial clause introduced by the subordinating conjunction *when* includes the verb *drives.*)
> *After the game was over,* the team shook hands with the opposition; then the players headed for the showers. (An adverbial clause introduced by a subordinating conjunction includes the

verb *was*. Note also that two coordinate clauses are joined by the conjunctive adverb *then*.)

A special kind of dependent clause is the *elliptical clause*. Such a construction is called elliptical because its subject and frequently its predicate are omitted and can be understood (inferred) from the independent clause.

> Although I was ill, I insisted on going to the party.
> *Although ill*, I insisted on going to the party. (elliptical clause)
> While she was eating, Ann looked at the newspaper.
> *While eating*, Ann looked at the newspaper.

Trouble—and sometimes laughter—arise when omitted, understood parts are *not* those of the independent clause.

> When six years old, my mother married for the second time.

G8c. USES OF DEPENDENT CLAUSES

Dependent clauses can perform the functions of various parts of speech.

Noun Clauses

A **noun clause** functions as a *noun* within the sentence. Noun clauses usually are introduced by *that, what, who, which, where, when, how,* or *why*.

> *Who came to the party* is no concern of yours. (subject)
> Kim wished *that she could ride a horse*. (object)
> We judge people by *what they do*. (object of preposition)
> The doctor came to the conclusion *that the patient was out of danger*. (appositive)
> One serious problem is *that there is no running water*. (predicate complement)

Adjective Clauses

An **adjective clause** acts as an *adjective*. Adjective clauses are usually introduced by a relative pronoun—*who, which, that*—or by a subordinating conjunction—*when, where, why*. The relative pronoun is sometimes left out. Clauses introduced by relative pronouns or adjectives are called *relative clauses*.

The bat *that you have used* has been broken. (adjectival clause modifying *bat*)

He knows the reason *why I could not come.* (adjectival clause modifying *reason*)

The job has been given to the person *whom you recommended.* (adjectival clause modifying *person*)

She is a girl *I never could stand.* (adjectival clause modifying *girl;* the relative pronoun *whom* is left out)

Adverb Clauses

An **adverb clause** modifies like an *adverb.* Introduced by subordinating conjunctions, adverb clauses can express several important relationships:

Time: *when, before, while, since*

When you row a boat, you must keep control of the oars. (adverbial clause modifies *must keep*)

Place: *where, wherever*

After finding the book *where I had left it,* I hurried back into the house. (adverbial clause modifies gerund *finding*)

Manner: *as, as if*

She kicked the can *as if it were a ball.* (adverbial clause modifies verb *kicked*)

Condition: *if, so, unless, provided that*

Unless you make the payment, service will be cut off. (adverbial clause modifies verb *will be cut off*)

Cause: *because, as, since*

The train, three hours late *because the locomotive had broken down,* was full of angry passengers. (adverbial clause modifies adjective *late*)

Purpose: *in order that, so that*

The students worked hard all day *so that the gym would be ready for the dance.* (adverbial clause modifies verb *worked*)

Result: *that, so that, so . . . that*

We were *so* hungry *that we ate stale crackers.* (adverbial clause modifies adjective *hungry*)

Degree or comparison: *than, as much as, as . . . as, just as*

Sally climbed farther *than you did.* (adverbial clause modifies adverb *farther*)

Concession: *though, although*

Although he did not score, he made the best play of the game. (adverbial clause modifies verb *made*)

EXERCISE 18

Number your paper from 1 to 15. Read the following clauses carefully and decide which are *independent* and which are *dependent*. If a clause is independent, write *I* next to its number. If it is dependent, write *D*.

1. the moon is blue
2. when the sun shone brightly
3. from her vantage point she realized
4. although the bluebirds have returned
5. from a distant hill he approached
6. after the train arrived
7. Andy Panda sat on the veranda
8. what is new is news
9. from Phoenix we returned to Albuquerque
10. inasmuch as Beverly asked your permission
11. the woman with the hat was smiling
12. when we were young
13. while you cried
14. not on your life
15. within the pages of this book are serious thoughts

EXERCISE 19

On a sheet of paper indicate the kind of dependent clause italicized in each of these sentences. List the function (use) of each.

1. The Smith family goes to the beach *whenever it is possible.*
2. Competing with a person *who is a better player* will help your tennis.
3. *Because I hate pizza,* I ordered a filet mignon.
4. The children play in the streets *wherever there is no traffic.*

5. Fishing for trout is *what I plan to do in Canada.*
6. Did David tell Santa Claus *what he wanted for Christmas?*
7. Sergeant Clancy is the police officer *who protected the demonstrators.*
8. We shall keep the puppies *until the owners come to take them away.*
9. You should decide *when you should return the used books to Miriam.*
10. This garden, *which was ravaged by the hurricane,* will grow back.
11. *Although the accident was a minor one,* I was badly shaken.

EXERCISE 20

On a sheet of paper copy the following sentences, leaving a blank space between each two lines. Underline each clause in each sentence. Above each underlined clause indicate by these abbreviations its function in the sentence: *Ind*—independent; *N*—noun; *Adj*—adjective; *Adv*—adverb.

1. Among other kinds of people we can single out these two: those who think and those who act.
2. The people of that section have been marketing a great quantity of vegetables in the city this summer.
3. He jumped up and down; he shouted and yelled; and yet, for some strange reason, no one paid him the slightest attention.
4. I recommend a visit to Chicago, but when you go, remember that your impressions will be determined by where you get off the train.
5. Whenever my high school friends assembled, we listened to the new records in anyone's collection.
6. I have often heard it said that people are funny, and I am sorry to have to admit that the statement is true.
7. As it was getting late, we began looking for a place where we might land and camp for the night.
8. Not all people in the library are scholars: across the table from me a boy is enjoying himself looking at the cartoons in a magazine; sitting farther away in a quiet corner are a boy and a girl reading newspapers.
9. The botanists who have been working in the experiment station are trying to develop a plant that will grow in any kind of soil.
10. The highlight of my childhood summers was a visit to my grandparents' farm; letting me do everything under the sun, it seemed, was their idea of showing me a good time.

G9. Sentences

G9a. DEFINITION

It is difficult to define a sentence satisfactorily. Traditionally, a sentence is defined as "a group of words containing a subject and predicate and expressing a complete thought." However, some sentences do not contain both an expressed subject and predicate. Furthermore, what exactly is a complete thought? Frequently, the completeness of a thought depends upon the statements that precede or follow it. (See Section S1.)

All that can accurately and fairly be said is that a **sentence** *is a stretch of prose (or poetry, for that matter) that a capable writer punctuates by beginning with a capital and ending with a terminal mark* (see Section PM1) *and that an educated reader will recognize and accept as a sentence.* (Perhaps you can do better with a definition of your own!)

G9b. SENTENCE MEANING

A sentence can be classified according to the kind of statement it makes. Sentences can be *declarative, interrogative, imperative,* or *exclamatory.*

A **declarative sentence** makes an assertion, either by stating a fact or by expressing an opinion. This assertion can be negative.

> Two and two equals four.
> That candidate will surely be elected.
> George isn't coming.
> Dessert may not be served.

An **interrogative sentence** asks a direct question.

> Is four really the sum of two and two?
> Do you think she will be elected?
> George isn't coming?

An **imperative sentence** expresses a request or command.

> Don't be shy.
> Forward, march.
> Fill out the application blank and mail it immediately.

An **exclamatory sentence** expresses strong, intense emotion.

> Let's get going!
> What a show!
> Oh, if only you had telephoned!
> Don't leave me!

G9c. SENTENCE STRUCTURE

Structurally, a sentence can be *simple, compound, complex,* or *compound-complex.*

A **simple sentence** includes only one act of predication. All simple sentences are basic sentence patterns. (See Section G9e.) A simple sentence may have more than one subject or more than one predicate, but all are unified into a single act of predication; that is, all the subjects must perform all the actions in the predicates.

> *Subject   Predicate*
> The *mule skinner fell* in the well.

> *Coordinate subject   Predicate*
> The *mule skinner* and his *mule fell* in the well.

> *Subject   Coordinate predicate*
> The *mule skinner*   *fell* and *got soaked* in the well.

> *Coordinate subject*
> The *mule skinner* and his *mule*

>   *Coordinate predicate*
>   *fell* and *got soaked* in the well.

A **compound sentence** includes two or more coordinate main clauses. A compound sentence is actually made up of two sentence patterns joined by a coordinating conjunction, a correlative conjunction, or a semicolon.

Coordinating conjunction:

> The applesauce was warm and sweet, *but* the sweet potatoes were burned to a crisp.

G 9

Correlative conjunction:

> *Not only* is she a candidate for a scholarship, *but* she is *also* holding down a part-time job.

Semicolon:

> I pulled guard duty today; tomorrow it will be someone else's turn.

Within a **complex sentence** there are one main clause and one or more dependent, or subordinate, clauses. Usually the subordinate clause modifies the main clause or some element in it. (See Section G8.) A complex sentence contains only one sentence pattern (see Section G9e), unless the clause functions as an integral part of the pattern. See the first example below.

Noun clause in act of predication of independent clause:

> *That the sun will rise* is indisputable. (subject)

Modifying like an adverb:

> *When she arrives,* Rachel will take charge. (modifies verb *will take*)

Modifying like an adjective:

> The city government, *which has serious financial problems,* will ask for a tax increase. (modifies noun *city government*)

A compound-complex sentence includes two or more coordinate independent clauses, along with one or more dependent clauses.

Dependent

> *When the legislature passed a sales tax*

Independent

> *many people complained; but the governor agreed to use most of the money for better schools.*

G9d. SENTENCE DIAGRAMING

Sentence diagraming is a way of graphically illustrating the grammatical functions of words within a sentence. Some experts consider diagraming of questionable value, whereas others think it is a legitimate and useful device. Both advocates and attackers of diagraming agree that it is only a means to an end. Advocates of diagraming insist that both means and ends are sensible and worthwhile; some of its attackers claim that neither the method of analysis nor the analysis itself is of much value.

In sentence diagraming, it is understood that every simple sentence and complete clause is made up of two elements, a subject part and a predicate part. The latter is present in every sentence and clause; the former is too, except in imperative sentences when it is implicit (understood).

Traditional diagraming shows relationships through the use of lines. (Other more complex methods of diagraming use different techniques, such as boxes.) The lines used in traditional diagraming are horizontal, perpendicular, slanting, curved, and dotted. The parts of a sentence are put on lines in the positions indicated in the following skeleton diagram. The three most important sentence elements (subject, predicate, object) are usually put on a horizontal line. Any modifiers are placed on lines underneath.

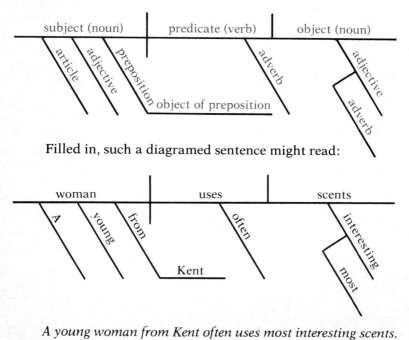

Filled in, such a diagramed sentence might read:

A young woman from Kent often uses most interesting scents.

The illustrations on this page and the next page show other elements of diagraming, as explained below.

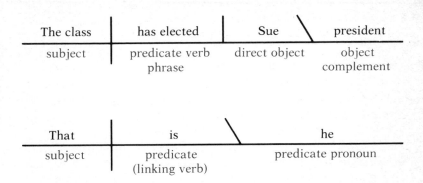

The simple subject, the simple predicate, the direct object (as above), and, when they appear, the object complement, the predicate noun or pronoun, and the predicate adjective are written on the main horizontal line. (If you do not know the meanings of these terms, look up each at its appropriate place in this handbook.) The subject and predicate are separated by a perpendicular line intersecting the horizontal line. A direct object is separated from its verb by a short perpendicular line extending up from the horizontal line. The object complement, the predicate noun or pronoun, and the predicate adjective are set off by short slanting lines extending up to the left from the horizontal line. When conjunctions appear, dotted lines are used to join.

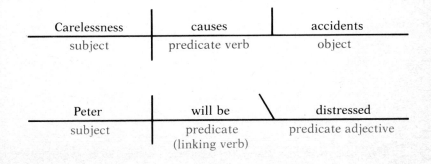

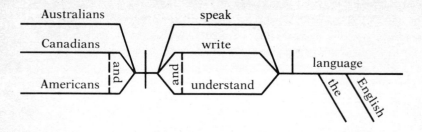

Several other types of sentences (compound, complex, compound-complex) and structures containing absolute phrases, expletives, infinitive phrases used as predicate nouns, etc., are not shown for two reasons: (1) fundamental principles remain identical with those shown and can be easily adapted; (2) diagraming is a game—useful or not—and should be kept no more involved than an individual or a particular class wishes it to become.

G9e. SENTENCE PATTERNS

A sentence is composed of a series of words. This series can convey meaning in English only because certain of those words are *structurally related to one another in such a way that they express an act of predication.* The patterns indicate the order in which English places these basic structural relationships.

The sentence patterns indicate the basic kinds of words which sentences contain. In other words, the patterns specify the types of words which must be present in a statement before it may be called a sentence.

In English, there are seven basic predication patterns:

Pattern 1

Subject	Predicate
People	talk.
Horses	jump.
Fires	burn.
We	sing.

This is the simplest predication pattern in English. It consists of only a noun or pronoun subject and a predicate. In this most basic pattern, the verb used in the predicate is called *intransitive*, that is, it asserts an action that does not carry across to an object. (See Section G3.) In Pattern 1 sentences an action, a state, or a quality of a subject is expressed by a predicate.

Pattern 2

Subject	Predicate	Direct Object
Musicians	play	instruments.
Birds	build	nests.
Children	prefer	candy.
You	need	me.

This is probably the most common predication pattern in English. In it, the action of a verb functioning as the predicate carries across to a noun or pronoun called its *object*. This kind of verb is called *transitive*, and the word functioning as the direct object answers the question "What?" or "Whom?"

Note that in the first two examples above, the verbs *play* and *build* can be classified as either transitive or intransitive, depending on how they are used. Both verbs can appear in Pattern 1 sentences: *Bill plays. Contractors build.*

In a Pattern 2 sentence, the predicate shows the relationship existing between the subject and the direct object.

Pattern 3

Subject	Predicate	Indirect Object	Direct Object
Bert	gives	Joan	presents.
Rebecca	wrote	him	letters.
Joyce	brought	Ted	books.

Note that in Pattern 3 sentences the relationship between the subject and the indirect object is different from the relationship between the subject and the direct object. The direct object answers the question "What?" or "Whom?" The indirect object answers the question *"To or for whom?"* It tells *to* or *for whom* the action of the predicate is done. For there to be an indirect object, the sentence must have a direct object that is either expressed or implied. The indirect object is placed somewhere between the predicate and the direct object.

Pattern 4

Subject	Linking Verb	Predicate Noun
Barry	is	a pilot.
He	was	the underdog.
Lisa	will be	an architect.
I	am	she.

In this pattern, special predication problems arise. First, notice that the verb does not state any specific action. The linking verb merely identifies or classifies the subject. In other words, it links the subject with the noun that follows the verb. In this pattern, the subject and the noun following the linking verb refer to one and the same person. *Barry* and *pilot*, in other words, are merely two ways of looking at the same person. In one case he is referred to as *Barry;* in the other, he is designated as *pilot*.

Notice that if we look at the first two words of the pattern, *Barry is*, a question arises. Barry is what? It may be that we simply want to say that a man named Barry in fact exists. If this is our intention, we have a Pattern 1 (Subject-Predicate, or S-P) sentence and can leave it at that: *Barry is*.

But if we wish to state more than the simple fact that Barry exists, we can complete a Pattern 4 predication with a noun. This noun is called a *predicate noun* or *predicate complement,* and the verb in the pattern is described as a *linking verb*.

NOTE: Observe that the predicate noun in the first three examples is preceded by a definite or indefinite article. These noun markers were omitted from the first three patterns in order to focus attention upon the bare essentials of those patterns. In a Pattern 4 sentence, however, an article is almost always used before the predicate noun. (However, note that in the fourth example, the pronoun stands without a marker.) Articles and other noun markers appear frequently in the other patterns also.

Pattern 5

Subject	Linking Verb	Predicate Adj.
Dogs	are	mean.
Ginger	is	tall.
Roses	smell	delightful.
It	seems	fine.

In this pattern, a linking verb is followed by an adjective that roughly answers the question "What sort of quality does the subject possess?" In Pattern 5 sentences, the predicate adjective describes or indicates a quality that the subject has.

NOTE: In this pattern verbs other than *to be* can function as the link between the subject and the predicate adjective; linking verbs such as *become, appear, seem, taste, grow*, etc., can work this way. These verbs generally express how things look or how we sense them. Note the following examples:

> Boys grow *tall*.
> Margaret became *angry*.
> The car seemed *fast*.
> Aunt Maria looked *young*.
> Pomegranates taste *tart*.
> The idea sounded *good*.
> Her face grew *purple*.
> The sky continued *cloudy*.

Note that in each of these sentences the adjective following the verb describes the subject. Note also that the sentences contain several noun markers.

It is important to remember that a predicate adjective always provides a description of the subject, not the verb. Confusion often arises because those words that *modify* verbs, called *adverbs*, often appear in the same pattern position as predicate adjectives.

> Boys grow *quickly*.
> Aunt Maria looked *away*.
> Ron appeared *immediately*.

To determine whether the word in this position is an adjective or an adverb, try it in the typical noun-modifying position, before the noun modified:

> tall boys   quickly boys
> young Aunt Maria   away Aunt Maria

It is clear that *quickly* and *away* are related to verbs in these sentences rather than to subject-nouns. Adverbs are never essential parts of basic sentence patterns.

Confusion about Pattern 5 can also arise when verbs appear in forms that use the verb *to be* as an auxiliary:

> *Subject*   *Predicate*
> Celia   is singing.
> Alison   was praying.

These are actually sentences employing Pattern 1 with the verb *to be* used as an auxiliary in forming a certain *tense*. (See Section U8.) Generally, a verb ending in *–ing* after a form of the verb *to be* is a form of the progressive tense. If the *–ing* word is asserting an *action* rather than a quality or description, you have a Pattern 1 predication. Further, the verb form may be modified by a word that looks like an adjective:

Subject	Predicate
Pedro	has been working hard.

Here simply place *hard* before "*Pedro*" in the noun-modifying position: *Hard Pedro has been working.* This does not make sense in the same way. It seems clear that *hard* is an adverb modifying *has been working.* There is no substitute for common sense or good judgment in deciding a problem like this.

Pattern 6

Subject	Predicate	Direct Obj.	Obj. Complement
Louise	named	her fish	Percy.
José	called	his friend	a fool.
They	elected	her	president.
Gwen	considered	Hans	her friend.

In this pattern, a predicate is followed by a direct object. In addition, another noun, called an *object complement*, follows the direct object and serves to complete the meaning of the predicate. There is a relationship between the direct object and its complement that resembles the relationship between the subject and the predicate noun in Pattern 4. That is, the linking verb *to be* is implied:

her fish (is) Percy
his friend (is) a fool
she (is) president
Hans (is) her friend

The object complement, in other words, serves to identify or classify the direct object.

Note that we could take a series of words like *Louise named her fish* and make a complete sentence which would be a Pattern 2 sentence. However, verbs that express action such as naming raise a natural question about their direct objects. In the examples, note that the object complement answers the question

"What?" Since the answer to the question is an integral part of the verb's act of naming, the object complement has a place in the predication pattern. Since the object complement completes a meaning relevant to the direct object, it is called the object complement.

NOTE: The sentences in the examples contain noun markers before some of the direct objects and object complements. (See Section G1.)

Pattern 7

Subject	Predicate	Direct Obj.	Adj. Complement
Rose	painted	the fence	green.
Marie	thought	her friend	loyal.
Joe	considered	the problem	difficult.
Fritz	made	the garden	beautiful.

As in Pattern 6, a predicate is followed by a direct object. In this pattern, however, the direct object is followed by a complement that is an adjective. The relationship between the direct object and the *adjective complement* is similar to the relationship between the subject and the predicate adjective in a Pattern 5 sentence. In other words, the verb *to be* may be understood between the direct object and the adjective complement: *the fence (is) green, her friend (is) loyal*, etc.

To make certain that the complement is an adjective, check by placing it before the word it complements (in the regular adjective-modifying position) and decide whether it applies in a sense that is in tune with the sentence. For example, *difficult problem* and *beautiful garden* make sense and therefore the words are obviously adjective complements.

G9f. EXPANDING SENTENCE PATTERNS

In the preceding section, the basic sentence patterns were illustrated by using only the minimum necessary words, except where noted. This was purposely done in order to focus your attention on the basic underlying structure of the various patterns. In actual speaking and writing, of course, such "barebones" sentences are rare.

There are many types of modifiers which serve to expand the basic elements of any pattern. The following are worth noting:

1. Definite and indefinite articles and other noun markers attach themselves to and signal nouns. Rare is the sentence without articles or noun markers.

   > *The* girls built *a* boat. (Pattern 2) (S-P-DO)
   > *My* brother lost *his* comb. (Pattern 2) (S-P-DO)

2. Single-word adjectives and adverbs frequently modify the elements of the basic patterns.

   > The *energetic* girls *quickly* built a boat. (Pattern 2) (S-P-DO)
   > She is an *accomplished* doctor. (Pattern 4) (S-LV-PN)
   > They elected a *capable* man governor. (Pattern 6) (S-P-DO-OC)
   > He works *well*. (Pattern 1) (S-P)

3. Phrases of various kinds (see Section G7) frequently modify the basic words in patterns.

   > *In the morning*, they left *for Tampa*. (Pattern 1) (S-P)
   > *Hoping to win the trophy*, Tom entered the race. (Pattern 2) (S-P-DO)
   > San Francisco, *a truly beautiful city*, is a popular place for tourists. (Pattern 4) (S-LV-PN)
   > *To get there on time*, Karen told the driver *to speed it up*. (Pattern 2) (S-P-DO)
   > He gave his parents a present *by staying out of trouble*. (Pattern 3) (S-P-IO-DO)

4. Clauses of various kinds (see Section G8) frequently modify basic words in patterns.

   > *Because he had failed twice alreay*, Ed lost his desire to try again. (Pattern 2) (S-P-DO)
   > Athens, *which enjoys a temperate climate*, is the capital of Greece. (Pattern 4) (S-LV-PN)
   > She always fought *for what she believed in*. (Pattern 1) (S-P)

In order to identify easily the basic patterns in expanded sentences, you must be able to distinguish modifying phrases and clauses. This is a relatively simple matter. Familiarity with prepositions, for example, will enable you to spot the phrases which they introduce. Similarly, a knowledge of the infinitive signal word *to*, the relative pronouns, the –*ing* forms of the participle and gerund, and the subordinating conjunctions will permit you to identify, respectively, infinitive phrases, adjective clauses, participial and gerund phrases, and adverb clauses.

When attempting to identify sentence patterns, be on your guard to avoid confusing dependent clauses with basic patterns. Since dependent clauses contain predications (subjects and predicates), they might be confused with the basic patterns. Keep in mind that there is no sentence pattern which makes provision for relative pronouns or subordinating conjunctions. Since both of these types of signal words are intimately connected with the predications that they introduce, they can never stand alone or fulfill the structural requirements of the basic patterns.

When infinitive and gerund phrases or noun clauses, however, serve as either subjects or objects, they may be considered as integral parts of basic patterns. Note the following examples:

> *To forgive* is divine. (Pattern 5) (S-LV-PA)
> The team tried *to win*. (Pattern 2) (S-P-DO)
> *Developing new territories* was the marketing manager's main responsibility. (Pattern 4) (S-LV-PN)
> They tried *growing hybrid plants*. (Pattern 2) (S-P-DO)
> *That she won* was obvious. (Pattern 5) (S-LV-PA)
> He knew *what to do*. (Pattern 2) (S-P-DO)
> *To be left alone* is *what I desire*. (Pattern 4) (S-LV-PN)

It is also worth noting that any essential part of a sentence pattern may be compounded through the use of a correlative conjunction. Compound subjects, predicates, and complements are considered as single units as far as the patterns are concerned.

G9g. VARIATIONS FROM THE BASIC PATTERNS

In the preceding section, the basic patterns of English sentences were discussed. You will note, however, that only sentences which constitute *direct statements* were included in the basic patterns. But there are a few other types of sentences in English. The following variations are common.

The Passive Variation

Sentences employing a verb in the passive voice (see Section G3d) are common in English. Such sentences are usually developed from Pattern 2 sentences. Take, for example, the following Pattern 2 sentences:

Subject	Predicate	Direct Object
Rita	jumped	the hurdle.
Captain Kidd	hid	the treasure.
Ms. Owens	built	a bookcase.
The sergeant	scolded	the troops.

The passive variation is formed by moving the direct object into the subject position and by making the subject into the object of a preposition in a prepositional phrase. The verb also changes to the passive voice, which is always made up of a form of the verb *to be* followed by the past participle:

Subject	Predicate	(Prep. Phrase)
The hurdle	was jumped	(by Rita).
The treasure	was hidden	(by Captain Kidd).
A bookcase	was built	(by Ms. Owens).
The troops	were scolded	(by the sergeant).

Note that the prepositional phrases appear in parentheses. This is to indicate that the phrase is optional. In some passive sentences, the prepositional phrase is omitted.

Pattern 6 and Pattern 7 sentences can also be changed into the passive voice. Note the changes that occur in the following examples:

Pattern 6: Louise named her fish Percy.
The fish was named Percy (by Louise).
Pattern 7: Rose painted the fence green.
The fence was painted green (by Rose).

Note that when a Pattern 2 sentence is changed into the passive, it becomes a Pattern 1 sentence. When Patterns 6 and 7 are changed, the revisions become Patterns 4 and 5, respectively.

The Question Variation

Sentences that ask questions are, of course, common in English or any other language. The question variation follows certain set patterns in English. These can be summarized as follows:

1. If an affirmative statement has a verb with one or more auxiliaries, the first auxiliary is switched so that it comes before the subject. Here are some examples:

Affirmative: The game was won.
The arrest will be made.
The deer was shot.
The house could have been repainted.
The guest has eaten.

Questions: Was the game won?
Will the arrest be made?
Was the deer shot?
Could the house have been repainted?
Has the guest eaten?

2. If the affirmative statement contains no auxiliary, some form of the verb *do* is placed in front of the subject. Here are some examples:

Affirmative: The boy runs fast.
Sara likes music.
Jane danced well.
Bill helps his friends.
Heather flew an airplane.
Carolyn likes mathematics.

Questions: Does the boy run fast?
Does Sara like music?
Did Jane dance well?
Does Bill help his friends?
Did Heather fly an airplane?
Does Carolyn like mathematics?

These same rules apply when questions begin with common question words like *where, when, why,* and *how.*

The Imperative Variation

The imperative mood in English is another basic variation. This variation may appear in any of the seven basic patterns. The imperative is commonly viewed as having the subject *you* understood, or implied. Here is an example of the imperative variation in each of the seven basic patterns:

Begin! (Pattern 1) (S-P)
Begin the game! (Pattern 2) (S-P-DO)
Give him a chance. (Pattern 3) (S-P-IO-DO)
Be a doctor. (Pattern 4) (S-LV-PN)
Remain silent. (Pattern 5) (S-LV-PA)
Name the dog Spot. (Pattern 6) (S-P-DO-OC)
Color his face red. (Pattern 7) (S-P-DO-AC)

EXERCISE 21

On your paper, number each of these sentences and indicate whether it is simple, compound, complex, or compound-complex.

1. Although few of the actors knew their lines, the rehearsal went well.
2. I want all of you to return to your rooms immediately.
3. Do the best you can; however, do not be discouraged by difficulties, which will surely occur.
4. Get me to the church on time.
5. When I first read *The Brothers Karamazov*, my favorite character was Ivan; but now I prefer Dimitri, who seems more believable.
6. Fish have to swim; birds have to fly.
7. During the 1920's, the Charleston was a very popular dance.
8. When the girls play field hockey, you yourself had better protect your shins; the girls are lethal competitors.
9. I lost my heart in San Francisco but not for long.
10. Dripping water in Wyoming's Fossil Mountain Ice Cave is transformed into sparkling columns of ice, and where water drops have splashed and frozen, the floor glitters as if it were covered with diamonds.
11. We dined and we danced.

EXERCISE 22

On your paper, number each of the following sentences and indicate its meaning and intent; declarative, imperative, interrogative, or exclamatory. Supply a suitable end stop (see Section PM1) for each sentence.

1. Do me a favor and sit down for a moment
2. It will cost $765.00 to repair a dented fender
3. That sum is highway robbery
4. All I want for Christmas is my two front teeth
5. When do you expect me to get all this painting done, Melvin
6. Drop those guns, Sheriff Murtz, or I'll have to ventilate you
7. Contact lenses can cause problems until one gets used to them
8. You want another ice-cream cone
9. What a magnificent sunset
10. Identifying sentences builds character

G
9

EXERCISE 23

Make two columns on your paper. Head one *Subject* and the other *Predicate*. From the following sentences, select those words that are fulfilling those functions and write them in the proper columns.

1. Kristin laughed.
2. Mother hurried.
3. The dog howled.
4. Father sang.
5. The car stalled.
6. Jody cried.
7. The candle melted.
8. Burr cooks.
9. The cat ran.
10. The fog lifted.

EXERCISE 24

Number your paper from 1 to 10. Arrange the following jumbled series of words into sentences. Write *Subject* and *Predicate* over the words acting in those functions.

1. awoke she early
2. rare Rover meat ate the
3. the well Juanita in fell
4. bought a farm Walter
5. the movie Johnny frightened
6. wore clown the a sign
7. her blew horn Denise
8. flew the ladybug home
9. a kite flew Sarah
10. his Christmas ate Jack pie

EXERCISE 25

Determine the sentence patterns in the following expanded sentences. Number a sheet of paper from 1 to 20. Next to each number, write the code for the pattern, following this example:

> Debbie bought her brother a tiny pup.
> *Answer:* Subject—Predicate—Indirect Object—Direct Object

1. Because they had to leave before sunrise, the scouts assembled their equipment the night before.
2. When the whistle blew, Patty sat down.
3. Unable to hold onto the cookie jar, Tim dropped it on the floor.
4. She had always been the best worker in the firm.
5. Frances, seeing that it was too early to get up, fell asleep for another few minutes.
6. The President awarded the hero the nation's highest decoration.
7. Although Fred had attempted to change her mind, Marie still thought him an extraordinary fool.
8. We pay our bills on the first of the month.

9. Ms. Simpson considered the former convict honest.
10. When Andrea came home, the house was a mess.
11. The woman knew a good bargain when she saw one.
12. Several qualified people had applied for the job without success.
13. The cool water tasted wonderful.
14. Virtue is its own reward.
15. Having looked all over town and having been convinced that a good used car could not be found for 50 dollars, the men, disillusioned but not completely hopeless, went home.
16. If we look hard enough, we might find a nice gift.
17. The passengers considered the day perfect for flying.
18. Many hours of work produced a beautiful garden.

EXERCISE 26

Change each of the following sentences into a passive, an imperative, and at least one type of question.

1. Bill sold apples.
2. The truck will deliver the furniture.
3. The children love my aunt.
4. Emily conducted the orchestra.
5. The children have built a new clubhouse.

EXERCISE 27

The following paragraph includes sentences with Pattern 1 predications only. Number your paper from 1 to 8. Extract the patterns from the sentences (there may be more than one pattern to a sentence) and write them after the number. Identify the words functioning as subject and predicate.

> We drove to the store. While Carlos waited, we shopped. I walked slowly, pushing the cart through the crowded aisles. The apples glistened with drops of water. And the shelves overflowed with cans. The checker smiled as Jane paid.

EXERCISE 28

Number your paper from 1 to 10. Write ten sentences, five including Pattern 1 and five including Pattern 2. Label those words in each sentence that are functioning as subject, predicate, and direct object.

EXERCISE 29

Number your paper from 1 to 5. Write five sentences illustrating Pattern 3. Label those words in each sentence that are functioning as subject, predicate, indirect object, and direct object.

EXERCISE 30

Number your paper from 1 to 10. Write five sentences illustrating Pattern 4 and five sentences illustrating Pattern 5. Label those words in each sentence that are functioning as subject, predicate, and predicate complement. Make sure to distinguish between the predicate noun and the predicate adjective.

EXERCISE 31

Number your paper from 1 to 10. Write five sentences illustrating Pattern 6 and five sentences illustrating Pattern 7. Label those words in each sentence that are functioning as subject, predicate, direct object, and object complement. Be sure to distinguish clearly between the noun and adjective complement.

G10. Glossary of Grammatical Terms

The following list defines briefly and sometimes illustrates those elements of grammar for which you will have greatest need. Refer to this glossary when you are in doubt about the meaning of a grammatical term. Most of the items listed in this quick-reference guide are treated fully at appropriate places within the text itself.

Absolute expression. An absolute expression usually consists of a noun or pronoun followed by a participle modifying it. The participle is usually expressed; it may be understood. The expression is absolute because it modifies no special word in the sentence; yet it does not stand alone as a sentence.

> *Two hours having elapsed,* we again set out on our journey.
> *The tire being flat,* we decided to pump it up.
> The little boat hugged the shore, *its sails flapping in the wind.*

Active voice. The form of an action-expressing verb which tells that the subject performs the action. See *Voice* below.

Agreement. Correspondence or sameness in number, gender, and person—between subject and predicate and between pronoun and antecedent. Subjects and predicates *agree* in number (both are singular or both are plural):

> *Martha is* my cousin. (Subject and predicate are singular.)
> *Martha and Sue are* my cousins. (Subject and predicate are plural.)

Pronouns agree with their antecedents in having the same gender, person, and number:

> *Liza* hopes to retain *her* youthful stamina.
> Many *persons* retain *their* youthful appearance.
> Gary is one of those *boys who* are always well-mannered.

Antecedent (meaning, literally, *going before*). The substantive (noun or pronoun) to which a pronoun refers or for which it is substituted. See Section U3.

> If *John* tries it, *he* will like it.
> *I* should have done it *myself.*
> *Neither* of the birds built *its* nest.

Although by definition the antecedent is placed before the pronoun, it is sometimes illogically, yet clearly, placed after:

> When *she* finally arrived, *Mother* explained why she was late.

Appositive. A substantive, usually a noun, added to or following another substantive to identify or explain it. The appositive signifies the same thing, and the second substantive is said to be in *apposition.*

More hardy than wheat are these grains—*rye, oats,* and *barley.*
(*Rye, oats,* and *barley* are in apposition with *grains.*)
One important product, *coffee,* this country has to import. *(Coffee
is in apposition with product.)*

An appositive agrees in number and case with the substantive to which it refers. It is set off by commas if its relationship is loose (nonrestrictive) and is used without punctuation
if the relationship is close (restrictive). See Section PM5b.

Auxiliary. A verb used to "help" another verb in the formation of
tenses, voice, mood, and certain precise ideas. *(Am, is, are,
was, were, been, have, has, had, do, does, can, could, may,
might, shall, should, will, would, must, ought, let, dare, need,*
and *used* are examples. See Section U7.

> Manuel *has* gone away for a visit.
> We *should have been* working with the stevedores on the dock.
> *Will* you please turn on the light?

Case. A term referring to the forms that nouns or pronouns have
(nominative, possessive, objective) to indicate their relation
to other words in the sentence. See Section U4.

Clause. A group of words containing a subject and predicate and
forming part of a sentence. A one-word *imperative,* with the
understood subject *you,* can serve as an independent clause.
See Section G8.

> When the cheering stopped, *Wilma was sad.* (independent)
> This is the present *that I bought.* (dependent adjective clause)
> *Wherever we travel,* we shall have fun. (dependent adverb clause)
> Charlie insisted *that he had tried to do it.* (dependent noun
> clause)

Comparison. The change in form of an *adjective* or *adverb* to
indicate greater or smaller degrees of quantity, quality, or
manner. Comparison is discussed and explained in some
detail in Section U10e.

> Positive: The *small* boy ran *swiftly.*
> Comparative: The *smaller* boy ran *more swiftly.*
> Superlative: The *smallest* boy ran *most swiftly.*

Complement. A word or expression used to *complete* the idea indicated or implied by a verb. A *predicate complement* (sometimes called *subjective complement)* may be a noun, a pronoun, or an adjective that follows a linking verb and describes or identifies the subject of the linking verb. See also *Object complement.*

> Ms. Jones is a *writer.*
> Jane is *cheerful.*
> The club members are *friendly.*

Complex sentence. A sentence containing one independent clause and one or more dependent clauses. See Section G9c.

> Although they try, the team cannot win a pennant.
> If they offer you the job, accept it.

Compound-complex sentence. A sentence containing two or more independent clauses and one or more dependent clauses. See Section G9c.

> You can send candy, or you can send flowers, but you must certainly send something because our friends expect a gift.

Compound sentence. A sentence containing two or more clauses that could stand as complete sentences. See Section G9c.

> The sun is bright and the sky is clear.

Conjugation. The changes in the form or use of a verb to show tense, mood, voice, number, and person. See these terms in this glossary.

Conjunction. A part of speech that connects words or groups of words. Conjunctions are of three types: coordinating, subordinating, and correlative. See Section U11.

Conjunctive adverb. A certain kind of adverb which can also be used as a conjunction coordinating two independent clauses: *also, furthermore, nevertheless, besides, however, therefore, thus, so, consequently, hence, likewise, still, then, moreover,* etc. See Sections PM2b and U11.

> The library is open on Saturday; *however,* it will be closed on Sunday.

Determiner. A determiner may be an article (*a, an, the*); a possessive (*my, your, her, its, their, his, our*); a demonstrative (*this, that, these, those*). Determiners usually occur with nouns but not with *all* nouns. Determiners do not appear with proper nouns, nor do *a* and *an* occur with such nouns as *courage* and *oxygen*. In general, a determiner is any member of a subclass of adjectival words that limits the noun it modifies.

Direct address. The noun or pronoun showing to whom speech is addressed (also called the *vocative*):

> *Babs*, are you there?
> After you mow the grass, *Fred*, take out the garbage.

Ellipsis (ellipsis mark). A mark of punctuation consisting of three spaced periods that indicates the omission of one or more words.

Elliptical clause. A clause with a word or words omitted. The omitted words are not needed because they are understood from other words or from context. An elliptical clause is occasionally an independent clause, but usually it is a dependent clause with its subject and part of its predicate omitted, since these are clearly understood from the main clause. In the following examples, the words shown in brackets are often omitted in speaking and writing.

> Some drove to Daytona, others [drove] to Palm Beach.
> She was fifteen years of age; her sister, [was] ten [years of age].

Expletive. When writers are at a loss about beginning a sentence or independent clause, they frequently resort to an *expletive* —a word or words not needed for the sense but used merely to fill out a sentence. The most common expletives are *it* and *there*. The most common expletive phrases are *there is, there are, there was, there were*. Usually, *there is* no weaker or less effective way to begin a sentence. Occasionally, however, expletives are desirable or even necessary, but as a general principle they should be avoided whenever *there is* a better, more effective way of beginning a statement. See Section D4d.

> *It* was Alice whom we saw.
> *It* is a truism that people love freedom.
> *There* are four hundred members present.

Finite verb. A verb form or verb phrase that serves as a predicate; it has number and person. (Opposed to the finite verb is the nonfinite verb form, which cannot serve as a predicate. Nonfinite forms are participles, gerunds, and infinitives. See Section G3g.)

> He *walked* to school.
> I *have finished* the job.

Gender. The classification of nouns or pronouns according to sex. The four genders are masculine, feminine, neuter, and common (either masculine or feminine): *boy, girl, it, individual.* Gender, when indicated, is clear from the noun or pronoun.

Traditional practice has been to generalize in the masculine to express common gender: "Each of the club members thought *his* job the most time-consuming." This practice has come under increasing attack by those who feel that it has unfairly excluded women. For further discussion of this issue and alternative practices, see Section U3e.

Gerund. A verbal noun ending in *–ing,* that is, a noun formed from a verb. A gerund has the same form as the present or perfect participle: "Your *speaking* is appreciated"; "Your *having spoken* to us is greatly appreciated." See Section G3g.

Grammar. The science dealing with words and their relationships to one another. *Grammar,* a descriptive statement of the way a language works, includes a discussion of the forms of words; their uses in phrases, clauses, and sentences; and their tenses, cases, or other changes in form according to their relationships with one another.

Idiom (idiomatic usage). Expressions peculiar to a particular language or a level of usage within that language. (See Section D7.)

Impersonal construction. A method of phrasing in which neither a personal pronoun nor a noun naming a person is stated as the actor. The passive voice or words like *it* or *there* are used.

> *It* is difficult to say.
> *It* is snowing.
> *It* remains to be seen.

Indirect object. A noun or pronoun preceding the direct object of a verb and before which the word *to* or *for* is understood. When such an object follows the direct object, the preposition *to* or *for* is used.

> Will you lend *him* your notes until Thursday?
> (Will you lend your notes *to him* until Thursday?)
> Yesterday I sent *her* a letter.
> (Yesterday I sent a letter *to her.*)

Indirect question. Restatement by one person of a direct question asked by another.

> Direct: Where will you stay?
> Indirect: Peggy asked where I would stay.

Indirect quotation. Restatement by one person, in different words, of the words written or spoken by someone else.

> Direct: Jim wrote, "I'll be there on Sunday."
> Indirect: Jim wrote that he will be here on Sunday.

Infinitive. A verb form that is the first of the three principal parts of a verb. The infinitive has the function of a verb (as part of the predicate), but it is also commonly used as a verbal or in a verbal phrase. When used as a verbal, it functions like a noun, adjective, or adverb and is usually preceded by the sign of the infinitive, the word *to.*

> to run, to jump, to laugh, to dream, to think, to explain

Inflection. A change in the form of a word to show a change in use or meaning. *Comparison* is the inflection of adjectives and adverbs; *declension* is the inflection of nouns and pronouns; and *conjugation* is the inflection of verbs.

> Examples: loud, louder, loudest; beautiful, more beautiful, most beautiful; I, me, mine; we, us, ours; he, him his; sing, sang, sung; have, has, had.

Intensifier. This is a word or element used to strengthen, increase, or enforce meaning. *Certainly, awful,* and *abominably* are examples of intensifiers.

Interjection. A part of speech—an exclamatory word—expressing strong feeling or surprise, which has little connection with the remainder of the sentence.

> *Oh*, that's what you mean.
> *Gosh!* What fun that will be.

Intransitive verb. A verb that does not require a direct object to complete its meaning. The meaning ends with itself, and the verb, therefore, may have adverbial modifiers but not an object. See Section G3b.

> The fearful shepherd *trembled* as he *spoke*.
> The mountain *roared* and issued forth a mouse.

Irregular verb. Irregular verbs do not follow a regular pattern in forming their principal parts. Instead, the principal parts are usually formed by a change in the vowel: *see, saw, seen; drive, drove, driven; choose, chose, chosen; lose, lost, lost.* Your dictionary is your guide. See Section U5 also.

Juncture. This word has several meanings, all of which involve the act or state of *joining*. In linguistics, the term has a somewhat specialized meaning relating to the fact that words as we speak them are not usually separated to the extent that they are in writing. Our words tend to flow together without the pauses which, in writing, are shown by spaces. If we speak the sentence, "The person who can do this well deserves praise," we would need briefly to interrupt our flow of sound after either *this* or *well* in order to be fully understood.

Linking verb (also called a *joining verb* or *coupling verb).* A verb which does not express action but only a state of being or a static condition. It serves to link the subject with another noun (*predicate noun*) or pronoun (*predicate pronoun*) or with an adjective (*predicate adjective*). These words following the linking verbs are called *predicate complements.* Common linking verbs are the forms of *to be, look, seem, smell, sound, appear, feel, become, grow, prove, turn, remain, stand*, etc. See Section U6.

> The other individual *was* his aunt.
> That *seems* reasonable.
> That flower *looks* pretty.

Modify. To describe or limit. Adjectives are used with nouns or pronouns, and adverbs are used with verbs, adjectives, or other adverbs to describe, limit, or make a meaning more definite. Descriptive: *gray* skies, *tall* buildings. Limiting: *six* envelopes, the *only* man.

Mood. A characteristic of verbs, revealing how action or expression is thought of: as a fact (*indicative mood*); as a possibility or something desired (*subjunctive mood*); or as a command or request (*imperative mood*). Other kinds of expression are possible through use of certain auxiliary verbs. See Section U9.

> He *is* my cousin. (indicative)
> I wish I *were* with you. (subjunctive)
> *Drop* that cupcake. (imperative)

Morpheme. Any word or part of a word not further divisible into smaller meaningful elements: *boy* and *–ish* in *boyish;* *ad–* and *vice* in *advice.*

Morphology. The patterns of word formation in a language. *Morphology* and *syntax* together form a basic division of grammar.

Nonfinite verb. A verb form which cannot serve as predicate, since it shows neither person nor grammatical number. Nonfinite verb forms—the verbals—are *gerunds, participles, infinitives.* See Section G3g.

Number. The change in form of a noun, pronoun, or verb to show whether one or more than one is indicated.

Object. The noun, pronoun, or noun clause following a preposition or following a transitive verb.

> Debbie is in the *room.*
> The carpenters built a *house.*
> He said *that he would go.*

Object complement. A noun or noun phrase used after a direct object of certain verbs to complete the meaning.

> We have elected Felicia *treasurer.*
> They called the dog *Jerry.*

Note that the verb is transitive in a sentence or clause containing an object complement. See *Complement*, also.

Participle. A verb form that functions (1) as part of a verb phrase or (2) as an adjective. The three forms are present participle, past participle, perfect participle.

> The student *sketching* the model is Kevin O'Shea.
> I have *finished* my essay.
> *Having finished* my essay, I turned it in.

Parts of speech. The classification of words. Every word must belong to one classification: *noun, pronoun, adjective, verb, adverb, preposition, conjunction, interjection.*

Passive voice. The form of an action-expressing verb which tells that the subject does not act but is acted upon. Literally and actually, the subject is *passive*. See *Voice*, also.

Person. The change in the form of a pronoun or verb to indicate whether the person used is the person speaking (*first person*), the person spoken to (*second person*), or the person or thing spoken about (*third person*): *I* play, *you* play, *she* plays, *it* plays, *we* play, *you* play, *they* play.

Phoneme. A group of closely related sounds regarded as a single sound. (These speech sounds are called *phones*.) A phoneme is the simplest possible significant classification of sound. Linguists differ in their analysis of sounds of our language but are generally agreed that some fifty phonemes exist in English.

Phonetics. The science of speech sounds and their production.

Phrase. A group of related words not containing a subject and a predicate and serving as a single part of speech. See Section G7.

Pitch. The combination of *pitch, stress,* and *juncture* (see entry) forms what is known as *intonation*. In linguistic terms, intonation is the significant speech patterns resulting from pitch sequences and pauses (juncture). *Pitch* is closely connected with *stress;* the latter, which refers to loudness, may be primary, secondary, tertiary, or weak. One linguist (Paul Roberts) uses the sentence "The White House is a white house" to indicate the different emphases given *White House* and *white house*. *Pitch* is usually numbered from 1 to 4 (low to high or high to low, depending upon which linguist is speaking or writing). Pitch helps distinguish spoken questions from statements just as question marks and periods do in writing.

Plural. A classification of nouns, pronouns, subjects, and predicates to indicate two or more units or members. Note that a subject with two or more singulars joined by *and* becomes plural.

Predicate. The verb or verb phrase in a sentence that makes a statement—an assertion, an action, a condition, a state of being—about the subject. A *simple predicate* is a verb or a verb phrase alone, without an object or modifiers. A *compound predicate* consists of two or more verbs or verb phrases. A *complete predicate* consists of the verb with its object and all its modifiers. See Section G9.

> Her brother *wrote* poetry. (simple predicate)
> Dolly Valdez *drove the ball nearly 200 yards.* (complete predicate)
> I *wrote* the letter yesterday *and mailed* it first thing this morning. (compound predicate)

Predicate adjective. An adjective used in the predicate after a linking verb; this adjective modifies the subject.

> Today seems *warmer* than yesterday.
> The backpackers appear *ready* for the trip.

Predicate complement, also called *subjective complement.* A *predicate noun* or *pronoun* or a *predicate adjective.* See *Complement,* also.

Principal parts. The three parts of a verb (*present infinitive, past tense,* and *past participle*) from which all other forms and uses of verbs (tense, mood, tone, voice) can be expressed, sometimes without, but most frequently with, the necessary auxiliary verbs. In learning the principal parts of unfamiliar verbs, consult your dictionary. See Section U5.

Reference. A word used with pronouns and their antecedents to indicate the relationship between them. The pronoun *refers* to the antecedent; the antecedent is indicated, or *referred* to, by the pronoun.

Regular verbs. These are the most common verbs in English because they usually form their past tense and past participle by adding *–d, –ed,* or *–t* to the present infinitive form: *move, moved, moved; walk, walked, walked; mean, meant, meant.* See Section U5.

Rhetoric. The art or science of literary uses of language. *Rhetoric* is concerned with the effectiveness and general appeal of communication and with methods of achieving literary quality and vigor. It is only loosely connected with correctness or with specific details of mechanics, spelling, and grammar, as such.

Root. In linguistics, the base of a word is a *root,* a morpheme to which may be added prefixes and suffixes. An approximate synonym for *base* and *root* in this sense is *stem;* all mean the part of a word to which suffixes and prefixes are added or in which phonetic changes are made. Thus we say that *love* is the root (stem or base) of the word *loveliness, form* of the word *reform,* and so on.

Simple sentence. A sentence containing one subject (simple or compound) and one predicate (simple or compound). See Section G9c.

> Anthony was a handsome baby.
> Sunshine and lollipops are Susie's wants for her birthday.

Singular. The number classification of nouns, pronouns, subjects, and predicates to indicate *one: woman, boy, student, I, he, she, it, is, has, was, goes.*

Subject. The person or thing (noun, pronoun, noun phrase, noun clause) about which a statement or assertion is made in a sentence or clause. A *simple subject* is the noun or pronoun alone. A *complete subject* is a simple subject together with its modifiers. A *compound subject* consists of two or more nouns, pronouns, noun phrases, noun clauses. See Section G9c.

Substantive. An inclusive term for a noun, a pronoun, a verbal noun (gerund, infinitive), or a phrase or a clause used like a noun. The practical value of the word *substantive* is that it saves repeating all the words that are included in this definition. The following italicized words are examples of substantives:

> The *porridge* was ten days old.
> *We* shall return in September.
> *From Portland to Bangor* is a great distance.
> Don't you realize *that Santa Claus will be here tomorrow?*

Syllable. In phonetics, a *syllable* is a segment of speech uttered with one impulse of air pressure from the lungs. In writing, *syllable* refers to a character or set of characters (letters of the alphabet) representing one sound. In general, *syllable* refers to the smallest amount or unit of speech or writing.

Syntax. Sentence structure; the grammatical arrangement of words, phrases, and clauses.

Tense. The time of the action or the state of being expressed by the verb: *present, past, future, present perfect, past perfect, future perfect.* The first three of these six are sometimes named the *simple* or *primary* tenses; the last three are sometimes named the *perfect* or *compound* or *secondary* tenses. See Section U8.

Tone. A word used in this handbook to distinguish a characteristic of tenses of verbs, indicating within any one tense or time limit *emphasis* or *progress* or *simple* time. See Section U8.

Transitive verb. A verb accompanied or followed by a direct object which completes its meaning. See Section G3b.

> Lisa *shook* the plum tree.
> Oscar *helps* the distressed.

Verb phrase. A verb together with an auxiliary or auxiliaries: *is going, was finished, shall have taken, will have been taken.* To distinguish between a *verb phrase* and a *verbal* (participle, infinitive, gerund), see Sections U7 and G3.

> Elena *has known* many people in her time.
> Carl's letter *was rewritten* several times.

Verbals. The verb forms—*participles, gerunds, infinitives*—when used as adjectives, adverbs, nouns, or parts of verb phrases. A verbal is never used alone as a verb. See Section G3g.

> *Skiing* is delightful. (gerund used as a noun)
> *To succeed* is exhilarating. (infinitive used as a noun)
> The *quaking* house may collapse. (participle used as an adjective)
> Miriam was glad *to have come.* (infinitive used as an adverb)

Voice. The change in the form or use of a verb—a transitive verb only—to indicate whether the subject is the performer of the action (*active voice*) or is acted upon (*passive voice*). In the formation of the passive voice, some form of auxiliary verb *to be* is used with the past participle. See Section G3d.

Word order. An English sentence does not consist of a string of words in free relationship to each other but of groups of words arranged in patterns. Words in an English sentence have meaning because of their position. That is, they may have one meaning in one position, another meaning in another position, and no meaning in still another position. Some linguists maintain that the basis of English grammar is word order. Certainly the order of words is a fundamental part of grammar and is basic in sentence construction. In addition, word order contributes to many effects of style, especially emphasis.

REVIEW EXERCISE 1

Write on your paper the number of each sentence. Beside the number, write the code indicating that the word, phrase, or clause italicized in each sentence has the *grammatical function* of one of the following parts of speech:

Noun—*N*	Adjective—*Adj*
Pronoun—*Pro*	Preposition—*Prep*
Verb—*V*	Conjunction—*Conj*
Adverb—*Adv*	

1. I mailed the package *today*.
2. Some people seem to have a sixth *sense* about coming troubles.
3. She left the hall *during* the lecture.
4. He is ready for whatever changes *develop* in the situation.
5. You know only a *tenth* of the problems we had.
6. I *am* not ready to leave yet.
7. It's possible to drive too *slowly* on this turnpike.
8. You have *still* another reason for studying hard.
9. You should learn *to read* more efficiently.
10. You eat your food faster *than* you should.

REVIEW EXERCISE 2

Follow the directions for Review Exercise 1.

1. We don't want the people *sitting* over there to hear us.
2. You should *at least* try to read the chapter.
3. I'd like to know who is *in charge*.

4. The ticket will be given to *whoever gets here first.*
5. *Insofar as* we can, we'll help you get the assignment.
6. Someone *has to have been fooling* with this apparatus.
7. *Doing* what you can is all anyone can expect.
8. You can count on me to help *to whatever extent* I can.
9. Your idea that something lies *at the bottom of this proposal* is probably right.
10. *Whomever you want to ask* to the party is all right with me.

REVIEW EXERCISE 3

In each of the following sentences three words are italicized. Write on your paper the number of each sentence and beside that number write the three abbreviations indicated to show the *parts of speech* involved.

Noun—*N*	Adjective—*Adj*
Pronoun—*Pro*	Preposition—*Prep*
Verb—*V*	Coordinating conjunction—*CC*
Adverb—*Adv*	Subordinating conjunction—*SC*

1. *If* George *comes,* will the others be *far* behind him?
2. The humidity decreased *greatly,* and we realized that a storm was *upon us.*
3. The *scarecrow fell to* earth at my brother's feet.
4. *Under* the *terms* of the agreement, the lawyer could not make *other* arrangements.
5. Nancy *frequently* peered *over* the *hedge* to watch her neighbors.
6. Cassie *made* her ice cream last as long as she *possibly could.*
7. *Skillfully* the *police* dispersed the *milling* crowd.
8. *By* the time Tanya is graduated, *she* should be a good *mathematician.*
9. *Everyone* gets *better* marks in the nuclear physics course *than* I do.
10. His manners are *disgusting,* and his personality is *barely tolerable.*
11. My friend *is* willing *but* not *able* to complete her obligations.
12. Valentino hurried *into* the *shelter* of an *overhanging* tent.
13. Do you *know whether* the team scored its last touchdown before or *after* Jones entered the game?
14. Dolores and Daniel *left* home *before 8* o'clock in the morning.
15. *I know that* the menu has been revised *greatly* since January.
16. Is *that* the *same* address you *had* before you went away to college?
17. *When* you find the scrapbook, set it *aside for* me.
18. *Look up* the *number* in the directory, please.

19. Valerie's *intellect was incredible.*
20. *At* the circus there are several activities in *which* all children find delight.

REVIEW EXERCISE 4

In each of the following sentences a phrase, clause, or complete statement (sentence) is italicized. Write on your paper the number of each sentence. Opposite that number write (1) the abbreviation (*P, C,* or *S*) to show whether it is a phrase, clause, or sentence. Then write (2) the proper abbreviation (from those below) to show what *kind* of phrase, clause, or sentence is involved.

Independent clause—*I Cl*	Noun phrase—*N Ph*
Noun clause—*N Cl*	Adjective phrase—*Adj Ph*
Adjective clause—*Adj Cl*	Adverb phrase—*Adv Ph*
Adverb clause—*Adv Cl*	Independent sentence—*I S*
Verb phrase—*V Ph*	

1. He promised to take us *into the clubhouse* next Sunday.
2. Integrity is *what every person should respect in others.*
3. The teacher *who lectured so well* is my roommate's aunt.
4. *In a dark blue Cadillac* the mayor could be seen bowing and smiling.
5. The teacher was told *that you were unable to be there.*
6. *The police officer hopes* that there will be no disturbances in the neighborhood.
7. *I neither want nor need your pity.* But I do need your money.
8. The Mets always seem to play better *in the evening.*
9. By this date the manuscript *should have been submitted.*
10. *She thought of her parents,* who had made so many sacrifices for her.
11. Jennifer spent too much time in the sun *when she was in Puerto Rico.*
12. *After their performance* the singers returned to the hotel.
13. They were chipmunks *who had invaded the vegetable garden.*
14. Eddie appeared *at the concert* wearing a striking red silk vest.
15. *Although in its infancy,* the new crafts gallery seemed promising.
16. The fire fighters rushed with their equipment *to the burning warehouse.*
17. The clock indicates that we *have been waiting* for three hours.

18. Cooking soup is easier than *cooking casseroles.*
19. *I expect you to deliver all the mail.*
20. The manual explains *that we shall then be subject to Canadian laws.*

REVIEW EXERCISE 5

Each item below consists of two sentences. Pick out the lettered word in the second sentence that has the same grammatical function as the italicized word in the first sentence. On your paper, write the proper capital letter.

Example: I *am* tired of all this talking.
             I think that he is willing to be on the team if we
                A   B C   D
             want him.
              E

Explanation: The answer is *B*, because *am* is a linking verb and *is* is the only such verb in the second sentence. Answer *A* is wrong because *I am tired* is functionally quite different from *I think that.* Answer *D* is wrong because *be*, though a linking verb, is in infinitive form.

1. She has the *irritating* habit of answering any question by asking another.

   With the top of the batting order coming up, our pitcher, obvi-
                              A

   ously tiring, cast appealing glances in the direction of the
       B   C

   dugout; but the manager, pretending interest in nothing but
                     D

   the scoreboard, had evidently decided on letting him take his
                                 E

   lumps.

2. She has the irritating habit of answering any question by *asking* another.

   (Use the same sentence for matching as in the preceding item.)

3. The wind rose, the sky darkened, and it began to rain *very* heavily.

What can have happened to my notebook is completely mysteri-
                                                  A

ous; I put it away only yesterday, and it ought to be right in this
        B   *C*   *D*   *E*

drawer.

4. If I had *had* a chance to advise you, I could have saved you some
trouble.

   He had always preferred the life of a simple country squire and
     A

   might well have finished out his life in that station had not the
     B   *C*   *D*

   whole American citizenry demanded that he lead them during
                                        E

   the crisis.

5. "If I had the Governor where the Governor's got me,/By next
   Tuesday morning the Governor'*d* be free."

   That so many great people have eagerly swallowed flattery and
                                             A

   have been ruled by favorites is one of the great puzzles of his-
     B   *C*

   tory, for most ordinary people despise flattery and will prove
                                            D

   resentful of it; just try it on a police officer or a flight attendant.
            E

Usage

U1. Levels of Usage

In today's society, few people fail to acknowledge the importance of using what is generally called "good English." It is important that we choose those expressions and grammatical forms that will convey to hearers and readers exactly the ideas and emotional tones we wish to present. On one occasion, we may wish to speak or write formally; on another, quite informally.

U1a. CHOOSE AN APPROPRIATE LEVEL OF USAGE.

The controlling guide to usage should always be the test of appropriateness: How can I best express what I have in mind so that it will be most effectively communicated to a specific reader (or listener)? In one set of circumstances, it might be appropriate to say, for instance, "Scram" or "Beat it" or "Get lost." In another situation, it would be more appropriate to say "Please leave" or "Au revoir" or "Godspeed." The appropriateness of a given level of usage depends upon the situation involved, that is, who is speaking to whom and about what.

U1b. DISTINGUISH AMONG VARIOUS LEVELS OF USAGE.

Within any language there are varieties of usage associated with geographic area (regional dialects), social status, educational background, individual style, and such special forms of communication as technical language, profanity, and slang.

In a broad sense, a distinction can be made between informal and formal usage. Actually, the problem of levels of usage is more involved than this; at least five levels can be mentioned. It is often difficult to tell, however, where one level ends and another begins.

1. **Carefully Selected Written English.** Precisely prepared and painstakingly edited books and magazines exhibit this level of usage. In addition, the writing of many educated men and women in all parts of the country falls into this category, which is largely (but not exclusively) the usage described and recommended in this handbook.

2. **General Written English.** Most newspapers, business letters and reports, and several widely circulated magazines employ this second level of usage. It does not involve all the niceties and "rules" of choice written English, but it is generally acceptable and represents the writing level that all serious students should try to attain.

3. **Choice Spoken English.** This is the language heard in serious or formal addresses and in the formal conversation of those people who also use carefully selected written English. It is neither so "correct" nor so inflexible as the two earlier varieties mentioned, because oral English is nearly always freer and less constrained than is written English.

4. **General Spoken English.** Most well-educated people employ this level in ordinary conversation. It is somewhat more easygoing than choice spoken English, employs more newer and shorter forms (slang, contractions), and is sometimes referred to as *colloquial* or *informal*.

5. **Nonstandard English.** This is a term used to characterize illiterate expressions. Such expressions, associated with the uneducated, appear also in the speech of many educated persons who choose to express themselves in ways sometimes considered uncouth. One who speaks vulgate (common) English is not necessarily vulgar any more than one who chooses to use carefully selected written English or choice spoken English is necessarily affected or snobbish.

The distinctions just made are somewhat arbitrary. Further, some expressions are identical on all levels. One who says or writes "I spoke slowly" is using an expression that has no distinct level of usage.

It is difficult to label constructions apart from their contexts, but the five levels mentioned can be illustrated:

Carefully Selected Written English:	I shall not speak.
General Written English:	I will not speak.
Choice Spoken:	I'll not speak.
General Spoken:	I'm not going to speak.
Nonstandard:	I ain't gonna say nothin'.

Although attitudes toward usage have become much less rigid in recent years, occasions arise for everyone in which a knowledge of acceptable, reputable English is either desirable or essential. You may not wish or need to use "correct" English at all times, but you should at least know, for those occasions when you will need it, what preferred usage directs.

EXERCISE 1

Each of the following sentences contains an error in usage, an acknowledged violation of reputable, acceptable written language practice. Make necessary corrections in each sentence. If any of the sentences give you trouble, study carefully Sections U2–U11, which follow.

1. I do not like them clothes as much as I do these.
2. She don't have to go unless she wants to.
3. This here model is difficult to build.
4. Mary and I we went to the party.
5. She is an intelligent person but she cannot learn me anything.
6. Just between you and I, the meat was badly cooked and served.
7. Every boy and girl in the class were shocked by the severity of the examination.
8. What I want to know is who did she give it to?
9. Joan just wanted to lay down and rest awhile.
10. The test was difficult for all of we students.

EXERCISE 2

Follow the instructions for Exercise 1.

1. After his illness, Bruce was unable to sleep good.
2. If I was you, I would not say nothing at all.
3. There is hundreds of people in the hall right now.
4. As soon as I was served, I set down and started eating.

5. Jack knew it was them who stole the car.
6. Helen is not even gonna give Herb a chance to apologize.
7. We can't hardly expect any more help from our friends.
8. Bill is not certain why Beulah give him help with his homework.
9. Betty and me were sorry to hear of your accident.
10. This outline, together with the charts, provide a clear idea of our plan.

EXERCISE 3

Follow the instructions for Exercise 1.

1. Renee asked me to do like she told me.
2. My opinion, like my presence here, are taken too much for granted.
3. Before the party, I made the discovery that the guests had broken into the refrigerator and drank most of the cokes.
4. Bill looked as if he was about to die from hunger.
5. Either you or Dolly writes better than her.
6. Everybody working on a holiday will have their pay doubled.
7. If we walk soft enough, we may be able to get close enough to take a picture.
8. Who do you take me to be anyway?
9. You should of told me about your problem before this.
10. The cause for all the noise and confusion were not clear to Berta and me.

U2. Subject and Verb Agreement

Grammatical agreement means oneness or harmony of parts of a sentence. Thus, when a subject agrees with its verb, both the subject and the verb in the predicate are alike in having the same *person* (first, second, third) and *number* (singular or plural).

U2a. A VERB MUST AGREE WITH ITS SUBJECT IN PERSON AND NUMBER.

Look for the person or thing about which the verb makes a statement. When you find it, you have the subject of the sentence. A subject is always a noun, a word or group of words used as a noun, or a pronoun.

> Our *football team* [subject] *plays* [verb] eight games each year.

In the preceding sentence, the subject and the verb are easy to find, but in some sentences the subject comes after the verb or is separated from the verb by other words. Before you try to make the verb agree with the subject, be sure that you have the *real* subject.

English verbs (except *to be*) have the same form (in the present tense) for singular and plural and for all persons except the third person singular.

Most nouns and verbs form their plurals in directly opposite ways; that is, most nouns form plurals by adding *–s* or *–es*, and most verbs add an *–s* in the third person singular. Remember that used as subjects, *I* and *we* are the forms for the first person; *you*, for the second person; *she, he, it*, and *they*, for the third person.

> The first concert helps us pay for new clarinets for the orchestra. (The noun *concert* is third person singular. The verb *helps* is also third person singular.)
>
> The sophomores invite the juniors to the first soccer game. (*Sophomores* is third person plural. The verb *invite* is also third person plural.)
>
> I choose a different girl for each team. (*I* is first person singular. The verb *choose* is also first person singular.)

NOTE: *Don't* means *do not*. It is used correctly with plural subjects and with *I* and *you* as singular subjects. Be careful not to use it with a third person singular subject like *he, the chair, the motor, Karen*. With such subjects use *doesn't*.

> Nonstandard: She *don't* play golf.
> Standard: She *doesn't* play golf.
> The meat *doesn't* need curing.
> Jim *doesn't* appear to be working well.

U2b. *THERE* AND *HERE* ARE NOT SUBJECTS.

After *there* and *here* we usually find the verb first and then the subject.

> Nonstandard: There *is* dances every Friday evening at the
> new gym.

Standard:	There *are* dances every Friday evening at the new gym.
Nonstandard:	Here *is* the tickets for the play.
Standard:	Here *are* the tickets for the play.

U2c. A PREPOSITIONAL PHRASE THAT FOLLOWS THE SUBJECT DOES NOT AFFECT THE NUMBER OF THE VERB.

Phrases such as *of the people, in the various groups,* and *to my cousins* are called prepositional phrases. The important words in a prepositional phrase are a preposition (*to, for, from, with, by, in, between, of,* and *near* are some common ones) and a noun or pronoun that is the object of the preposition. Do *not* make the verb agree with the object of a preposition.

Nonstandard:	Personnel managers from the Pearce Company *interviews* students in our senior class every year. (The word *Company* is the object of the preposition *from. Managers* is the subject.)
Standard:	Personnel managers from the Pearce Company *interview* students in our senior class every year.
Nonstandard:	One of the members *preside* at each meeting.
Standard:	One of the members *presides* at each meeting.

U2d. SINGULAR PRONOUNS REQUIRE SINGULAR VERBS.

These pronouns are singular: *another, anybody, anyone, anything, each, either, everybody, everyone, everything, many a one, neither, nobody, no one, one, somebody, someone.* They require a singular verb form.

Nonstandard:	Each of the campers *cook* some dish well.
Standard:	Each of the campers *cooks* some dish well.
Nonstandard:	Everyone in the Hawaiian Islands *were* concerned about the danger of invasion.
Standard:	Everyone in the Hawaiian Islands *was* concerned about the danger of invasion.
Nonstandard:	Neither of the senators *show* any uncertainty.
Standard:	Neither of the senators *shows* any uncertainty.

Nonstandard: Either of the twins *like* to go swimming in the nearby lake.

Standard: Either of the twins *likes* to go swimming in the nearby lake.

NOTE: Certain nouns or pronouns are considered singular or plural according to the singular or plural number of the key word in a modifying phrase. Examples are *none, some, all, any, half, what,* and *which*.

> *Some* of my *allowance has* been spent.
> *Some* our our *athletes have* been awarded letters.
> No ice is left; *all* of *it has* melted.
> No skaters are left on the frozen pond; *all* of *them have* gone inside to get warm.
> *Half* of this *report is* to be completed by Saturday.
> *Half* of the *dresses* in the store *are* imported from England.
> *Which* [one] of the cars *is* reserved for the guest speaker?
> *Which* [ones] of the cars *are* reserved for the town officials?

None (literally *no one*, but frequently meaning *not any*) may be followed by either a singular or a plural verb. Studies of the use of *none* have revealed that it is as often followed by a plural as by a singular verb, especially when the phrase that modifies *none* contains a plural noun.

> *None* [no one] of the players on our team *is* likely to make varsity.
> *None* [not any] of the players on our team *have* failed to pass their examinations.

U2e. WORDS JOINED TO A SUBJECT BY *WITH*, *TOGETHER WITH*, *IN ADDITION TO*, *AS WELL AS*, AND *INCLUDING* DO NOT AFFECT THE VERB.

> Our allies, as well as the enemy, *were* suffering.
> My whole equipment, including fishing rods, tackle, and knapsack, *was* lost on the trip.

U2f. A COLLECTIVE NOUN USUALLY TAKES A SINGULAR VERB.

Common **collective nouns** are *army, assembly, clergy, committee, company, couple, crew, crowd, family, flock, group, herd, jury, mob, multitude, orchestra, pair, personnel, squad, team, union.*

U
2

These collective nouns take a singular verb and singular pronouns when the collection of individuals is thought of as a unit. However, they take a plural verb and plural pronouns when the members of the group are thought of as individuals, acting separately.

> The jury [a unit] *is* going to reach a verdict before 6 o'clock.
> The jury [members] *have* ordered their suppers and are going to eat them in the jury room.
> The committee [a unit] *has* appointed a new secretary.
> The committee [members] *have* been unwilling to charge for personal expenses.
> The couple [a unit] at the head table *is* named Johnson.
> The couple [members] *were* assigned simple tasks during the service.
> Our platoon [a unit] *marches* very well.
> The family [members] *disagree* about my plans.

U2g. FOR NOUNS PLURAL IN FORM BUT SINGULAR IN MEANING, USE A SINGULAR VERB.

> Calisthenics *is* included in our physical fitness program.
> Mumps *is* a contagious disease.
> Economics *was* Dan's major in college.

Although authorities differ in their opinions about the number of some of these nouns, the following are usually considered to be singular: *physics, economics, news, politics, ethics, measles.* Consult your dictionary for guidance.

Subjects plural in form, which describe a quantity or number, require a singular verb when the subject is regarded as a unit.

> Ten miles *is* too far to walk.
> Two from five *leaves* three.
> Five dollars *was* the price of the book.
> Two-thirds of a gallon *does* not seem enough.

A title of a book, play, film, painting, musical composition, or other such work is singular.

> *Pride and Prejudice* is my favorite novel.
> *The Frogs* is a play by Aristophanes.

U2h. BE CAREFUL OF THE PLURALS OF NOUNS OF FOREIGN ORIGIN.

Singular	*Plural*
datum	data
phenomenon	phenomena
genus	genera
synopsis	synopses
alumnus	alumni

Synopses of two stories *were* submitted.
The alumni *were* in favor of building the stadium.

NOTE: *Data* is correctly used as a plural, though many now use it as a singular.

U2i. FORMS OF *TO BE* AGREE WITH THE SUBJECT, NOT WITH THE PREDICATE NOUN OR PRONOUN.

When a form of the verb *to be (am, is, are, was, were, have been, has been)* comes between two nouns or pronouns, the noun or pronoun coming first is considered the subject.

The hardest part of the job *is* the bending and lifting.
Bending and lifting *are* the hardest part of the job.

U2j. A COMPOUND SUBJECT JOINED BY *AND* REQUIRES A PLURAL VERB.

French and biology *are* my favorite subjects.
Television and radio *have* revolutionized social habits.
On the landing field *stand* a jet and a small helicopter.

NOTE:

1. When the two nouns or pronouns form a single thought, have a closely related meaning, or mean one thing or one person, a singular verb is used.

The secretary and treasurer of our club *is* named Benno Curtis.
Bread and peanut butter *is* my favorite snack.
My comrade and friend *was* with me.
Spaghetti and meatballs *is* forbidden on my diet.

2. If *each* or *every* precedes two or more singular subjects joined by *and*, the verb is singular.

> Every girl and boy in the auditorium *applauds* when the principal appears on the stage.
> Each boy and girl *has* received a letter from the dean.

U2k. IF TWO SUBJECTS ARE JOINED BY *OR*, *EITHER* . . . *OR*, *NEITHER* . . . *NOR*, THE VERB AGREES WITH THE SUBJECT NEARER IT.

> Neither the student president nor her friends *want* to see Janice elected.
> Either new athletic fields or a swimming pool *is* to be provided in the spring.
> Either they or I *am* at fault.
> Either some of her classmates or Bill *is* willing to volunteer.
> Either Bill or some of her classmates *are* willing to volunteer.

U2l. A RELATIVE PRONOUN (*WHO, WHICH, THAT*) IS SINGULAR OR PLURAL ACCORDING TO THE WORD TO WHICH THE PRONOUN REFERS.

The only way to tell whether a relative pronoun is singular or plural is to examine the part of the sentence that precedes it and decide which word in the sentence the pronoun refers to. This word is called the *antecedent* of the pronoun. If the antecedent is singular, the pronoun will be singular, and the verb that goes with it must be singular.

> Margie is the only one of the golfers who *has* maintained a consistently good score (*Who* is the subject of the relative clause. It refers to *one* and is therefore singular.)
> Monieka is one of the six mission stations that *are* supported by our church. (*That* is the subject of the relative clause. It refers to *stations* and is plural.)

EXERCISE 4

Write on your paper the number of each sentence. Beside it write the subject of each incorrect verb and the correct form of that verb. Be prepared to explain in class why you have made the correction. If the sentence is correct, write *C* after its number.

1. For those who want to join clubs there is the ski club, the drama club, and the chorus.
2. The real meaning of success for many people are making more and more money.
3. Semantics is a good thing for a student to be interested in, and so is athletics.
4. The loss of three friends and a job were the price Carl had to pay for his curiosity.
5. Fifteen dollars were all the Old Stone Peers could collect for playing at the dance.
6. Either you or I are going to have to push the car out of the ditch.
7. Except for a few scattered cousins, the seven aunts was all the family Wesley had.
8. The tastiest part of most school lunches are the spaghetti and meatballs.
9. Your letter, together with your check, was received yesterday.
10. Everybody, students and instructors alike, are glad that school is opening.
11. Dolores insisted that champagnes from a domestic stock was not to be considered.
12. Whoever finds Margaret Mead a dull and uninteresting writer are, I fear, devoid of intellectual curiosity.
13. Each of the girls in the drama club is an aspiring television star.
14. Measles, for adults, are often a serious disease.
15. Dave smilingly disgreed when someone remarked that *The Dynasts* were great literature.
16. *Westward the Worms* are one of the finest novels ever to come from Shillingbreek's typewriter.
17. For Monica 20 miles of hiking over rugged terrain were no challenge.
18. Beside the cottage stands a pine tree, a willow, and a maple.

EXERCISE 5

Follow the directions for Exercise 4.

1. George Appleby was discharged because the spelling on the memoranda he wrote to his boss was so bad.
2. Cursing and pleading are not going to help us find our way out of the jungle, Deirdre.

3. Important in a person's development is the schools she or he has attended.
4. The senior class is having their pictures taken at five-minute intervals this afternoon.
5. In the States, shooting people or their families are against the law.
6. The fatheadedness of my two assistants were simply indescribable.
7. Each of the school regulations have a different purpose.
8. Monique is one of the most sophisticated women that has ever lived in this community.
9. It was one of the roads that leads to Wichita, and that was all that mattered.
10. The superintendent, with two members of the board of directors, inspects the heating plant every fall.
11. There is a Montgomery Ward, a J. C. Penney, a Woolworth, and two large banks in town.
12. Violet is a good student who has no trouble at examination time.
13. You forget, Gina, that your mother and I am aging fast.
14. Hernandez was one of those clumsy and inartistic matadors that sometimes wangles an engagement in the off-season.
15. Jay soon realized that politics were not for him.
16. Harry and Hilda meets each other after every class.
17. There was certain moments when little Karl feared he could bear the pain no longer.
18. The plans for the celebration of St. Patrick's Day was kept a closely guarded secret.
19. It seems that either she or I have to make all the decisions.
20. I told Gloria that eight dollars was too little for a day's work.

EXERCISE 6

If a sentence contains a verb not in agreement with its subject, write the proper form of the verb. Some sentences contain no error.

1. There are a shoe store, a supermarket, and a toy store in this shopping center.
2. Each of the actors seems suitable for this demanding role.
3. Eleven dollars were what we earned by selling tickets.
4. Eloise or I are willing to help deliver gifts to hospitals.
5. For Betty a three-day visit with her grandparents were a great treat.

6. The most difficult aspect of raising some flowers are the proper use of chemical nourishment and water.
7. Near the Ferris wheel stands the leader, the campers, and a crowd of onlookers.
8. None is better qualified to succeed in this endeavor than Ned.
9. Everybody, teachers and parents alike, hope that the junior class play will be well received.
10. Neither Wonder Woman nor Superman are capable of handling this threat to the safety of the city.

U 3

U3. Pronouns and Antecedents

Our writing would be dull if we repeated nouns again and again. Consequently, we use a pronoun (*pro–* meaning "for") instead of repeating the noun.

U3a. A PRONOUN SHOULD AGREE WITH ITS ANTECEDENT IN GENDER, NUMBER, AND PERSON.

The meaning of the pronoun will not be clear unless it has the same gender, number, and person as the noun for which it stands. This noun is called the **antecedent.** Its relationship to the pronoun must be unmistakably clear if your reader is not to be confused.

> Orlon is an important synthetic material. *It* is said to be better than nylon. (*It* refers to *orlon*, the antecedent. Both *orlon* and *it* are neuter gender, singular number, third person.
> The woman put on *her* gloves. (Singular antecedent, feminine.)
> The women put on *their* gloves. (Plural antecedent, feminine.)

(Pronouns do not necessarily agree with their antecedents in case. In the sentences above, *woman* and *women* are nominative, *her* and *their* are possessive. See Section U4.)

U3b. SINGULAR PRONOUNS REFER TO SINGULAR ANTECEDENTS.

The words *each, either, neither, somebody, anyone, anybody, everybody,* and *nobody* are singular, and in formal English a pronoun referring to any one of these words should be singular (*she, her, hers, he, him, his, it, its*).

In spoken English and informal writing, the rule stated above is frequently ignored, however. Speakers who wish their language to sound casual and relaxed often use *their* to refer to *everybody.* And when the sense of *everybody, anyone,* etc. is *many* or *all,* the plural personal pronoun referring to these indefinite pronouns is frequently found in both formal and informal English: "Everybody is expected to do *their* share of the work." Such use is preferable to the somewhat artificial and even awkward "Everybody is expected to do *his or her* share of the work." Notice, however, that a singular, not a plural, verb form is used.

> Informal: Everybody took *their* heavy coat to camp.
> Formal: Everybody took *her* heavy coat to camp.
> Informal: Each of the boxers was accompanied by *their* manager.
> Formal: Each of the boxers was accompanied by *his* manager.
> Informal: Anyone can try *their* luck at this game.
> Formal: Anyone can try *her or his* luck at this game.

U3c. A COLLECTIVE NOUN USED AS AN ANTECEDENT TAKES A SINGULAR PRONOUN IF THE GROUP IS THOUGHT OF AS A UNIT AND A PLURAL PRONOUN IF THOUGHT OF IN TERMS OF ITS INDIVIDUAL MEMBERS.

> The crowd took off *their* hats. (The crowd acted as individuals.)
> The crowd shouted *its* overwhelming approval. (The crowd acted as a unit.)

NOTE: Once you decide whether a collective noun is to be singular or plural, stick to your decision. If you use it as the subject with a singular verb, make sure that all pronouns referring to it are singular; and if you use it with a plural verb, make sure that all pronouns are plural.

> Nonstandard: The family *was* discussing *their* problems.
> Standard: The family *was* discussing *its* problems.
> Standard: The family *were* discussing *their* problems.

U3d. A NOUN OR AN INDEFINITE PRONOUN USED AS AN ANTECEDENT TAKES A PRONOUN IN THE THIRD PERSON.

All nouns and indefinite pronouns are in the third person, except when they are used in direct address or in apposition with a pronoun of the first or second person. Aside from these two uses, all nouns and indefinite pronouns require a third-person pronoun. A phrase such as *of us* or *of you* coming between the pronoun and its antecedent does not affect the person of the pronoun.

Nonstandard:	If a man wants to succeed, *you* must work hard.
Standard:	If a man wants to succeed, *he* must work hard.
Nonstandard:	Neither of you has finished *your* lunch.
Standard:	Neither of you has finished *her* lunch.

U3e. WHEN THE ANTECEDENT IS A SINGULAR NOUN OF COMMON GENDER, TRADITIONAL PRACTICE HAS BEEN TO USE A MASCULINE PRONOUN UNLESS THE NOUN CLEARLY REFERS TO A WOMAN.

Each member of the drama club indicated *his* choice of a play for the annual production.

Each member of the girls' glee club was asked to name *her* favorite Christmas carol.

NOTE: This practice has come under increasing attack. Critics feel that the use of the masculine pronoun unfairly excludes women. Although the standard practice described above is still acceptable, many sensitive writers will try to avoid this construction. Some alternatives are as follows:

Use *he or she*. (This expression tends to be awkward, however, and should be used sparingly.)

Each committee member did *her or his* assigned work.

Change the wording from the singular to the plural.

All committee members did *their* assigned work.

Reword the sentence to avoid the generic pronoun.

Each committee member performed an assigned job.

U3f. A PRONOUN AGREES WITH THE NEARER OF TWO ANTECEDENTS.

Occasionally, two antecedents, different in gender or number, occur in a sentence. With two antecedents and only one pronoun, the pronoun referring to the nearer antecedent should be used.

> He loves everybody and everything *that* is connected with his work.
> He loves everything and everybody *who* is connected with his work. (However, *that* would also be correct. See Sec. U3g.)
> In this cool room, neither the gardenia nor the roses will lose *their* freshness.

U3g. *WHO* REFERS TO PERSONS, *WHICH* REFERS TO THINGS, AND *THAT* REFERS TO PERSONS OR THINGS.

> The individual *who* told me the story is your doctor.
> My battered but loved desk, *which* I discarded reluctantly, joined the rest of the furniture donated to the charity auction.
> The flier *that* took her plane on a round-the-world trip has been awarded a medal.

U3h. *WHAT* SHOULD NOT BE USED TO REFER TO AN EXPRESSED ANTECEDENT.

> Nonstandard: The book *what* you sent me as a graduation present arrived yesterday.
> Standard: The book *that* you sent me arrived yesterday.
> Standard: I heard *what* you said.

U3i. THE ANTECEDENT OF A PRONOUN SHOULD BE EXPRESSED, NOT MERELY IMPLIED.

The relation of a pronoun to its antecedent must be clear and unmistakable. The reference word should be placed close to its antecedent in order that no intervening words may cause confusion. A *relative pronoun* must be in the same sentence as its antecedent, but *personal* or *demonstrative pronouns* may be placed some distance away, frequently in other sentences, if there is no intervening noun or pronoun to cause confusion.

Implied reference occurs when the antecedent of a pronoun is not actually expressed but must be inferred from the context. One of the most common forms of implied reference is the use of the pronouns *it, this, that,* or *which* to refer to an entire preceding statement rather than to some noun or pronoun in that statement. You, as a writer, must decide whether such words refer to an implied antecedent or whether their antecedent occurs in a preceding or even following statement. Frequent use of implied reference is found in the work of many reputable writers, and when confusion is not possible, the use may be effective.

Faults in the implied reference of *it, which, this, that, these, those,* etc., may be corrected by (1) summing up the idea of the preceding statement in a noun that acts as the antecedent; (2) rephrasing the sentence so as to eliminate the pronoun or to give it a clear and appropriate antecedent.

Vague:	I worked for the post office last Christmas vacation and enjoyed *it* very much.
Improved:	I was employed by the post office last Christmas vacation and enjoyed the work very much.
Vague:	Wednesday morning I was ill but *it* became steadily better during the day.
Improved:	Wednesday morning I was ill but felt steadily better during the day.
Vague:	You will have a lot of hiring and firing to do, and *this* takes a great deal of diplomacy.
Improved:	You will have a lot of hiring and firing to do, a task that demands a great deal of diplomacy.
Vague:	At the beach we saw the lavish fireworks display. *This* concluded our celebration.
Improved:	When we saw the lavish fireworks display at the beach, we concluded our celebration.
Vague:	Strewn over the floor was everything from broken bottles to old rotor heads. *That* solved the mystery.
Improved:	Strewn over the floor was everything from broken bottles to old rotor heads. That mess solved the mystery.
Vague:	He was in bad shape, *which* was made obvious by his persistent bleeding.
Improved:	He was in bad shape, a condition that was made obvious by his persistent bleeding.

U
3

U3j. AVOID THE INDEFINITE USE OF *IT* AND *THEY*.

It as a third person singular pronoun, neuter, should usually have an appropriate antecedent. Also, when *it* is used impersonally and acceptably (*it* seems, *it* is possible, *it* is raining, etc.), do not use another *it* in the same sentence to refer to a definite antecedent. See Section U3k.

They, *their*, *theirs*, and *them* should have definite antecedents: plural nouns or other pronouns in the plural. Otherwise, do not use these pronouns.

> Vague: In this article, *it* shows that war is horrible.
> Improved: This article shows that war is horrible.
> Vague: *They* have good roads in Delaware.
> Improved: Delaware has good roads.
> Vague: *They* say that Argentina is a wealthy nation.
> Improved: Economists say that Argentina is a wealthy nation.

NOTE: *It* is sometimes used impersonally to introduce an idea.

> It will be clear tomorrow.
> It was Lincoln who made the "House Divided" speech.

It is necessary, it is true, it is certain, it is likely, and *it is imperative* are correct expressions.

U3k. DO NOT USE IMPERSONAL *IT* AND THE PRONOUN *IT* IN THE SAME SENTENCE.

> Vague: We can send the refrigerator today, or we can keep *it* in the factory for a few days if *it* is necessary.
> Improved: We can send the refrigerator today, or we can keep *it* for a few days.

NOTE: In informal English, *it* sometimes refers to an idea instead of a single antecedent.

> Informal: He was nervous, but he tried not to show it.
> Formal: He was nervous, but he tried not to show his uneasiness.

U3l. IN FORMAL WRITING AVOID THE USE OF *YOU* TO MEAN PEOPLE IN GENERAL.

In informal speech, expressions such as "You can see how important money is" or "Dancing makes you graceful" are permissible. Formal English requires the use of *one* or *anyone* in these statements.

> Anyone can see how important money is.
> Dancing makes one graceful.

U3m. AVOID THE USE OF *SAME* IN PLACE OF A PERSONAL PRONOUN.

> Vague: Please fill out the blank and return *same* to us.
> Improved: Please fill out the blank and return *it* to us.

U3n. AVOID DOUBLE REFERENCE FOR A PRONOUN.

Double reference occurs when two antecedents are possible for a single pronoun. The pronoun reference is therefore ambiguous. Instead, the antecedent should be clear and definite.

Ambiguous reference can be corrected by (1) repeating the antecedent, (2) using a synonym for the antecedent, (3) changing the wording of the sentence so that the antecedent of each pronoun is unmistakable.

> Vague: When a mother hands over the car to her daughter, *she* is not always sure it is in good condition.
> Improved: A mother is not always sure the car is in good condition when she hands it over to her daughter.

> Vague: The actor told Bob that *he* should move upstage. (Who should move: *Bob?* The *actor?*)
> Improved: The actor said, "I shall move upstage." (The *actor* will move.)
>   The actor told Bob of his intention to move upstage. (The *actor* will move.)
>   The actor advised Bob to move upstage. (*Bob* should move.)

EXERCISE 7

Write on your paper the number of each sentence. Then write the correct form in formal English of any pronoun that is nonstandard or doubtful. Beside the correct form of the pronoun, write the antecedent of the pronoun that you have corrected. If a verb requires change, make this alteration also. If an indefinite pronoun must be removed, rewrite the entire sentence. If a sentence is correct, write *C* next to its number.

1. Both Lennie and his partner Joe knew how to handle himself in an Indian fight.
2. You can tell when you have a fish on your line because you can feel them struggle.
3. In the advertisement it explained why Twodekay is popular with youngsters.
4. If every member of the class does their best, we should finish *Giants in the Earth* by April.
5. When a student doesn't have a car, they must take a bus or hitch-hike to town.
6. A blond wig can be carefully curled, and which can be an expensive hairdo.
7. You know very well that the Smithfield Grange always has their suppers on Friday nights.
8. No one wanted to go back to work because they are watching the pigeons.
9. My aunt is an archeology professor. This is an unusual position.
10. Coach Redblood instructed the team doctors to stand by with their Novocain.
11. The Finch family was an industrious group that never tired of their work.
12. When I look into your deep purple eyes, Minerva, I get that old thrill.
13. The teacher promised that each child would have a chance to make their speech.
14. That company has a particularly good retirement policy for their employees.
15. They say that falling in love is wonderful.
16. Never touch a high-voltage wire without throwing the switch; they may kill you.
17. A person likes to vote for a candidate that they can feel proud of.
18. I want you to unbuckle those galoshes for the children and then tell them to put them away when they are out of them.
19. Marsha's glance gave Marvin that sinking feeling.

20. Bill attended a party occasionally, but he always left before they started dancing.
21. One should always do what your conscience tells you.
22. Did anyone find my sunglasses?
23. Each girl in the band practiced their music after school.
24. After each student finished the exam, they put down their pens and turned over their papers.
25. The club sent out an announcement to their members.

U

3

EXERCISE 8

Follow the directions for Exercise 7.

1. We tried to explain to Grandfather that a man of sixty-five would only make a spectacle of themselves in ballet.
2. If a person on our campus needs some guidance, they simply find Professor Corvelle and ask her.
3. As soon as the customers left the tables, the waiters cleaned them.
4. Everyone should outline his research paper before writing it, not afterward.
5. Neither the hot sun nor the gentle rains will have their usual effect on the tourists this year.
6. When you play with matches, you often get burned.
7. As each worker reached headquarters, they gave the battery clerk the information they had gathered.
8. Neither Josh nor his brother was permitted to own a car until they got licenses.
9. Every grocer that raises every price will be boycotted.
10. The sergeant discovered, too late, that one of his soldiers had neglected to brush their teeth.
11. Even someone like Doris has his problems.
12. In that particular discotheque it was difficult to hear every note of the music.
13. If you've never watched a finch gobbling up their suet, you've missed one of nature's loveliest sights.
14. Either the lecture or the slides will have their special appeal for the audience.
15. Lolly's mother is a lion tamer. That is a tricky business.
16. Never fell a eucalyptus tree in a high wind; they may fall the wrong way and hurt someone.
17. When you find the scissors, will you please give it to me?

18. Selma took the children from the buses and sent them to the zoo.
19. In the notice it says that parking fees will be increased 15 dollars a year.
20. Sandra is one person I always enjoy seeing at the library.

EXERCISE 9

If a sentence contains a pronoun not in agreement with its antecedent, state the proper form. Some sentences contain no error.

1. That person likes a book that they can read quickly and easily.
2. Neither the sun nor the wind will have its effect on the flowers at this time.
3. Neither Jennie nor Will was allowed to own a car until they got a license.
4. The interior decoration was elegant; even the draperies had gold thread running through it.
5. If someone in our home wants to locate something, they must find me and ask for help.
6. It was fully evident that the mayor and his aide had their own ideas about the celebration.
7. No one wanted to return to work because they were enjoying the delightful summer weather.
8. Since the baseball team has three excellent pitchers, they should win a lot of games.
9. When you finish reading the newspaper, will you give it to me?
10. Through careful practice in writing, one eventually learns to express themselves effectively.
11. If one wants to succeed, you have to work hard.
12. None of the children would admit that they liked spinach.

U4. Case Forms of Pronouns

Case is a grammatical term referring to one of the forms that a noun or pronoun takes to indicate its relation to other words. The three cases in English are *nominative, objective,* and *possessive.*

The following principles for use of nominative and objective cases rarely apply to nouns but are a guide for use of pronoun forms. Learn the different forms of personal, relative, and interrogative pronouns.

Personal Pronouns			
	Nominative	*Objective*	*Possessive*
	Singular		
1st person	I	me	my, mine
2nd person	you	you	your, yours
3rd person *feminine* *masculine* *neuter*	she he it	her him it	her, hers his its
	Plural		
1st person	we	us	our, ours
2nd person	you	you	your, yours
3rd person *(all genders)*	they	them	their, theirs
Relative and Interrogative			
	Singular and Plural		
	who	whom	whose

U
4

When there are two possessive forms of the personal pronoun, the first one given in the list above is followed by the noun it qualifies as a possessive adjective; the second is used alone, as a possessive pronoun.

> *My* book is on the desk; *yours* is on the shelf.
> The book on the desk is *mine*.
> *Her* appointment is in the morning; *his* is in the afternoon.

No change in form occurs in the use of *that* and *which*.

U4a. THE SUBJECT OF A VERB IS IN THE NOMINATIVE CASE: *I, YOU, HE, SHE, IT, WE, YOU, THEY.*

> Sarah and *I* have eaten too much candy.
> When Ned comes, *he* and *I* are going to build a fire.
> *We* boys can do a better job without your help.

U4b. A PRONOUN FOLLOWING ANY PART OF THE VERB *BE* (*AM, IS, ARE, WAS, WERE, BEEN, BE*) AND REFERRING TO THE SUBJECT IS IN THE NOMINATIVE CASE. IT IS CALLED A PREDICATE NOMINATIVE.

> The officers of the class are *Carol, Alfred,* and *I.*
> It was *they* who telephoned last night.
> Do you think it could have been *she* who sang on the radio?

NOTE: Controversy exists over "This is *I*" or "It is *I*" versus "This is *me*" or "It is *me*." In one opinion poll among competent judges, 59 percent labeled the *me* use acceptable. Studies have shown that both "It is *I*" and "It is *me*" are avoided by careful speakers and writers in favor of "This is Jones" or "This is *she*" or a simple "Yes" to the question, "Is this Jones?"

U4c. THE OBJECT OF A VERB OR A PREPOSITION IS IN THE OBJECTIVE CASE: *ME, YOU, HER, HIM, IT, US, THEM.*

Watch particularly the second member of a compound object. Both members must be in the same case.

> Mother met *Hilda* and *me* at the airport. (*Hilda* and *me* are objects of the verb *met.*)
> Abbie Fulton had invited *her* and *me* to a party. (*Her* and *me* are objects of the verb *invited.*)
> Between *Jack* and *him* there has always been a good understanding. (*Jack* and *him* are objects of the preposition *between.*)
> All the plans for the party were made by *Elena* and *him.* (*Elena* and *him* are objects of the preposition *by.*)

U4d. THE INDIRECT OBJECT IS IN THE OBJECTIVE CASE.

The **indirect object** precedes the direct object and tells *to* whom or *for* whom the action of the verb is done. It is the noun or pronoun before which *to* or *for* is understood.

> Uncle Fred sent *me* a bracelet from India. (*Me* is the object of *to* understood; *bracelet* is the direct object.)
> Save *me* a piece of that cake. (*Me* is the object of *for* understood; *piece* is the direct object.)

U4e. IN AN ELLIPTICAL CLAUSE BEGINNING WITH *THAN* OR *AS*, USE THE FORM OF THE PRONOUN CALLED FOR IF THE CONSTRUCTION WERE COMPLETED.

An **elliptical clause** is one with a word or more missing; the omitted word or words are understood from other parts of the sentence. If you supply the missing word or words, you should have little trouble deciding the correct case form for the pronoun.

> My sister is taller than *I*. (*Than* introduces the elliptical clause *I am. I* is the subject of the verb *am* understood.)
>
> Tom is just as good an actor as *she*. (*She* is the subject of *is* understood.)
>
> Nobody cares more about your happiness than *he*. (*He* is the subject of *does* understood.)
>
> I like Katerina better than *her*. (*Her* is the object of *like* understood.)
>
> This television program pleased you much more than *me*. (*Me* is the object of *pleased* understood.)

U4f. THE SUBJECT OF AN INFINITIVE IS IN THE OBJECTIVE CASE.

The **infinitive** is the form of the verb that usually has *to* in front of it:

> I wanted *him* to run for class secretary. (The whole group of words is the object of *wanted; him* is the subject of *to run*.)
>
> Lee expected *me* to wait for her.
>
> Joan asked *me* to go to the museum.
>
> The music teacher let *Gordon and me* sing a duet. (A verb used after *let* is an infinitive although it is used without *to*. *Gordon and me* are subjects of the infinitive *to sing*.)

U4g. THE OBJECT OF AN INFINITIVE, GERUND, OR PARTICIPLE IS IN THE OBJECTIVE CASE.

> The librarian wants to see *us*. (*Us* is the object of the infinitive *to see*.)
>
> Finding *you* here is a surprise. (*You* is the object of the gerund *finding*.)
>
> Having recognized *her* instantly, I hurried across the street. (*Her* is the object of the participle *having recognized*.)

U
4

U4h. THE OBJECTIVE COMPLEMENT OF THE INFINITIVE *TO BE* IS IN THE OBJECTIVE CASE WHEN THE SUBJECT OF THE INFINITIVE IS EXPRESSED.

This construction may cause some trouble because it requires an objective case after a linking verb. It may help to remember that the objective case will occur after *to be* only when two conditions prevail: (1) The sentence must use the infinitive form of the verb *to be*. (2) The subject of that infinitive must be expressed. Notice the difference in these examples:

> I thought you were *he*. (Here, the form *were* is not an infinitive.)
> I took you to be *him*. (In this sentence, *you* is the subject of the infinitive *to be*. The subject of an infinitive is in the objective case. Then the objective case must follow.)
> Aunt Jane took Lucy to be *me*.

The construction is an awkward one and can be avoided.

U4i. AN APPOSITIVE MUST BE IN THE SAME CASE AS THE NOUN OR PRONOUN THAT IT IDENTIFIES OR EXPLAINS.

> The principal wants us all — Alice, Roslyn, and me — to run for the office. (*Alice, Roslyn, me* are in apposition with *us* and must be in the same objective case.)
> We, you and I, are the only persons here not wearing hats. (nominative)

U4j. THE POSSESSIVE CASE OF A NOUN OR PRONOUN SHOULD BE USED BEFORE A GERUND.

The possessive case with a gerund is usually clear, whereas the objective case with a gerund may not be. Here are some examples of possessives with gerunds.

> I do not approve of *his* playing football. *(Playing* is the gerund. It is the object of the preposition *of.)*
> My teachers were not sure of *my* winning the prize. *(Winning* is the gerund.)
> *Her* singing could be improved. (*Singing* is the gerund.)

NOTE: Be sure to distinguish between gerund and participle. The latter is used as an adjective and does not have a possessive case preceding it.

> We saw him standing on the corner. *(Standing* is a participle modifying *him.)*

U4k. ***WHO* AND *WHOEVER* ARE USED AS SUBJECTS OF VERBS OR PREDICATE PRONOUNS. *WHOM* AND *WHOMEVER* ARE USED AS OBJECTS OF VERBS AND PREPOSITIONS.**

Many grammatical errors arise from misunderstanding the pronoun forms *who* or *whom* and *whoever* or *whomever.*

1. The following sentences illustrate proper use of *who* and *whoever,* nominative forms serving as subjects of the verbs in the dependent clauses:

> I demand the opportunity for *whoever* wishes it. *(Whoever* is the subject of the verb *wishes;* the whole dependent clause is the object of the preposition *for.)*
> The question of *who* can seize the opportunity must be answered. *(Who* is the subject of *can seize;* the whole dependent clause is the object of the preposition *of.)*
> I cannot tell *who* is *who* in the present student council, but I can tell *who* was *who* in last year's council. (Each *who* before *is* and *was* is the subject; each *who* after *is* and *was* is a predicate pronoun.)

In other words, the subject of a verb takes precedence over the object of a preposition or verb when pronoun case forms are in question.

2. The following sentences illustrate proper use of *whom* and *whomever,* objective forms serving as objects in the dependent clauses:

> This is the interesting girl *whom* I met at the party. (Direct object of *met.)*
> Bring *whomever* you like. (Direct object of *like;* the dependent clause is the object of *bring.)*

The statement began, "To *whom* it may concern." (Direct object of *concern;* the dependent clause is the object of the preposition *to.*)

The new father offered a cigar to *whomever* he met that morning. (Direct object of *met;* the dependent clause is the object of the preposition *to.*)

3. The nominative and objective cases are frequently confused because of intervening words. The case of a pronoun depends upon its use in the sentence and must not be influenced by words that come between the pronoun and its antecedent.

He asked us *who* we supposed would be elected. (Check by omitting *we supposed.*)

Who do you imagine would ever do such a thing? (Check by omitting *do you imagine.*)

I danced with the boy *whom* no one would have dreamed I could like. (Check by omitting *no one would have dreamed.*)

4. Whenever you are in doubt about *who* or *whom*, substitute either *she* and *her* or *he* and *him* to see which makes sense:

Who/whom are you speaking to? (To *who/whom* are you speaking?

He/him are you speaking to? (To *he/him* are you speaking?)

She is the kind of leader *who/whom* we admire. (We admire *who/ whom.*)

NOTE: Current usage studies indicate that the distinction between *who* and *whom* is breaking down, partly because keeping them straight is difficult and partly because many people start a sentence or clause with *who*, not knowing how they are going to end. One dictionary says of *whom:* "the objective case of *who; who* is often used colloquially instead of *whom*" *(Webster's New World Dictionary)*, i.e., in informal English *who* may replace *whom* when it stands before a verb or preposition of which it is the object. Some speakers and writers probably will still observe the conventional distinctions of *who* versus *whom: who* only as subject, *whom* only as object.

EXERCISE 10

Write on your paper the number of each sentence, and beside it write the appropriate pronoun or noun forms from the choices provided. Be prepared to explain in class why you have made each choice.

1. Let Susan and (*I, myself, me*) wire your chicken house.
2. Give the flowers to (*whoever, whomever*) comes to the door and mention (*who, whom*) sent them.
3. Fire over the head of (*whoever, whomever*) crosses the river, Paula; David and (*I myself, me*) will try to get at the position from the rear.
4. That is the opinion (*who, that*) is held by a woman (*who, that*) ought to know.
5. (*She, Her*) and (*I, me*) often shoot ducks together.
6. Don't you realize that Manuel is richer than you and (*I, me*)?
7. The speaker said that the future of civilization depended largely on (*we, us*) plumbers.
8. Between you and (*I, me*), Cathy, this new volleyball coach doesn't know what she's talking about.
9. For (*they, them*) who have to work for a living (*she, her*) and Dennis have the deepest compassion.
10. I thought it was (*they, them*) who felt that tennis knew no better coach than (*him, he*).

U 4

EXERCISE 11

Follow the directions for Exercise 10.

1. (*She, Her*) and the cobra get along better now, thanks to (*their, them*) discovering a mutual interest in music.
2. "It isn't a question of (*my, me*) going to Europe," said Jesse, "only of (*who, whom*) I should go with."
3. At (*who, whom*) did the child smile, Valerie—you or (*I, me*)?
4. Just between you and (*I, me*), what's the chance of the (*team, team's*) winning next week?
5. Among (*we, us*) six who received the penalty, five were innocent.
6. I hurt (*myself, me*) as much as I did (*her, herself*).
7. What puzzled Harry and (*I, myself, me*) was not so much the presence of (*she, her*) and Clifford at the diplomatic reception as (*their, them*) being permitted to sit at the same table with those of (*we, us*) who were high officials.
8. Of (*who, whom*) are you speaking, Lisa or (*I, me*)?
9. Mr. Throop wandered through the forest with his dog beside (*him, himself*).
10. (*We, Us*) Americans are rightly proud of (*Earhart, Earhart's*) flying alone across the Atlantic in 1932.

EXERCISE 12

Follow the directions for Exercise 10.

1. The new counselor is a woman (*who, whom*) we're quite sure will be able to control the girls.
2. Jay's boss isn't fond of (*his, him*) leaving work early.
3. Dolores and (*I. myself, me*) are very good friends, but she has never approved of (*me, my*) playing the banjo.
4. (*We, Us*) three—you, Cliff, and (*I, myself, me*)—have been elected to the dishwashing detail.
5. Those boys will get (*themselves, theirselves*) in trouble if they keep on getting to school late.
6. Last night Mandy introduced her new friend to (*us, we*) girls.
7. Just (*who, whom*) do you think you are?
8. (*Martin, Martin's*) carrying on disturbed Agnes as well as (*I, me*).
9. Do you think (*she, her*) and Louinda really ought to go alone?
10. My friends certainly had (*themselves, theirselves*) a time on the class trip while I was sick in bed.
11. For (*who, whom*) are you looking?
12. Did (*he, him*) go with you?

EXERCISE 13

Follow the directions for Exercise 10.

1. We thought it was (*they, them*) who believed that politics knew no better candidate than (*her, she*).
2. The recent graduates had (*themselves, theirselves*) a difficult time locating summer jobs.
3. Jenny blamed (*herself, her*) more than (*myself, me*).
4. (*Barney's, Barney*) stupid behavior upset his sister as well as (*I, me*).
5. Of (*whom, who*) are you speaking, Connie or (*I, me*)?
6. Give the lottery tickets to (*whoever, whomever*) arrives first to explain (*who, whom*) requested them.
7. Geraldine's friend isn't fond of (*her, hers*) working late at the garage every night.
8. That is an opinion (*who, that*) is held by anyone (*who, that*) thinks logically.
9. It's time for (*me, I*) to realize that she is smarter than (*I, me*).
10. (*We, us*) three—you, Clara, and (*I, myself, me*)—have been chosen as delegates to the convention.

U5. Principal Parts of Verbs

In every language, verbs have principal parts, sometimes three, as in German, sometimes five, as in French, Spanish, and Italian. The English verb has three principal parts: *present tense* (present infinitive), *past tense*, and *past participle*, for example: *eat, ate, eaten*. An excellent way to recall the principal parts of a verb is to substitute those of any verb for the following:

I *eat* today.	I *walk* today.
I *ate* yesterday.	I *walked* yesterday.
I *have eaten* every day this month.	I *have walked* every day this month.

Almost a principal part and a necessary verb form is the *present participle*, formed by adding *–ing* to the present infinitive form. This "fourth part," if in any way irregular, is given in your dictionary. Examples are *eating, walking, working, starting, doing, finding*. The present participial form has constant use both as part of the predicate and as an adjective.

The *past* and the *past participle* of many English verbs are formed by adding *–d*, *–ed*, or *–t* to the present. These are called *regular* verbs.

Present	Past	Past Participle
save	saved	saved
talk	talked	talked
ask	asked	asked
mean	meant	meant
spend	spent	spent
wish	wished	wished

There are, however, other verbs, which do not follow this pattern. These are called *irregular* verbs, and they form the past tense and past participle in several ways. Although it is impossible to establish a rule for these changes, groups of these words do often fall into a special pattern. One group has a vowel change in the past tense and, in some cases, in the past participle as well.

Present	Past	Past Participle
drink	drank	drunk
sing	sang	sung
cling	clung	clung
fight	fought	fought

sit	sat	sat
shoot	shot	shot
come	came	come
run	ran	run
find	found	found

Some verbs in this group, in addition to the vowel change, add *–n* to the past participle.

Present	*Past*	*Past Participle*
grow	grew	grown
break	broke	broken
fly	flew	flown
freeze	froze	frozen
drive	drove	driven
write	wrote	written
eat	ate	eaten
ride	rode	ridden
fall	fell	fallen

Another group changes its form completely in the past tense and past participle.

Present	*Past*	*Past Participle*
bring	brought	brought
think	thought	thought
buy	bought	bought
stand	stood	stood
go	went	gone
do	did	done
lie	lay	lain
catch	caught	caught
wind	wound	wound

A few verbs change the last consonant, but not the vowel.

Present	*Past*	*Past Participle*
make	made	made
have	had	had
build	built	built

A few others have the same form for all three principal parts.

Present	*Past*	*Past Participle*
cut	cut	cut
burst	burst	burst
hurt	hurt	hurt

set	set	set
spread	spread	spread
cast	cast	cast
put	put	put

If you are uncertain about the correct verb form, consult your dictionary.

Following is a list of troublesome verbs. Study them; put them into the three expressions suggested in the first paragraph of page 99.

bear	bore	borne (born, *given birth to*)
begin	began	begun
bid	bid	bid *(as in an auction)*
bid	bade	bidden *(as in a command)*
bite	bit	bitten (bit)
blow	blew	blown
break	broke	broken
burst	burst	burst
catch	caught	caught
choose	chose	chosen
come	came	come
dig	dug	dug
dive	dived	dived
do	did	done
drag	dragged	dragged
draw	drew	drawn
drink	drank	drunk
drown	drowned	drowned
eat	ate	eaten
fall	fell	fallen
fly	flew	flown
forget	forgot	forgotten (forgot)
freeze	froze	frozen
get	got	got (gotten)
go	went	gone
hang	hung	hung *(object)*
hang	hanged	hanged *(person)*
know	knew	known
lay	laid	laid *(put or set)*
lead	led	led
lend	lent	lent
lie	lay	lain *(recline)*
lie	lied	lied *(falsehood)*
lose	lost	lost

U
5

pay	paid	paid
raise	raised	raised
ride	rode	ridden
ring	rang	rung
rise	rose	risen
run	ran	run
set	set	set
sing	sang	sung
sit	sat	sat
speak	spoke	spoken
swim	swam	swum
take	took	taken
tear	tore	torn
wake	waked (woke)	waked (woken)
wear	wore	worn
wring	wrung	wrung
write	wrote	written

U5a. DO NOT CONFUSE THE PAST TENSE AND THE PAST PARTICIPLE.

The past tense, or the second principal part of a verb, is used without an auxiliary.

The past participle, the third principal part, makes a compound tense of the verb only when it is accompanied by some part of *have* or *be*.

Present	Past	Past Participle
see	saw	seen
do	did	done
go	went	gone

Seen, *done*, and *gone* are past participles and form tenses only with the aid of some part of the verb *have* or *be*.

> Nonstandard: I *seen* the flames reach the top of the building.
> Standard: I *had seen* the flames reach the top of the building.
> Standard: I *saw* the flames reach the top of the building.
> Nonstandard: I *have saw* several ice hockey games.
> Standard: I *have seen* several ice hockey games.
> Standard: I *saw* several ice hockey games.
> Nonstandard: I *done* it myself.
> Standard: I *did* it myself.

Be careful not to write *of* for *have*.

Nonstandard:	I could *of gone* to the game.
Standard:	I could *have gone* to the game last week.
Standard:	I could've *gone* to the game.

U5b. DO NOT CONFUSE AN IRREGULAR VERB WITH A REGULAR VERB.

Confusion or carelessness may cause you to add regular verb endings to irregular verbs or to treat an occasional regular verb like an irregular verb.

Nonstandard:	She *drawed* a bucket of water from the well.
Standard:	She *drew* a bucket of water from the well.
Nonstandard:	Last night the wind *blowed* at 30 miles an hour.
Standard:	Last night the wind *blew* at 30 miles an hour.
Nonstandard:	I *throwed* it to him fast.
Standard:	I *threw* it to him fast.

EXERCISE 14

Write on your paper the number of each sentence, and next to it place the correct form of the verb that appears in parentheses. When in doubt about the correct form, restudy Section U5 or consult your dictionary.

1. Martin missed his appointment because he had (lie) in bed until 8:30.
2. Jenny (arise) every day at dawn and walked ten miles.
3. He was glad that he had not (drown).
4. Joan feared that she and her friends would be (throw) out of the theater.
5. After eating for an hour and a half, the glutton realized that he (begin) to lose his appetite.
6. Barbara stuck her head out and nearly got it (shoot) off.
7. The phone had (ring) several times before Stella answered it.
8. The presence of Colonel Hogben (lend) an air of dignity to the meeting.
9. As the passengers threw coins into the water, children (dive) for the money.
10. So far Doris had (bear) the slipshod service patiently.

EXERCISE 15

Follow the directions for Exercise 14.

1. Ricardo had apparently (drink) both bottles.
2. Chuck did not look like someone who had (swim) the Channel, and he hadn't.
3. The day the water mains (burst), we irrigated our tomatoes.
4. It was Ethel; she had (take) the plane from the hangar.
5. Had he only (dive) a little more to the left, he would have hit the water.
6. The swimmer caught the line and was (drag) onto the lobster boat.
7. Just then someone (begin) to pull rabbits out of the hat.
8. Her father's spirits (sink) when Mary declined the offer.
9. I fear, Debbie, that you have (draw) the shorter straw.
10. Who knows how long this jet has (fly) in the wrong direction?

EXERCISE 16

Follow the directions for Exercise 14.

1. Because she had other fish to fry, she (know) the little perch would survive.
2. Why buy new overalls, Harry, when a patch may be (sew) on your old ones?
3. Janet declared that she'd rather be (hang) than miss the opening of the deer season.
4. Steven had (prove) to his own satisfaction that castor oil tastes awful.
5. Gladys (speed) across the lawn, the storm drawing ever closer.
6. It was good to hear the old familiar songs being (sing).
7. If he said his hen (lay) sixteen eggs in three days, he lied.
8. For the next two days the prisoner was (bind) hand and foot.
9. When the old general entered the room, we all (rise) from our chairs.
10. Theresa (bid) her friends a sad farewell and drove away.

U6. Linking Verbs

Most verbs assert action, but a few express a static condition or state of being (no action). Most of these "inactive" verbs are called *linking* (or *joining*) *verbs*. They serve the purpose of coming between, or *coupling*, two substantives or a substantive and an adjective. The substantive following the linking verb is a *predicate noun* or *predicate pronoun*. It is never a direct object. An adjective following the linking verb is a *predicate adjective*, for it modifies the subject, not the predicate.

The most common linking verb is *to be*, in its various forms of number, person, tense, and mood. Other common linking verbs are *appear, become, feel, grow, look, prove, remain, seem, smell, sound, stand, taste, turn.* Except for forms of *to be*, these other linking verbs are followed by adjectives—rarely, if ever, by pronouns or nouns as predicate substantives. When these verbs are followed by nouns or pronouns as *direct objects*, they are not linking verbs, but imply or express action. They are linking verbs if you can substitute some form of *to be* for them, especially *is, are, was, were.* In the following examples, the linking verbs are in italics; the words linked are in small capitals.

> This HAMBURGER *is* THIN.
> JONES *is* my ROOMMATE.
> That PLAY *was* GOOD.
> The new AUDITORIUM *is* MULTILEVEL.
> The DIRECTOR *will be* FAMOUS tomorrow.
> The STUDENT *seems (is)* SHY today; next week HE may *turn (grow, become, be)* BOLDER.
> Their SUSPICION *became (seemed, grew, was)* HEAVIER as fresh evidence was turned up.
> Those SHARKS *appear (look, seem, are)* COFFEE COLORED.

U6a. DISTINGUISH BETWEEN A LINKING VERB AND ONE THAT EXPRESSES ACTION

Note the difference between verb words when they assert action of the subject and when they do not state action but serve merely as links.

> The sky *looks* cloudy this morning. (linking)
> Bill *looks* at Mark as though he hates him. (action)
> The coffee *tasted* too sweet. (linking)
> Betty cautiously *tasted* the steaming-hot soup. (action)
> The team did not *feel* bad about its defeat. (linking)
> If you cannot see in the dark, try to *feel* your way along. (action)

EXERCISE 17

Write two sentences using each of these linking verbs. In the first sentence, the verb should be in the present tense, in the second, the past tense. Example: Roland appears tired today. The river appeared muddy yesterday.

become	smell
feel	sound
grow	stand
look	taste
seem	turn

EXERCISE 18

Write on your paper the number of each sentence. After the number, write *linking* or *action* to describe the function of each italicized verb.

1. As a good chef Henry *tasted* the unsavory mess wryly.
2. The moon, riding high above the clouds, *appeared* ghostly.
3. Gardeners have never seen flowers *grow* so rapidly.
4. If the crowd *turns* surly, we shall *turn* around rapidly and head for the hills.
5. The child *looked* ashamed of herself after the third spanking.
6. Throw the meat away; it *smells*.
7. You have learned to pick up your feet; you *are becoming* graceful.
8. When you get high marks, you certainly *feel* good.
9. On a hot day a glass of lemonade *smells* good and *tastes* better.
10. When a man has a good friend, he feels sure that he *is* fortunate.
11. The cake *tastes* delicious.
12. Peter *felt* the knicks in the wood.

U7. Auxiliary Verbs

An **auxiliary verb** "helps out" a main verb. That is, it aids in forming the tense, mood, and voice of a main verb. An auxiliary verb has little meaning of its own; rather, it changes the meaning of the main verb. In the following sentences, the italicized form is an auxiliary verb. The form in small capitals is the main verb.

Mary *has* LEFT the city.
The machine parts *will be* SHIPPED early this afternoon.
As we *were* LEAVING, we *were* STOPPED by a guard.
I *did* MAIL the letters this morning.

The meanings of the commonly used auxiliary verbs are contained in your dictionary. These verbs and their uses may be summarized as follows:

1. **To be**—Used in all tenses in forming the progressive tone and the passive voice.

2. **To have**—Used in the present perfect, past perfect, and future perfect tenses; also in the perfect infinitive and the perfect participle.

3. **To do**—Used to express emphasis (emphatic tone) in the present and past tenses.
   —Used to avoid repetition of a verb or full verb expression: "John slept as soundly as I *did*." "We shall start out when they *do*."

4. **Shall**—Used as the precise auxiliary for the first person, future and future perfect tenses.
   —Used in the second and third persons to express command or determination: "You *shall* be more prompt in the future."

5. **Will**—Used as the precise auxiliary for the second and third persons, future and future perfect tenses.
   —Used in all three persons to express willingness or consent: "I *will* take the examination."
   —Used in the first person to indicate determination or resolution: "We *will* pay the bill immediately."

   NOTE: The word *precise* used in explaining the functions of *shall* and *will* may itself not be precise. Perhaps it would be better to say that only scrupulously careful or fastidious users of the language make the distinctions indicated. In almost all speaking and writing, *shall* and *will* are now used interchangeably.

6. **Should**—Used as a kind of past tense of *shall,* in the first person, but weaker in emphasis: "I *should* not scold the little boy." "I *should* hope for the best."
   —Used frequently in a conditional meaning: "If I *should* make other plans, I shall let you know." "If Anita *should* want soda, we can provide some."

—Used in all three persons to express duty or propriety or necessity: "You *should* organize your work." "He *should* be quite proud of her."

—Used in all three persons to express expectation: "We *should* be flying over Savannah now." "The letter *should* reach her on Monday."

7. **Would**—Used as a kind of past tense of *will*, in the second and third persons, but less strong in meaning: "You *would* scarcely bother about them."

NOTE: If the verb in the independent clause is in the past tense, use *would* to express futurity in the dependent clause. If the verb in the independent clause is in the present tense, use *will* in the dependent clause: "John *told* me he *would* write." "John *tells* me he *will* write."

—Used frequently in a conditional meaning or after a conditional clause: "If you *would* agree, they would be pleased." "If the traffic were heavy, Beth *would* take another route." "If I could, I *would*."

—Used to express determination: "She *would* try, no matter how difficult the undertaking appeared to be."

—Used in all three persons to express repeated or habitual action: "Last winter we *would* play ice hockey every day."

—Used infrequently to express wish or desire: "*Would* that we all had done otherwise!"

8. **May**—Used to express permission: "*May* I have your name?" "You *may* keep the book." "If I *may* say so, that color scheme is terrible."

—Used to express probability or a wish: "It *may* hurt a little." "*May* your trip be a pleasant one!"

9. **Might**—Used as a kind of past tense of *may* to express the same ideas of possibility or probability in a weaker manner: "You *might* be interested in astrology."

10. **Can**—Used to express ability or power or the idea of being able to: "I *can* meet him at 7 o'clock." "My daddy *can* fix anything."

11. **Could**—Used as a kind of past tense of *can* to express the same ideas in a weaker manner: "Stuart *could* not haul in the heavy anchor."

12. **Must**—Used to express obligation or compulsion. "Every girl *must* help in the Camp Follies."
—Used to express reasonable certainty: "Gloria was here promptly at 7 o'clock, so she *must* have set her alarm clock." "I hear thunder, so there *must* be a storm coming."

13. **Ought to**—Used to express duty or obligation: "You *ought to* learn French, Jill." "Every boy *ought to* keep his shoes shined."

    NOTE: *Have* and *had* are never used before *ought* or must.

    Nonstandard: I *had ought* to start studying.
    Standard: I *ought to have started* studying long ago.

14. **Let**—Used to express the ideas of allowing or permitting, suggesting, ordering: "*Let* me follow her." "*Let's* have a picnic." "*Let* me think a minute." "*Let* him finish his milk."

15. **Need**—Used to express necessity or obligation: "I *need* not give her my pony." "They *need* only speak up and speak out."

    NOTE: As an auxiliary verb, the third person singular form is also *need:* "He *need* not take my advice."

16. **Used to**—In the past tense only, *used to* expresses custom or habitual action: "I *used to* cry a lot when I was a child." "It *used to* rain every day in Kensington."

17. **Dare**—Used, usually with *say*, to express probability: "I *dare* say that's true." "I *dare* say the choice will be difficult to make."

EXERCISE 19

For each italicized verb in the following sentences, indicate the verb's auxiliary, if it has one. Then explain the purpose that the auxiliary serves or the meaning that it expresses.

1. Eloise should *keep* a diary; I could certainly *profit* by reading it.
2. You may *catch* the fish, but can you *cook* it?
3. Jim used to *think* he was an expert sailor; not he *is* not so sure.
4. She ought to *saw* tree branches carefully; otherwise, she may *find* herself out on a limb.
5. Have you *tried* sky diving? It might *amuse* you.
6. I will never *allow* a child of mine to be without memories.

7. Let no one *forget* the fight; it will *do* us all harm.
8. Must we *go?* We have not *been* here long.
9. When I *was* a boy, Mother would *assign* me new chores every other day.
10. We should have *served* the fried chicken; in fact, we might have *served* it if our cook had not *dropped* it in the sand.

U8. Tense and Tone

Tense shows the time of the action or state of being expressed by a verb. The three divisions of time—past, present, future—are shown in English by six tenses. The three *primary,* or *simple,* tenses are the *present* tense, the *past* tense, and the *future* tense. The three *perfect* (*secondary* or *compound*) tenses are the *present perfect,* the *past perfect,* and the *future perfect.*

Within some tenses, verbs also have certain *tones,* which express precisely what the writer wishes to say: *simple* tone (I read); *progressive* tone (I am reading); and *emphatic* tone (I do read).

U8a. USE THE CORRECT TENSE TO EXPRESS PRECISE TIME.

The following brief table and comments on each tense should help you to use the precise tenses needed to convey your ideas:

Active Voice	
Present	I hear (am hearing)
Past	I heard (was hearing)
Future	I shall hear (shall be hearing)
Present perfect	I have heard (have been hearing)
Past perfect	I had heard (had been hearing)
Future perfect	I shall have heard (shall have been hearing)

Passive Voice	
Present	I am heard (am being heard)
Past	I was heard (was being heard)
Future	I shall be heard
Present perfect	I have been heard
Past perfect	I had been heard
Future perfect	I shall have been heard

Verbals *(Nonfinite Verb Forms)*	
Present infinitive	to hear (to be hearing)
Perfect infinitive	to have heard (to have been hearing)
Present participle	hearing
Past participle	heard
Perfect participle	having heard (having been hearing)
Present gerund	hearing
Perfect gerund	having heard (having been hearing)

U
8

1. **Present tense** indicates that the action or condition is going on or exists now:

> He *eats* a big breakfast every morning.
> The scores *are* posted.

2. **Past tense** indicates that an action or condition took place or existed at some definite time in the past:

> Yesterday she *gave* an impressive speech.
> They *were* married on Saturday.

3. **Future tense** indicates that an action will take place or that a certain condition will exist in the future:

> We *shall move* to Iowa next week.
> The cruise ship *will be sailing* at midnight.

The future may be stated by the present tense accompanied by an adverb (or adverbial phrase) indicating time. Such constructions as the following are common:

> I am going downtown later on today.
> This Friday the plane takes off for Tahiti.

4. **Present perfect tense** indicates that an action or condition was begun in the past and has just been completed or is still going on. The time is past but it is connected with the present. The present perfect tense *presupposes* some relationship with the present:

> We *have lived* in Chicago for 15 years.
> The water *has been* too cold for swimming.
> I *have* long *been* a friend of Senator Twitchell.
> We *have waited* here long enough.

5. **Past perfect tense** indicates that an action or condition was completed at a time now past. It indicates action "two steps back." That is, the past perfect tense presupposes some relationship with an action or condition expressed in the past tense:

> The market place was crowded because a new shipment *had arrived* early that morning.
> She was employed by the Browne Company. She *had worked* there for a month.

6. **Future perfect tense** indicates that an action or condition will be completed at a future time:

> By the time you arrive, I *shall have finished* lunch.
> The ice *will have broken* up before the ship reaches this harbor.

The three perfect tenses always indicate *completed* action, whether it be in the present (present perfect tense), in the past (past perfect tense), or in the future (future perfect tense).

U8b. WATCH CAREFULLY THE SEQUENCE OF TENSES.

When only one verb is used in a sentence, it should express the precise time involved. When two or more verbs appear in a sentence, they should be consistent in tense. Most importantly, remember that the tense of a verb in a subordinate clause depends on the tense of the verb in the main clause.

1. The present tense is used in a dependent clause to express a general truth:

> At that time, most people could not understand that the earth *is* round.

The present tense is used alone to express a "timeless" truth.

> An ounce of prevention *is* worth a pound of cure.

Do not use the past tense if logically the present tense is called for: "Last summer we visited a village in Lapland. The people of that community *were* hardy and resourceful." It is possible that the community no longer exists or that its people have since become weakened, but is that what is meant?

Passages in some short stories and novels are written in the present tense, although the action occurred in time which is past. This use of what is called the *historical present* sometimes makes narrative more vivid, but it quickly becomes monotonous.

2. Use a present infinitive except when the infinitive represents action completed before the time of the governing verb:

> I made a note *to talk* [not *to have talked*] with you about it.
> The coach is happy *to have made* Sally a member of the team.

3. A present participle indicates action at the time expressed by the verb; a past participle indicates action before that of the verb:

> *Eating* in so many restaurants, Lena *is* introduced to some exotic foods.
> *Having been* a benched player himself, he *felt* sympathy for Bob.

4. When narration in the past tense is interrupted for reference to a preceding event, use the past perfect tense:

> Last week they *fixed* the pipes, which *had been frozen* all winter.
> She *confided* that she *had been* in the city for over a month.

As a summary, these two formulas for the sequence of tenses may be helpful to you:

PAST ◄————————PRESENT➤FUTURE
PAST PERFECT ◄—PAST————►FUTURE

U8c. USE THE CORRECT TONE TO EXPRESS PRECISE MEANING.

The **simple tone** is a concise statement of a "snapshot" or instantaneous action of a verb: I *walk* (present tense); I *walked* (past tense); I *shall walk* (future tense); I *have walked* (present perfect tense); I *had walked* (past perfect tense); I *shall have walked* (future perfect tense).

The **progressive tone,** showing action in progress, consists of a form of the verb *to be* and the present participle of the main verb: I *am walking, was walking, shall be walking, have been walking, had been walking, shall have been walking.*

The **emphatic tone,** which indicates emphasis, consists of a form of the verb *to do* and the present infinitive of the main verb. The emphatic tone is used only in present and past tenses: I *do walk,* I *did walk.*

EXERCISE 20

On your paper write the number of each sentence below. Opposite the number, write any verb that appears in the wrong tense, and then write the correct form.

1. Some historians think that Napoleon's chief hope in conquering Italy was that he may win the admiration and love of Josephine.
2. I ought to have paid this utilities bill before the discount period ends.
3. After Cortez subdued the Aztecs, all Mexico will be quickly explored by the Spanish.
4. By the time the new hay crop was ready, the barns are almost empty.
5. When the Yankees lost, Francine felt that life is no longer worth living.
6. When the plumbers laid the pipeline on the surface, they forgot that water became solid at below-freezing temperatures.
7. Cynthia believes that the principal effect of *Hamlet* was catharsis.
8. After we went a half-dozen miles, we ran out of gas.
9. Unfortunately I had not had time to have played the entire concerto.

10. When the teacher explained that all bodies are subject to the law of gravity, my visiting brother, a former paratrooper, yells "Amen!"
11. Do you think he should have gone?
12. By the time we finish our homework, the television show is over.
13. The current edition of the encyclopedia, which I saw yesterday, said that cloning is possible.
14. If you wanted to go, you should.
15. Do you think that because he was sick yesterday he isn't going to tomorrow's party?

U 8

EXERCISE 21

Follow the directions for Exercise 20.

1. Last week I was just too tired to have pruned the peach trees.
2. By the time we reached Washington, we were too low on money to have stayed at the Marriott Motor Hotel.
3. After he had pacified the usher, Jack leads his seven aunts down the aisle.
4. Modern historians have concluded that Troy had been besieged for commercial rather than personal reasons.
5. When Marlena sees the grade on her term paper, she screamed like a wounded panther.
6. When I stopped at the teacher's desk, as he requested, he says to me, "Where's your term paper?"
7. Harvey circled until he saw an opening; then he grabs the giraffe by the ears.
8. Vivian wanted desperately to have received an A in history.
9. Having opened the manuscript, the editor lunges for her blue pencil.
10. After my parents lived on a farm for ten years, they moved into town.

EXERCISE 22

Follow the directions for Exercise 20.

1. If you had a bit of common sense, Tony, you will stay off roller skates.
2. We analyzed "The Turn of the Screw" to determine whether it was a psychological study or a ghost story.

3. A straight and narrow path is one that had no primroses on it.
4. After his dad punishes him, my buddy was angelic for a week.
5. If we could find out who released the spiders, we can take the proper steps.
6. At barbecues, Professor White used to remind us that humans are carnivorous animals.
7. Linda explained patiently that amperes were coulombs per second.
8. If the tobacco seedbed was not burned over before the seeds are planted, the weeds will sprout.
9. Had the distance from the pool to the house not been so great, Gladys might have escaped from the lightning.
10. This is my parents' anniversary; they had been married for 21 years.

U9. Mood

Verbs appear in one of three moods: *indicative, imperative,* or *subjunctive.* Nearly all verbs that you use appear in the indicative mood because this is the mood for making a statement, expressing a fact, or asking a question. Of the other two moods, only the subjunctive causes trouble.

U9a. USE THE INDICATIVE MOOD TO EXPRESS A FACT OR TO ASK A QUESTION OF FACT.

> Who *designed* the house? (question of fact)
> Rosemary *made* the blueprints. (statement of fact)
> The construction *is* faulty. (statement of fact)

U9b. USE THE IMPERATIVE MOOD TO EXPRESS A COMMAND, A POLITE OR STRONG REQUEST, OR AN ORDER.

> *Shut* the door. (command)
> *Come* and *bring* a friend. (polite request)
> Please *be* there on time! (strong request)
> *Come* home at once! (order)

U9c. LEARN TO RECOGNIZE THE SUBJUNCTIVE FORMS.

Present Indicative		*Present Subjunctive*	
I am	we are	(if) I be	(if) we be
you are	you are	(if) you be	(if) you be
he is	they are	(if) he be	(if) they be
Past Indicative		*Past Subjunctive*	
I was	we were	(if) I were	(if) we were
you were	you were	(if) you were	(if) you were
he was	they were	(if) he were	(if) they were
Present Indicative		*Present Subjunctive*	
I come	we come	(if) I come	(if) we come
you come	you come	(if) you come	(if) you come
he comes	they come	(if) he come	(if) they come

NOTE:

1. Distinctive subjunctive verb forms in current English have disappeared or are disappearing in favor of more commonly used indicative verb forms:

    Former use: If it *be* possible, I shall come.
    The student, if he *write* well, will receive a high grade.
    Current use: If it *is* possible, I shall come.
    The student, if he *writes* well, will receive a high grade.

2. Our language still retains a number of subjunctive forms in sayings handed down from times when this mood was more widely used: *Heaven forbid, Thy Kingdom come, if need be, she need not speak, suffice it to say, come what may,* etc.

U9d. USE THE SUBJUNCTIVE *WERE* TO EXPRESS A CONDITION THAT IS HYPOTHETICAL, IMPROBABLE, OR IMPOSSIBLE.

If I *were* you, I'd refuse to let her use my car.
I we *were* at home, we could consult our unabridged dictionary for the derivation of the word.

(I am not you. We are not at home. Hence the statements in the preceding examples are contrary to fact.)

CAUTION: Not every clause that begins with *if* requires a subjunctive.

If he *was* out late last night, he is probably still asleep. (The speaker thinks he may have been out late.)
If she *was* there, I didn't see her. (The speaker is willing to accept the fact that she was there even though the speaker did not see her.)

U9e. USE THE SUBJUNCTIVE *WERE* AFTER *AS THOUGH* OR *AS IF* TO EXPRESS DOUBT OR UNCERTAINTY.

He talks as if he *were* the only intelligent person in the group.
She looked as though she *were* completely exhausted.

NOTE: Do not use the subjunctive after *though* when it is not preceded by *as*.

Even though he *is* deaf, he doesn't have to shout.
Though she *can*, she won't.

U9f. USE THE SUBJUNCTIVE IN *THAT* CLAUSES EXPRESSING NECESSITY OR A PARLIAMENTARY MOTION.

I move that the committee *be appointed* by the president.
It is essential that she *appear* at the meeting.
It is expected that we all *pay* our own way.
The committee insisted that she *tell* the whole story.
I suggest that the topic *be considered* at our next meeting.
The motion is that the committee *be authorized* to proceed.

U9g. IN PARALLEL CONSTRUCTIONS, DO NOT SHIFT THE MOOD OF VERBS.

Nonstandard: If I *were* in your position and *was* offered a trip to Europe, I'd certainly go.

Standard: If I *were* in your position and *were* offered a trip to Europe, I'd certainly go.

Nonstandard: If Lee *were* to resign and Dee *was* elected, we should have better leadership.

Standard: If Lee *were* to resign and Dee *were* elected, we should have better leadership.

EXERCISE 23

Number each of the following sentences on your paper. Opposite each number write the form of the italicized verb that you prefer, and indicate whether it is indicative or subjunctive.

1. If she were that intelligent and (*was, were*) modest also, she would be a remarkable person.
2. Charles sometimes wondered if Althea (*was, were*) pulling his leg.
3. I think Jerry tries not to be concerned, but he (*is, be*).
4. Gladys feared that the dog (*was, were*) only a step or two behind.
5. Audrey couldn't save herself even if she (*was, were*) given an oar to pull with.
6. (*Were, Was*) he really an honest man, he wouldn't have agreed with the professor.
7. The regulations require that an athlete in training (*is, be*) in bed by 10 o'clock.
8. (*Is, Be*) Shillingbreek's new novel worth reading?
9. Sometimes I wish that my mother (*was, were*) as avant-garde as Maria's.
10. Glory (*is, be*) to God for dappled things.

EXERCISE 24

Follow the directions for Exercise 23.

1. If that (*is, be*) she, as I believe, let her in.
2. Be sure the tent is secure, David, lest it (*washes, wash*) away in the monsoon.

3. If I (*was, were*) late seven times, as my instructor says, I certainly didn't know it.
4. I move that the treasurer (*explains, explain*) how he became rich enough to buy a racehorse.
5. How my little sister wishes she (*was, were*) a sky diver!
6. I don't care if the business (*fails, fail*), Donald, if we still have each other.
7. Suzanne sometimes acts as if she (*was, were*) the only intelligent person in the school.
8. If Martha be not worthy of promotion, who (*is, be*)?
9. I fear that I (*was, were*) responsible for the hysteria.
10. Tony smilingly insisted that the infinitive (*is, be*) split.

U10. Adjectives and Adverbs

We have little difficulty in deciding whether we should use an adjective *or* an adverb in a given sentence. (Actually, most writers use more of both than they should, thus making their work wordier than it should be.)

Keep in mind these three statements about the use of adjectives and adverbs:

1. After a linking verb, use an *adjective* if reference is to the subject. Use an *adverb* if reference is to the verb.
2. Idiomatic usage often violates the distinction between *adjectives* and *adverbs*.
3. Some *adjectives* and *adverbs* have identical forms.

Adjectives

An **adjective** modifies a noun or pronoun by describing, limiting, or otherwise making its meaning more nearly exact. Adjectives are of three general types: descriptive (a *yellow* dress, a *broad* horizon, a *tired* laborer); limiting (the *third* phase, her *given* name, *several* weeks); proper (an *American* policy, a *Florida* orange).

Some adjectives—indeed most—have endings that mark them as adjectives. The most important of these include:

–able (–ible):	workable, serviceable, combustible
–al:	partial, radial, experimental, optional
–ary:	auxiliary, beneficiary, primary, arbitrary
–en:	golden, smitten, hidden, rotten
–ful:	sinful, rueful, scornful, dutiful
–ic:	artistic, pessimistic, altruistic, rustic

–ish:	slavish, peevish, reddish, babyish
–ive:	restive, festive, corrosive, explosive
–less:	faultless, guileless, fearless, mindless
–ous:	marvelous, viscous, luscious, amorous
–some:	lonesome, fearsome, awesome
–y:	sticky, risky, funny, catty, dreamy

**U
10**

An adjective may modify a noun directly (*the* violet *shadows lengthening along the sand*) or indirectly (*the prisoner,* wan *and* shabby, *was led gently from the stand*). In sentences such as "The seat felt *hard*" and "The path is *treacherous*," each adjective is related to the subject, the word it modifies, by a linking verb. (A linking verb has little meaning of its own; it serves primarily as a connection between subject and predicate noun or predicate adjective.) In the sentences above, *hard* and *treacherous* are called *predicate adjectives*, or *complements*.

Adverbs

An **adverb** modifies a verb, adjective, or other adverb. Adverbs generally tell *how, when, where, why, how often,* and *how much.* In "The high cliff loomed *forbiddingly* above him," the adverb modifies the verb *loomed* and tells *how.* In "We are *nearly* ready for supper," the adverb modifies the adjective *ready.* In "Close the hatch *very* quickly," the adverb modifies the adverb *quickly.*

Adverbs have the following characteristics:

1. Adverbs are frequently, but not always, distinguished from corresponding adjectives by the suffix *–ly: true, truly; poor, poorly; sharp, sharply.*
2. Certain adverbs are distinguished from corresponding nouns by the suffixes *–wise* and *–ways: sideways, lengthwise, clockwise, counterclockwise.*
3. Certain adverbs are distinguished from corresponding prepositions in not being connected to a following noun:

   > Adverb: She fell *down.*
   > Preposition: He fell *down* the staircase.

4. Like adjectives, but unlike nouns and verbs, adverbs may be preceded by *intensifiers* such as *very, least,* etc.:

   > It was the *least expensively* furnished house.
   > We must see her *right now.*

U10a. BE SURE TO USE AN ADVERB TO MODIFY A VERB.

The form of a word does not always reveal whether it is an adjective or adverb. Most words ending in *–ly* are adverbs, but *holy, sickly, motherly, unruly* are adjectives. Also, some adjectives and adverbs have the same form: *quick, little, early, fast, kindly*. Finally, a few adverbs have two forms quite different in meaning: *late, lately; sharp, sharply.*

> Nonstandard: He spends his money too *rapid*. (*Rapidly*, an adverb, should modify the verb *spends; rapid* is an adjective.)
> The dog barks *loud* when he spies the cat. (Use *loudly*.)
> She spoke to him *motherly*. (in *a motherly way*)
> The officer spoke *sharp* to me. (*sharply*)

U10b. BE SURE TO USE AN ADVERB TO MODIFY ANOTHER ADJECTIVE.

> Nonstandard: She is a *real* good basketball coach. (Use *really,* an adverb.)
> The sailor made the knot *plenty* tight (Use *very,* or *quite,* or *exceedingly.*)

U10c. AFTER SUCH VERBS AS *APPEAR, BE, BECOME, FEEL, LOOK, SEEM, SMELL,* AND *TASTE,* THE MODIFIER SHOULD BE AN ADJECTIVE IF IT REFERS TO THE SUBJECT, BUT AN ADVERB IF IT DESCRIBES OR DEFINES THE VERB.

> Standard: This pastry tastes *good.* (adjective)
> The sunshine felt *wonderful.* (adjective)
> Carl appeared *happy* when he came. (adjective)
> She looked at him *tenderly.* (adverb)
> Fred feels *keenly* that he was cheated. (adverb)
> Josephine speaks *deliberately* when addressing a class. (adverb)

U10d. BE ACCURATE IN USING WORDS THAT MAY BE EITHER ADJECTIVES OR ADVERBS.

Standard:	Sam's father, the *late* mayor, had a small estate. (adjective)
	Marshall has been studying French *lately*. (adverb)
	Skippy is a *little* beagle. (adjective)
	Put the lamp a *little* farther back. (adverb)
	Grandfather was a *kindly* man. (adjective)
	She treated all of us *kindly*. (adverb)
	Sandy is my *best* friend. (adjective)
	Who knows *best?* (adverb)

U10e. BE ACCURATE IN THE USE OF COMPARATIVES AND SUPERLATIVES.

Most adjectives and adverbs change their forms to show a greater or smaller *degree* of the quality they express. This change of form is called *comparison*. The three degrees of comparison are *positive, comparative,* and *superlative*.

Positive	Comparative	Superlative
happy (adj.)	happier	happiest
soon (adv.)	sooner	soonest

In comparisons that indicate *less* of a quality, the words *less* and *least* are used with all adjectives and adverbs that can be compared.

Positive	Comparative	Superlative
ill	less ill	least ill
afraid	less afraid	least afraid
honest	less honest	least honest

This construction, however, can be avoided if it seems awkward.

Formal:	She is less ill than she was this morning.
Better:	She is not so ill.
	She is better.

Most adjectives and adverbs of one syllable form the comparative degree by adding –*er* and the superlative degree by adding –*est*.

Positive	Comparative	Superlative
tall	taller	tallest
cheap	cheaper	cheapest
tough	tougher	toughest

Although adjectives of two syllables usually add –*er* for the comparative and –*est* for the superlative, there are times when such adjectives have two forms for both comparative and superlative.

Positive	Comparative	Superlative
portly	more portly or portlier	most portly or portliest
rotten	more rotten or rottener	most rotten or rottenest

Adverbs that end in –*ly* and adjectives of more than two syllables usually form the comparative and superlative by prefixing *more* and *most*.

Positive	Comparative	Superlative
beautifully	more beautifully	most beautifully
rapidly	more rapidly	most rapidly
nearly	more nearly	most nearly
dutiful (adj.)	more dutiful	most dutiful
efficient (adj.)	more efficient	most efficient

Some adjectives and adverbs form their changes irregularly.

Positive	Comparative	Superlative
good (adj.)	better	best
well (adv.)	better	best
bad (adj.)	worse	worst
badly (adv.)	worse	worst

When using the comparative and superlative degrees, keep in mind the following guidelines:

1. The comparative is used for comparing two persons or objects or actions; the superlative is used for comparing more than two.

I bought two new outfits. Which do you think is *more suitable?*
Which of your friends is the *better* athlete?
Caribbean water is *greener* than Atlantic water.
Lynn's was the *most artistic* of all the flower arrangements.

In informal English, the superlative is often used when only two things are compared.

2. Avoid double comparatives and superlatives; that is, when *–er* or *–est* has been added to form the comparative or superlative, do not use *more* or *most* before the word.

Nonstandard:	She is more older than her sister.
Standard:	She is older than her sister.

3. Choose the comparative form with care. Do not confuse the comparative of an adjective with that of an adverb.

Nonstandard:	He carries trays steadier than Tommy does.
Standard:	He carries trays more steadily than Tommy does.

4. A few adjectives, like *parallel, unique, square, round,* and *equal,* are logically incapable of comparison because their meaning is absolute. Two lines, actions, or ideas are parallel or they are not. They cannot logically be more parallel. However, these words have somewhat lost their superlative force and in informal English are often compared. Even good writers use adverbs like *entirely* or *quite* before them.

5. Avoid including the subject in a comparison if the subject is part of a group with which it is being compared. Use *else* or *other* in such cases. (See Section S13.)

Illogical:	Our boat is larger than any in the fleet.
Better:	Our boat is larger than any *other* in the fleet.
Illogical:	Mary is smarter than anyone in her class.
Better:	Mary is smarter than anyone *else* in her class.

EXERCISE 25

On your paper number each of the following sentences. Next to the number write the word or phrase that is modified by the italicized word. If the italicized word is unsuitable, write a better form.

1. Thelma skipped *nimble* up the steps just ahead of her sister.
2. There were just two cookies left on the plate, and so I took the *biggest* one.
3. The creamed spinach made our happiness *complete*.
4. The team felt *badly* about losing the swimming meet.
5. Let's all patronize *local* owned stores.
6. Martin certainly looks *nicely* in sideburns.
7. You did *good* to accede to their request.
8. I *sure* would be happier without these snakes.
9. Just then a *beautiful* dressed couple walked into the room.
10. My classmates tell me that I write *fluent*.

EXERCISE 26

Follow the directions for Exercise 25.

1. Until we get clear of the cobras, Kurt, we had better step extremely *careful*.
2. The trail was *ruggeder* than the campers thought it would be.
3. Julia will become much more *confidently* as she gets older.
4. Daisy decided that going to camp was a *real* fine idea.
5. Fearing that he did not smell *well*, Robert tried another shaving lotion.
6. Mrs. White discovered that the car overheated very *easy*.
7. Little Edson blinked back the tears and smiled *bravely*.
8. We agreed that it was a *most unique* sunset.
9. The rats were still waiting *patient* in the corner of the room.
10. My brother acts much too *cautious*.

EXERCISE 27

Follow the directions for Exercise 25.

1. Rosalynn looked *furtive* at the goldfish.
2. To everyone's surprise the play turned out *successful*.
3. Twirling his cane, William strolled *slowly* through the meadow.
4. The sign read "Drive *slow*."
5. Greg applied himself and became an *extreme* successful sales representative.
6. Harriet thinks her car handles *easier* than mine.

7. His leg seems entirely *well* again.
8. When I returned to the house after having shoveled snow for three hours, the hot apple pancakes tasted *good* indeed.
9. Terri grows very *dubious* begonias.
10. Dating is a *real* popular leisure activity among teenagers.

U11. Conjunctions

U11a. A CONJUNCTION IS A LINKING WORD USED TO CONNECT WORDS OR WORD GROUPS.

There are two main kinds of conjunctions, *coordinating* and *subordinating*.

Coordinating Conjunctions

Coordinating conjunctions join words or word groups of equal rank. The principal coordinating conjunctions are:

and	nor
but	either
or	neither
for	yet

Marcia *and* Jesse were invited to the game.
The keys are in the car *or* in your pocket.
I don't feel good *but* I am determined to go.

Subordinating Conjunctions

A **subordinating conjunction** begins an adverb clause, joining the dependent adverb clause to the rest of the sentence. Some principal subordinating conjunctions are:

after	before	since	until
although	how	so that	when
as	if	though	where
because	in order that	unless	while

Jason did not look in my direction *because* he was angry.
If that is your opinion, speak up.
She offered me the money *so that* I could pay the bill.
I won't leave *unless* you go with me.

Correlative Conjunctions

Certain coordinating and subordinating conjunctions are sometimes joined to form what are known as **correlative conjunctions.** The principal pairs of correlative conjunctions are:

both . . . and   so . . . as
either . . . or   whether . . . or
neither . . . nor   not only . . . but also

Both Susie *and* Mark are working on the problem.
Either the points *or* the spark plugs need changing.
Whether I vote *or* not is none of your business.

Conjunctive Adverbs

Another kind of conjunction is called a **conjunctive adverb** because it has an adverbial function but can be used to connect two sentences or two main clauses. Among numerous conjunctive adverbs, the following appear frequently:

also	however	otherwise
anyhow	in addition	still
besides	in fact	then
consequently	likewise	therefore
furthermore	nevertheless	thus

Learn to speak more slowly; *otherwise,* no one can understand you.
You seem to be certain of your facts; *however,* I do not agree.
The politician spoke indistinctly; *besides,* she had no real facts.

NOTE: A conjunctive adverb joining two main clauses is preceded by a semicolon.

U11b. CHOOSE THE CONJUNCTION THAT CONVEYS THE MEANING YOU DESIRE.

Depending on your purpose, ideas may be coordinated or subordinated in several ways. Unless you know the meanings of conjunctions and conjunctive adverbs, you will have trouble. If your purpose in a sentence is to express the idea of "along the same line" or "in the same direction of thought," then use one of these:

and	in addition
both . . . and	indeed
not only . . . but also	likewise
also	moreover
besides	similarly
furthermore	whereupon

Note these ten additional purposes you might have in writing a sentence and the proper conjunctions for you to choose from:

1. Purpose: *contrast*

    although, but, however, instead, nevertheless, not only . . . but also, notwithstanding, still, whereas, yet

2. Purpose: *affirmative alternation*

    anyhow, either . . . or, else, moreover, or, still, whereas, whether

3. Purpose: *negative alternation*

    except that, however, instead, neither, neither . . . nor, nevertheless, nor, only, whereas

4. Purpose: *reason, result, purpose, cause*

    accordingly, as, as a result, because, consequently, for, hence, inasmuch as, in order that, since, so, so that, that, thereby, therefore, thus, whereas, why

5. Purpose: *example*

    for example, indeed, in fact, namely

6. Purpose: *comparison*

    indeed, in fact, moreover, so . . . as, than

7. Purpose: *time*

    after, as long as, as soon as, before, henceforth, meanwhile, once, since, then, till, until, when, whenever, while

8. Purpose: *place*

    whence, where, wherever

9. Purpose: *condition*

> although, as if, as though, if, lest, once, provided, providing, though, unless

10. Purpose: *concession*

> although, insofar as, notwithstanding the fact that, though, unless, while

U11c. CORRELATIVE CONJUNCTIONS SHOULD CORRELATE ONLY TWO IDEAS.

> Nonstandard: *Both* her poise, charm, wit, *and* talent attracted us. (Delete *both* or two of the four subjects.)
>
> Standard: Her poise, charm, wit, and talent attracted us. *Both* her poise *and* wit attracted us.
>
> Nonstandard: *Neither* noise, a crowded room, *nor* the scorn of her roommate could keep Maria from concentrating on algebra. (Delete one of the three subjects or rephrase the sentence.)
>
> Standard: *Neither* noise *nor* the scorn of her roommate could keep Maria from concentrating on algebra.
>
> Noise, a crowded room, and the scorn of her roommate could not keep Maria from concentrating on algebra.

U11d. BE CAUTIOUS IN USING *LIKE* AS A SUBORDINATING CONJUNCTION.

The use of *like* in clauses of comparison has increased greatly within the past few years: "It looks *like* I might go." A certain brand of cigarette makes the claim that it "tastes good *like* a cigarette should." We do not avoid the use of *like* "like we once did." However, in standard English *like* is used as a preposition with no following verb: "She looks like an intelligent woman." In strictly formal English, use *as* or *as if* for clauses of comparison:

> You must march *as* I tell you (not *like* I tell you).
> My ankle felt *as if* I had broken it (not *like* I had broken it).
> I am being generous to you *as* my brother was generous to me (not *like* my brother was generous to me).

EXERCISE 28

Write on your paper the number of each sentence. If the italicized conjunction is satisfactory, write *S* after the number. If the conjunction is not acceptable, supply a better one.

1. The jacket fitted Henry perfectly, *while* the pants had to be shortened.
2. Neither the ice *or* the slush caused me to slow down.
3. *Although* some skill is necessary, prowess of Olympic caliber is not required in order to make our swimming team.
4. The fat was Mrs. Spratt's favorite part of the pork chop, *whereas* Jack preferred the lean.
5. *Being as how* Amy loves to travel, she visited Europe as well as Japan.
6. Marvin has measles, *but* he would have joined us today.
7. Helen doubted the wisdom of their action; *however*, she determined not to stand in their way.
8. *Both* persimmon *and* burnt sienna are shades of orange.
9. It seems *like* every time I want to visit a foreign country, that country has a revolution.
10. My closest friends are Chuck, Bill, Harvey, *and* Mike.

EXERCISE 29

Follow the directions for Exercise 28.

1. The huge boulder looked *like* it would topple over and crush us.
2. Beatrice could not make up her mind *if* she would wrestle the crocodile.
3. Bonnie not only found herself flat broke *but* discovered her friends had vanished completely.
4. The cannibal wanted stew, *and* there was nobody to put into the **pot**.
5. We had feared that you would give up, *or* you did.
6. Family *and* friends are waiting for me in Bridgewater.
7. Fred told her *how that* his heart started pounding when the barking dog began running after him.
8. She was so wrapped up in her own problems *until* she did not want to listen to mine.
9. I heard on the radio *where* apple pie is losing its eminence as America's favorite dessert.
10. I do not care for that expensive blue shirt he chose, *and* I will pay for it anyway.

U
11

EXERCISE 30

Follow the directions for Exercise 28.

1. Both the Colts *and* the Vikings need to improve their standings in the league.
2. My wet coat felt *like* it weighed 50 pounds.
3. Neither sunshine *or* moonlight has any effect on my moods.
4. They are not sure *if* they will have enough time for the party.
5. She was so fond of nuclear physics *until* she didn't want to think or talk about anything else.
6. Jo finished high school with honors *while* her older brother never got through the sixth grade.
7. We read in the newspaper *where* twenty people were injured in that accident.
8. Pot roast is my father's favorite meat, *whereas* I prefer a good broiled steak.
9. The teacher disagreed with what I said, *and* she earnestly defended my right to my own opinions.
10. It seems *like*, in every trial, the defense attorney claims that the jury has been prejudiced in some way.

REVIEW EXERCISE 1

The following sentences contain various faults in usage. On your paper, number each sentence and rewrite it, correcting all errors.

1. For many years our family has went to Florida for their vacation; this is a trip my mother and brother always chose because of his asthma, and my father and me enjoyed the fishing.
2. If he had been given a job, like he was promised before he became desperate, you would never have read of him saying such anti-social things.
3. In today's paper it says as how the earth is gradually growing warmer, the reason being that the sun is getting closer to the earth.
4. The teacher said she was happy that Clara and myself was doing so good. She thought we would even fuller understand if we applied ourselves.
5. The automobile problem in the United States has went from bad to worse recently because so many of them are on the road and people will not learn to drive slow.
6. It says in the report that they frequently employ children to do

this work, which is very dangerous unless carefully regulated.

7. If I was a farmer that lived in some parts of the United States, I would be real afraid of tornadoes because they strike without warning but do much damage.

8. Ms. Jones informed Cathy that her house had been burglarized, that they had stole all they could carry, and that they had wrecked things as if it was a maniac.

9. My Uncle Matt, one of my mother's brothers, have lived at our house until he died last year, which was sure a blow to me.

10. The leader of all seven patrols are to keep contact with headquarters; if any survivors were found, they should report them by messenger.

11. I didn't want to have nothing to do with it.

U
R

REVIEW EXERCISE 2

Each of the following sentences contains a form wrongly used. Write each on your paper, underline the faulty expression, and label the error, using the following abbreviations: *Agr*—lack of agreement between subject and predicate: *Mood*—wrong mood; *Tense*—wrong tense; *Verb*—wrong verb form; *Case*—wrong case; *Ant*—lack of agreement between pronoun and antecedent; *Ad*—confusion of adjective and adverb.

1. Nancy sighed disconsolately, wishing she was out of school.
2. My father took it very good when I broke my arm while I was skating.
3. In the film, the sheriff hung the cattle rustler, and we cheered at this display of frontier justice.
4. Either my brother or I are going to have to stay home and babysit.
5. Nice children don't hit whomever angers them.
6. Gracie's mother picked her up and swang her into the high chair.
7. The first report, happily erroneous, was that Russell had hit the referee.
8. Between her and I, we have kept expenses to a bare minimum.
9. The teacher praised the sonnets of Shakespeare, but Lorraine heartily disagrees.
10. When the rudder broke off from the boat, Alicia jumped into the bay and swum to shore for help.
11. I have a cow that gives homogenized milk that might interest you.

12. Louise was so tired from tennis that she laid right down beside the court and took a nap.
13. I'll tell you what I'd do if I was he.
14. I greatly admired Keith giving in to his brother in order to prevent a fight.
15. Sandra whistled lowly, and the others came into the room.
16. How sweetly clover blossoms smell in the early morning air.
17. As it turned out, it was Stan and myself who were marked tardy.
18. Let's occupy ourselves by making a list of who is debating who at the final competition.
19. Gladys dived nimbly under the rope and run down the steps.
20. The expression "a loaf of bread, a jug of wine, and thou" are one poet's idea of bliss.
21. A quiet student in the rear responded with a delicate phrased explanation.
22. As soon as she saw Faye, Marsha asked her to dinner, but Ellen asked her last week.
23. By the time the horses were lined up at the gate, each spectator has figured the odds and made a bet.
24. Doctor Perkins was persuaded to remove the bullet, but it got him into trouble.
25. Sammy felt that the insults of his younger tormentor was worse than the torture.

REVIEW EXERCISE 3

Write on your paper the number of each sentence. Beside the number, write the correction or corrections necessary and give the reason for each correction. If a sentence contains no errors, write *C* beside the number.

Examples:	1.	Jerry went with Gene and I.
	2.	Each of the students had their own books.
Corrections:	1.	me—object of the preposition *with*
	2.	his or her—pronoun and antecedent agreement.

1. If it had been necessary, Alberta could beat any of the chess players.
2. We did not think that the project would turn out very good.
3. The young girl's eyes mirrored the gratitude that laid in her heart.
4. When I left, after being with the company for ten years, I felt like a piece of my life was gone.

5. He shall not use my money. I will see that he does not.
6. We recommend that there be appointed an experienced parks commissioner.
7. Because of the heat wave, air conditioning sold very satisfactory that month.
8. The firm objects to me studying Spanish because every woman and man in the office have spent a good deal of time on some similar subject that have not helped their work.
9. The beach was so pleasant I could of laid for hours in the sun.
10. If I was her, I'd make a new start.
11. Each of the ten drivers were issued a separate warning.
12. The trophy was to be awarded to whomever made the highest score in the race series, but I never thought it would be me who would win it.
13. A first prize of an expense-paid trip to Mexico will be given to whoever can solve the Spanish riddle.
14. If you won a nomination against Robert Story, you have did very good indeed.
15. I have always felt like I'd like to be a lawyer.
16. Keith has never been strong; so he don't go hiking like the rest of us do.
17. I drunk a huge glass of iced tea when I come home from the movies.
18. Digging a tunnel into the hillside, the boys went away and left it.
19. Headlines in the newspaper is arranged so that it attracts attention.
20. Every evening there has been some sort of meeting; and although I would have liked to have attended all of them, it was physically impossible.

REVIEW EXERCISE 4

Follow the directions for Review Exercise 3.

1. This camp is different than all of the other camps I have attended.
2. The partners wish to express their appreciation for your patronage during the year and welcomes this opportunity to wish you a merry Christmas.
3. Since one photograph is worth a thousand words, advertisers are turning to them to sell products.
4. It was not prudent of you to have given her your diary.
5. Losing his fortune in a real estate investment, he begun working again at fifty.

6. New cars don't jump direct from the drafting board to the production room like some people think they do.
7. People said he behaved as a fool at the wedding.
8. Since you invited Paul and I for a visit, our mother has been terrible ill; so we will not be able to accept your invitation.
9. The dance will probably last until midnight; so there is no point in you waiting up any longer.
10. A mysterious stranger whom, we discovered later, met Father last winter, crosses the lake and ties up at our dock.
11. When you consider that neither of us have did any water skiing for two years, we are not doing so bad.
12. Neither Mother nor I are surprised to hear that Agnes failed; she didn't do her assignments careful at all.
13. I wish I was able to tell Carla and she the dreadful secret.
14. Since the computer checking system has been used successful, most of our banks have adopted it.
15. He told Ms. Kenworth that she was sure to be made a director.
16. The lifeguard said that the boys almost drownded because they swum out too far.
17. After we helped sweep out the dining room, we arranged chairs for the meeting.
18. The satellites that we launch makes life more and more complex.
19. I'm afraid his foot is froze.
20. I could have come if I had knew that you were coming.

Punctuation and Mechanics

PM
1

Punctuation is a method by which the meaning of written communication is made clear through the use of certain marks.

  Mechanics, a rather vague word, applies to the use of capital and small letters; italics (underlining); abbreviations; the representation of numerals in either words or figures; and the spelling of English words and phrases.

  The most significant marks of punctuation are

.	period	,	comma
?	question mark	;	semicolon
!	exclamation point	:	colon
—	dash	" "	double quotation marks
-	hyphen	' '	single quotation marks
'	apostrophe	( )	parentheses

  Each of these marks is a sort of shorthand device, or road sign, that assists the reader. Every mark of punctuation is effective if it helps the reader understand. The presence or absence of every mark is harmful if it impedes the flow of thought from your mind to that of your reader. Punctuation usually serves one of four general purposes:

1. To *end* or *terminate* a statement—use a period, a question mark, or an exclamation point.

   Snow flurries were predicted.
   Have you been home?
   What a surprise!

2. To *introduce* — use a comma, a colon, or a dash.

   He needed only one thing, encouragement.
   My purpose is simple: to succeed in life.
   My goal in life is simple—success.

3. To *separate* parts of a sentence or word—use a comma, a semicolon, a dash, a hyphen, or an apostrophe.

> If you have any influence at all, try to have me excused.
> Some people prefer steak for breakfast; others prefer it for dinner.
> Sneezing, wheezing, and coughing—these are symptoms of the common cold.
> Judy Nash was elected vice-president.
> It will soon be 3 o'clock.

4. To *enclose* parts of a sentence or a whole section—use commas, dashes, quotation marks, single quotation marks, parentheses, or brackets. Enclosure marks are usually used in pairs.

> An energetic woman, Ms. Boylen, was my favorite grade school teacher.
> Ms. Boylen, an energetic woman, was my favorite grade school teacher.
> My favorite grade school teacher was Ms. Boylen, an energetic woman.

> You are not—and everyone around here knows it—a very careful driver.
> You are not a careful driver—and everyone around here knows it.

> "The word 'lousy' is not in reputable use as a term in literary criticism," said the lecturer.
> You are referred to the United States Constitution (see especially Article VII).
> The article began: "People these days are to [*sic*] busy to think about problems that arise more than 100 miles from their homes."

PM1. End Stops

Punctuation appearing at the end of a sentence is called an **end stop.** Sometimes called "terminal marks," end stops include periods, question marks, and exclamation points.

A story is told that Victor Hugo, the famous nineteenth-century French writer, wrote the shortest letter on record. Wishing to know how his latest novel was selling, he sent a sheet of paper to his publisher on which appeared a single question mark. His publisher, pleased to report good news, replied with a single exclamation point. If you wish to know your standing with an absent sweetheart, you might copy Hugo's letter, but you run the risk of receiving in reply another question mark or, worse luck, a period.

The Period

PM1a. USE A PERIOD AT THE END OF A DECLARATIVE SENTENCE.

PM
1

School will be dismissed early today.
Ralph prefers driving to flying.

PM1b. USE A PERIOD AFTER MOST ABBREVIATIONS.

Mr. and Mrs. Robert Manley
Jane L. Freeman, M.D. (b. 1908, d. 1967)
Nov. 5, Fla., St., Ave., A.M., oz., bbl.

PM1c. USE THREE SPACED PERIODS TO INDICATE AN INTENTIONAL OMISSION.

Such periods, called **ellipses,** indicate an omission of one or more words within a sentence or quotation. If the omission ends with a period, use four spaced periods.

"Finds tongues in trees, books . . . in brooks, sermons in stones,
. . . good in everything."
The tiger crept stealthily toward its prey. . . .

Exclamation Point and Question Mark

PM1d. USE THE EXCLAMATION POINT TO EXPRESS SURPRISE, COMMAND, EMPHASIS, OR STRONG EMOTION.

What nerve you have!
I tell you—bluntly!—leave me alone.
So you have changed your mind after all!
So that's what he's after!

Use the exclamation point sparingly. The emotion, command, or surprise involved must be strong enough to justify an exclamation point.

Use a period, not an exclamation point, after an only mildly imperative sentence.

> Drive slowly, and watch out for falling rocks.

PM1e. USE A QUESTION MARK AT THE END OF EVERY DIRECT QUESTION.

> You commented—did I understand you?—that you disliked all TV programs.
> Do you really think I am that silly?
> Joe asked politely, "May I borrow a dollar?"

However, use a period, not a question mark, after an indirect question.

> Kindly tell me when you will wish this returned to the library.

And use a period, not a question mark, after a polite request or an only superficially interrogative sentence.

> "May I see you to the door" is a remark of courtesy more than of interrogation and does not require a question mark.

PM1f. USE QUESTION MARKS TO INDICATE A SERIES OF QUERIES IN THE SAME SENTENCE OR PASSAGE.

> Are you staying? Is your brother? Carol? Marie?
> Do you remember when cars had rumble seats? When boys wore knickers? When grandparents were elderly?
> Who's going to volunteer? Diane? Andy?

EXERCISE 1

On your paper copy each of the following sentences and supply periods, exclamation points, or question marks where they are needed.

1. Now you never connect a white wire to a black wire except when you are working on the discarded models
2. The Rt Rev Chauncey Cummins will speak at 7:00 PM on Sunday evening, Aug 4, in place of Cecil Bustem, PhD, DD
3. How could a person answer a question like that before a whole group of strangers Why, the whole situation was ridiculous Absurd Preposterous
4. On St Sebastian's Day we had cookies, turtle soup, pancakes Have you ever tried St Sebastian's Day pancakes What a wonderful day it was
5. The other channel Of course you may watch the other channel
6. Drop that gun Hold up your hands Who are you, anyway
7. My brother longs to be able to write "BA, MA, PhD" after his name, but my sister says he's going to have to start studying before that ever happens
8. Look out There's no guardrail Nothing to stop us if we slip off the road
9. Ours isn't all just run-of-the-mill work; even though our day-to-day operations are largely routine, we get some fun out of the ordinary assignments
10. During the summer session, classes are held as early as 7 AM but never run later than 2 PM

PM
.1

EXERCISE 2

Follow the directions for Exercise 1.

1. That electrician Do you know what he charged Fifty dollars
2. George Harris was graduated from Harvard with a BA (1956) and from Brown with an MA (1958)
3. Mr and Mrs Wolverton visited twenty-eight European cities in twenty-three days
4. Help Help I'm trapped inside of a closet Help
5. Ms Zickefoose will address the board of trustees at 7 PM this evening.
6. You take that roast back to the butcher and have all the fat trimmed off Now get going, Sam
7. The litter of kittens strolled calmly across the schoolyard
8. I saw him—what's his name—at the movies last Friday night
9. Ms Plunkett, our advisor, ordered six pizzas for the party
10. The plane for Paris is due to depart at 8 PM, not 9 PM
11. Who went with you to the lake Debbie Louise
12. The door creaked open and

PM2. The Semicolon

The **semicolon** (;) is a mark of separation, or division. It is never used to introduce, enclose, or end a statement. It is a stronger mark than the comma, signifying a greater break or longer pause between sentence elements. But it is weaker than the period and other terminal marks (question mark, exclamation point) and cannot be used to end a sentence. Its use indicates that two or more statements are not sufficiently related to require commas but are too closely related to justify being put in separate sentences separated by a terminal mark.

PM2a. USE THE SEMICOLON TO SEPARATE INDEPENDENT CLAUSES NOT JOINED BY A COORDINATING CONJUNCTION (*AND*, *BUT*, *OR*, *NOR*, *FOR*).

> The stupid believe that to be truthful is easy; the artist, the great artist, knows how difficult it is. (Willa Cather)

> One can never pay in gratitude; one can only pay "in kind" somewhere else in life. (Anne Morrow Lindbergh)

> A little neglect may breed mischief: for want of a nail the shoe was lost; for want of a shoe the horse was lost; for want of a horse the rider was lost. (Benjamin Franklin)

PM2b. USE THE SEMICOLON TO SEPARATE INDEPENDENT CLAUSES JOINED BY A CONJUNCTIVE ADVERB.

Conjunctive adverbs, special kinds of adverbs that can also be used as conjunctions, include *also, anyhow, as a result, besides, consequently, for example, furthermore, hence, however, in addition, indeed, in fact, instead, likewise, meanwhile, moreover, namely, nevertheless, otherwise, similarly, still, then, therefore,* and *thus.*

> We regret that we have sold all of the shirts in blue; *however,* we have the same style in white.
> Dorothy's brother is a busy boy; *in fact,* he works harder than she does.

He ran a high fever for three days; *then* he admitted defeat and let his brother summon a doctor.

She expected a reward for her diligent efforts on behalf of the party; *instead,* she was punished.

PM2c. USE A SEMICOLON TO SEPARATE INDEPENDENT CLAUSES JOINED BY A COORDINATING CONJUNCTION IF THE CLAUSES ARE LONG OR CONTAIN COMMAS.

When the scorpion stung the man, he felt a sharp pain in his foot; but since there was no swelling, he thought that he had not been injured.

Roberta, a very good friend of mine, wants me to go to camp with her; but because I have been to camp for three years in succession, I am undecided.

Success in school, so some maintain, requires intelligence, industry, and honesty; but others, somewhat fewer in number, insist that only personality and contacts really count.

PM2d. USE A SEMICOLON TO SEPARATE THE MEMBERS OF A SERIES IF ANY OF THEM CONTAIN COMMAS.

The ones chosen to represent the school were Nancy Black, president of the debating society; Jack Smoak, boys' varsity baseball captain; and Gene Toale, active in school dramatics.

Down the field came the newly organized, somewhat incompetent band; three cheerleaders in white, spangled skirts; and the team, muddy and wretched.

PM2e. DO NOT OVERUSE THE SEMICOLON.

The semicolon has its special uses and should be employed only in the situations described above. Avoid using semicolons in the following ways:

1. Do not use a semicolon between an independent clause and a dependent clause or a phrase.

The semicolon has the same function as a period: it indicates a complete break and marks the end of one thought and the beginning of another. Except for the special situations noted in the two previous rules, a fairly safe guide is no period, no semicolon. Phrases and dependent clauses cannot be set off by periods and thus cannot be marked by semicolons.

Faulty: Since Megan wants to go with us; we must revise our plans. (The opening dependent clause should be followed by a comma, not a semicolon.)

Faulty: Being aware of the high cost of living; I am sympathetic to your predicament. (The opening participial phrase requires a comma at the end, not a semicolon.)

2. Do not use a semicolon to introduce statements or lists.

The semicolon is not a mark of introduction and should never be used for this purpose.

Faulty: His goal is simple and direct; to make the debating team. (Use a colon or dash, not a semicolon.)

Faulty: Dear Sir; Dear Ms. Woods; (Use a colon or a comma, not a semicolon.)

3. Do not use a semicolon to indicate a summary.

Faulty: Sweeping, dusting, mopping; these were my household chores. (Use a colon or dash, not a semicolon.)

EXERCISE 3

On your paper copy the following sentences and supply semicolons where they are needed.

1. Oscar suddenly found himself eye to eye with a rattler he was unable to move a muscle.
2. The customs inspector looked suspicious as she checked the declaration statement: a camera, complete with flash attachments a portable typewriter valued at 50 dollars and a machine gun, loaded and ready for use.
3. Mehitabel would not give up easily there was life in the old cat yet.
4. This is Homecoming Weekend, and we have to look our best furthermore, our team must win Saturday's game.
5. The camp nurse told Lulu to open her mouth and stick out her tongue the latter action Lulu performed with extraordinary expertness.

6. Stephanie's Christmas list grew: Billy, a green-and-blue striped tie Doug, a plaid tie Harry, a plain knitted tie.
7. I relax by listening to my stereo Lee prefers to watch television.
8. When we met Nancy and George, they had just returned from school they greeted us warmly.
9. In spite of the election ratings, Mayor Hinkle remained confident nevertheless, he did not order refreshments for his partisans.
10. We were there when Olga sang in Stratford the appreciative audience would not let her stop singing.

EXERCISE 4

Follow the directions for Exercise 3.

1. Uncle Ned hates to shave he also hates beards.
2. The highest-ranking students were Ronald George of Erebob, Ohio Sylvia Marteney of Sillabub, Maine Mary Jenkins of New Orleans and I.
3. My Aunt Louise lives in a Greenwich Village garret therefore she lacks the room a grand piano requires.
4. All of the Disney pictures are suitable for all members of the family this is but one reason for their great popularity.
5. When they watch television together, they always argue about what programs to see they seem to enjoy these arguments.
6. Fly-fishing has its unique appeal however, I prefer using lures.
7. A rainy spell set in, and construction was halted for a week consequently, we were free from Monday through Friday.
8. Three and twenty pigeons were perched upon the ledge therefore, we crossed to the other side of the street.
9. "Let's all go to the art exhibit," she said 15 minutes later, we were on our way and had a wonderful time.
10. Springtime in Vermont is every bit as lovely as the song suggests all skiers will not agree.

PM3. The Colon

The main purpose of the **colon** (:) is to tell the reader to watch for what is coming. That is, it signals that the next group of words will provide a further explanation or illustration of what has just been said.

PM3a. USE THE COLON TO INTRODUCE A WORD, PHRASE, OR CLAUSE, OR AFTER AN INTRODUCTORY STATEMENT THAT SHOWS THAT SOMETHING IS TO FOLLOW.

Only one other possibility remains: to travel by bus.
My aim in this course is easily stated: a high grade.
This is my problem: Where do I go from here?
Do this before you leave: Buy traveler's checks, check your passport, have your smallpox vaccination.

PM3b. USE THE COLON TO SEPARATE INTRODUCTORY WORDS FROM A LONG OR FORMAL QUOTATION THAT FOLLOWS.

Deems Taylor concluded his article on Richard Wagner with these words: "The miracle is that what he did in the little space of seventy years could have been done at all, even by a great genius. Is it any wonder that he had no time to be a man?"

PM3c. USE THE COLON AS A SEPARATING MARK IN SPECIAL SITUATIONS.

1. *In business letters*, the salutation is separated from the body of the letter by a colon.

   Dear Madam: Dear Mr. Clark: Gentlemen: My dear Ms. Swan:

2. *Titles and subtitles of books* can be separated by a colon.

   Education for College: Improving the High School Curriculum
   The English Novel: A Panorama

3. *Hour and minute figures* in writing time can be separated by a colon.

   8:17 P.M.; 3:26 A.M.

4. *Acts and scenes of plays* can be separated by a colon.

   Twelfth Night, II:v

5. *Chapters and verses of the Bible* can be separated by a colon.

   James 3:16

6. *Volume and page reference* can be separated by a colon.

   The History of the English Novel, V:83

7. *A publisher's location and name* can be separated by a colon.

   New York: Harper & Row, Publishers, Incorporated

8. *In stating proportions*, both a single colon and double colon can be used.

   2:4::4:8 (2 is to 4 as 4 is to 8)

PM 3

PM3d. DO NOT OVERUSE THE COLON.

The colon is a useful mark that adds clarity to writing, but it should be used only as suggested above. Do not use the colon in other ways, such as those listed below:

1. Do not place a colon between a preposition and its object.

   I am fond of: New York, Washington, and Miami. (There is no need for the colon or any other mark of punctuation after *of*.)

2. Do not place a colon between a verb and its object or object complement.

   He likes to see: TV, plays, movies, and baseball games. (Use no mark of punctuation after *see*.)
   She liked a number of activities, such as: dancing, cooking, and swimming. (Use no mark of any kind after *such as*.)

EXERCISE 5

On your paper copy the following sentences. Supply colons where they are needed.

1. At 630 the next morning what everyone had been expecting occurred murder.
2. I know only one passage, Karen, that will give you the answer to your question Exodus 614.
3. Of the performance of a celebrated violinist, Dr. Johnson once said "Difficult do you call it, Sir? I wish it were impossible."
4. Donovan refused to economize on the necessities of life, such as good dinner wines, adequate theater seats, and competent valet service.

5. The only magazines she ever reads are *Ms., Time,* and *Harper's Bazaar.*
6. Then from a gloomy corner on the north side of the waiting room came the awful words of the stationmaster "The 945 train for Denver will never leave this station."
7. For Tuesday's assignment we are to read poems by the following Poe, Thoreau, and Dickinson.
8. My cousin has only one responsibility left to find a home for her aging beagle.
9. Dan chose his car after carefully examining all the compact cars manufactured by the Chrysler Corporation, the Ford Motor Company, and General Motors.
10. The minister took her text from Psalms 133.

PM4. The Dash

The **dash** (—) is most often used to indicate a sudden interruption in thought. Some other mark of punctuation can usually be substituted for a dash. However, a dash lends a certain air of surprise or emotional tone and, if used sparingly, is a device for adding movement, or a sense of movement, to writing.

PM4a. USE THE DASH TO INDICATE A SUDDEN BREAK OR SHIFT IN THOUGHT.

Here is a fuller explanation—but perhaps your students will not be interested.
She is the most despicable—but I should not say any more.

Breaks or shifts in thought and the use of dashes to indicate them should both be rare.

PM4b. USE A DASH TO INTRODUCE A WORD OR GROUP OF WORDS THAT YOU WISH TO EMPHASIZE.

There is only one other possibility—to travel by car.
There is only one thing he needs for his complete happiness—love.

Either a colon or comma could be used in such constructions as these, but the dash adds emphasis, vigor, and emotional tone.

PM4c. USE DASHES TO SET OFF AN ABRUPT PARENTHETICAL ELEMENT.

> My advice—if you will pardon my impertinence—is that you apologize to your friend.
>
> My brother is not afraid—he is a surgeon, you know—of performing the most delicate operation.
>
> I was pleased—delighted, I should say—to hear your news.
>
> She was aware—she must have known—that the proposal was hopeless.

PM 4

PM4d. USE A DASH TO INDICATE OMISSION OF LETTERS AND WORDS AND TO CONNECT COMBINATIONS OF LETTERS AND FIGURES.

> Representative B— was an excellent orator.
>
> We were in one h— of a spot when we landed.
>
> May—August (May to or through August)
>
> She lived in that city 1962—1967.
>
> Joe Pear is a pilot on the New York—Chicago run.
>
> The First World War, 1914—1918, was fought to end all wars.

A hyphen (-) might be substituted in typing or handwriting in each of the examples above except the first two, where a double dash could also be used.

Do not use a dash in such expressions as those above when the word *from* or *between* appears.

> from May to (or though) August (not *from May—August*)
>
> between 1956 and 1963 (not *between 1956—1963*)

EXERCISE 6

Copy the following sentences on your paper and supply dashes when needed in each sentence.

1. No, no, Ed, not that switch, the one with the for heaven's sake look out!
2. The stock market crash of 1929 it began on October 24 of that year brought many a paper millionaire to beggary.
3. The mysterious woman asked Uncle Julian to mind her Pekingese while she but that's another story.

4. Excuse me, sir, I didn't mean to why, if it isn't my old friend Leonard.
5. The lawyer briefly sketched the main facts of her wait, haven't I said that before?
6. Well, I'll be
7. The coach called the team together they were in the clubhouse where they had dressed for the game and reminded them "This game will decide the league championship. Do your best. That's all I ask."
8. Call Linda she insists on being involved and then report back to me.
9. I saw a John Wayne movie I forget the title of it in which he didn't win the war single-handedly.
10. Monica swam the river believe it or not wearing sneakers.

PM5. The Comma

Because the **comma** (,) serves many different purposes, it is the most widely used of all punctuation marks. This mark of punctuation, more than any other, helps to clarify the meaning of writing. But its overuse and misuse also obscure meaning more than the misapplication of any of the other marks.

Here are three important facts about the comma that you should keep in mind:

1. It is a relatively weak mark compared to the period, semi-colon, and colon.
2. It is always used *within* a sentence.
3. It has three primary purposes: (a) to *separate* sentence elements that might be misread; (b) to *enclose* or *set off* constructions within a sentence that act as interrupters; (c) to set off certain *introductory* sentence elements.

PM5a. USE A COMMA TO SEPARATE WORDS OR OTHER SENTENCE ELEMENTS THAT MIGHT BE MISREAD.

The single most important use of the comma is to prevent misunderstanding. Look at this statement: "Ms. Jones our neighbor is an attorney." Is this a statement to or about Ms. Jones? Make your meaning clear by writing "Ms. Jones, our neighbor is an attorney" or "Ms. Jones, our neighbor, is an attorney."

Try reading these sentences, omitting each comma:

> Outside, the house needs a coat of paint; inside, the walls need replastering.
> The day after, a sales representative called with the same product.
> In 1977, 984 first-year students appeared on our campus.
> Instead of a hundred, thousands came.

1. Separate two main clauses joined by a coordinating conjunction.

A comma between two such clauses will prevent misunderstanding on first reading. Consider these sentences:

> Last week I was sick with a cold and my brother took charge.
> I do not care for the job isn't important.
> We ate waffles and our leader had eggs.

Inserting a comma after *cold, care,* and *waffles* will prevent a reader from thinking that the subject of the second clause in each sentence is an actual part of the first clause.

If the clauses are short, the comma may be omitted before the conjunction. This brings up the question "How short is short?" If each independent clause consists of only subject and predicate, or of three or four words each, then the comma can be omitted.

> The rains came and the rivers rose.
> In the final judging, Mary did not win nor did Jane.

Fairly long clauses are sometimes written without a comma between them if their connection is particularly close or if the subject of both clauses is the same.

> Henry read the assignment over hurriedly and then he began a more careful rereading of it.

2. Separate elements in a series.

This rule applies to words, phrases, and clauses that follow each other and might be misread if not separated.

> You will find Gloria around somewhere: in the living room, in the basement, or out in the garden.

> She whispered, she muttered, but finally she shouted.
> I have brought my textbook, my notebook, and some theme paper with me.
> Stop, look, and listen.

One kind of series is represented by A, B, and C—three or more words, phrases, or clauses, with a conjunction joining the last two members.

Some writers omit the comma before the conjunction and use A, B and C. Since greater clearness is frequently obtained by the use of the comma before the conjunction, present practice favors the comma.

Another kind of series is represented by A, B, C—three or more words, phrases, or clauses, with no conjunctions. Commas are used after each member except *after* the last, unless the clauses are all independent.

> This store sells newspapers, magazines, books on weekdays only.

Do not use commas when a conjunction joins each pair of a series (unless emphasis is desired).

> I have read nothing by Swift or the Brontë sisters or Poe.
> I have thought and pondered and reflected and meditated—and I still don't know what to do.

3. Separate two or more adjectives when they equally modify the same noun.

> I bought an old, dilapidated chair and a new, ugly, badly faded rug.

When the adjectives are not coordinate, commas are omitted.

> The old oaken bucket was covered with wet green moss.

Notice that a comma is never used to separate the last adjective from the noun.

Sometimes there may be doubt about whether the adjectives are coordinate, as in "an old, dilapidated chair" above. Several tests, although not infallible, may help. One way of testing is to insert *and* between the adjectives. If the *and* fits, use a comma when it is omitted, otherwise do not. Another test: If the position of the adjectives can be reversed, the adjectives are coordinate.

6. Percentage

The interest rate is 5%.
10 percent, one-half of 1 percent, 4¼ percent bonds

7. Money

$4.55, $0.50, 50 cents, $6 per bushel, 35¢ apiece

8. Chapters and page numbers

Chapter 6, p. 483, pp. 20-32, p. 1654

EXERCISE 19

Copy the following sentences and correct each error that occurs in the use of numbers and abbreviations.

1. They enjoyed a 3-mo. tour of It. and Fr. but did not get to Ger.
2. The contractor ordered ninety one-inch pieces of weather stripping.
3. The class pres.'s mother, who is a prof at the univ., comes home at 4 P.M.
4. That minister has a D.D. degree but prefers to be known as Rev.
5. 4 members of our team had scored 4 points by Jan. 3rd, 1978.
6. The banker says that the bond will mature on 1/15/85.
7. It is my painful duty to report that a large % of the sophs failed their tests and will be summarily dismissed.
8. Two hundred fifty a mo. is too much for an apartment on E. 14th Street or even on West End Dr.
9. Geo. and Nan were late that day for their psych. class.
10. The official address is 1620 Lane Street, Scranton, Pennsylvania.

EXERCISE 20

Follow the directions for Exercise 19.

1. Mister Jones and Pres. Jones are brothers, and, coincidentally, each makes twelve thousand three hundred dollars a year.
2. N.Y.C. is large; its central boro is Manhattan, which lies s. of the Bx. and e. of the N. Riv.
3. On Ap. twenty-third, 1949, my parents were married at seventeen Lawn Ter., Broadhurst, Kansas.
4. R. C. Groggins, our grocer, once remarked that he had trusted people for 47 yrs and never been cheated out of a $.

5. The ratio of profits to sales varied during the decade from 4 to nine percent.
6. When Ellen was 5 and Mike 3½, we took them to the zoo in S.F. to see the pachyderms.
7. Waterloo is the name of a univ. in the prov. of Ont.
8. That famous speech appears in *Hamlet*, Act III, Scene Two.
9. 873-1046 turned out to be the telephone number of an apt. house in L.A.
10. Rev. Gilhooley told my sisters Lil and Eliz. that the bazaar will be open until 1:30 A.M.

PM15. Spelling

The first and most important step in correct spelling is to have the *desire to learn*, really to want to become a competent speller. The second is to devote the *necessary time* to learning. The third is to use *all available means* to learn.

In addition to desire, time, and means, it should be easy to improve if you habitually do these seven things:

1. Pronounce words correctly.
2. Mentally *see* words as well as hear them.
3. Use a dictionary to fix words in your memory.
4. Use memory devices (mnemonics) to help remember troublesome words.
5. Learn a few spelling rules.
6. Write words carefully in order to avoid errors caused not by ignorance but by carelessness.
7. *List* and *study* the words you most frequently misspell.

PM15a. PRONOUNCE WORDS CORRECTLY.

A definite relationship exists between pronunciation and spelling. The former is not an infallible guide to the latter nor the latter to the former. Nevertheless, mispronouncing words usually makes them harder to spell because, for many words, pronunciation is closely connected with spelling. Cultivate the habit of spelling troublesome words aloud, syllable by syllable, writing them, and then spelling them aloud again in order to relate the sound to the spelling.

PM15b. ACTUALLY SEE WORDS AS WELL AS HEAR THEM.

One method of improving spelling is to look at, or repeat, a word until you really *see* it. Look at the word alone or in its context, pronounce it, study it, write it, see it with your eyes shut, write it again, see whether it is correct, write it again, pronounce it. This method of studying words until you can *see* them is particularly valuable when dealing with tricky words that for no apparent reason may drop letters; add or transpose letters; change one or two letters for others; or contain unpronounced letters: *proceed* but *procedure; repeat* but *repetition; fire* but *fiery; explain* but *explanation; pronounce* but *pronunciation; curious* but *curiosity; maintain* but *maintenance.*

PM
15

PM15c. USE THE DICTIONARY TO HELP IN YOUR SPELLING.

When you are unsure of the spelling of any word, check its spelling immediately in the dictionary. If you cannot find it, look up and down the column, since a silent letter may be causing the trouble; *aghast* will be there, but not *agast*. If the initial letters confuse you, ask someone for suggestions: you will never find *mnemonics* under *n, philosophy* under *f, pneumonia* under *n, psychology* under *s.*

Knowledge of the etymology (origin, derivation) of a word also helps you to spell correctly. For example, if you know that *preparation* is derived from the prefix *prae* plus *parare* (to make ready), you will not spell the word *prepEration*. If you know that *dormir* is the French word for *sleep* (from Latin *dormitorium*), you will not spell *dormitory* with an *a* for the *i*. Sometimes, too, spelling the simpler or root form of the word helps: *finite, definite, infinite,* not *definate, infinate; relate, relative,* not *relitive; contribute, contribution,* not *contrabution; ridicule, ridiculous,* not *rediculous; please, pleasing, pleasant,* not *plesant*. But watch the tricky words that vary from their roots: *fiery, explanation, curiosity, repetition, pronunciation, procedure, maintenance.*

PM15d. USE MEMORY DEVICES TO HELP YOU REMEMBER TROUBLESOME WORDS.

One kind of memory device has the rather imposing name of **mnemonics**. The word is pronounced ne-MON-iks and comes from a Greek word meaning "to remember." A *mnemonic* is a special aid to memory, a memory trick based on what psychologists refer to as association of ideas, remembering something by associating it with something else. Any mnemonic is a sort of crutch, something you use until you can automatically spell a given word without even thinking.

Here are a few examples of mnemonics. They may not help you because they have no personal association, but they will provide ideas for the manufacture of your own.

> *argument*—I lost an *e* in that *argument*.
> *business*—*Business* is no *sin*.
> *corps*—Don't kill a live body of men with an *e* (corpse).
> *dessert*—Strawberry sundae (two *s*'s).
> *potatoes*—*Potatoes* have eyes and *toes*.

PM15e. LEARN A FEW SIMPLE RULES FOR SPELLING.

Numerous rules for spelling cover certain words and classes of words, but remember that the words came *first*, the rules *second*. These rules are generalized statements applicable to a fairly large number of words, but not all. Consequently, every rule has its exceptions.

The rules that follow are easily learned; mastering them will eliminate many recurring errors. Memorizing a simple key word or a common example of each rule can help you both to memorize the rule and to recite it from your example.

1. **Words containing *ei* or *ie***

> Write *i* before *e*
> Except after *c*,
> Or when sounded like *a*
> As in *neighbor* and *weigh*.
> *Either, neither, leisure, seize*
> Are exceptions; watch for these.

This rule or principle applies *only* when the pronunciation of *ei* or *ie* is a long *e* as in *he* or the *a* sound as in *pale*. A memory device for remembering whether the *e* or *i* comes after the *c* or *l* is the key word *Celia* (or *police*, or *lice*). Another memory device: *ie* is the usual spelling when an *r* follows: *cashier, fierce, pier*.

If the sound of *ei* or *ie* is other than long *e* or *a*, the principle does not apply: *conscience, foreign, height, their*.

2. Final *y*

The basic principle of spelling words ending in *y* is this:

a. Words ending in *y* preceded by a consonant usually change *y* to *i* before any suffix except one beginning with *i* (such as –*ing*, –*ish*, –*ist*).

activity, activities	copy, copies, copying
library, libraries	beauty, beautiful
carry, carries, carrying	easv, easier
modify, modified, modifying	lucky, luckily
study, studies, studying	lively, livelihood

b. Words ending in *y* preceded by a vowel do not change *y* to *i* before suffixes or other endings.

day, days	annoy, annoyed, annoying
turkey, turkeys	array, arrayed, arraying
valley, valleys	obey, obeyed, obeying
monkey, monkeys	spray, sprayed, spraying

Important exceptions; *day, daily; lay, laid* (but *allay, allayed*); *pay, paid; say, said; slay, slain*.

3. Doubling final consonant

When ending in a single consonant (except *x*) preceded by a single vowel, one-syllable words and words of more than one syllable that are accented on the last syllable, double the consonant before adding an ending that begins with a vowel.

Common endings beginning with a vowel are the following: –*ed*, –*es*, –*ing*, –*er*, –*est*, –*able*, –*ible*, –*ance*, –*ence*, –*ish*, and –*y*.

admit, admitting	forget, forgettable
refer, referring	wet, wettest

Important exceptions: *transferable, transference, gases, gaseous*.

Note, also, if the accent is shifted to an *earlier* syllable when the ending is added, the final consonant is not doubled: *prefer, preferred,* but *preference; refer, referred,* but *reference.*

4. The one-plus-one rule

When the prefix of a word ends in the same letter with which the main part of the word begins or when the main part of the word ends in the same letter with which the suffix begins, be sure that both letters are included. Otherwise, do not double the letters.

The same rule applies when two main words are combined, the first ending with the same letter with which the second begins.

dissatisfied	overrun	accidentally
dissimilar	unnoticed	coolly
illiterate	underrate	occasionally
bathhouse	bookkeeping	shirttail
irresponsible	misspell	cruelly
brownness	meanness	suddenness

Exception: *eighteen,* not *eightteen; pastime,* not *pasttime.*

Naturally, three identical consonants or vowels are never written solidly together: cliff-face, not cliff*ff*ace; shell-like, not shell*ll*ike; still-life, not stil*ll*ife; cross-stitch, not cros*ss*titch; sight-seer, not sights*ee*er.

5. Final silent *e*

A final silent *e* is an *e* ending a word but not pronounced. Its function is to make the vowel of the syllable long: *rate* (but *rat*); *mete* (but *met*); *bite* (but *bit*); *note* but *not*); *cute* (but *cut*).

a. Most words ending in silent *e* drop the *e* before a suffix beginning with a vowel but keep the *e* before a suffix beginning with a consonant.

argue, arguing	ice, icy	safe, safety
arrive, arrival	live, livable	sincere, sincerely
believe, believing	true, truism	sure, surely
come, coming	bare, bareness	tire, tiresome
guide, guidance	hope, hopeless	use, useful

Exceptions: When final silent *e* is preceded by another vowel—except *e*—the final *e* is not retained before a suffix beginning with a consonant: *argue, argument; due, duly; true, truly; agree, agreement.*

b. Words that end *–ce* or *–ge* retain the *e* when *–able* and *–ous* are added, in order to prevent giving a hard sound to the *c* or *g:*

marriage, marriageable	change, changeable
notice, noticeable	courage, courageous
service, serviceable	outrage, outrageous

c. The few words ending in *ie* (pronounced like long *i*), in which the *e* is also silent, change *ie* to *y* before *–ing*, perhaps to prevent two *i*'s from coming together: *die, dying; lie, lying; vie, vying.*

d. The silent *e* is retained in the *–ing* forms of *dye, singe,* and *tinge (dyeing, singeing, tingeing)* to distinguish these words from *dying, singing,* and *tinging.*

6. *–cede, –ceed, –sede* words

The problem with these words is simple because only thirteen words are involved.

Only one word in English ends in *–sede: supersede.* It has this ending because it comes from the Latin word *sedeo,* meaning "to sit."

Only three words end in *–ceed: exceed, proceed,* and *succeed.*

Of the remaining words ending with a "seed" sound, only a few are in common use. The list of nine words is as follows:

accede	concede	recede
antecede	intercede	retrocede
cede	precede	secede

PM15f. DO NOT CARELESSLY MISSPELL WORDS

Many spelling errors are caused by carelessness, not ignorance. The careful student, realizing these facts, will proofread written work once or twice solely for the purpose of finding misspelled words.

PM

15

The simple, easy words, not the difficult ones, cause most trouble in careless misspelling. The following words, which probably everyone could spell correctly in a test, are nevertheless frequently misspelled in student papers:

> *acquaint, against, all right, amount, appear, arise, around, basis, before, begin, careless, clothes, coming, consider, decide, extremely, field, finish, laid, likely, lonely, mere, noble, paid, passed, past, piece, prefer, prepare, sense, simple, stories, strict, therefore, those, tries, truly, until, whose, woman.*

Do not omit letters, carelessly transpose letters of words, or write two words as one when they should be written separately.

PM15g. KEEP A LIST OF THE WORDS YOU MOST FREQUENTLY MISSPELL.

Learning to spell correctly seems a hopeless task because so many thousands of words must be mastered. But no one is expected to be able to spell all words, on demand, and only a comparatively few words are the most persistent troublemakers. Curiously, words like *Mississippi, Tennessee, literature,* and *extracurricular* are not frequently misspelled, even when frequently used; rather, words like *too, all right, it's, its, there, their* most often are the offenders.

Keep a list of words that you misspell and study the words until you thoroughly learn their spelling.

According to several estimates, a basic list of only 1000 words appears in 90 percent of all writing. Several of these words appear on the following list of frequently misspelled words. Your own list of misspelled words may not contain all of the words listed here; the listing is prepared from general experience with students and should be expanded by you to fit your particular needs.

absence	all right	among	argument
absurd	already	anxiety	arithmetic
accepted	altogether	anxious	arrival
across	always	apartment	assemblies
afraid	amateur	apparatus	audience

awkward
beginning
believe
biscuit
brief
business
buying
cafeteria
captain
certain
cheerful
chief
choose
coming
copies
courtesy
cried
decide
definite
descend
describe
desirable
despair
destroy
develop
difficulties
dining room
disabled
disagree
divide
doesn't
during
easily
eighth
embarrass
enemies
excellent
exercise
existence
experience

familiar
fierce
fiery
foreign
forty
fourth
friend
frivolous
fulfilled
furniture
generally
governor
grammar
guard
hammer
handkerchief
heroes
humorous
hurried
imaginary
immediately
independent
influence
intellectual
invitation
itself
jewelry
judgment
knowledge
laboratory
ladies
laid
library
lightning
loneliness
lying
magazine
marriage
mathematics
meant

messenger
minute
misspelled
mortgage
mountain
muscle
mystery
necessary
neighbor
neither
niece
nineteen
ninety
ninth
oblige
occasionally
occurred
offered
omission
opportunity
paid
parallel
partner
peculiar
perhaps
pilgrim
pleasant
possession
potato
prison
privilege
probably
pronunciation
realize
really
receive
repetition
replied
representative
respectfully

rhyme
riding
running
safety
seize
sense
sentence
separate
shepherd
shining
shoulder
similar
sincerely
speech
strength
stretch
strictly
studying
summarize
superstitious
surely
surprise
thorough
toward
tragedy
tries
truly
twelfth
until
using
usually
village
villain
Wednesday
woman
women
writer
writing
written
yacht

EXERCISE 21

Insert *ei* or *ie* in the following:

1. ach____ve
2. bel____f
3. br____f
4. c____ling
5. conc____t
6. dec____ve
7. for____gn
8. financ____r
9. misch____vous
10. n____ghbor
11. n____ther
12. perc____ve
13. p____ce
14. rec____pt
15. rel____ve
16. rev____w
17. sh____ld
18. shr____k
19. v____l
20. y____ld

EXERCISE 22

Add *–ed* and *–ing* to the following:

1. array
2. copy
3. dally
4. delay
5. deny
6. destroy
7. empty
8. hurry
9. imply
10. marry
11. pity
12. play
13. pray
14. pry
15. rally
16. rely
17. reply
18. stay
19. toy
20. try
21. annoy
22. relay
23. say
24. sway

EXERCISE 23

Add *–ing* and *–ment* to each of the following:

1. abridge
2. acknowledge
3. advise
4. amuse
5. atone
6. argue
7. excite
8. judge
9. move
10. settle

EXERCISE 24

Add *–ed* and either *–able* or *–ible* to the following:

1. avail
2. comprehend
3. depend
4. dismiss
5. excite
6. like
7. presume
8. reverse
9. suggest
10. value

EXERCISE 25

From many verbs, nouns may be formed that end in *–ance, –ence; –ar, –or, –er; –ary, –ery.* Examples: *contribute, contributor.* Form a noun from each of the following words.

1. act
2. adhere
3. beg
4. carry
5. collect
6. confer
7. counsel
8. defer
9. defy
10. distill (distil)
11. lecture
12. lie
13. occur
14. prefer
15. protect
16. provide
17. repent
18. station
19. subsist
20. visit

EXERCISE 26

Supply the missing letter in each of the following.

1. appar____nt
2. cors____ge
3. crim____nal
4. def____nite
5. friv____lous
6. gramm____r
7. ignor____nt
8. instruct____r
9. irresist____ble
10. livel____hood
11. nes____le
12. priv____lege
13. p____rsue
14. r____diculous
15. sacr____fice
16. su____prise
17. tra____edy
18. tres____le
19. vulg____r
20. We____nesday

EXERCISE 27

Some of the following words are correctly spelled, some incorrectly. If a word is spelled correctly, write *C* next to its number. If it is misspelled, spell it correctly.

1. accommodate	8. environment	15. perseverance
2. atheletic	9. height	16. reccommend
3. competition	10. mischieveous	17. safty
4. desireable	11. naturally	18. suppress
5. discipline	12. obstacal	19. vengeance
6. dissappointed	13. occassion	20. villain
7. embarassed	14. outragous	

EXERCISE 28

The following words have variant spellings. For each word, write *P* if the spelling given is the preferred one. If it is not, indicate what the preferred spelling is.

1. analyze	8. esthetic	15. sextet
2. armor	9. fulfil	16. sulphur
3. canyon	10. instalment	17. theatre
4. catalogue	11. judgment	18. tranquillity
5. center	12. medieval	19. traveler
6. defense	13. monologue	20. vigor
7. dialogue	14. savior	

EXERCISE 29

Write the plural of each of the following words.

1. appendix	11. loss
2. attorney	12. mass
3. book	13. piano
4. cargo	14. sky
5. chief	15. strawberry
6. city	16. table
7. crisis	17. tax
8. criterion	18. tomato
9. dynamo	19. turkey
10. hero	20. zero

REVIEW EXERCISE 1

Each item below begins with a correctly punctuated sentence. You are instructed to change it in a specific way. Rewrite the sentence in your head or on a sheet of paper, making only necessary changes in wording or word order. Then answer the question about the rewritten sentence.

1. The bungalow is really a very attractive one; however, the site is not pretty.
   [Change the semicolon to a comma.]
   The rewritten sentence contains the word
   A. however
   B. nevertheless
   C. although
   D. still
   E. since

2. The men of Company K, who were the first to reach the edge of the wood, shouted for the rest to follow them.
   [Take out the commas.]
   In the rewritten sentence, compared to the original sentence, the number of men described as reaching the edge of the wood is
   A. greater
   B. less
   C. the same
   D. uncertain; there is no way to tell

3. As soon as the lake quieted down, we launched the canoes and returned to camp.
   [Begin the sentence with the words *we launched.* . . .]
   The rewritten sentence contains
   A. one comma
   B. one semicolon
   C. a comma and a semicolon
   D. a dash
   E. no punctuation within the sentence

4. "Even the best of those going out for gymnastics aren't very promising," the coach complained.
   [Rewrite the sentence in the form of indirect discourse—without quotation marks.]
   The rewritten sentence contains
   A. one comma
   B. two commas
   C. a colon
   D. a comma and a colon
   E. no punctuation within the sentence.

PM
R

5. There can be only one outcome in this election, for the people will turn the rascals out.

   [Take out the word *for*.]

   In the rewritten sentence, the mark of punctuation after *election* that would best signal the reader to expect the meaning in the second part of the sentence is

   A. a comma
   B. a semicolon
   C. a colon
   D. an exclamation point

6. I wrote to her asking if she couldn't come to visit us the following month.

   [Put what was written in the form of direct discourse—within quotation marks.]

   The end punctuation of the rewritten sentence is

   A. month."
   B. month".
   C. month?"
   D. month"?

7. While the other pupils kept on working, the girls who had finished the examination passed quietly out of the room.

   [Enclose *who had finished the examination* in commas.]

   The rewritten sentence implies that

   A. some of the girls remained in the room
   B. there were some boys taking the examination
   C. it was a short examination
   D. only girls took the examination
   E. none of these things; there is no way to tell

8. The physics course is an example of those courses that can hardly be run without the aid of technical apparatus.

   [Substitute *for example* for *is an example*.]

   The rewritten sentence contains

   A. no internal punctuation
   B. one comma
   C. parentheses
   D. two commas
   E. a dash or dashes

9. "As far as I am concerned," Maya said, "you can go whenever you like."

   [Change *As far as I am concerned* to *It is no concern of mine*.] The rewritten sentence contains the combination

   A. , "you
   B. , "You
   C. ; "you
   D. ; "You

10. This machine deeply breaks up the soil, and it cuts the weed roots at the same time.
    [Take out the word *it*.]
    The rewritten sentence contains
    A. one comma
    B. two commas
    C. a semicolon
    D. a dash
    E. no punctuation within the sentence

11. Arrowheads were often made of volcanic glass in the absence of metal.
    [Begin the sentence with the words *In the absence of metal*, keeping the sentence otherwise unchanged.]
    Is there a comma in the rewritten sentence?
    A. Definitely yes; it is necessary.
    B. Definitely no; it would be misleading.
    C. Possibly yes, in formal or strict punctuation; preferable here.
    D. Possibly no, in informal or open punctuation; preferable here.

12. He said evenly, "You owe me nothing," and that was all.
    [Take out the *and*.]
    The rewritten sentence contains the combination
    A. ,"
    B. ",
    C. ";
    D. ;"
    E. !"

13. I'd appreciate your looking over this manuscript when you have some free time.
    [Add the phrase *that is* to the end of the sentence.]
    The word *manuscript* in the rewritten sentence would be most effectively followed by
    A. a comma
    B. a semicolon
    C. a colon
    D. a dash
    E. nothing (no punctuation)

14. With her usual tendency to overstatement, this author writes, "Our government has *never* invoked the Monroe Doctrine for the purpose originally intended."
    [Insert the phrase *my italics* after *never*.]
    The inserted phrase is best marked by
    A. enclosure in commas
    B. enclosure in parentheses

PM
R

    C. enclosure in brackets
    D. underlining to indicate italic printing
    E. nothing (no punctuation)

15. The prosecutor asked the witness whether she was absolutely sure that she had heard the man cry for help.
[Keeping *help* as the last word in the sentence, put both the speech of the prosecutor and the cry of the man in direct discourse—within quotation marks.]
The end punctuation of the rewritten sentence is
    A. !"?
    B. !?"
    C. '!"?
    D. !"?'
    E. ?'!"

REVIEW EXERCISE 2

Each item begins with a correctly punctuated sentence. Rewrite it as directed, in your head or on a sheet of paper. Then select a capital letter indicating that the shift from the original to the rewritten sentence requires you to:

    A insert or change a mark to a semicolon or semicolons
    B insert or change a mark to a colon or colons
    C insert or change a mark to a dash or dashes
    D take out one of the marks above, or change it to a comma
    E keep the punctuation as in the original

1. A cat when lapping up milk cups its tongue backward, not, as many suppose, forward, in a rapid series of dipping and shoveling motions; this fact is one of the curious revelations of high-speed photography.
[Take out *this fact is*.]
2. You can hardly be a success in politics without being your own convinced disciple, but the reverse proposition is unfortunately not true.
[Change *but* to *however*.]
3. The accident occurred at 12 minutes after three in the afternoon.
[Put the time in numerical and abbreviated form.]
4. The army expects of its rank and file one thing above all, and that is obedience.
[Take out *and that is*.]
5. Because of a rainy spell, construction was halted for a week, so we were free from Monday through Friday.
[Change *so* to *consequently*.]

6. One of the texts required in the course is *Western Art.*
   [Lengthen the title by adding *The Renaissance*]
7. The finalists in the competition for scholarships were Honor Blackman, Bess Sanborn, and Stephen Dobbs.
   [Reverse each name, putting the surname before the given name.]
8. Animals that prey on other animals move upwind when hunting, and for related reasons animals that are preyed on flee downwind when hunted.
   [Take out *and*.]
9. The minister took his text from the third chapter, eleventh verse, of Second Corinthians.
   [Put the citation in numerical notation.]
10. I can tell you in confidence that Mr. Snodgrass has been paying particular attention to me lately, and I really think the poor man is smitten.
    [Give only the first letter of *Snodgrass*, the rest of the name being merely indicated.]

PM

R

REVIEW EXERCISE 3

Add commas, semicolons, colons, dashes, quotation marks, apostrophes, and hyphens as needed in the following passage. Use no additional periods. (This item does require paragraph breaks, but ignore that fact for the purpose of this exercise.)

One of our neighbors Mr. Watchung got into a little trouble with the police the other day. Mr. Watchung used to have a dairy farm near Beauville Wisconsin but a year or so ago he moved west buying a house and lot at 263 Cedar Street Denver Colorado just a few doors down the street from us. Mr. Watchung is a quiet taciturn self reliant man you know the type and his neighbors saw very little of him perhaps we might have saved him some trouble and expense if he had talked to us more. It seems that Watchung got to brooding about his cows thinking how much had gone out of his life when he sold them he finally decided to start a little dairylike project right here in Denver. He had only a moderately large city lot however that didnt stop him. He poked along with the work building a dairy barn very small but complete right in his backyard. Because he is handy with tools he was able to do all the work himself foundation framing plumbing wiring everything consequently he didn't come in contact with the authorities. In fact his design was not surely known until one morning when Ms. Bolliver his next door neighbor looked out her window and saw six sleek Holstein cows marching along the walk between her kitchen and Mr. Watchungs. Well the police arrived eventually and made him get rid of them moreover they made him pay for damage to Ms. Bollivers geraniums. For my part I hated to see that barn go to waste. Look Mr. Watchung I said having met him in front of his house one morning why not turn the barn into a youth center? Listen he replied if I catch any youth cantering around my barn I'll yell and holler and make an awful fuss. Ill enjoy it too he added grinning fiendishly. He must have still been mad with the police and with city ways.

Diction

When you talk or write, you *have* to have something to say and *should* have some interest and purpose in expressing that something. Therefore, you call on your vocabulary, or word supply, and select those expressions that will best communicate to others what you have in mind.

This process of selecting is called **diction:** "the choice of a word or group of words to express ideas." Thus defined, diction applies to both speaking and writing. However, *diction* has further meanings when applied to speech since it involves voice control, voice expression, pronunciation, and enunciation.

Our thinking is done in words. We are constantly using words in thinking and in attempts to express our thinking. In a real sense, our thinking can be no better than our word supply.

Diction also plays a large part in telling others about who and what we are. Therefore, all of us who put pen to paper, who even start to speak, should try to improve our choice and use of words.

D1. Levels of Diction

D1a. APPROPRIATE DICTION

Any rule for the choice and use of words *must* bend to the test of what is appropriate in a given situation. Word selection is not rigidly "good" or "bad," or standard or nonstandard. Usage depends upon considerations of place, time, occasion, and the circumstances of who is speaking (or writing) to whom and about what. No standard of diction is, or ever can be, absolute.

The words we use in talking with a friend or classmate might be inappropriate in conversations with a school official, a teacher, or a parent. The words used in an informal and highly personal letter to a friend may be suitable for that purpose but might be faulted if used in a formal paper prepared for class.

A word or phrase in suitable usage a generation ago may now be outmoded. An expression appropriate in one section of the country may be unclear and therefore ineffective in another. A technical term that is appropriate when used before a specialized group of listeners might be misunderstood by people in general and therefore be unsuitable for use in ordinary conversation.

The best course to follow is to try to choose words and expressions that are normally employed at this time by reputable speakers and writers in all sections of the country. That is, diction is always both appropriate and effective when it is in *present, reputable,* and *national* use.

The best and safest guide concerning words in present, reputable, and national use is a dictionary. A reliable dictionary records; it does not dictate. It labels words and expressions for users. By paying attention to the information provided in your dictionary, you can learn what current practice is and be guided accordingly.

Usage can be divided into *standard* and *nonstandard* varieties. Standard usage can be further divided into *formal standard* and *informal standard* usage.

D1b. STANDARD ENGLISH

The written and spoken language used by educated persons is *standard.* People who write for newspapers, authors of books, preachers, courtroom lawyers, and public lecturers normally employ standard English. Their usage differs, depending upon circumstances, but generally their choice and use of words follow certain conventions that are widely observed.

This language of educated people known as standard can be either *formal* or *informal.* Formal English is that kind considered appropriate for public addresses, sermons, formal reports, book reviews, and many carefully edited books and magazines. Formal English, especially formal written English, includes words that are rarely used in ordinary conversation. It is also likely to contain few contractions, no slang, and few if any words considered colloquial. Formal standard English can be referred to as the language of formal dress: careful, conventional, and precise.

The use of informal standard English is much more widespread than that of formal standard. It is the language most people use most of the time. It is the language used in telephone conversations, personal letters, many newspapers, and the give-and-take of radio and television interviews. Informal standard English employs fewer learned and difficult words than does formal standard. It usually contains contractions and occasionally a slang expression. In short, it compares to formal English as do a T-shirt and jeans to a dress or suit.

Look at these two sentences. Each is in standard English, but the first is formal, the second informal:

> I am not inclined to make a donation to that campaign.
> I'm not willing to give money to that cause.

Informal diction is always informal, but it should be pointed out that the act of speaking is usually more relaxed and free of conventions than is informal writing. However, both informal and formal varieties of standard English should be tested for appropriateness. Either may be out of place in a given set of circumstances. Further, informal English is often more effective than formal simply because our ears and minds are more accustomed to it.

D1c. NONSTANDARD ENGLISH

Standard and nonstandard English are not different languages, but they do differ widely in their use of pronouns and verbs. A user of standard English would say or write "they were," but a nonstandard user would say "they was." A nonstandard speaker would say "they hurt theirselves," but a standard user would say or write "they hurt themselves." Nonstandard English is filled with ungrammatical expressions, excessive and clumsy use of slang, and strictly local dialect. Expressions such as these are characteristic of nonstandard English:

dassent (for *don't*)	talks bad (for *talks badly*)
I is (for *I am*)	didn't ought (for *shouldn't have*)
us are (for *we are*)	can't never (for *can't ever*)

D
1

them there (for *those*)   Sue she says (for *Sue says*)
they does (for *they do*)   we drunk (for *we drank*)

How would a nonstandard user of the language have expressed the statement given above: "I'm not willing to give money to that cause"? Possibly like this: "I ain't gonna give nothin' to that racket."

In your own speaking and writing, try to use only standard English, no matter how informally. And if in doubt, use the information in this text as a guide to standard usage.

EXERCISE 1

Assume that the standard of word choice is that of careful but not affectedly formal American speech and writing. By such a standard, each of the following sentences contains one or more questionable expressions. On your paper, number each sentence; next to the number write the faulty expression and substitute a word or phrase that would be acceptable.

1. I can't hardly understand why Mr. White never graduated high school.
2. I stayed home from school that morning but attended baseball practice latter in the day.
3. Lug in a chair for Lady Percy, Ronald.
4. The manager's attention was arrested by Paula's ability to fix up any problem that might arise.
5. Why do you reckon she went that way?
6. But I shall not come except we all can come.
7. Martin was acting in his officious capacity as justice of the peace.
8. Consuela is the sort of woman with whom one likes to converse with.
9. I see no favorable factors in your case, so I shall have to answer in the negative.
10. The coroner is now examining the corps.

EXERCISE 2

Follow the directions for Exercise 1.

1. We're liable to meet the football captain at Jerry's party on Saturday.

2. The little boats averaged in length a length of 11 feet.
3. Leave go of her this instant.
4. What do you think you are, a television censure?
5. Adele is terribly perceptive, isn't she?
6. Unfortunately, Mother did not put meat enow in the stew.
7. Riding in his car alone by himself, he repeated her name over again and again.
8. He was caught in the immutable web of fate and never reached the goal of his aims.
9. We didn't know it, but this was an exceptionally unique opportunity.
10. Your investigative paper is not exceptable, Anna.

EXERCISE 3

Follow the directions for Exercise 1.

1. The poor loser always gets it in the neck.
2. Although he ordinarily liked the delectable crustacean, he lifted one of the toothsome morsels in a timorous fashion and devoured it with a rueful grimace.
3. I liked her manner but not the way of speaking.
4. We must push on, Scott, irregardless of the danger.
5. We worked late into the night because we were truly impelled to solve the problem.
6. She took on when she discovered that her diary was missing.
7. It was sure a delicious supper, was it not?
8. I really resent your illusion, Sybil.
9. All hands on deck! In this holocaust of misfortune you must not leave a stone unturned.
10. Let us initiate movement toward the portal.

D2. Vocabulary Growth

Each of us has three vocabularies. First, we have an active *speaking* vocabulary, a working supply of words that we use daily in our speech. Second, we have a *writing* vocabulary, some of whose words we do not usually use in our speech. In addition to these two active vocabularies, each of us has a *potential*, or *recognition*, vocabulary, which is the largest of the three. This potential vocabulary consists of the many words we recognize and partly understand, possibly from the context, but which we would not be able to use in our own speaking and writing. However, until we use such words—start them working for *us*—they are not really ours.

Consistent effort is needed to move words from your potential to your active vocabulary. It is, however, the best way to begin vocabulary improvement, for the good reason that these words are already somewhat familiar to you.

You should constantly try to expand your vocabulary, not only because doing so will enhance your reading, writing, and speaking, but because a good vocabulary will be increasingly important in your life. As Johnson O'Connor, a scientific investigator, has stated:

> An extensive knowledge of the exact meanings of English words accompanies outstanding success in this country more often than any other single characteristic which the Human Engineering Laboratory has been able to isolate and measure.

D2a. MAKE FRIENDS WITH YOUR DICTIONARY.

The most important element in vocabulary growth is the *will* to learn new words. But wide reading and intelligent listening should lead straight to a good dictionary.

If in reading you dislike breaking the chain of thought by looking up words in a dictionary (although the very necessity for using a dictionary has already broken that chain!), jot down unfamiliar words and look them up as soon as possible. Keeping a notebook nearby is a good idea. And be sure, after you have thoroughly studied a new word, to use it in speaking and writing until it is yours.

D2b. STUDY SYNONYMS AND ANTONYMS.

Collecting lists of synonyms and distinguishing their meanings is an effective way to enlarge your vocabulary. Many dictionaries include listings and explanations of hundreds of synonyms. When looking up a word, carefully study the synonym entries. If you do this, you may be able to choose a more exact and effective word and at the same time enlarge your active vocabulary.

For example, after becoming aware of synonyms, will you necessarily have to write that the baby is *cute*, the game *thrilling*, the idea *interesting,* the dress *glamorous* or *chic,* the play *exciting?* A study of synonyms for *old* might add to your vocabulary these, among other words: *immemorial, aged, ancient, aboriginal, decrepit, antique, hoary, elderly, patriarchal, venerable, passé, antiquated, antediluvian.*

Similarly, studying antonyms will also contribute to vocabulary growth. For example, seeking antonyms for *praise* may add to your vocabulary such words as *vilify, stigmatize, lampoon, abuse, censure, blame, deprecate, condemn, impugn, denigrate, disparage,* and *inveigh against.* Even such a simple word as *join* has numerous approximate opposites, among them *uncouple, separate, sunder, unyoke, cleave, disconnect,* and *dissever.*

D2c. STUDY PREFIXES AND SUFFIXES.

Another method of adding to your vocabulary is to make a study of prefixes and suffixes. A **prefix** is an element placed *before* a word or root to make another word; a **suffix** is placed *after* a word or root. You can add to your vocabulary by learning the meanings of several prefixes and suffixes. Here is a brief list of the most common:

D 2

Prefixes

ante–	before	antedate, anteroom
anti–	against	antisocial, antiwar
hyper–	beyond the ordinary	hypercritical, hyperactive
il–, in–, im–, ir–	not	illogical, indefinite, impossible, irresponsible
poly–	many	polygon, polysyllable
post–	after	postseason, postwar

Suffixes

–ful	characterized by, or as much as will fill	beautiful, spoonful
–hood	state, condition, character	childhood, falsehood
–less	without	faultless, hopeless
–ly	like	saintly, bravely
–meter	measure	speedometer, thermometer
–polis	city, or resident of	metropolis, cosmopolitan
–ship	condition, character, skill	friendship, statesmanship
–some	tendency	loathsome, meddlesome

D2d. STUDY COMBINING FORMS.

A **combining form** is a term for a word element that rarely appears independently but does form part of a longer word. *Graph*, for example, although a word itself, appears most frequently as a combining form in words such as *photograph* and *lithography*. Knowing the meanings of such forms as the following will help in increasing your vocabulary:

anima	life, breath	animal, animation
aqua	water	aquarium, aqualung
bios	life	biopsy, biosphere
culpa	fault	culprit, culpable
domus	house	domicile, domestic
ego	I	egoism, egocentric
facilis	easy	facile, facilitate
gramma	letter	grammar, grammatical
lex	law	lawyer, legal
liber	book	library, libretto
locus	place	locality, local
navis	ship	navigate, navy
opus	work	opera, operation
populus	people	population, populate
sanctus	holy	sanctuary, sanctify
sophia	wisdom	sophomore, sophisticated
tacitus	silence	tacit, taciturn
thermo	heat	thermometer, thermal
umbra	shade	umbrella, umbrage
vita	life	vital, vitamin

EXERCISE 4

On your paper write the words in the following list. Then write opposite each word the letter of the group of words in the second column that defines it. Use your dictionary early and often.

1. reciprocity
2. amphibious
3. arbitration
4. allocate

a. to set apart for a special purpose
b. to make payment for expense or loss
c. skillful management to get the better of an opponent
d. decrease in value through use

5. amortization e. property or cash possessed by a company
6. reimburse f. mutual exchange
7. strategy g. having to do with farm matters
8. agrarian h. capable of working on both land and water
9. reparations i. an addition to a will
10. depreciation j. security pledged for payment of a loan
11. codicil k. make easier
12. collateral l. become worse
13. facilitate m. compensation by a defeated nation for damage after a war
14. dilemma n self-governing, independent
15. autonomous o. amount subtracted from a bill for prompt payment or other special reason
16. assets p. gradual payment of a debt before the due date
17. curtail q. to reduce, diminish
18. deteriorate r. a difficult or embarrassing situation
19. discount s. contact between persons or groups working together
20. liaison t. settling a dispute by discussing and coming to an agreement

D
2

EXERCISE 5

Follow the directions for Exercise 4.

1. ambidextrous a. a hater of humanity
2. assiduous b. haughtily disdainful
3. cacophony c. cowardly
4. elucidate d. disgrace or reproach incurred by conduct considered shameful
5. grandiose e. formal expression of praise
6. innocuous f. logically unsound
7. invective g. able to use both hands equally well
8. misanthrope h. constant in application
9. ostentatious i. false argument
10. supercilious j. not harmful
11. vicarious k. affectedly grand
12. encomium l. make clear
13. concatenation m. experienced in place of another
14. abscond n. having one's identity concealed
15. fallacious o. harsh sound

16. nebulous
17. pusillanimous
18. sophistry

19. incognito
20. opprobrium

p. to run away to avoid legal process
q. vague, hazy, cloudy
r. an utterance of violent reproach or accusation
s. state of being linked together
t. characterized by show

EXERCISE 6

List the synonyms given in your dictionary (or in a thesaurus) for each of the following words. Prepare for class a written or oral presentation (as your teacher assigns) of the likenesses and differences among the synonyms given for *two* of the words.

1. street
2. opposite
3. frank
4. answer
5. trite

6. defame
7. yield
8. magic
9. tolerant
10. effort

EXERCISE 7

Give one or more antonyms for each of the following. Use your dictionary if you think it will help.

1. professional
2. solicitous
3. huge
4. repudiate
5. dark

6. decrease
7. grave
8. sophisticated
9. fine
10. arrogant

EXERCISE 8

Give the meaning of each of the following prefixes and list five words containing each.

1. mono–
2. non–
3. pseudo–
4. semi–
5. over–

6. micro–
7. auto–
8. sub–
9. bi–
10. multi–

EXERCISE 9

Give the meaning of each of the following suffixes and list five words containing each.

1. –est
2. –able
3. –ment
4. –graph
5. –ish

6. –let
7. –ness
8. –like
9. –er
10. –ine

EXERCISE 10

Give the meaning of each of these combining forms. Use a word involving this form in a sentence.

1. *aristos*
2. *beatus*
3. *causa*
4. *decem*

5. *hostis*
6. *mater*
7. *pedi*
8. *petra*

D
3

D3. Words as Symbols

Words are actually symbols that single out or point to something else. Certain words (such as conjunctions and prepositions) are symbolic only in a limited way. Also, the things that words symbolize vary widely. Words may stand for concrete objects such as *house* or *horse*, for imagined objects such as *elves* and *pixies*, or for nonphysical things such as *honor* or *horror* or *pity*. They may also stand for varied other actions, qualities, and abstractions. Frequently, a word suggests many different things at once. What, for instance, is it that the word *America* corresponds to—an area of earth, a people, a culture, a form of government?

D3a. DISTINGUISH BETWEEN THE DENOTATIONS AND CONNOTATIONS OF A WORD.

Words have an exact meaning (**denotation**) and a suggested or implied meaning (**connotation**).

Denotation

The exact, literal meaning of a word is referred to as its *denotation*. A denotation is a dictionary definition of a word, the meaning recognized by all speakers of a language. It is thus different from an associated meaning, or connotation, that the word might have for an individual (or group) because of personal experience. The denotation of *wind* is "air in natural motion," although the word may have individualized meanings for persons recalling their own experiences with wind. "A certain breed of dog" is the denotation of *Labrador retriever*, a term generally agreed upon and understood by all users of the English language.

In writing exposition and argument, you should try to use words as exact, as specific, and as literal in meaning as possible. Clearness should be the basic guiding principle. In all forms of writing, however, even in exposition and argument, it is impossible always to avoid words that express more than their literal meanings. But we should make the attempt to avoid associated meanings for words unless, of course, we are deliberately trying to appeal to the emotions of readers.

Assume that you see a small four-footed animal on the street and refer to it as a *dog*. If your purpose in using the word is to refer to the animal in reasonably exact terminology, you have succeeded in applying a denotative term that is plain, straightforward, and objective. But suppose that one grandparent of the dog was a fox terrier, another was a bulldog, the third was an Irish terrier, and the fourth was a collie. You can denotatively express these facts by referring to the animal you see as a *dog of mixed breed*. Here you have continued to use objective phrasing. But if your purpose is to speak exactly and clearly, it would be unwise to call the dog a *mongrel*. True, this last term means the same as a *dog of mixed breed*, but it is likely to arouse mingled feelings of approval or disapproval toward that dog. In short, when appropriate to do so, use words that do not suggest associated meanings and that do not suggest or imply emotional meanings.

Can you think of other words besides *mongrel* that have either favorable or unfavorable associated meanings?

Connotation

Nearly all words mean more than they seem to mean. They have associated meanings, a surrounding fringe of suggestive, or connotative, values. As discussed above, the bare, literal meaning of a word is its *denotation*. The *connotation* of a word, on the other hand, is the suggestions and associations that attach to it. For example, a dictionary definition of the word *gold* is "a precious yellow metal, highly malleable and ductile, and free from liability to rust." But with gold have long been associated riches, power, happiness, evil, unhappiness. Around the core of meaning that the dictionary definition gives are associations, suggestions, implications. These connotations are not always present, but one should be aware of this suggestive power in words.

A writer's obligation is to convey sensible comments clearly. But good writers search for words that suggest more than they say, that stimulate the reader's imagination. These words, having connotative values, suggest associated meanings: *baby sister*, not *girl; enigma*, not *problem; home*, not *house; mother*, not *woman*. By exact, or *denotative*, definition, a horse is "a large, solid-hoofed, herbivorous mammal," but to anyone who has ever owned, loved, and cared for a horse, the word suggests many associated meanings. New Orleans is "an industrial and trade center," but its name suggests such images as Crescent City, Old French Quarter, Mardi Gras, Sugar Bowl, Superdome, and Dixieland jazz.

D
3

Use your imagination in writing, but try not to let it get out of hand. A profusion of connotative words in one short theme will render it less, not more, effective.

D3b. THINK OF MOST WORDS AS SYMBOLS.

A significant phase of word study is called *semantics*. Specifically, **semantics** refers to that branch of linguistics that deals with word meanings and historical changes in meaning. Semantics also involves a study of the relations among signs (words, symbols), their meanings, and the mental or physical actions called forth by them.

A word has three relationships: (1) with other words with which it is used, (2) with the thing it represents, the *referent*, and (3) with the persons who speak, write, and hear it.

The relationship of words with each other is a matter of *grammar*. The relationship of words to the things they represent, their referents, is the basic concern of semantics. The relationships between words and people is the primary concern of *general semantics.*

Semantics

Strictly speaking, words exist in people's minds, and since all minds are dissimilar, no word can have a meaning that it precisely and inevitably calls up in everyone. But it is true that people do commonly agree on the association of certain words with certain thoughts. If a given word did not generally symbolize a given idea, we could hardly communicate with each other.

You can use the word *peach* as a symbol to express your thought about a particular fruit, "a subacid, juicy, drupaceous" food; the fruit is the *referent* of peach. By general agreement, those who use English employ this symbol when they think of a specific kind of fruit. And yet the symbol would not work if the writer or speaker were thinking of the peach tree itself, or of a certain color, or of something made or cooked with peaches or with a flavor like that of a peach. And the symbol would be far afield if the writer used it to express an opinion of someone especially admired.

Remember that the meanings of many words have two overlapping aspects. A word has its *denotation,* a certain set of things that it stands for and about which most people generally agree. It also has its *connotation,* a set of feelings and associations that it arouses in the people who use it.

Words are symbols whose arbitrary relationships to the things they represent must always be kept in mind. Again, this relationship is the concern of semantics.

General Semantics

So far as we now know, humans are the only animals capable of inventing symbol systems, such as mathematics and the English language, with which to record the past, evaluate the present, and plan the future. The systematic study of the role of human symbols in the lives of individuals and groups is called **general semantics.** This branch of semantics is concerned with meanings in more than just their dictionary sense. It involves several kinds of verbal and nonverbal meanings and the importance of those meanings in our private lives and public affairs.

General semanticists recognize that, like words, sentences and paragraphs, chapters, essays, songs, plays, poems, and books have meaning.You cannot find the meaning of a sentence, a paragraph, or a poem by looking up each of its words in a dictionary. Nor will you, as Wendell Johnson once remarked, find the meaning of a particular sunset in a dictionary.You will find its meaning only in yourself, in your thoughts and feelings. The meanings of words are no more in the words than the meaning of a maple tree is in a maple tree. The meanings of words, claim general semanticists, are in the person who uses them or responds to them, just as the meanings of "a green meadow are the children who chase butterflies across it, the artist who paints it, the cows which graze upon it, or the old soldier who remembers the battle that once was fought across its green slope" (Johnson).

To the general semanticist, a study of words is not merely the study of words or paintings or musical scores. Rather, the study of words includes a study of people and what words and paintings and musical scores mean to them. To discover what such things mean to people is to observe what people do to, with, and about them. General semantics deals with symbolic behavior, its patterns, its principles, its effects on us and our world, and the conditions of its changes from time to time in the lives of people and societies.

In summary, general semantics is concerned not only with word meanings but also with human beings and what words mean to them at different times and under different circumstances.

EXERCISE 11

Distinguish carefully the words in the following groups of synonyms or related words:

1. car, automobile, jalopy, limousine
2. dishonor, disgrace, ignominy, shame
3. wealthy, affluent, rich, opulent
4. school, academy, institute, college, university
5. fat, portly, stout, obese, corpulent

EXERCISE 12

For each of the following (next page), provide a word or phrase with about the same denotation but a different connotation. Example: *scholar* for *pedant*.

1. sophistication
2. amorous
3. hick
4. eccentric
5. egghead
6. cynic
7. politician
8. mossback
9. beatnik
10. fun-loving

EXERCISE 13

For the italicized words in the following phrases substitute words or phrases that convey stronger attitudes of *approval*.

1. so-and-so's *boorishness*
2. *swilling* her coffee
3. a *garrulous* companion
4. *shrewd* in her dealings
5. a government *spy*
6. to speak *arrogantly*
7. so-and-so's *stupidity*
8. rather *pleasant*
9. the children who were *flogged*
10. a *silly* baby

EXERCISE 14

For the italicized words in the following phrases, substitute words or phrases that convey stronger attitudes of *disapproval*.

1. the *odor* of onions
2. a *convivial* weekend
3. a *famous* gate-crasher
4. to be *excluded*
5. *careful* with his money
6. a *corpulent* man
7. a *precise* speaker
8. a *strict* parent
9. *liberal* with his money
10. a *tolerant* attitude

EXERCISE 15

Discuss the connotation and, where possible, the denotation of each of the following:

1. reactionary
2. extremist
3. bureaucrat
4. bleeding heart
5. brainwashing
6. vested interests
7. thought control
8. do-gooder
9. senior citizen
10. welfarism

EXERCISE 16

Write a paragraph of fifty to seventy-five words using as many of the terms in the preceding exercise as you sensibly can.

EXERCISE 17

Comment on the use (meaning) of words in the following sentences. Point out any shifts in meaning or emotionally toned words that you find.

1. No race is inferior; in fact, some are superior.
2. "A pickpocket is obviously a champion of private enterprise." (G. K. Chesterton)
3. Of course, I am not a liar; I'm only a prevaricator.
4. America must be a welfare state because the Constitution requires the government to promote the general welfare.
5. "The movie is the diversion of slaves, the pastime of illiterate wretches harried by wants and worries, the astutely seasoned pabulum of a multitude condemned by the forces of Moloch to this vile degradation." (Georges Duhamel)

D4. Conciseness

To be effective, diction must be economical. It is difficult, even impossible, to write forcefully when using three or four words where one would be sufficient.

D4a. AVOID USING MORE WORDS THAN NECESSARY TO EXPRESS AN IDEA.

The moral of few words for many is in the following: To the simple question of whether rules should be observed, an administrator wrote, "The implementation of sanctions will inevitably eventuate in subsequent repercussions." What might have been said, simply, was "Yes."

Examples of some wordy expressions and their concise counterparts are:

I would appreciate it if	please
in the month of June	in June
it has come to our attention that	(begin with the word following *that*)
it is interesting to note that	(begin with the word following *that*)
in the event that	if
at the present time	now
on condition that	if
in regard to	about
inasmuch as	since
are of the opinion	believe
in accordance with	by

When meaning is expressed or implied in a particular word or phrase, repeating the idea by additional words is useless. One word of two or three expresses the idea, and the other words add nothing. Common examples are using *again* with many verbs beginning with *re–*; using *more* or *most* with absolute-meaning adjectives; and using *more* or *most* with adjectives and adverbs already ending in *–er, –est.* The following list provides examples of such repetitious expressions.

repeat again	recur again
more better	necessary need
long length	first beginnings
endorse on the back	each and every one
completely unanimous	cooperate together
rise up	fellow classmates
most perpendicular	more perfect
more paramount	resume again
loquacious talker	meet up with
audible to the ear	consensus of opinion
more older	many in number
most unkindest	visible to the eye
descend down	final end
individual person	revert back
join together	reduce down
complete monopoly	cover over
this afternoon at 3 P.M.	back up
most unique	talented genius

D4b. AVOID NEEDLESS REPETITION OF A WORD OR PHRASE.

The following sentences illustrate repetition that is faulty because of a lack of ideas or carelessness or both:

> My coming to college was made possible by some money which was made possible by a job I had last summer.
> His solution involved public support of a mass transit system to move large masses of people.
> Crop rotation, used on many farms, is the use of a plan by which various fields vary in their crops each successive year.
> Organized charitable organizations carry on charitable work in my community.

D4c. AVOID REPETITION OF TOPIC SENTENCES.

The flaw of meaningless, useless repetition of a topic sentence within a paragraph is so common that it deserves mention. Aimless repetition of an idea in the same or different words, phrases, or sentences is called **tautology.** Note the inadequacy of this repetitious (tautological) paragraph:

> Some people pay too much attention to their diet. They spend hours every day wondering if they should eat this or that. They are too concerned about their digestive processes. One would think their greatest concern was low-calorie food, and their talk shows that it is. Diet is not nearly so important as these people think it is; it's the amount they eat. Paying so much attention to diet does not warrant so much concern. They just pay too much attention to it.

D4d. AVOID OVERUSE OF *THERE IS, THERE ARE, THERE WAS,* ETC.

Usually such "there" beginnings are superfluous words. Occasionally they may be effective, as in "there are four genders in English," and you will find them used by many writers. But each time you see such a beginning, determine whether the writer could have been more concise.

Wordy: *There were* ten lead soldiers broken in half.
Concise: Ten lead soldiers were broken in half.
Wordy: In the bakery *there are* many cakes awaiting your selection.
Concise: In the bakery, many cakes await your selection.
Wordy: In our apartment building *there* live ten families.
Concise: Ten families live in our apartment building.

EXERCISE 18

Apply principles of conciseness to the following sentences:

1. There were only about one-third of our platoon who made it back.
2. There should be greater emphasis placed on our tutoring program.
3. Saturdays are the only days I am able to have the car.
4. When I ask for a raise in my allowance, my parents' answer is usually in the negative.
5. In the event that I make the honor roll, I plan to have a party.
6. Some people are resentful with regard to the way the dues have been raised.
7. The story was basically dreary, and it was plain to see that the author had tried to enliven it.
8. I had hoped to become a good student in the field of mathematics.
9. It was at midnight that I awoke to a most astounding sight.
10. It was after the 1975 drought that my father dug himself another well.

EXERCISE 19

Follow the instructions for Exercise 18.

1. In case I am offered the opportunity, I may fly to Chicago.
2. We heard that stores would remain open a longer length of time during the Christmas season.
3. I have always shied away from the field of mechanical engineering.
4. About 20 miles north of Sommerville is a camp called Whistlewood; this is my summer camp.

5. It has been called to my attention by the secretary that a board of directors meeting has been scheduled for June 8.
6. I do not feel the necessity for a conference at the present time.
7. Upon arriving at the Bar-X Ranch, we were assigned horses for the pack trip into the hills.
8. There is still a great deal to be explained in the area of flying saucers.
9. I would like to take this opportunity to introduce myself.
10. I endorsed on the back a check for $10 that my aunt had sent me for expenses.

EXERCISE 20

Rewrite the following sentences, correcting faulty repetition.

1. The ducks were flying well, and they were decoying to my decoys.
2. I had never eaten turnips until the summer of 1976. During the summer of 1976, I paid a short visit to an aunt and uncle of mine, and they gave me turnips to eat.
3. The most important decision is deciding what should be one's aim in life.
4. All students in college are required to take placement tests. These placement tests are for the purpose of determining what classes, regular or advanced, the students should be placed in.
5. My final statement relates to a relationship that I have with a relative.
6. After buying our tickets, we came to another waiting line. This line was formed inside the auditorium to await the start of the next show.
7. I got my homework done and got the car out and got off to school.
8. To give you some idea of where I live, I will use the use of Interstate Highway 96.
9. I did not enjoy jet flights as much as I enjoyed them in past years, and I enjoyed watching my sister on her first jet flight.
10. I made a B on yesterday's exam. That was my French exam, and that gives me a B average for the year.

D5. Exact Diction

The exact use of words depends upon *clear thinking*. If an idea is vague, we are likely to express it vaguely, using the first words that come to mind. But if we know *exactly* what we have in mind, we will search for the words that will most clearly express it to others.

For example, let us consider one of the most overworked words in the language, *nice*. We speak of a nice trip, a nice person, a nice day, and so on. The word *nice* carries a somewhat general meaning and cannot be called incorrect, but does it express exactly what we want to convey? Perhaps a trip would be more accurately described as *interesting, comfortable, successful, exciting, eventful, pleasant, exhilarating, inspiring, rewarding,* or *well-organized.* These words are not all synonyms for *nice,* but perhaps one of them might more exactly describe our impression than the now somewhat dull and ineffective *nice.* If we will think carefully, draw on the resources of our vocabularies, and use a dictionary or a thesaurus, we will have no great difficulty in finding the right word for the thought.

To select the exact word for the context, you must become aware of shades of meaning. When you wish to describe that characteristic of molasses that, particularly in winter, hampers its swift flow from the jug, will you use *thick, viscous, dense, sticky, adhesive,* or *gluey?* Choose always the word that shows most exactly the meaning you intend. Which is most appropriate and exact for your context: *quarrel, altercation, fight, wrangle,* or *brawl?*

D5a. PREFER CONCRETE TO ABSTRACT WORDS

An *abstract* word gives no clear picture; it is often a general word. A *concrete* word expresses something tangible, something usually discernible by at least one of the senses: *roses, tap dance, serrated, clove-scented, aquamarine, soft.* Examples of concrete words are *onomatopoetic* words, words that express or suggest sounds: *crackle, hoot, rustling, murmuring, meow, hiss, singsong, roar, staccato.*

Concrete nouns, colorful and vigorous adjectives and adverbs, verbs that describe action (motion) or relate to the senses (emotion), concrete phrases—all these make our writing forceful and vivid.

D5b. PREFER SPECIFIC TO GENERAL WORDS

Exact and emphatic diction uses expressive nouns, adjectives, verbs, and adverbs. A *general* word names a broad concept: class names of nouns (*flower, food, car*); conventional verbs (*say, come, put*); and vague adjectives and adverbs (*nice, slow, bad, gladly*). Especially dull diction results from overuse of the forms of *to be* (*is, am, are, was, were,* etc.).

A *specific* word names a narrow concept—*lilac, spaghetti, jeep, shout, swoop, cram, captivating, inching, excruciating, jubilantly.* Each of these could be narrowed still further.

The following ineffective words and phrases can surely be replaced with more specific words: *item, element, case, phase, asset, condition, situation, instance, feature, factor, cute, nature, interesting, quality, nice, persuasion, degree, lot, personality, state, job, thing, along the line of, in respect to, with regard to, according as to whether, in the case of, sort of, on this account.*

Vague and indefinite:	a nice person
	the time factor
	thing used for any idea or object, as in "another thing about it"
Specific:	a cordial person
	timing
	another characteristic

D5c. AIM FOR SIMPLICITY IN DICTION

By *simplicity* is certainly not meant writing down to your readers, thus risking insult to their intelligence. Rather, the word means expressing an idea in terms that are clear and specifically geared to the level (age, education, etc.) of the persons for whom you are writing.

If we can choose between a polysyllabic and a short word, we should use whichever is clearer and more precise—usually, but not always, the short word. Short words are often sharper and more vivid than polysyllables and, being crisp and to the point, leave as little doubt as possible in the minds of those who are reading or hearing us. But whether we choose long or short words, diction should be as simple and clear as we can make it so that our ideas will flow smoothly.

D5d. AVOID EXCESSIVE EXAGGERATION.

To *exaggerate* is to misrepresent by overstatement: "I thought I'd die of embarrassment"; "That outfit is ten years older than Noah"; "That is a horrible [or ghastly or frightful] tie you are wearing."

Occasionally, exaggeration can be used to good effect, but it is *never* exact and is not intended to be taken literally. It is more often misleading and ludicrous than it is appropriate and picturesque. Be cautious when using such words as *gigantic, tremendous, wonderful, phenomenal, staggering, thrilling, terrible, gorgeous, horrible, marvelous,* and *overwhelming.* Avoid writing noted for its overuse of intensifiers, its exaggeration, and its gushiness.

D5e. USE TECHNICAL WORDS APPROPRIATELY.

It is especially important to be careful and exact when you use *technical* words. These are words that have special meanings for people in particular fields. To such words approximately fifty "special subject labels" are attached by dictionary makers: astronomy, engineering, entomology, psychology, and the like.

Examples of technical words are *cuprous* (chemistry), *sidereal* (astronomy), *broadside* (nautical), *lepidopterous* (zoology), *coniferous* (botany), *stratus* (meteorology). Some have crept into popular use: *telescope* (astronomy), *virtuoso* (music and art), *stereo* (sound reproduction), *computer* (electronics).

A specialist writing for specialists uses many technical words. If the writing is meant for others in the same general field, fewer technical terms or less difficult ones will be used, and the more specialized terms will be defined. If the specialist is writing for the nonspecialist and the general reader, no technical terms at all will be used or at least those used will be defined.

EXERCISE 21

Rewrite each of the following sentences, substituting more exact and precise words for any you consider weak. You may rephrase the sentences if you wish, but do not alter the sense.

1. Information letters can notify the same event to many people.
2. I try to put off eating that horrible old cereal until the last minute.
3. The easiest thing in school is home economics.
4. By exercising, I reckoned I could pull my weight down.
5. It was a little funny to Jim not to play in the games.
6. The study of the theories that are attributed to the many flying saucer sightings is very interesting.
7. During my first term I gained the girls' hockey club and the Graphic Arts Society.
8. Cousins are a wonderful thing, and I am grateful for having such thoughtful cousins.
9. The problem of finding and keeping kitchen help is another obstacle that must be accounted for by the summer camp.
10. One of the greatest things a parent can teach is respect for elderly people.

EXERCISE 22

Follow the directions for Exercise 21.

1. The most important happening to our school was its founding in 1960 by Octavius C. Silversmith.
2. I shall always remember my father informing me to work a little harder.
3. Our new gym is one of the prettiest in the city.
4. At commencement everyone is obsessed with a wonderful feeling.
5. It's perfectly splendid that you are trying so hard for the job.
6. There have been many boats at the marina that have used sails from Essex.
7. I have trouble with the proper sequence of subjects in my paragraphs.
8. My friend told me about her first office job and warned me about doing the same.

9. The library provides a numerous amount of information to help students in their homework assignments.
10. Playing that role was my biggest thrill yet, but an even bigger one was coming.

EXERCISE 23

With the aid of your dictionary, substitute words or phrases that seem more exact and emphatic (concrete and specific) for the italicized parts of the following phrases. Example: *Walking* from the room—stalking, trudging, slinking, ambling.

1. a *pleasant* party
2. a shabby *structure*
3. a *short* man
4. a *blunt* instrument
5. a *bright* girl
6. he *laughed* strangely
7. a *bad* girl
8. a *grand* day
9. a *terrible* assignment
10. an *anxious* moment

EXERCISE 24

Follow the instructions for Exercise 23.

1. a good *picture*
2. he *went* home
3. a blunt *instrument*
4. a *sad* face
5. a *fine* thing
6. in the *automobile*
7. to *go* away
8. a fine *situation*
9. a *funny* lecture
10. a *poor* cake

EXERCISE 25

Make a list of ten technical words or expressions that you know for some reason but that you think may mystify some of your classmates and the general public. Provide definitions for each term listed.

EXERCISE 26

With what sports or games are the following associated? (If you do not know from direct experience, consult your dictionary. Consult it anyhow.)

1. strike	10. spare	19. double fault
2. jibe	11. grand slam	20. frame
3. rabbit punch	12. ringer	21. bull's-eye
4. fall	13. set point	22. break
5. K.O.	14. javelin	23. mousetrap
6. birdie	15. ace	24. deuce
7. love	16. chucker	25. goalie
8. baby split	17. double dribble	26. bank shot
9. half nelson	18. lateral pass	27. foul

EXERCISE 27

In literary criticism, what specialized meanings do these terms have?

1. essay	7. climax	13. character
2. meter	8. novel	14. antihero
3. verse	9. tragic hero	15. archetype
4. setting	10. plot	16. protagonist
5. theme	11. style	17. point of view
6. accent	12. fatal flaw	18. stream of consciousness

**D
6**

D6. Affected Diction

Affectation is artificial behavior or manners designed to impress others. In language, it is evident in pronunciation and in the use of words not customary or appropriate for the writer or speaker employing them.

D6a. AVOID "FINE WRITING."

"Fine writing" is anything but fine. It is stilted, artificial, insincere, and flowery. Fine writing is characterized by four main faults: overuse of polysyllabic words; the use of too many modifiers; overuse of foreign words and Briticisms; and the use of poetic words.

1. Avoid fine writing by not overusing "big" words.

Choose the short word if it will serve as well. Short words are usually clearer and more natural than long words.

Too many long words will make a piece of writing seem heavy or pedantic. A series of long words will also tend to interrupt the smooth, even flow of a sentence. Compare the effect of the following sentences:

> Long words: After liquidating his indebtedness, he was still in possession of sufficient funds to establish a small commercial enterprise.
>
> Short words: After paying his debts, he still had enough money to set up a small business.

This does not mean that long words should never be used. A writer with a mature style will, of course, use many long words; but they will be used only to express particular meanings for which shorter words may not exist. There are no short words, for example, to express the exact meanings of *jurisdiction, epilogue,* or *appendicitis.* But compare the following: *repast* and *meal; retire* and *go to bed; epistle* and *letter; ratiocinate* and *think; pulchritude* and *beauty; comestibles* and *food.* In these expressions, the simple words express quite clearly what the writer wishes to say and are in better taste.

2. Avoid the overuse of modifiers.

Use necessary words to give your reader a clear understanding of your meaning; however, avoid piling on descriptive words for their own sake or for false impressiveness. Try to avoid a writing style like the following:

> A penetratingly loud and constantly insistent buzzer sounded, waking me out of a blissfully pleasant and dream-free sleep. As I rose slowly and regretfully to dress, I could see through the gracefully flowing and swaying open draperies that colorful, Jack-Frost-touched autumn had begun its annual artistic change of dress. The trees with long, yearning, outstretched branches shook violently and fearfully as the caressing gusts of wind nudged their multicolored overcoats of green, brown, red, and yellow.

3. Avoid foreign words and Briticisms.

A bit of Latin or French sometimes seems impressive, and the inexperienced writer may be tempted to sprinkle writing with foreign phrases. Actually they are ostentatious and should be avoided except in a very few instances when there is no English equivalent.

Briticisms (British rather than American expressions) also make writing seem stilted. Use *gasoline* not *petrol, elevator* not *lift,* and *lawyer* not *barrister.*

4. Avoid the use of poetic words in prose.

Words that have been used in poetry but not in prose are known as *poetic diction.* "Poetic" words, sometimes so designated in dictionaries, are usually archaic words found in poetry composed in (or intended to create the aura of) a somewhat remote past. Examples of these are certain contractions such as *'tis, 'twas;* the use of *–st, –est, –th, –eth* endings on present tense verbs: *dost, would'st, doth, leadeth*; and words like *'neath, oft, ofttimes,* and *ope.*

D6b. AVOID USING EUPHEMISMS IN ALL WRITING.

Specifically, a **euphemism** is a softened, bland, totally inoffensive expression used instead of one that may suggest something unpleasant. In avoiding the use of such nonreputable expressions as *croak, turn up one's toes to the daisies, kick the bucket,* and *take the last count,* you may be tempted to write *pass away* or *depart this life* rather than the short, direct word *die.* Other examples of euphemisms to be avoided: *perspire* for *sweat, prevaricate* for *lie, expectorate* for *spit, mortician* for *undertaker, separate from school* for *expel, intoxicated* for *drunk, abdomen* for *stomach, obsequies* for *funeral.*

D6c. DO NOT USE OBSOLETE OR ARCHAIC WORDS.

An **obsolete** word is one that has completely passed out of use, in form or in one or more of its meanings. An *obsolescent* word is one that is becoming obsolete. Because the status of such words is difficult to ascertain, compilers of dictionaries usually label obsolete or obsolescent words "rare" or "archaic."

An **archaic** word is old-fashioned, a word that was once common in earlier speaking and writing. In special contexts, such as legal and Biblical expressions, it may be retained, but it has almost entirely disappeared from ordinary language.

D
6

D6d. AVOID THE USE OF GOBBLEDYGOOK.

Gobbledygook is a special kind of fine writing. The term was coined by a former United States congressman, grown weary of involved government reports, who possibly had in mind the throaty sounds uttered by a male turkey.

The term *gobbledygook* is applied to government and bureaucratic announcements that have been called "masterpieces of complexity." For example, in a pronouncement from a Washington bureau, "the chance of war" was referred to, in gobbledygook, as "in the regrettable eventuality of a failure of the deterrence policy."

Another example is the plumber who wrote to inform an agency of the United States government that he had found hydrochloric acid good for cleaning out pipes. Some bureaucrat responded with this gobbledygook: "The efficiency of hydrochloric acid is indisputable, but the corrosive residue is incompatible with metallic permanence." The plumber responded that he was glad the agency agreed. After several more gobbledygookish letters, an official finally wrote what he should have originally: "Don't use hydrochloric acid. It eats the inside out of pipes."

Possibly realizing how absurd gobbledygook is will ensure your never using it. Who, for instance, would prefer "Too great a number of culinary assistants may impair the flavor of the consommé" to "Too many cooks spoil the broth"?

D6e. AVOID THE USE OF JARGON.

Jargon has two basic meanings: (1) the language of a particular trade, profession, or group, such as *legal* jargon or *medical* jargon; (2) unintelligible or meaningless talk. The first of these meanings is discussed elsewhere under the topics of *technical words* and *slang*.

As a contributor to "fine writing," jargon involves the use of vague terms, "big" words, and indirect, roundabout ways of expressing ideas. The vague and pretentious language of gobbledygook is one form of jargon.

In an attempt to make writing "fine," the users of jargon will write "The answer is in the negative" rather than "No." For them, "bad weather" is "unfavorable climatic conditions."

Jargoneers also employ what has been called "the trick of elegant variation." They may call a spade a spade the first time but will then refer to "an agricultural implement."

EXERCISE 28

Rewrite each of the following sentences, correcting flaws in diction.

1. Our cooking class serves a luncheon of succulent viands on the first Tuesday of each month.
2. There should be no evidences of expectoration on this doorstep.
3. She plays along the manner of Joan Baez but, as regards her singing ability, the answer is in the negative.
4. A penny saved is a copper coin received in compensation.
5. A luminous shape, distinctly discernible to the eye, invaded the darkness of the cave.
6. On the regrettable eventuality of the failure of his deterrence policy, General Flap later made little comment.
7. Not until then was Macbeth ready to seize the knife and clobber the sleeping King.
8. We had a groovy time at the hop last Friday night.
9. At work, Aretha pursued her tasks with great diligence and was soon promoted.
10. The famous actor stepped onstage to give out with the immortal speech.

D 6

EXERCISE 29

Follow the directions for Exercise 28.

1. To be elected was indeed a great honor; I would not have swapped it for a king's ransom.
2. Mr. Bloomer told Sam to change his attitude or be separated from school.
3. In my youth I burned the midnight oil, but today I am content to be a vendor of footgear.
4. In my biology class, we discussed the reasons why feathered bipeds of similar plumage will live communally.
5. At the race track, Lisa had been given a bum tip about the winning horse.
6. To prevaricate about your marks is useless, Martin.

7. I will make my plans according as to whether Nancy likes playing tennis better than swimming.
8. Jennifer bought some red flannel underwear to keep her limbs warm.
9. Attending the obsequies may delay my departure.
10. After buying some eats at the delicatessen, they drove to the beach.

EXERCISE 30

Following are three statements, as reported by the Associated Press, concerning a promotion refusal. Which is the least and which is the most effective? Why?

1. Verbal contact with Mr. Blank regarding the attached notification of promotion has elicited the attached representations intimating that he prefers to decline the assignment.
2. I have spoken to Mr. Blank about this promotion; he does not wish to accept the post offered.
3. Blank doesn't want the job.

EXERCISE 31

The following letter of seventy-eight words can be written in clear, simple language in about thirty words. See how close to that number you can come in your revision.

Dear Sir:

We are in receipt of your favor of the tenth instant in re order for five television sets and wish to advise that according to our records your order was shipped on Oct. 19. Inasmuch as the order was carefully checked on this end, we would ask you to wait for three days. If the material has not been received in that time, we would ask that you use the card attached hereto and give us due notice.

EXERCISE 32

Sometimes a renowned writer may be accused of "fine writing." In the following paragraph from *The Return of the Native*, do you think Thomas Hardy should be accused of or defended from the charge of fine writing?

> That night was an eventful one to Eustacia's brain, and one which she hardly ever forgot. She dreamt a dream; and few human beings, from Nebuchadnezzar to the Swaffham tinker, ever dreamed a more remarkable one. Such an elaborately developed, perplexing, exciting dream was certainly never dreamed by a girl in Eustacia's situation before. It had as many ramifications as the Cretan labyrinth, as many fluctuations as the Northern Lights, as much colour as a parterre in June, and was as crowded with figures as a coronation. To Queen Scheherazade the dream might have seemed not far removed from commonplace; and to a girl just returned from all the courts of Europe it might have seemed not more than interesting. But amid the circumstances of Eustacia's life it was as wonderful as a dream could be.

D
6

EXERCISE 33

What are American equivalents for the following Briticisms? (1) *tram*, (2) *treacle*, (3) *wireless*, (4) *stay-in-strike*, (5) *hire-purchase system*, (6) *lorry*, (7) *chemist*, (8) *blackcoat worker*.

EXERCISE 34

From your reading, collect as many examples of archaic, obsolete, or poetic expressions as your teacher directs. A suggestion: read several of the older English or Scottish popular ballads and almost any English and American literature written before 1800 and not "modernized."

EXERCISE 35

Read or reread one of Shakespeare's plays. From it, compile a list of archaic and obsolete words containing as many items as your teacher directs.

EXERCISE 36

Rewrite the following sentence in plain, understandable language.

1. You should manufacture desiccated alfalfa during solarized incandescence.

2. A fact is a statement of an empirically verifiable phenomenon within a conceptual scheme.

3. The capital of the Papal States was not constructed during a diurnal revolution of the globe.

4. It has come to our attention that herbage, when observed in that section of enclosed ground being the property of an individual other than oneself, is ever of a more verdant hue.

5. Seeking a suitable place for the purpose of courting a state of dormant quiescence during the first part of the crepuscular period and forsaking said suitable place during the first part of the matinal period results in myriad benefits to *homo sapiens*, among which benefits may be noted a substantial increase in body soundness, monies, and sagacity.

EXERCISE 37

Follow the instructions for Exercise 36.

Much of an organization's effectiveness depends upon the adequacy of the data and information with which its employees work. The multifarious overlapping planning units have produced fragmented data, oriented toward single uses of land, and as these data were used by employees organized into single-use office groupings, the problem was exacerbated.

D7. Idiomatic Usage

Idioms are forms of expression peculiar to a language. Idiomatic expressions conform to no laws or principles; each idiomatic expression is a law unto itself. It may violate grammar or logic or both and still be acceptable, because the phrase is familiar, deep-rooted, widely used, and easily understandable—for the native-born.

Only a few generalized statements can be made about the many idiomatic expressions in our language. One is that several words combined may lose their literal meaning and express something only remotely suggested by any one word: *birds of a feather, blacklist, lay up, toe the line, bed of roses, dark horse, heavy hand, open house, read between the lines, no axe to grind, hard row to hoe.*

A second statement about idioms is that parts of the human body and words expressing activity have suggested many of them: *burn one's fingers, all thumbs, fly in the face of, stand on one's own feet, keep body and soul together, keep one's eyes open, step on someone's toes, rub elbows with, get one's back up, keep one's chin up.*

A third generalization is that hundreds of idiomatic phrases contain adverbs or prepositions with other parts of speech. No rule covers their use; yet certain combinations are acceptable and clear while others are not. Here are some examples:

> *walk off, walkover, walk-up;*
> *run down, run in, run off, run out;*
> *get nowhere, get through, get off*

agree:	*to* a proposal; *on* a plan; *with* a person
contend:	*for* a principle; *with* a person; *against* an obstacle
differ:	*with* a person; *from* something else; *about* or *over* a question
impatient:	*for* something desired; *with* someone else; *of* restraint; *at* someone's conduct
rewarded:	*for* something done; *with* a gift; *by* a person

D7a. USE ACCEPTABLE IDIOMATIC EXPRESSIONS.

Usage should conform to idiomatic word combinations that are generally acceptable. A good dictionary contains explanations of idiomatic usage following key words that need such explanation. It is important to consult your dictionary when using certain words, i.e., *prepositions* with nouns, adjectives, or verbs. Examples of idiomatic and unidiomatic expressions containing troublesome prepositions are the following:

Idiomatic	Unidiomatic
accord with	accord to
according to	according with
acquaint with	acquaint to
adverse to	adverse against
aim to prove	aim at proving
among themselves	among one another
angry with (a person)	angry at (a person)
as regards	as regards to
authority on	authority about
blame me for it	blame it on me
cannot help talking	cannot help but talk
comply with	comply to
conform to, with	conform in
correspond to (a thing)	correspond with (a thing)
desirous of	desirous to
graduated from (high school)	graduated (high school)
identical with	identical to
in accordance with	in accordance to
in search of	in search for
prefer (one) to (another)	prefer (one) over (another)
prior to	prior than
responsible for (to)	responsible on
superior to	superior than
treat of (a subject)	treat on (a subject)
unequal to	unequal for

It should be pointed out that many educated users of the language do not always follow accepted idiomatic usage. In everyday conversation, such a speaker is as likely to say "blame it on me" as "blame me for it" and "angry at" a person as "angry with." But in careful writing, the distinctions made above should be followed.

Collecting idioms can be an enjoyable pastime. Analyzing their structure and meaning can be even more fun. For instance, what can you make of these idioms?

make a date; make as if; make believe; make a fool of; make heavy weather of; make good; make off; make ready; make up; make a meal of; make it; make over; make mincemeat of; make do; make merry; make a fuss; make trouble; make a pass

Or of these?

> break one's heart; have one's heart in the right place; wear one's heart on one's sleeve; change of heart; after one's own heart; heart and soul; set one's heart on; eat one's heart out; take to heart; cold hands—warm heart; one's head rules one's heart; sick at heart

EXERCISE 38

Use correct prepositions with each of the following verbs to form common idiomatic combinations:

1. acquaint
2. concentrate
3. wait
4. part
5. center

6. acquiesce
7. engage
8. sympathize
9. listen
10. collide

EXERCISE 39

Use correct prepositions with each of the following adjectives to form common idiomatic expressions:

1. independent
2. unmindful
3. adverse
4. identical
5. sick

6. worthy
7. obedient
8. superior
9. angry
10. peculiar

EXERCISE 40

What is the meaning of each of the following idiomatic expressions? Be prepared to discuss in class the difference between the meaning of the idiomatic expression and the individual words considered separately.

> petty cash, square dance, pilot plant, oxygen tent, olive branch, king's evil, second fiddle, scorched earth, automatic pilot, salad days, far cry, round robin, blue laws, match play, rabbit punch, near miss, list price, flying saucer, walking papers, to the ends of the earth

EXERCISE 41

Number your paper from 1 to 20. For each sentence, provide a
preposition for the blank space.

1. Do not infer ____ my statements that I dislike you, Ted.
2. She was not desirous ____ running afoul of the law.
3. Nightingales think suet superior ____ seeds.
4. Stanley said he was not averse ____ the idea.
5. Gladys was admitted ____ the principal's office.
6. It is difficult to accommodate ourselves ____ that tight schedule.
7. Bobby is dependent ____ his big brother for dates.
8. I didn't agree ____ any such thing.
9. Contrast this photograph ____ that one.
10. He will never comply ____ your request.
11. Let's not be unmindful ____ the panthers, Dick.
12. I think pimento farms are peculiar ____ Tasmania.
13. Students often are apprehensive ____ their grades.
14. Her mother grew impatient ____Carla's experiments.
15. I am not capable ____ controlling that horse.
16. What do you imply ____ your remark?
17. Two hours prior ____ leaving, Judy opened the letter.
18. The difficulty inheres ____ her method of approach.
19. The six characters were in search ____ an author.
20. Marguerite tried to substitute cleverness ____ valid argument.

D8. Colloquialisms

A **colloquialism** is a conversational expression that is permissible in an easy, informal style of speaking and writing. Indeed,
colloquialisms are often indispensable in ordinary conversation.
A colloquialism is *not* an illiteracy. It is *not* incorrect, *not* in bad
taste, and *not* substandard. Colloquialisms *are* expressions more
often used in speech than in writing and are more appropriate in
informal than in formal writing.

D8a. USE COLLOQUIALISMS APPROPRIATELY AND EFFECTIVELY.

The test for the use of colloquialisms is appropriateness. There is
no objective test or exact rule to enable you to determine when

colloquialisms may be used. Certainly it is better to employ them than to avoid them and make your writing seem artificial and awkward. In fact, in informal English, colloquialisms are actually desirable for smoothness, clarity, and power of communication. But in formal, well-planned writing they should be avoided unless they are deliberately used to achieve some stylistic effect. Consult the dictionary to determine whether a word is considered colloquial.

Some words are colloquial in all their meanings. Others are colloquial only in one or more of several meanings or combinations. Examples:

> brass tacks (facts), shape up, nervy, ad, gumption, hasn't got any, take it, fall for, jinx, moxie, come-on, show up, try and, goner (a person dead, lost, or in deep trouble), fizzle (fail), flop (to fail or break down), root for (cheer).

EXERCISE 42

From any two pages in your dictionary, list the words or word meanings labeled "colloquial" or "informal." What general statement can you make about the words on your list?

EXERCISE 43

What are the colloquial (informal) meanings of the following words and expressions?

> burg, mum, numbskull, primp, uppish, fizzle, type, catch (n.), rambunctious, middy, highfalutin, lab, bossy, grapevine, fluke, preachify, sleuth, buddy, buck fever, pass the buck, pitch in, freeze out, war-horse, small potatoes, yes-man, yours truly, square shooter, blue streak, rubber stamp, Dutch treat, salt away, close call, play up to, walking papers, make time, sweet tooth, fill the bill, cut a figure.

D9. Slang

Slang is a label for a particular kind of colloquialism. It may be defined as language that consists of very current terms having a forced or fantastic meaning or displaying eccentricity. Such expressions may capture the popular fancy or some segment of it (college slang, musical slang, baseball slang), but in the main they are nonstandard. Even so, slang may for a while be used over a broad area, and a large number of words and phrases bear the "slang" label in dictionaries. If such expressions survive, they may in time receive the respectable label "colloquial." Some of the following examples appear in dictionaries with the "slang" label; some may appear there eventually; and some will not appear at all, because their vogue is too short-lived.

Slang expressions appear as one of several forms:

1. Words formed from others by abbreviation or by adding endings to change the part of speech: *VIP* or *V.I.P.* (Very Important Person), *psych out, C-note, groovy, snafu* (situation normal; all fouled up), *phony, chintzy, nervy, mod.*

2. Words in otherwise acceptable use given extended meanings: *chicken, grind, corny, guts, lousy, swell, buck, jerk, square, dish, grub, sack, bad* (meaning "good" or "beautiful").

3. Words formed by compounding or coalescing two or more words: *whodunit, stash* (*sto*re and ca*che*), *egghead, high-hat, slanguage* (*sl*ang and *l*anguage), *attaboy* (that's the boy), *screwball, slithy* (*sli*my and li*the*).

4. Phrases made up of one or more newly coined words (neologisms) or one or more acceptable ones: *goof off, blow one's top, bum steer, shoot the bull, live it up, get in orbit, in cahoots, on the skids, deadbeat, have a ball, off one's rocker, conk out, cut out, shoot the works, cool it.*

D9a. AVOID SLANG IN FORMAL WRITING.

Slang, although popular, has little place in formal writing. Sound reasons exist for guarding against it.

First, many slang words and expressions last for a relatively brief time and then pass out of use, becoming unintelligible to many readers and listeners.

Second, using slang expressions keeps you from searching for the exact words you need to convey your meaning. Many slang expressions are only rubber stamps. To refer to a person as a "swell gal" or a "lemon" hardly expresses exactly or fully any critical judgment or intelligent description.

Third, slang does not serve the primary aim of writing: conveying a clear message from writer to reader.

Finally, slang is not suitable in most formal writing because it is not in keeping with the context. Words should be appropriate to the audience, the occasion, and the subject.

However, some do argue in favor of slang in certain places. It does express feeling, although boisterously and sometimes ludicrously. It also makes effective shortcuts in expression and often prevents artificiality in writing. Furthermore, it should be used in recording dialogue to convey the flavor of the speech actually used. But for reasons already set down, an excessive use of slang expressions should be carefully avoided.

D 9

D9b. USE NEOLOGISMS SPARINGLY AND ONLY WHEN THEY ARE APPROPRIATE.

Neologisms are newly coined words. Not all of them are slang, but many of them are. Not all of them are contrived and artificial, but the majority are. You are advised not to overuse them, but to employ them when no adequate substitutes are available.

New words are coined in various ways. Some are adaptations of common words: *millionheiress*. Some, the so-called *portmanteau* words, are combinations of common words: *brunch* (*br*eakfast and l*unch*), *smog* (*sm*oke and f*og*). Some are formed from the initial letters of common words: *loran* (*lo*ng *ra*nge *n*avigation), *radar* (*ra*dio *d*etecting *a*nd *r*anging). Some are virtually new formations, like *gobbledygook*, modeled on the meaningless sounds of a turkey's gobble. Discoveries, new inventions, and occupations inspire new coinages: *A-bomb, rhombatron, transistor, programmer*. Registered tradenames or trademarks are in the same classification: *Dacron, Technicolor, Kodak, Xerox*. Events, like depresssions and wars, create words: *Hooverville, jeep, foxhole, blitz*.

New words that appear in dictionaries may have no label or be labeled "slang" or "colloquial." Some neologisms, like *motel*, change to permanent status and become common words.

EXERCISE 44

As your teacher directs, prepare a brief paper or a short talk for class delivery comparing and contrasting the meanings provided by your dictionary for the following terms:

1. argot   5. lingo
2. cant   6. shoptalk
3. dialect   7. slang
4. jargon   8. vernacular

EXERCISE 45

Look up in your dictionary the meanings of the following slang words and phrases:

1. sound off   11. kibosh
2. on the make   12. pork barrel
3. shyster   13. high-hat
4. cahoot   14. long green
5. get one's goat   15. goo
6. stool pigeon   16. on the loose
7. sad sack   17. jittery
8. hooey   18. stuffed shirt
9. nix   19. mooch
10. tizzy   20. a yard

EXERCISE 46

Provide a slang meaning for each of the following. Then, when possible, provide a less informal, more acceptable meaning for each word. Be prepared to discuss in class whatever connection there may be between the slang meaning and the less informal meaning of each word.

1. pinch   7. salted
2. rat   8. plug
3. oyster   9. noodle
4. stall   10. pony
5. stuff   11. ham
6. applesauce   12. sap

13. bushwa	17. grind
14. goof off	18. yellow
15. guy	19. beatnik
16. flame	20. clod

EXERCISE 47

Bring to class a list of as many neologisms as your teacher suggests. Compile the list from reading several newspaper columnists and a few issues of *Time* magazine and by recording coinages that you hear on television and radio.

D10. Illiteracies and Improprieties

Illiteracies are words and expressions not accepted in either colloquial or formal language. **Improprieties,** unlike illiterate words, are standard English words that are misused in function or meaning. In an impropriety, the word itself is acceptable; it is the misuse of that word that causes the error in diction.

D10a. AVOID USING ILLITERATE WORDS AND PHRASES.

Characteristic of uneducated speech, illiteracies are to be avoided in writing except as quotations of people you are characterizing or, on very rare occasions, for purposes of humor.

In dictionaries some illiteracies are so labeled, but what may be marked *illiterate* in one dictionary may be termed *dialect* or even *colloquial* in another. Because most dictionaries primarily record standard usage, few examples may be recorded. When they are, do not assume that you can use them in your writing simply because they appear in the dictionary; be careful to read the label attached to them. The following words and phrases are examples of those that you should guard against: *acrossed, ain't, anywheres, borned, boughten, brung, disremember, drownded, et* (past of *eat*), *excessible, hisself, I been* or *I done, irregardless, kepted, losted, mistakened, nohow, nowheres, ourn, snuck* (past of *sneak*), *vacationize, youse.* Note that a not uncommon illiteracy consists of an –*ed* added to past participle forms of verbs.

D10b. AVOID IMPROPRIETIES IN GRAMMATICAL FUNCTION.

One classification of improprieties includes words acceptable as one part of speech but unacceptable as another: nouns improperly substituted for verbs, verbs for nouns, adjectives for nouns, adjectives for adverbs, adverbs for adjectives, prepositions for conjunctions. Another includes misuses of principal parts of verbs.

A word identified as more than one part of speech may be so used without question, but do not remove a word from one part of speech and place it in another until standard usage has sanctioned this new function. Examples of grammatical improprieties:

Nouns used as verbs:	*grassing* a lawn; *suppering;* to *party; ambitioned; passengered*
Verbs used as nouns:	a *sell; advise*
Adjectives used as adverbs:	dances *good, awful* short, etc.
Verb forms:	*come* for *came; don't* for *doesn't; says* for *said; done* for *did; hadn't ought; set* for *sit; of* for *have*
Other combinations:	*this here; them there; them kind; being that, being as,* or *being as how* for *because* or *since; except as* for *unless*

For guidance, consult your dictionary, which labels every word according to the part or parts of speech that it is. Note also the usage label—colloquial, dialect, slang, etc.—since the same word may be acceptable as one part of speech but not as another.

D10c. AVOID IMPROPRIETIES IN MEANING.

Another classification of improprieties includes words similar or vaguely similar to other words and used inaccurately or wrongly in their place. Such words include *homonyms* and *homographs.*

Homonyms are two words that have the same or almost the same pronunciation but are different in meaning, in origin, and frequently in spelling; for example, *real* and *reel; made* and *maid; hour, our,* and *are; accept, except.*

Words that are near-homonyms may also cause confusion: *farther* for *further, father* for *farther, genial* for *general, stationary* for *stationery, morass* for *morose, loose* for *lose, imminent* for *eminent.*

> A person of such distinction is certainly one to *immolate.*
> The tennis player *lopped* the ball to the back of the court.
> To be an engineer, one has to be able to use a *slight* rule.

Such confusions may result from hearing words inexactly rather than seeing them in print and relating their meaning to their appearance as well as their sound.

Homographs are two or more words that have the same spelling but are different in meaning, origin, and perhaps pronunciation. Examples: *slaver* (a dealer in slaves) and *slaver* (drool or drivel); *arms* (parts of the body) and *arms* (weapons); *bat* (club, cudgel) and *bat* (flying mammal). Homographs cannot cause misspelling, but they can cause confusion or ambiguity.

**D
10**

EXERCISE 48

As your teacher directs, prepare a short presentation for written or oral delivery that summarizes what your dictionary informs you about these terms: *vulgarism, solecism, impropriety, illiteracy, barbarism.* If available, use dictionary examples of each.

EXERCISE 49

Use correctly in sentences ten of the pairs of words listed in Section D13.

EXERCISE 50

From your dictionary, find the answers to the following questions. If the answer is "yes," explain. Can the following words be used as indicated?

1. *Corp* as the singular of *corps?*
2. *Conjugate* as an adjective?

3. *Pshaw* as a verb? An interjection?
4. *Rose* as a verb?
5. *Holp, holpen* as past tense and past participle?
6. *Contrariwise* as an adjective?
7. *Quarry* as a verb?
8. *Throw* as a noun?
9. *Cool* as a noun?
10. *Complected* as a variant for *complexioned?*
11. *Stratums* as a plural?
12. *Ditto* as a verb?
13. *Quail* as a verb?
14. *Wrought* as a past participle of *work?*
15. *Hardy* as a noun?
16. *Sure* as an adverb?
17. *Equal* as a noun?
18. *Appropriate* as an adverb?

D11. Triteness

Triteness, sometimes referred to as *clichés*, applies to words and expressions that are worn out from overuse.
Trite language spares writers the burden of expressing exactly what they mean, but its use results in stale and ineffective writing. Clichés may seem humorous; indeed, they are often used to express humor or irony. When used seriously, however, they indicate that the writer or speaker is naïve.

D11a. AVOID THE OVERUSE OF TRITE LANGUAGE

Trite expressions often are expressive and colorful. If they were not, they would never become hackneyed. But here are examples of colorful expressions now stale from overuse:

abreast of the times	at a loss for words
add insult to injury	at an early date
all the luck in the world	at your earliest convenience
all work and no play	be that as it may
along these lines	be there with bells on
are in receipt of	better half
as big as a house	bigger and better
as luck would have it	bitter end

bolt out of the blue
budding genius
busy as a bee
by and large
by leaps and bounds
captain of industry
center of attraction
checkered career
clinging vine
cold as ice
conspicuous by her absence
deadly earnest
deem it an honor and a
  privilege
deepest gratitude
depths of despair
do justice to a dinner
each and every
esteem it a great honor
exception proves the rule
festive occasion
few and far between
first and foremost
fools rush in
goes without saying
good time was had by all
great open spaces
green with envy
heartfelt thanks

hit an all-time low
hungry as a bear
ignorance is bliss
in this day and age
irony of fate
last but not least
level best
makes the world a better
  place to live in
meets the eye
method in his madness
milestone on the road of life
needs no introduction
nipped in the bud
none the worse for wear
out of a clear sky
proud possessor
red as a rose
ripe old age
shot heard around the world
take this opportunity
the good life
the worse for wear
time marches on
time of my life
tired but happy
to make a long story short
too full for utterance
words fail to express

D
11

D11b. AVOID THE OVERUSE OF FILLERS AND CONVERSATIONAL TAGS.

This section applies more to speaking than to writing, but it does deal with an important aspect of triteness. As we talk (and occasionally as we write) we tend to throw in tags and fillers that add little or nothing to what we are trying to communicate. For instance, if we need time to think about what we are going to say next, we will pause and say "uh" or "y'know" or "well." When we cannot think of anything else to add, we end a statement with "and all like that" or "and everything."

Fillers listed here can successfully be used in talking, but the talk you hear is probably overloaded with them. What about your own talk?

and all	on the average
as a matter of fact	say
by the same token	so
curiously enough	still and all
first of all	strangely enough
frankly	strictly speaking
interestingly enough	that is to say
know what I mean?	uh

EXERCISE 51

Prepare a comment (written or oral as your teacher directs) on the meanings given in your dictionary for these terms:

1. trite
2. stereotyped
3. hackneyed
4. commonplace
5. banal
6. cliché
7. platitudinous
8. bromidic
9. corny

EXERCISE 52

Substitute more effective expressions for those that you consider trite in the following sentences:

1. After all, one does not have to stay out to the wee small hours of the morning simply because it is New Year's Eve.
2. When I applied for my first job, I must admit that I had butterflies in my stomach.
3. The movie ended with the hero driving down the highway, like a ribbon winding over the hills, and into the reddening glow of the setting sun.
4. Her marks have improved by leaps and bounds. The main underlying reason for it is that she has worked like a dog.
5. At a ripe old age she died, having lived out her life in the wide open spaces.
6. Last but not least, we have scheduled two concerts for our summer schedule.
7. She spent every penny she earned. She saw no sense in putting money aside for a rainy day when she could have been living it up. After all, you can't take it with you.

8. First and foremost, your dinner was wonderful.
9. I can't wait to see my friends again and taste some of that good old home cooking.
10. Suffice it to say, I think it's wacky to worry in this day and age.

D12. Mixed Figures of Speech

A **figure of speech** is a method of using words out of their literal, or ordinary, sense in order to suggest a picture or image. "He is a saint" and "sleeping like a baby" are illustrations of, respectively, the two most common figures of speech: *metaphor* and *simile*. A metaphor is a term applied to something to which it is not literally applicable. Associated with metaphor in meaning, a simile expresses resemblance of one thing to another but does so by using the words *like, as,* or *as if.* "She is *like* a cool brook." Figurative language, often vivid and imaginative, can add color and clarity to writing. But it can also result in confusion, distraction, or even amusement.

Found occasionally in prose are the following figures of speech, which, like parts of speech, appear in both writing and speaking. In addition to *metaphor* and *simile,* these include:

1. **Synecdoche:** A figure of association. Use of a part or an individual for the whole class or group, or the reverse. Part for whole: "We have fifty *head* of cattle on our farm." Whole for part: "Central defeated Gardner High in the homecoming game"; i.e., the two schools did not play, but their football teams did.

2. **Metonymy:** A figure of association, somewhat like synecdoche. Use of the name of one thing for that of another suggested by it. "We all agree that the tailor *sews a fine seam*" (i.e., does good tailoring).

3. **Personification:** Giving nonhuman objects the characteristics of a human being: "The waves *murmured*, and the moon *wept* silver tears."

4. **Hyperbole:** Exaggeration, or a statement exaggerated imaginatively, for effect; not to be taken literally. Some similes and metaphors express hyperbole: "The young student, innocent *as a newborn babe*, eagerly accepted the bet." "The sweet music *rose and touched the farthest star*."

D
12

Because figurative language is colorful and imaginative, it adds vigor and effectiveness to writing. But do not think of figurative language as a mere ornament of style; do not use it too frequently; do not shift abruptly from figurative to literal language; and bear in mind that a direct simple statement is usually preferable to a series of figures and always preferable when the figures are artificial, trite, or overly elaborate. Many worn-out similes are trite phrases: *happy as a lark, cool as a cucumber, busy as a bee, mad as a hornet, quick as a wink, smooth as silk, right as rain, quiet as a mouse, hot as blazes, sleeps like a newborn baby.*

D12a. AVOID USING MIXED AND INAPPROPRIATE FIGURES OF SPEECH.

Mixed figures are those in which the images suggested by the words and phrases are obviously unrelated. Similes or metaphors are especially likely to become mixed through inconsistency, overelaborateness, and incongruity. Here are examples of mixed and inappropriate figures:

> After football season many a football player who was a tidal wave on the football field has to put his nose to the grindstone and study.
>
> Three of us were sure the kingpins on the roost in our high school.
>
> At any party there is always a rotten apple that throws a monkey wrench in our food and drink.
>
> I hope to get to be a big wheel here at high school, but I don't expect to do much trotting around when I get out.
>
> When I graduate, I hope to become a well-oiled cog in the beehive of industry.

EXERCISE 53

Point out any inconsistent figurative language in the following, and rewrite the sentences containing it.

1. Someday we will make a start on pruning the vines of bureaucracy, but we must unite, for there are sharks in these waters.
2. There were four of us in the boat; and when we got to shore that night, we were dead.
3. My sister is always on her toes when she is driving a car.

4. I received many valentines, but Harvey's jealousy put a big dent in my enthusiasm.
5. We are going to have to look the situation in the eye with an open mind.
6. Now that I have learned to organize my time, I have attained a foothold by which I can police myself.
7. The spirit of the student body is keyed to only one goal; to cheer their team on to the championship.
8. When you drive a foreign car, you have your feet firmly on the ground.
9. As dishwasher at the cafeteria, I am literally cut to ribbons every day by the great quantities of knives and forks piled in the sink.
10. She was at that awkward age that whenever she opened her mouth, she put her foot in.

D13. Words Often Confused

It is all too easy to use a word that resembles another in some way but actually is chosen because of ignorance, confusion, or carelessness.

D13a. DO NOT CONFUSE ONE WORD WITH ANOTHER.

Watch out for the following, which are merely a sampling of the many words in English that can and do cause trouble:

Ability, capacity. *Ability* means the power to do something, mental or physical *(ability* to manage an office). *Capacity* is ability to hold, contain, or absorb (a suitcase filled to *capacity).*

Accept, except. *Accept* means "to receive" or "to say yes to"; *except* means "to exclude" or "to exempt." (I *accept* the terms of this contract. Jane was *excepted* from the general invitation.) As a preposition, *except* means "other than." (No one *except* me knew the combination.)

Affect, effect. *Affect,* as a verb, means "to assume," or "to influence." (Her voice *affected* me strangely.) *Effect,* as a verb, means "to cause"; as a noun, it means "result." (Being captain *effected* a change in his attitude. The decision had a profound *effect* on labor relations.)

All right, alright. The former expression is correct but has been overworked to mean "satisfactory" or "very well." *Alright* is not an acceptable word in standard usage.

Already, all ready. The former means "earlier," "previously." (When she arrived, he had *already* left.) *All ready* means "all are ready." (They will leave when they are *all ready*.)

Altogether, all together. *Altogether* means "wholly," "completely." (He was not *altogether* pleased with his purchase.) *All together* means "all in company" or "everybody in one place." (The family was *all together* for the holidays.)

Among, between. The former indicates a relationship of more than two objects. *Between* refers to only two or to more than two when each object is considered in relation to the others. (The land was divided *among* seven farmers. The rivalry *between* Joe and Sam is intense. Trade *between* nations is desirable.)

Anyway, anyways. *Anyway* means "in any case," "anyhow." (She was planning to go *anyway*.) *Anyways* is considered either dialectal or colloquial. (*Anyway* [not *anyways*], I want to go too.)

Apt, liable, likely. *Apt* suggests fitness or tendency.(She is *apt* in arithmetic.) *Liable* implies exposure to something burdensome or disadvantageous. (You are *liable* for damages.) *Likely* means "expected," "probable." (We are *likely* to have snow next month.) *Likely* is the most commonly used of the three terms. Distinction in meaning has broken down somewhat, but *apt* and *liable* used in the sense of "probable" are sometimes considered colloquial or dialectal.

Awful, awfully, abominably. These and such other expressions as *terrible*, *ghastly*, and *horrible* are loose, overworked intensifiers. If you really need an intensifier, use *very*. (See *Very*, Sec. D14.)

Bad, badly, ill. *Bad* is an *adjective* meaning "not good," "not as it should be." *Badly* is an *adverb* meaning "harmfully," "wickedly," "unpleasantly," "inefficiently." *Ill* is both an adjective and an adverb and means "sick," "tending to cause harm or evil," or "in an evil manner," "wrongly." (He was very *ill*.) *Bad* and *badly* are often incorrectly used with the verb *feel*. (I feel *bad* today [not *badly*, unless you mean that your sense of touch is impaired].)

Balance, remainder. *Remainder* means "what is left over." *Balance* has many meanings, but its use as "remainder" is considered colloquial. (She finished the *remainder* [not *balance*] of her chemistry homework.)

Beside, besides. *Beside* is normally a preposition meaning "by the side of." *Besides* is an adverb meaning "moreover," and, infrequently, is a preposition meaning "except." (The young mother sat *beside* the cradle. I am angry because he left suddenly, and *besides*, he owes me money.)

Can, may, might. *Can* suggests "ability," physical and mental. (She *can* sing beautifully when she wants to.) *May* implies permission or sanction. (You *may* borrow my suitcase.) The distinction between *can* and *may* (ability versus permission) is illustrated in this sentence: "I *can* swim, but Mother says I *may* not." *May* also expresses possibility and wish (desire): "It *may* turn cold this evening" (possibility); "*May* you have a safe journey" (wish, desire). *Might* is used after a governing verb in the past tense, *may* after a governing verb in the present tense: "She *says* that we *may* proceed"; "She *said* that we *might* proceed."

Common, mutual. The former means "belonging to many or to all." *Mutual* means "reciprocal." (Airplanes are *common* carriers. Our respect and love were *mutual*.) Avoid the redundancy of such a statement as "He and I entered into a mutual agreement."

Compare, contrast. *Compare* is used to point out likenesses, similarities (used with the preposition *to*), and to examine two or more objects to find likenesses or differences (used with the preposition *with*). *Contrast* always points out differences. (The poet *compared* her child *to* a frisky kitten. The teacher *compared* my paper *with* Henry's and found no signs of copying. In *contrast* to your work, mine is poor.)

Complement, compliment *Complement* means something that completes. (This hat will *complement* your wardrobe.) A *compliment* is a flattering comment. (When she remarked that he was handsome, Ted thanked her for the *compliment*.)

Continual, continuous. In some uses, these words are synonymous. A subtle distinction is that *continual* implies "a close recurrence in time," "in rapid succession." *Continuous* implies "without interruption." (I object most to my sisters'

D
13

continual quarreling. The *continuous* dripping of water from that leaky faucet unnerved me.)

Council, counsel. *Council* means "an assembly," "a group." (A *council* of labor leaders voted on the proposal.) *Counsel* is both a noun and a verb and means "advice" or "to advise." ("Work hard and save your money" is indeed wise *counsel*. Our minister will *counsel* me whenever problems arise.)

Disinterested, uninterested. The former means "unbiased", "not influenced by personal reasons." *Uninterested* means "having no interest in," "not paying attention." (The minister's opinion was *disinterested*. I was completely *uninterested* in the play.) As a colloquialism, *disinterested* is often used in the sense of "uninterested," "indifferent."

Either . . . or, neither . . . nor. The former means "one of two." *Neither* means "not one of two." *Or* is used with *either*, *nor* with *neither*. The use of *either . . . or* and *neither . . . nor* in coordinating more than two words, phrases, or clauses is approved by some dictionaries but not by others. (*Either* of you *is* satisfactory for the role. *Neither* the boys *nor* the girls wished to dance.)

Emigrate, immigrate. The former means "to leave"; the latter means "to enter." (Our supervisor *emigrated* from Russia in 1948. In the future, a great number of people from the Latin countries will *immigrate* to the United States.)

Envelop, envelope. The verb *en-vel′ op* (accent on second syllable) means "to cover," "to wrap." (Fog will soon *envelop* the island.) *En′vel-ope* (accent on first syllable) is a noun meaning "a covering." (Your invoice is contained in this *envelope*.)

Farther, further. These are interchangeable; however, some writers prefer *farther* to indicate "space," "a measurable distance," and *further* to indicate "greater in quantity, degree, or time," and also "moreover," "in addition to." (I drove eight miles *farther*. Let us give the matter *further* consideration.)

Fewer, less. Both of these words imply a comparison with something larger in number or amount. Although *less* is widely used in place of *fewer*, particularly in informal writing and in speech, the distinction between them seems useful. *Fewer* applies to number. (*Fewer* horses are seen on the streets these days.) *Less* is used in several ways; *less* material in the dress, *less* coverage, *less* than a dollar. (The *less* money we have the *fewer* purchases we can make.)

Formally, formerly. The first word means "in a formal manner," "precisely," "ceremonially." The latter means "in the past." (The artist was *formally* introduced to the President. I was *formerly* treasurer of my class.)

Fort, forte. *Fort* means an "enclosed place," a "fortified building." *Forte* means "special accomplishment or ability." (The old *fort* has been turned into a museum. I am not a golfer; tennis is my *forte.*)

Good, well. The former is an adjective with many meanings: a *good* time, *good* advice, *good* Republican, *good* humor. *Well* functions as both adjective and adverb. As an adjective it means "in good health," and as an adverb it means "ably" or "efficiently." (I feel *well* once again. The sales force worked *well* in the campaign.)

Got, gotten. The principal parts of *get* are *get, got, got* (or *gotten*). Both *have got* and *have gotten* are acceptable terms. Your choice will depend upon your speech habits or on the rhythm of the sentence you are writing or speaking. *Got* is colloquial when used to mean "must," "ought," "own," "possess," and many other terms. (I *ought* [not *got*] to go.) (See *Have got to,* Section D14.)

Gourmand, gourmet. These words have to do with eating, but they are different in meaning. A *gourmand* is a large eater. (Teenage boys are notorious *gourmands.*) A *gourmet* is a fastidious eater, an epicure. (Les Chevaliers du Tastevin is an association of well-known *gourmets.*)

Hang, hung. The principal parts of *hang* are *hang, hung, hung.* However, when the word refers to the death penalty, the parts are *hang, hanged, hanged.* (The pictures are *hung.* The cattle rustler was *hanged.*)

Healthful, healthy. These words are often used interchangeably, but *healthful* precisely means "conducive to health"; *healthy* means "possessing health." In other words, places and foods are *healthful*, people and animals are *healthy*. (Athletes must be *healthy* people because of their *healthful* daily workouts.)

Human, humane. The term *human* refers to a person. Some particularly precise writers and speakers do not use the word alone to refer to a person; instead they say or write *human* *being*. However, use of the word alone as a noun has a long and respectable background. *Humane* means "tender," "merciful," "considerate." (The general insisted upon *humane* treatment of all prisoners.)

If, whether. In standard English, *if* is used to express condition. *Whether*, usually with *or*, is used in expressions of doubt and indirect questions expressing condition. (*If* it isn't raining, we'll be in the garden [simple condition]. I am wondering *whether* he can do it [doubt]. She asked *whether* the car had stopped [indirect question].) In standard English *if* is not used with *or*. (I do not know *whether* [not *if*] I am rich *or* poor.)

Imply, infer. To *imply* is to suggest a meaning hinted at but not explicitly stated. (Do you *imply* that the cashier is dishonest?) To *infer* is to draw a conclusion from statements, circumstances, or evidence. (From your reply I *infer* that you would rather stay at home.) Do not confuse these two words in use.

Impractical, impracticable. Distinctions in the meanings of these words have broken down somewhat, but the former means "speculative" or "theoretical." *Impracticable* means "not capable of being used," "unmanageable." (His plan is *impractical* and his instructions are *impracticable*.)

Is, was, were. These are parts of the verb *to be*. It may help you to remember that *is* is singular in number, third person, present tense. (*She* [or *He* or *It*] *is* in the room.) *Was* is singular, first or third person, past tense. (*I* [or *He* or *She* or *It*] *was* in the room.) *Were* can be either singular or plural, second person in the singular and all three persons in the plural, and is in the past tense. (*You* [both singular and plural] *were* in the room. *We* [or *You* or *They*] *were* in the room.) The two most frequent errors in using *to be* are employing *was* for *were* and vice versa and using *is* in the first or second person instead of in the third.

It stands to reason. A cliché.

Its, it's, its'. This little three-letter combination causes more errors than any other grouping of letters in the English language. However, the distinctions among them are simple and easily learned. *Its* is the possessive form of *it*. (The dress has lost *its* shape.) *It's* is a contraction of *it is* and should never be used unless it means precisely this. (I think *it's* [it *is*] going to rain.) *Its'*? There is no such form or word in the language.

Jealous, zealous. The former means "resentful" or "envious"; idiom decrees that *jealous* should be followed by *of*, not *for*. (Ingrid is *jealous* of Margaret's ring.) *Zealous* means "diligent," "devoted." (They were *zealous* workers on behalf of their candidate.)

Later, latter. The spelling of these words is often confused. They also have different meanings. *Later* refers to time. (The train arrived five minutes *later* than usual.) For *latter*, see *former, latter*, Section D14.

Lead, led. These words show the confusion that our language suffers because of using different symbols to represent one sound. *Lead* (pronounced *lēd*) is the present tense of the verb and causes little or no difficulty. *Led* (pronounced like the name of the metal) is the past tense and is often misspelled with *ea*. (*Lead* the horse around the paddock. She *led* the horse around the paddock yesterday.)

Learn, teach. Standard English requires a distinction in meaning between these words. (I'll *learn* the language if you will *teach* me.) The expression "*to learn* someone something" is an illiteracy.

Least, lest. The former means "smallest," "slightest." The latter means "for fear that." (It was the very *least* I could do. Close the door *lest* our secret be overheard.)

Leave, let. Both words are common in several idiomatic expressions implying permission, but *let* is standard whereas *leave* is not. (*Let* [not *leave*] me help you wash the dishes.)

Legible, readable. These terms are synonymous in the meaning of "capable of being deciphered or read with ease." *Readable* has the additional meaning of "interesting or easy to read." (Your handwriting is *legible*. This book is *readable*.)

Lie, lay, lye. The first of these words is the present tense (infinitive) of a verb meaning "to be in a recumbent or prostrate position." As a noun, it means "falsehood." (Please *lie* down. Never tell a *lie*.) *Lay* has several meanings, but it is most often used as the past tense of *lie*. (He *lay* down for a nap.) *Lye* is an alkaline substance. (Some soaps contain *lye*.)

Loan, lend. Many careful writers and speakers use *loan* only as a noun (to make a *loan*) and *lend* as a verb (to *lend* money).

D 13

Because of constant and widespread usage, *loan* is now considered a legitimate verb to be avoided only in strictly formal English.

Loose, lose, loss. *Loose* means "not fastened tightly." (This is a *loose* connection.) *Lose* means "to suffer the loss of." (Don't *lose* your hard-earned money.) *Loss* means "a deprivation," "a defeat," "a reverse." (The coach blamed me for the *loss* of the ball.)

Lousy. This word actually means "infested with lice." It is constantly used as a slang expression, however, to mean "dirty," "disgusting," "contemptible," "poor," "inferior," and "well supplied with" (as in *lousy with money*). Use it in only the most informal of informal conversations. You can startle or impress your friends by using *pediculous*.

Luxuriant, luxurious. The former term refers to abundant growth; *luxurious* pertains to luxury. (The blooms in her garden were *luxuriant*. Silk curtains gave the simple room a *luxurious* touch.)

Maybe, may be. The first means "perhaps." (*Maybe* I will go bowling today.) *May be* (two words) is used to express possibility. (There *may be* some food in the refrigerator.)

Most, almost. *Most* is the superlative of *many* and *much* and means "greatest in amount, quality, or degree." *Almost* indicates "very nearly," "all but." *Most* is colloquial when used for *almost*. (Audrey has *almost* [not *most*] come to a decision.)

No place, nowhere. The former is a perfectly sound phrase (There's *no place* like home), but in standard English it cannot be a synonym for *nowhere*. (She could find her purse *nowhere* [not *no place*].) Be certain to spell *nowhere* correctly; *nowheres* is as dialectal as *no place*.

O, oh. The former is usually part of a vocative (direct address), is normally capitalized, and is rarely followed by any mark of punctuation. *Oh* is an interjection, may be followed by a comma or exclamation point, and is capitalized according to the usual rules. (*O* Dave! Stop your clowning. Yet, *oh*, what a happy ending! *Oh*, what gorgeous eyes!)

Oral, aural, verbal. *Oral* means "spoken." (The order was *oral*, not written.) *Aural* means "received through the ear," or "pertaining to the sense of hearing." (After the concussion,

Jane's *aural* sense was below normal.) *Verbal* means "of, in, or by means of words." In such a sentence as "Our contract was *verbal*," it means "unwritten." *Oral* and *verbal* are thus often confused in everyday use.

Party, person, individual. Except in telephone and legal language, *party* implies a group and should not be used to refer to one person except in a colloquial sense. *Individual* refers to a single, particular person. As nouns, *individual* and *person* are synonymous. As an adjective, *individual* means "single," "separate," and is therefore unnecessary and repetitious when used to modify *person* or when "each" has been used. Both *individual person* and *each individual member* are wordy phrases.

Passed, past. The first word is the past tense of the verb *to pass*. In its use as a verb, the latter is the past participle. (She *passed* quietly by the open doorway. The years of struggle are now *past*.) *Pass* is not only a verb; it is also a noun. In one or the other of these two categories, it appears in many expressions that are either colloquial or slangy, among them *pass the buck, make a pass at, a pretty pass, pass up, pass out*.

Percent, per cent. This word (from Latin *per centum*, meaning "by the hundred") may be spelled as either one or two words. *Percent* is colloquial when used as a substitute for *percentage* (the noun). *Percentage* is colloquial when used in the meaning of "profit" or "advantage," as in "What's the *percentage* in hard work?"

Principal, principle. *Principal* is a noun indicating "sum of money" or "a chief person," and an adjective meaning "chief" or "main." *Principle* is a noun only, meaning "a rule of conduct," "a doctrine," "a governing rule or truth." (Both *principals* endorsed the request for funds, less for the money itself than for the *principles* that were involved.)

Quiet, quit, quite. *Quiet* means "still" or "calm." (Later, at a *quiet* meeting in the boardroom, he announced his resignation.) *Quit* means "to stop," "to desist." (He *quit* his complaining.) *Quite* means "positively," "entirely." (You are *quite* sure?)

Rang, rung, wrung. *Rang* is the past tense and *rung* is the past participle of the verb *ring*, meaning "to give forth a sound." (I *rang* the bell and then entered. I have *rung* the bell five times and no one has come to the door.) *Wrung* is the past tense of the verb *wring*, "to press or squeeze." (I *wrung* the water from my socks.)

Refer, refer back. *Refer* means "to direct attention" or "to make reference"; therefore, *back* is superfluous. (Please *refer* [not *refer back*] again to my statement.) The same faulty diction occurs in *repeat again* and *return back*.

Regard, regards. *Regard* is used with *as* to mean "consider" or "think." (They *regard* me as a friend.) *In regard to* and *with regard to* are idiomatically sound, but both phrases are wordy and jargonistic. In these same phrases, *regards* is nonstandard. Limit your use of *regards* to the third person singular, present tense form of the verb, as in "He *regards* her as his sister," and to the plural form of the noun *regard*, "Please give your aunt my *regards*."

Saw, seen. The principal parts of *to see* are *see, saw, seen. Seen* is improperly used as the past tense; *saw* is incorrect as the past participle. (I *saw* [not *seen*] my lawyer this morning. I *have seen* [not *have saw*] my lawyer every morning this week.)

Sensual, sensuous. The first refers to gratification of bodily pleasures or appetites. *Sensuous* suggests the appeal of that which is pleasing to the senses. (The movie served no purpose other than to arouse *sensual* desires. The velvet had a *sensuous* softness.)

Shall, will. Distinctions in the use of *shall* and *will* have largely broken down, but a few careful speakers and writers still observe them.

1. Use *shall* in the first person and *will* in the second and third persons to express simple futurity. (I *shall* arrive. You [or She or He or They] *will* arrive.)

2. For *emphasis*, to express determination, command, intention, or promise, use *will* in the first person and *shall* in the second and third persons. (I *will* pay him back, no matter how long it takes. You *shall* pay him back [meaning *must*].)

Should, would. In general, use *should* and *would* according to the rules for *shall* and *will* (see *Shall, will*). The following may be helpful:

1. *Should*

   Obligation—I *should* exercise regularly.

Expectation (a corollary of obligation)—They *should* be on the next train.

Condition—If she *should* be late, telephone her assistant.

Simple future (first person only)—I *should* feel sorry to hear it.

2. *Would*

Habitual action—He *would* walk in the garden during lunch hour.

Condition (*after* a conditional clause)—If it weren't raining, he *would* walk in the garden.

Determination—She *would* do it, even if we objected.

Wish or desire—*Would* that I had accompanied her!

Simple future (second and third persons only)—He said that he *would* go. (If the governing verb is in the past tense, use *would* to express futurity, as above. If the governing verb is in the present tense, use *will:* She *states* that she *will* come with us.)

D
13

Sit, set. *Sit*, predominantly an intransitive verb, not requiring an object, has the meaning of "to place oneself." *Set*, predominantly a transitive verb requiring an object, means "to put" or "to place." (*Set* the lamp by the fireplace and come *sit* by me.) *Set* used for *sit* in the meaning shown is dialectal or an impropriety. However, both words have several special meanings. For example, *set* has an intransitive use, as in "The sun *sets* in the west."

Stationary, stationery. The former means "having a fixed or unmoving position." (Prices remained *stationary* for six months.) *Stationery* means "paper for writing." (My name and address are printed on my *stationery*.)

Statue, stature, statute. A *statue* is a sculptured likeness. (A *statue* of General Grant may be found in the park.) *Stature* can mean "status" and "prestige" or "natural height." (She has great political *stature*. He was a man of tall *stature*.) A *statute* is a law. (This *statute* is unenforceable and should be stricken from the book.)

Tasteful, tasty. The former means "having or showing good taste, sense, or judgment." *Tasty* means "flavorful," "savory," "having the quality of tasting good." (She made a *tasteful* arrangement of linen, china, and silverware. It was her *tasty* casserole of veal, however, that won first prize.) *Tasteful* for *tasty* is in rare or archaic use; *tasty* for *tasteful* is colloquial.

Their, there, they're. These simple and common words cause much difficulty, but they are easy to keep straight. *Their* is a possessive pronoun. (This is *their* house.) *There* means "in or at that place." (Were you *there* when she arrived?) *They're* is a contraction of *they are*. (We are disappointed because *they're* not coming.)

Then, than. These words are often confused in writing and sometimes in pronunciation. *Than* is a conjunction used in clauses of comparison. (Kate made a better score *than* Harvey did.) *Then* is an adverb of time. (You may *then* proceed to clean up.)

These kind, those kind, these sort, those sort. *Kind* and *sort* are singular nouns; *these* and *those* are plural modifiers. Say and write *this kind, those kinds, this sort, those sorts*. (See *Kind of a, sort of a*, Section D14.)

Till, until, 'til. Each of these words means "up to the time of." *Till* and *'til* (a shortened form of *until*) have the same pronunciation and are more often used within a sentence than at the beginning. *Until* more often appears at the beginnings of sentences and is sometimes considered somewhat more formal than its two synonyms. All three terms are correct in standard English.

To, too, two. Correct use of these words is largely a matter of careful spelling. *To* is a preposition (*to* the gate) and the sign of an infinitive (*to* hurry). *Too* is an adverb meaning "also" or "overabundance of." (I *too* am impressed, but Mary is *too* sophisticated *to* show surprise.) *Two* is the number after one. (The *two* soldiers were *too* exhausted *to* run.)

Try and, try to. The correct idiom is *try to*. However, *try and* is in everyday use and has been for a century. Standard English would have you write "*Try to* [not *try and*] finish your work early."

Unmoral, amoral, immoral. *Unmoral* means "having no morality," "nonmoral," "unable to distinguish right from wrong." Thus we may say that an infant or a mentally disordered person is *unmoral*. *Amoral* means "not concerned with moral standards," "not to be judged by criteria or standards of morality." Animals for example, may be called *amoral. Immoral* means "wicked," "contrary to accepted principles of right and wrong." The acts of thieves, murderers, and embezzlers may be called *immoral.*

Unpractical, impractical, impracticable. The first two of these terms are interchangeable, although *impractical* is considered slightly more formal and refined. Each means "not practical," "lacking practical usefulness or wisdom." *Impracticable* means "not capable of being carried out, used, or managed." (It is *impractical* to suggest that a boy be sent on a man's errand. Because of the wind, our leaf-raking methods were *impracticable.*) (See *impractical, impracticable.*)

Who, whom. The former is the nominative case, the latter the objective. When in doubt, try as a memory device the substitution of *she* or *he* for *who,* and *him* or *her* for *whom:* "I am wondering *who* [or *whom?*] we should hire. Should we hire *her?*" Therefore: "I wonder *whom* we should hire."

Who's, whose. The former is a shortened form of *who is.* (*Who's* ahead in the race?) *Whose* is the possessive case of *who.* (*Whose* toes did I step on?)

D
14

D14. Glossary of Misused Words

The following glossary, alphabetically arranged for easy reference, contains words and expressions often misused. A few of these expressions are always to be avoided, but many are unacceptable only in *formal English.* Remember especially that no stigma attaches to the label "colloquial"; it indicates that a given expression is generally more appropriate in conversation and in informal discourse than it is in formal writing.

Usage is so constantly changing that expressions now restricted in some way may later be considered standard. Furthermore, because no dictionary or grammar is a final authority, some usages are disputed. And probably, no two linguists would agree on all the comments that follow. But this illustrative list should be serviceable as a starter.

A, an. *An* should be used before an initial vowel sound, *a* before a word that begins with a consonant sound: *an* answer, *a* battery, *an* honor, *a* hotel.

Absolutely. This word means "perfectly," "wholly," "complete-ly." Besides being greatly overused as an intensifier, it is both wordy and faulty in an expression such as "*absolutely* complete." Never use *absolutely* or any other such modifier with words like *complete, perfect, unique.* (See *Unique.*)

Ad. A colloquial abbreviation, much used for *advertisement.* In strictly formal writing, avoid such abbreviations as *ad, auto* for *automobile, phone* for *telephone, exam* for *examination.*

Advise. This word means "to give advice to." It is overused to mean "tell," or "inform." (I am pleased to *inform* [not *advise*] you that the check has been received.)

Ain't. This contraction is considered illiterate or dialectal and is cautioned against in standard English, both written and spoken. However, the word, which stands for *am not,* is often informally used even by educated people. But it has not been accepted in the sense that *isn't* (for *is not*), *aren't* (for *are not*), and *weren't* (for *were not*) have been.

And etc. A redundant expression. *Etc.* is an abbreviation for the Latin phrase *et cetera,* meaning "and so forth." Omit the *and* in "and etc." (See *Etc.*)

As. One of the most overworked words in the English language. It is a perfectly good word, but *since, because,* and *when* are more exact and effective conjunctions. (*Since* [not *as*] we were alone, we could speak frankly.) *As* is also often misused in place of *that* or *whether.* (I felt *that* [not *as*] I was right.) In negative comparisons some writers prefer *so...as* to *as...as.* (She is not *so* graceful *as* her cousin.) In general, use *as* sparingly; nearly always, a more exact and effective word can be found.

As good as, if not better than. A correctly phrased but awkward and mixed comparison. A statement will be more effective when *if not better* is put at the end. (Awkward: His style is *as good as, if not better than,* your style. Improved: His style is *as good as yours, if not better.*)

Being as. A colloquial or illiterate substitute for *since, because, inasmuch as,* etc. (*Since* [not *being as*] I have a cold, I'll stay indoors.)

Be sure and. This expression is considered both colloquial and unidiomatic. (When you reach Detroit, *be sure to* [not *be sure and*] telephone us.)

Broke. This word has standard uses, but it is a colloquialism or slang when used to mean "out of money." To *go broke* (become penniless) and *go for broke* (dare or risk everything) are slangy expressions.

Cancel out. Omit the *out*. This wordy expression is often used, perhaps by analogy with *cross out* or *strike out*.

Cannot help, cannot help but. The first of these expressions is preferable in such statements as "He *cannot help* mentioning it." The *but* should be omitted since its addition results in a double negative: *cannot help* and *can but*.

Can't hardly. Omit the *not* in the contraction. (I *can* hardly hear you.) *Can't hardly* is a double negative.

Continue on. This is a wordy phrase. *Continue* means to "endure," "to last." Hence *on* is unnecessary.

Cool. In the sense of "lacking warmth," "moderately cold," and several other meanings, *cool* is a useful and correct word. But it is informal or slangy when used to mean "actual" (a *cool* million dollars), "great," and "excellent." It is also highly informal in such debatable expressions as "cool jazz," "cool cat," and "cool customer."

Could of. An illiteracy. Probably because of its sound, it is sometimes written for *could have*. (The rusty nail *could have* [not *could of*] hurt you.) (See *Would of, etc.*)

Data. This word was originally the plural of the Latin *datum* and means "facts and figures from which conclusions can be drawn." Purists consider the word to be plural and use it with a plural verb, but its use with a singular verb is becoming more widespread. (*These* data *are* not reliable. *This* data *is* not reliable.)

Different from, than, to. *Different than* and *different to* are considered colloquial by some authorities, improper and incorrect by others. Even so, these idioms have long literary usage to support them and certainly they are widely used. No one ever objects on any grounds to *different from*. Use *different from* and be safe.

Disremember. An illiteracy. Never use this word in standard English.

Done, don't. The principal parts of this verb are *do, did, done*. *Done* is frequently used incorrectly as the past tense of *do*. We *did* [not *done*] our work early today.) *Don't* is often used incorrectly for *doesn't*. (It *doesn't* [not *don't*] make much difference to me.)

Each . . . are. *Each*, even if not followed by *one*, implies one. Any plural words used in modifying phrases do not change the number. (Each *is* [not *are*] expected to contribute *his or her* time. *Each one* of you *is* a fraud.)

Etc. *Etc.* is an abbreviation of the Latin *et cetera* and means "and so forth." It looks somewhat out of place in formal writing and tends to be overused. Furthermore, it cannot be pronounced in speech without sounding individual letters or giving the entire phrase. Sometimes we use *etc.* at the end of a list to suggest that much more could be added. But do we really have anything in mind? (See *And etc.*)

Faze. The word, which means "to disturb" or "to agitate," is considered informal (colloquial) in this spelling by some authorities. The word *phase* has entirely different meanings.

Feature. As both verb and noun, *feature* is an overworked colloquialism in the sense of "emphasize" or "emphasis." *Feature* is slang in the expression "Can you *feature* that?" meaning, presumably, "Can you imagine that?"

Fed up. An expressive but slangy term meaning "to become disgusted, bored." Do not use it when you are trying to impress an intellectual.

Fine. The word is much overused in the general sense of approval. It is colloquial when used as an adverb. (Mona sang *well* [not *fine* or *just fine*].)

First-rate, second-rate. These words suggesting rank or degree of excellence are vastly overused. *First-rate* is colloquial in the sense of "very good" or "excellent" or "very well."

Fix. This is a word of many meanings. In standard English it means "to make fast." As a verb, it is informal (colloquial) when used to mean "to arrange matters," "to get revenge on," "to repair." As a noun, it is used colloquially for "difficulty."

Folks. This word is colloquial when used to refer to "relatives" and "family." Both dialectal and colloquial is the expression *just folks*, meaning "simple and unassuming people." *Folksy* is a colloquial word for "sociable."

Former, latter. *Former* and *latter* refer to only two units. To refer to a group of more than two items, use *first* and *last* to indicate order.

Free from, free of. The former is idiomatically correct. *Free of* is considered either colloquial or dialectal.

Graduate. This word has several meanings, all of which are in some way related to marking in steps, measuring. Idiom decrees that one *graduate from* (not *graduate*) a school.

Guy. This word has several meanings, but we most often use it colloquially to refer to a man or boy. Some experts regard this use of the word as slang; it should be avoided in formal standard English. To *guy* someone is a highly informal way to express the sense of teasing or joshing.

Have got to. A colloquial and redundant expression for "must," etc. (I *must* [not *have got to*] do my laundry today.) (See *Got, gotten*, Section D13.) *Have* is a useful verb and appears in many expressions we use constantly. In standard English we should avoid using such expressions as *have a check bounce, have cold feet, have a lot on the ball, have it in for someone*. In these expressions the *have* is only partly responsible for the colloquialism.

In accordance to, with. *In accordance with* is the preferred idiom. However, the phrase is wordy and trite.

In back of. This phrase is colloquial for "behind." However, *in the back of* and *in front of* are considered standard terms, although both are wordy. *Behind* and *before* are shorter and nearly always will suffice. (*Behind* [not *in back of*] the counter were six crates. *Before* [or *in front of*] the mirror stood a weary actor.)

In regards to. Omit the *s* in *regards*. Better yet, substitute *concerning* or *about* for the entire phrase; one word is usually more effective than three (See *Regard, regards* in Section D13.)

Inside of, off of, outside of. The *of* in each of these expressions is superfluous. (*Inside* [not *inside of*] the barn the horses are eating hay. The girl fell *off* [not *off of*] her tricycle. Will you travel *outside* [not *outside of*] the state?) When these expressions are not prepositional, the *of* should be included: the *outside of* the house, the *inside of* the tent.

Irregardless, disregardless. Each of these words is an illiteracy. That is, neither is a standard word and neither should be used under any circumstances, formal or informal. The prefixes *ir–* and *dis–* are both incorrect and superfluous in these constructions. Use *regardless.*

Is when, is where. These terms are frequently misused, especially in giving definitions. Grammatically, the fault may be described as using an adverbial clause in place of the noun phrase or clause that is called for. "A subway *is where* you ride under the ground" can be improved to "A subway *is* [or *involves*] an electric railroad beneath the surface of the streets." "Walking *is when* you move about on foot" can be improved to "Walking *is the act of* [or *consists of*] moving about on foot."

Kid. The word means "a young goat," in which sense it is rarely used. But *kid* in two other senses is one of the most common words in the language. We use it to refer to a "child or young person" and we use *to kid* when we mean "to tease, banter, jest with." In both uses the word is dubious in formal standard English.

Kind of a, sort of a. In these phrases the *a* is superfluous. Logically, the main word (which can be *kind, sort,* or *type*) should indicate a class, not one thing.(*What kind of* [not *what kind of a*] party is this?) Although *kind of* and *sort of* are preferred in this construction, these same phrases are often used colloquially to mean "almost," "rather," "somewhat." (She was *rather* [not *kind of*] weary. Martha was *almost* [not *sort of*] resigned to his leaving.)

Knock. In the primary sense of "strike" and in several other meanings, *knock* is a legitimate word on any level of usage. We should avoid its use in such phrases and terms as *to knock* (colloquial for "to criticize"), *to knock about* (colloquial for "to wander"), and *to knock down* (colloquial in the sense of "to embezzle" or "to steal"). *Knock off,* meaning "to stop," as in "to knock off work," is even more frequently heard, but it is still considered colloquial by most authorities.

Let. This word, with a primary meaning of "allow," "permit," has many legitimate uses. Such phrases involving *let* as the following, however, are colloquial and should not be used in standard English: *let on* (in the sense of "pretend"), *let out* (as in "school let out"), *let up* (meaning "cease"). *To let one's hair down* is both colloquial and trite. (See also *Leave, let* in Section D13.)

Line. This standard word has several nonstandard uses. It is considered slang in such expressions as *come into line* (meaning both "agree" and "behave properly"); *get a line on; he gave* [or *fed*] *Joe a line.*

Might of. An illiteracy. (If you had asked, I *might have* [not *might of*] accompanied you.) (See *Would of*, etc.)

Mighty. This word means "strong" or "powerful." When it is used to mean "very" or "extremely," it is considered a colloquialism. (Tom was a *very* [not *mighty*] lucky boy.) (But see *Very*.)

Muchly. An illiteracy. Despite the fact that you may often hear the word, it really does not exist—at least not in standard English. Use *much* instead.

Of. *Of* is an exceedingly common word with a variety of standard uses. However, it is not an allowable substitute for *have* after auxiliary verbs in such expressions as *could of, would of, might of, should of.* (You *should have* [not *should of*] been here yesterday.)

O.K. This everyday term is colloquial or business English for "all right," "correct," "approved." It is occasionally spelled *OK*, or *okay*.

Once-over. A slang term meaning "a swiftly appraising glance."

Pass out. In the sense of "to faint" or "to become unconscious," *pass out* is a useful term but, as slang, should not appear in standard English.

Phony. As both adjective and noun, this word is slang. As a quick and easy substitute for "not genuine," "fake," *phony* is so often used that, presumably, it will in time be acceptable in standard English. Until then, no.

Plenty. This word is colloquial when used to mean "very," "fully." (The water is *very* [not *plenty*] hot today.) But see *Very*.

Quite a. This phrase is colloquial when used to mean "more than." In standard English avoid using such phrases as *quite a few*, *quite a bit*, and *quite a party*.

Real. In the sense of "really" or "very," *real* is an impropriety. (Are you *really* [or *very*, not *real*] certain of your figures?) Adverbial use of *real* is increasing.

Reason is because. In standard English, the construction beginning "The reason . . ." is followed by a noun or a noun clause usually introduced by *that*. Yet we often hear such a sentence

D
14

as "I couldn't go; the *reason was because* I had to work." In spite of its form, the construction introduced by *reason was* is a noun clause rather than an adverbial one. But such a use should appear only in colloquial speech. Standard writing requires "I couldn't go; the *reason was that* I had to work."

Reason why. A redundant expression. Omit *why* and, in most constructions, also omit *reason.* "The *reason why* I like this job is the salary I get" can be improved by writing "I like this job because of the salary."

Setup. In the sense of "an easy victory," this term is slang. More importantly, *setup* is now being used widely to refer to anything related to organization, conditions, or circumstances. (He's got a great *setup.*) The term is vague, at best. Try to find something less used and more exact.

So. *So* is correctly used as a conjunctive adverb with a semicolon preceding, and it is frequently used between independent clauses with only a comma before it. The chief objection to *so* in such constructions is simply *overuse.* In constructions like those below, *so* can often be replaced by *therefore, thus, accordingly,* and the like, or predication may be reduced.

> Ineffective: The jazz concert was canceled, *so* we decided to go to the movies.
> Improved: *Since* the jazz concert was canceled, we decided to go to the movies.

In correcting the overuse of *so*, guard against a worse error, that of using another conjunctive adverb with a comma before it and thus writing an unjustifiable comma splice.

> Wrong: The jazz concert was canceled, *therefore* we decided to go to the movies. [Use a semicolon or a period.]

Sometimes *so* is misused when the writer means *so that* or *in order that.*

> Ineffective: Is it possible to buy potatoes in quantity *so* each potato may cost us less?
> Improved: Is it possible to buy potatoes in quantity *in order that* each potato may cost us less?

Sure. This word is used as adjective or adverb, but it is colloquial in the sense of "surely," "certainly," "indeed." (She was *certainly* [not *sure*] sad to see him go.) *Sure* is also colloquial in such expressions as *sure enough* (meaning both"certainly" and "real") and *surefire* (meaning "certain to be successful"). See *Be sure and.*

Sure thing, a. A slang expression.

Swell. This word is not acceptable in standard English as a modifier. It is colloquial when used to mean "stylish," "fashionable," and it is slang when used as a general term of approval meaning "excellent." (He gave *an excellent* [not *a swell*] lecture.) In the meaning of "conceited," *swelled head* is considered colloquial or slangy.

Thusly. An illiteracy. Use *thus.*

Unique. This word means "having no like or equal" and expresses absoluteness as do words such as *round, square, perpendicular.* Logically, therefore, the word *unique* cannot be compared; something cannot be more unique, less unique, more round, less round. If a qualifying word such as *nearly* is used, the illogicality is removed. "This is the *most unique* statue in the park" is not standard, but "This is the *most nearly unique* statue . . ." is.

Up. This useful little word appears in many verb-adverb combinations (*grow up, give up, take up, use up*). In other phrases it adds nothing to the meaning of the verb; *up* is colloquial (and wordy) in such expressions as *choose up, divide up, finish up, increase up, wait up. On the up and up* is slang. *Up against* (meaning "face-to-face with") and *up against it* (meaning "in difficulty") are colloquial. *Up on* (meaning "informed about") and *up to* (meaning "scheming" or "plotting") are colloquial. *Up-and-coming* and *up one's alley* are other phrases to avoid in standard English. *Open up* is wordy in the sense of "give access to" and is colloquial when used to mean "speak freely."

Used to, use to. In the phrase *used to*, the *d* is often elided in speaking so that it sounds like *use to.* In writing, the *d* must be included.

Very. *Very*, like *so, surely, too, extremely, indeed*, has been so overused that it has lost some of its value as an intensifier. Use these words sparingly and thoughtfully; consider whether your meaning is just as emphatic without them: "You are [very] certain of your position." *Very* is used colloquially to qualify participles; formal use has adverbs like *greatly.*

D
14

Colloquial: I was *very irritated* by his comments.
Formal: I was *greatly irritated* by his comments.
Colloquial: I am *very obliged* to you for giving me the benefit of the doubt.
Formal: I am *much obliged* to you for giving me the benefit of the doubt.

Want for, want in, want out. The *for* in *want for* is dialectal. (She *wants* [not *wants for*] to buy groceries.) Neither *want in* nor *want out* is acceptable in formal English. (The prisoner *wants to get out* [not *wants out*].)

Where. This is a useful word, but it should not be substituted for *that* in standard English. (We saw *that* [not *where*] another dishwasher was needed.)

Where at. This phrase is redundant for *where*. In standard English avoid such a statement as "Steuben couldn't say *where* he was *at*."

Worst kind, worst sort, worst way. Slang terms for *very much, greatly, intensely,* and the like.

Would of, could of, might of, should of. These terms are all illiteracies probably resulting from attempts to represent what is pronounced. In rapid and informal speech, *would have (would've)* has the sound of *would of*. In each phrase, *have* should replace *of*.

You all. In the sense of "all of you," this phrase has a recognized and standard plural meaning. When used to refer to one person, it may be considered either dialectal or an illiteracy.

REVIEW EXERCISE 1

In this exercise, assume that the standards of word choice are those of careful but not overly refined or affectedly fine speech and writing. On a sheet of paper write the capital letter indicating what you would have to substitute (in one or more places) in order to make the sentence acceptable.

A the correct *form* of a word or phrase (for an impropriety or illiteracy)
B a *current* American expression (for a regional, British, or old-fashioned one)
C a *more formal* expression (for slang)

D   a *fresher or simpler* expression (for hackneyed language, jour-
    nalese, or other professional or occupational jargon)

E   a more *straightforward or frank* expression (for euphemism,
    would-be elegance, or affectedly fine writing)

If the sentence fits more than one category, choose the first one
it fits.

1. In the event of your requiring further information in connection
   with this matter, please contact our Cleveland office.
2. I admit it was a pretty crummy thing to say, but she had had it
   coming to her for a long time.
3. Much to my surprise, I found on entering that Mother had summoned a happy gathering to celebrate this anniversary, which
   marked my arrival upon this earth.
4. The mortician concluded his arrangements for the obsequies of
   the dear departed.
5. I wasn't much enthused by the prospect of another lecture on
   driving, but there was no doubt I was in for one.
6. As Doris waited on the corner, the snow drove through her sheer
   stockings, and by the time the bus came her limbs were nearly
   frozen.
7. I've seen some flaky cats before, man, but this one is really off the
   wall.
8. Quite a crowd had gathered outside, and I told them to vamoose,
   but they still wanted in.
9. If the adversary seizes certain available options, a significant es-
   calation of our military involvement is inevitable.
10. The misfortunate boy finally reached dry ground, only to discov-
    er that someone had made off with his clothes.

REVIEW EXERCISE 2

Using diction that is exact, concrete, and effective, write one sentence describing the details involved in each of these situations:

1. The elevator in which you are riding suddenly stalls between
   floors.
2. On the boardwalk, children are watching a Punch-and-Judy
   puppet show.
3. You have just awakened on your first morning at camp and are
   looking out at the woods surrounding you.
4. You are emerging from a movie theater where you have been
   watching an absorbing drama.

5. At a restaurant, you observe a young person attempting to use chopsticks for the first time.

REVIEW EXERCISE 3

Orally or in writing (as your instructor suggests) show different meanings for each of the words given by using the word in a different context—for example, *sharp:* sharp knife, sharp reply, sharp dresser.

1. love	6. fool
2. drill	7. pin
3. window	8. scatter
4. wet	9. slow
5. dull	10. lazy

REVIEW EXERCISE 4

For the italicized words in the following phrases, substitute words that convey a stronger connotation of approval—for example: "a *sickly* girl" could be changed to "a *fragile* girl."

1. A *muddled* report.	6. A *radical* idea.
2. A *snide* comment.	7. A *bigoted* group.
3. A *snobbish* person.	8. A *tyrannical* coach.
4. The child *whined.*	9. A *cowardly* act.
5. They are *moody.*	10. They *gossiped.*

REVIEW EXERCISE 5

For each of the following phrases write (or say) several words that have the same general meaning as the italicized word but are more exact (specific, concrete).

1. A *luscious* cake.	8. This *weapon.*
2. A *bleak* day.	9. A *fearful* day.
3. A *drawn* face.	10. A *confused* child.
4. A *wretched* play.	11. A *riotous* party.
5. He *sighed* strangely.	12. A *strange* feeling.
6. A *fine* solution.	13. A *sweet* person.
7. A *terrible* situation.	14. They *came* home.

15. A *tall* person.
16. The *lazy* clerk.
17. A *bad* suggestion.
18. In the *box*.
19. An *awkward* gesture.
20. A *silly* story.

REVIEW EXERCISE 6

Each sentence in the numbered pairs below may contain a word that does not mean what the writer intended. Select the capital letter indicating that in this respect

    A   the first sentence only is acceptable
    B   the second sentence only is acceptable
    C   both sentences are acceptable
    D   neither sentence is acceptable

1. Vegetation is sparsely scattered to make the most of available water.
   To possess a heated swimming pool is my idea of really luxuriant living.
2. On this sample ballot, recumbent candidates are marked with an asterisk.
   Dictatorial governments are always afraid of dissent.
3. The broken idyl lay prone beside its pedestal with eyes staring at the vacant sky.
   This punishment goes beyond his just desserts.
4. By rights her fellow wrights should be present at the last rites.
   There was no dissent to the charge that this descent from the standard of the club was not decent.
5. These new satellites travel at an incredulous velocity.
   For several years the Mendel family lived next store to us.
6. Many a person has been persuaded to a course of action without being convinced that it was right.
   I was unable to convince him to join our party after the show.
7. There is some nobility in your defying accepted opinion and flaunting conventional beliefs provided the consequences fall on you alone.
   Your account of the affair is favorable to everybody concerned, but I reject it because it is simply not creditable.
8. From the earliest times, marital music has been used to improve military morale.
   She applied to the French consul to have her visa renewed.
9. If you look up that word, you will find that it has a curious entomology.
   I refuse to answer without advice of council.

10. The corps of archers gained access to the fort.
    They wrung the whole sordid story out of him.
11. Some soldiers quickly become adopted to life in the Arctic.
    So far nobody has discovered an anecdote for this poison.
12. The bass singer usually plays the villain in an opera.
    She wore the most bazaar costume at the masquerade.
13. A hundred statutes were passed in the closing session of the legis-
    lature.
    The kind of life she than lead would go against my conscience.
14. The driver of a car with bad brakes gambols with death and may
    lose the bet.
    Plants are classified by genius and species.
15. Her attorney waived the right of cross-examination.
    The sun shone brightly as the ship moved into its berth at the end
    of the pier.

KK 15

The Sentence

All writing of whatever kind is dependent upon that basic unit of composition called the **sentence.** It is not entirely correct to say that we think in terms of words, phrase our thoughts in sentences, and write in paragraphs. But it is true that everyone uses words to form sentences that are then tied together in paragraphs. A sentence is a link between a thought and the full expression of that thought in a paragraph or group of paragraphs. Like all links, the sentence is important. If it is true—and it is—that good sentences derive at least in part from good diction, it is equally true that effective paragraphs and compositions stem from effective sentences.

You would be helped in learning to write effective sentences if you could be provided with a positive statement of what a sentence is. But no fully satisfactory definition is possible. A usable opinion is this: "A sentence consists of one or more words conveying to the reader (or listener) a sense of complete meaning." Another traditional definition is that a sentence is "a group of words containing a subject and a predicate and expressing a complete thought." But problems immediately arise with both definitions. Sentences do not always contain expressed subjects and predicates and, more significantly, do not always express fully complete thoughts.

Normally, we cannot express a fully complete thought until we have written or spoken a series of sentences. A pronoun in one sentence may take its meaning from an antecedent in another. Such words as *again, thus,* and *these* and such phrases as *on the other hand* and *for example* reveal that the thought in one sentence is related to the thought in another. This interrelationship and interdependence of sentences provide further proof of their importance in building larger units of composition—the paragraph and the theme.

A sentence should indeed contain a group of words that is grammatically self-sufficient as, for example, "She was one of the great romantic figures of history." This sentence has a subject, *she*, and predicate, *was;* it begins with a capital letter and ends with a period. But its complete meaning depends upon other sentences that tell us that *she* refers to Cleopatra and that Cleopatra was a great romantic figure because she was a queen of Egypt, because she led a revolt supported by Julius Caesar, because she married two of her own brothers and was mistress to Caesar, to whom she bore a son, because she had a love affair with Marc Antony, because she died from the bite of an asp, and because she was acknowledged to be a fabulously alluring woman.

Learning to write effective sentences is a central goal of education. But your efforts to learn the meanings of the parts of speech and the distinctions between the kinds, uses, and patterns of sentences will be wasted until that knowledge operates upon the sentences that you write or speak. The following sections are designed to help you write sentences that are grammatically correct and rhetorically effective and to enable you to see why and how you do so.

S1. The Sentence Fragment

All groups of words that make sense to the reader or hearer can be called sentences. However, to be coherent, a sentence must be *complete.* That is, it must contain both a subject and a predicate (verb) that are expressed or clearly implied. Also, it must not begin with a connecting word such as *because, before,* and *while* unless an independent clause follows immediately in the same construction. An incomplete sentence, one that does not meet the previous two requirements, is called a **sentence fragment.**

For example, the statement "Susan has cut her hair" is a coherent and complete sentence. But it could not stand by itself if the subject, *Susan,* were omitted or if the verb, *has cut,* were replaced by a compound participle such as *having cut.* Moreover, the use of some connecting word such as *because* before *Susan* will make the sentence incomplete: "Because Susan has cut her hair" requires the support of some other statement. The fully coherent sentence could be "Because Susan has cut her hair, she no longer resembles my sister."

In oral communication, sentence fragments are common and even effective, as is noted in Section S1d. Also, you must have noticed that many advertisements make use of incomplete sentences both to conserve space and to focus on key words. Neither of these practices should be used as excuses for sentence fragments in carefully prepared papers.

S1a. AVOID SETTING OFF A PHRASE AS A SENTENCE.

A phrase is only part of a full sentence. It should be attached to the sentence with which it belongs. Or it should be made to stand by itself through the addition of a subject, a predicate, or both.

Incomplete: *Spring having come late that year.* The lilacs were not yet in bloom.

Improved: Spring having come late that year, the lilacs were not yet in bloom.
Spring came late that year, and the lilacs were not yet in bloom.

Incomplete: Mary constantly talks about herself. *Without regard for other people's interests.*

Improved: Mary constantly talks about herself without regard for other people's interests.

Incomplete: I have two purposes in dieting. *To trim my waistline and to save money.*

Improved: I have two purposes in dieting. I wish to trim my waistline and to save money.
I have two purposes in dieting: to trim my waistline and to save money.

S1b. AVOID SETTING OFF A DEPENDENT CLAUSE AS A SENTENCE.

Adjective and adverbial clauses are frequently mistaken for sentences. The adjective clause may be wrongly set off as a sentence when it properly should be at the end of an independent clause. Similarly, the adverbial clause may be wrongly set off as a sentence when it properly should be at the beginning or end of an independent clause.

A dependent-clause fragment can often be corrected, with no change in wording, by substituting a small for a capital letter and replacing a period with a comma or no mark at all. Or a dependent adjective clause can be made independent by changing the relative pronoun into a personal pronoun and an adverbial clause be made independent by omitting the subordinating conjunction.

Incomplete: We have talked with a marine biologist. *Who is convinced that the seas can feed the world.* (adjective)

The desk had a secret drawer. *Into which I stuffed the muddy bills.* (adjective)

Wadsworth gave up hope. *When suddenly a ship appeared on the horizon.* (adverbial)

Unless all planes are grounded. We shall take off for Denver in less than an hour. (adverbial)

Improved: We have talked with a marine biologist who is convinced that the seas can feed the world.

We have talked with a marine biologist. He is convinced. . . .

The desk had a secret drawer into which I stuffed the muddy bills.

Wadsworth gave up hope. Suddenly a ship appeared on the horizon.

Unless all planes are grounded, we shall take off for Denver in less than an hour.

S1c. AVOID STARTING A STATEMENT WITH ONE CONSTRUCTION AND THEN STOPPING OR SHIFTING TO ANOTHER.

An unfinished or incomplete sentence results when a writer begins a statement and then shifts thought, adding words, yet stopping before giving meaning to the opening words. Or the writer may start with an independent clause but then add an unfinished statement and forget to coordinate it with the first independent statement. In correcting such unfinished constructions, the writer should determine carefully what is missing and then supply it, in proper grammatical elements:

Incomplete: An injured man in the apartment, who, because he had become progressively more lame, was forced to use a cane and then to be confined to a wheelchair.

Improved: An injured man in the apartment, who, because he had become progressively more lame, was forced to use a cane and then to be confined to a wheelchair, ordered the landlord to install a telephone in his kitchen.

Incomplete: I thought that preparing dinner for eight guests would be a simple matter, but after deciding on a menu and shopping for the food, being very careful to stay within my budget, and then spending hours over a hot stove that burned the lima beans and three of my fingers.

Improved: I thought that preparing dinner for eight guests would be a simple matter, but after deciding on a menu and shopping for the food, being very careful to stay within my budget, and then spending hours over a hot stove that burned the lima beans and three of my fingers, I realized that a dinner party is a formidable undertaking.

S1d. USE ONLY JUSTIFIABLE SENTENCE FRAGMENTS.

A sentence, when defined grammatically, consists of a subject and predicate and expresses a complete thought. Yet, various statements without an actual or implied subject and verb can also express a full thought. Expressions such as *hello, what a day, sure, ouch, enough for now* are *grammatically* only sentence fragments; otherwise, they are clear and forceful. They are often found in dialogue because they represent normal conversation. Put in context, they amply serve to answer questions and to give details after general statements. Sentence fragments in the following piece of dialogue, for example, are fully justifiable:

"Where are you going tonight?"
"To the concert."
"You have tickets?"
"Sure."
"Lucky you."
"I know."

EXERCISE 1

Correct the unjustifiable sentence fragments in the following by attaching them logically to materials with which they belong.

1. There are many words that he uses incorrectly. Such as *have went* for *have gone*, *I seen* instead of *I saw*, and many, many others.
2. Since school afforded few extracurricular activities of any kind. I participated in all those that were offered.
3. Senior week we shall never forget. The magnificent prom, a great picnic, and much fun.
4. Winter does something to me. When the snow leaves a white blanket over the ground.
5. My clothing bill for this summer was $415. This being more than double what I expected to spend.
6. Then Mother begins preparing Thanksgiving dinner. Roast turkey and dressing, mashed potatoes and gravy, baked beans, coleslaw, pickles, radishes, and carrots.
7. I slid through high school as an otter slides down a snowy hill. Free and easy without a care in the world. Not caring about anything.
8. The next experience that I recalled happened to Carlotta and me. Carlotta being the driver, of course.
9. The plane rose higher and higher. Its wings swept back and its nose piercing the air.
10. Magazine rates for three-year subscriptions are cheaper. Thereby saving the subscriber a considerable sum of money.
11. Knowing that he did well on the exam. Bob was greatly relieved.

EXERCISE 2

Expand into sentences the unjustifiable sentence fragments in the following statements.

1. I wish I could go back to my first year in high school. With the knowledge I have now about how important study is and the importance of good study habits.
2. New York City—a place everyone would like to visit.
3. A man of average height and rugged build, with silvery gray hair, his hair indicating that he was in his fifties.
4. In college there is nobody to tell you to get up in the morning. Nobody to make you study.

5. The whine continued and Janice got more and more nervous. If only she could stop the noise.

6. The name of our farm is The Oaks. Named thus because of the abundant growth of oak trees.

7. Fraternities want you to be a "big activities" man on the campus. Get you into all the activities they can load you down with and then they wonder why your grades in school are so low.

8. Experience is a good but expensive teacher. Although after making a costly mistake, one usually never lets it take place again.

9. The card catalog has three divisions. The first of which contains the author cards.

10. Thoughtless, self-centered drivers can cause accidents. Where if they had yielded the right of way, lives could have been saved.

S2. The Comma Splice

When our thoughts stray from or dart ahead of our writing, we may find that, instead of setting down full sentences one at a time, we are splicing, or joining, with a comma statements that should be separated by a period or should be linked by a semicolon, a colon, or a conjunction *and* a comma. Such **comma splices,** considered faulty in both punctuation and in sentence construction, are serious flaws because the reader cannot determine where one sentence ends and the next one begins.

S2a. AVOID UNJUSTIFIABLE COMMA SPLICES.

Comma splices, or *comma faults*, occur in several forms:

1. Two statements that are not grammatically related but that are related by content

   Our alumni dinner will be held on Friday evening, the new Dean of Admissions will be introduced.

2. Two related statements, the second of which begins with a personal pronoun whose antecedent is in the first

   The sentry bent over the crumpled form, he let out a low, soft whistle.

3. Two related statements, the second of which begins with a demonstrative pronoun or adjective (*that, this, those, these, such*)

> Make use of the suggestions on the label, these are very helpful.

4. Two statements, the second of which begins with or contains a conjunctive adverb (*nevertheless, however, then,* etc.)

> I made the four-o'clock train, however, my brother couldn't meet me.

There are several ways to correct a comma splice error:

1. Use a period after the first statement and capitalize the first letter of the second.
2. Use a semicolon between the statements.
3. Place a conjunction between the statements, or as a substitute for the conjunctive adverb, and retain the comma.
4. Subordinate one of the statements and retain the comma.

One or more of these methods can be used to correct the comma splices illustrated above. Be careful to avoid a succession of short, choppy sentences, and do not attempt to show a causal relationship where in fact it does not exist without proper subordination.

S2b. USE A JUSTIFIABLE COMMA SPLICE WHEN IT IS EFFECTIVE AND APPROPRIATE.

Many writers and editors carefully avoid all comma splices on the grounds that a comma splice is a serious error that always confuses the reader. However, occasional examples of such faults have been deemed justifiable because they are stylistically effective in certain constructions. In such cases the independent clauses are short and closely related in form and meaning. Consider, for example, the following:

> It bubbled, it welled, it shot into the air.
> You do not show courage, you show recklessness.
> That is the library, this is the Town Hall.
> *Philosophy* comes from two Greek words: *philos* means "loving," *sophia* means "wisdom."

EXERCISE 3

Correct all the comma faults in the following sentences. If possible, correct each one by all the methods suggested above. Arrange corrected versions in the order of most effective to least effective.

1. Our farm is not too large, it consists of 200 acres.
2. One defect is incorrect spelling, the other is the occasional use of faulty diction.
3. Baseball would probably die out if the typical spectators didn't like to criticize, thus when they attend a game, they can really blow off their steam.
4. Let's share our vacation experiences, here are mine.
5. The streets are not clean, the buildings lining the streets are old, dirty, and broken-down.
6. The students and the teacher did not get along properly, therefore, about all I remember was a riot each day.
7. Most students do not find the subject matter too hard, instead they find it hard to adjust to the new way of college life.
8. "We do not have a thirteenth floor," she explained, "it is a superstition of the hotel."
9. A town that should be interesting to you is Harrisburg, it is the capital of Pennsylvania.
10. It seemed to me that the day nursery school would be much more suitable to me than teaching, consequently I changed my course of study.

EXERCISE 4

Follow the directions for Exercise 3.

1. First he was a rail-splitter, then several years later he became a lawyer.
2. Dee sends away for dozens of free samples, she has acquired a large collection of them.
3. We forgot to bring the hamburgers, this made the picnic less successful than it could have been.
4. This teacher gives few high grades, however, he is popular.
5. Whenever Juanita goes to the beach, it rains, we seldom go swimming with Juanita.
6. Send all the pizzas to Ms. Oliver's house, she has ordered them for a birthday party.

7. Give your ticket to the attendant, someone will take you to the parking lot.
8. I worked on that paper for a month, nevertheless, it received a low grade.
9. We want two quarts of strawberries, these seem like good ones.
10. The kennel was closed on Sunday, we returned the next day to get our dog.

S3. The Fused Sentence

An error even more serious than a comma splice is the **fused sentence.** In the former, at least some indication of separation between statements is given. In the latter, two complete sentences are fused or pushed together with no punctuation at all. The reader is therefore unable to tell where one full thought ends and another full thought begins.

S3a. DO NOT WRITE TWO SENTENCES WITH NO PUNCTUATION BETWEEN THEM.

A sentence should always be followed by a *terminal mark:* a period, question mark, or exclamation point.

> Fused: The Depression deepened its hold on American business thousands of people lost their jobs and breadlines became a common sight.
>
> When he left the Army, Herbert took up horseracing this activity is often called the sport of kings.

Judged by grammatical standards, each of the above "sentences" contains two independent and distinct statements that can be written separately. If the writer decides that two statements are sufficiently related in thought, they may be connected more closely with punctuation that is not terminal.

> Improved: The Depression deepened its hold on American business. Thousands of people lost their jobs, and breadlines became a common sight.
>
> When he left the Army, Herbert took up horseracing. This activity is often called the sport of kings.
>
> When he left the Army, Herbert took up horseracing, often called the sport of kings.

S3b. AVOID CORRECTING A FUSED SENTENCE BY PLACING A COMMA BETWEEN ITS PARTS.

Two complete sentences should never be fused. However, to separate them with a comma would result in another violation of unity: the comma splice. A comma splice is about as grave an offense as the fused sentence. (See Section S2.) A comma is not adequate in a sentence such as this: "We lived in Springdale two years ago our house was in the center of town." To correct a fused sentence, use the same methods that would correct a comma splice. (See Section S2a.)

> We lived in Springdale two years ago. Our house was in the center of town.
> We lived in Springdale two years ago; our house was in the center of town.
> We lived in Springdale two years ago, and our house was in the center of town.
> When we lived in Springdale two years ago, our house was in the center of town.

EXERCISE 5

Correct the following by using terminal marks of punctuation or by subordination.

1. Then suddenly we knew what was wrong the man in the middle had no face.
2. She is an excellent performer, one of the best in the state, I think do you think so, too?
3. I'm afraid dinner will be delayed the French fried potatoes are acting up again.
4. Curtis was too shy to play the piano before so many strangers moreover he had no piano.
5. Lucy remained in Germany for two years when she returned to enter college.
6. "Help Help" the man cried I hurried to the edge of the river, but I could see that he was only playing.
7. Concita was garrulous I did not pay any attention to her harangue.
8. I'll tell you one thing it surely is hard to eat peas in a small airplane.
9. But how could Ronald get into the laboratory to release the mice with whose connivance could he have entered the building?

10. I'll show you how to do it just break off the neck of the bottle and jump back.
11. All at once we knew the answer we knew John was telling the truth.

EXERCISE 6

Follow the directions for Exercise 5.

1. When the roar of the engines is loudest, I hold my ears I like to spend hours at the airport watching arrivals and departures.
2. The coach was pessimistic her players were not.
3. The most difficult putts in golf are often short they require the utmost concentration.
4. The artist's garden overlooked the river the neighbors coveted her superb view.
5. Paddy ran the mile in 4:02 we had no idea he could run so fast.
6. The scarecrow did not frighten the wily birds it attracted them in flocks.
7. They could sterilize the outside of a space vehicle they could not kill all the germs inside without ruining electronic equipment.
8. The stags fought viciously the spectators stood at a safe distance.
9. The whistle sounded the beginning of the game the players tensed their muscles.
10. I don't know how it happened I just took my eyes off the road.

S4. Unity

Unity, which means "singleness of purpose," demands that a sentence express a single thought or group of closely related thoughts. Sentence unity has little to do with sentence length. A long sentence may contain several references to people, places, things, or ideas and still be unified. A short sentence may refer to one person only and yet be ununified. This extended sentence shows unity of thought: "Although her friend claimed that Winona made the honor roll without effort, often at midnight she could be found at her desk, nibbling on a favorite snack of peanut-butter crackers as she painstakingly reread all of her written homework." But this next sentence, only a fraction as long, lacks unity: "Winona was a good student, and she liked peanut-butter crackers."

S4a. AVOID RAMBLING SENTENCES THAT CONTAIN TOO MANY DETAILS.

Rambling: As I grew older, my desire to play basketball grew also, and when I entered high school I was too small to play my first two years of school, being only five feet tall, so I had to sit on the bench, but later in high school I began to grow, and before I graduated my senior year I was playing center on the first team, for I had grown 13 inches in two years.

Improved: Although my interest in basketball had grown with the years, I discovered upon entering high school that my physical growth had not kept pace with my desire to play. For two years my five-foot frame glumly occupied the bench. Before I graduated, however, I was playing center on the first team. The reason is a simple one: in the years between I had grown 13 inches.

S4b. AVOID PLACING UNRELATED IDEAS IN THE SAME SENTENCE.

When unrelated ideas occur in the same sentence, unity can sometimes be achieved by showing some evidence of relationship or by subordinating one idea to another. If the ideas are not closely related and cannot be made to link, use separate sentences. If no relationship whatever exists, one of the ideas should be omitted.

Unrelated: His brother was a tall man, and he was a good sprinter.

Improved: His brother, a tall man who loved to run, was a good sprinter.
His brother was a tall man. He was also a good sprinter.

EXERCISE 7

Rewrite the following sentences, making one idea subordinate to the other in sentences where the parts are sufficiently related. If the parts are not sufficiently related, divide them into two sentences.

1. My cousin was given a handsome watch for graduation, and he has gone to Philadelphia on the senior trip.
2. I want to get a good liberal education, and history, which is a required course, is difficult for me.
3. Karin's roommate is the most absentminded girl I have ever known, and she comes from San Francisco.
4. We paid a guide ten dollars for taking us across the island-studded bay, and the scenery was very beautiful.
5. The asphalt highway was slippery when it was wet, and it led from Islip to Center Moriches.
6. Chicago is a city with a large metropolitan population, and it is located on Lake Michigan.
7. My sister is an excellent swimmer and was born on the Fourth of July.
8. Last summer my family and I went on a long trip through the West, and I have always liked to drive.
9. Carlos said to Jane, "I love you; will you please lend me five dollars until tomorrow?"
10. July 1 is Dominion Day in Canada, and large uranium discoveries have been made there.

EXERCISE 8

Divide the following into unified sentences, supplying or deleting words where necessary.

1. The band was astonished to learn that it was to play an engagement in Oyster Junction, a whistle-stop a day's drive from Wichita with no suitable hotel accommodations, and they blamed their manager, Freddie Swange, a fellow with a good business head but little interest in music, for booking them where they couldn't even get a decent meal.

2. Because the need to meet our nation's ever-increasing energy demands has become a major area of concern, whether the energy is gasoline for cars, or gas or electricity for homes and industry, many people feel that we should make greater efforts to apply solar energy, which is a free and self-replenishing energy supply, as well as a strict conservation measure.

3. The job was a good one for Mr. Ashe, who couldn't get around very well because of his foot trouble, a recurrent tendonitis that had not responded very well to the treatment prescribed by Dr. Goslin, who had been trained at the Mayo Clinic and who should have been able to cure tendonitis if anyone could.

S5. Misused Dependent Clauses

All dependent clauses have the functions of one of three parts of speech—noun, adjective, adverb. To substitute one such clause for another is as serious an error as, for example, misusing an adjective for an adverb. The most common misuses are (1) an adverbial clause used for a noun clause, (2) an adverbial clause used as a substitute for a noun, (3) a full sentence used for either a noun clause or a noun.

S5a. DO NOT USE AN ADVERBIAL CLAUSE AS A NOUN CLAUSE.

A noun clause is properly the subject of a verb, the object of a verb, or a predicate nominative—an adverbial clause is not. To correct a misused adverbial clause, change it into a noun clause or supply a verb that the adverbial clause can modify.

> Faulty: Rafael remembered *where the radio said* the stock market is dropping.
> *Because there was no use in her staying* was the reason Sandy left the meeting.
> Improved: Rafael remembered *that the radio said* the stock market is dropping.
> Sandy left the meeting *because there was no use in her staying.*

S5b. DO NOT USE AN ADVERBIAL CLAUSE IN PLACE OF A SINGLE NOUN OR NOUN PHRASE.

For reasons similar to those that apply above, avoid using adverbial clauses for single nouns or noun phrases. *When, where,* and *because* clauses are frequent offenders, as in the following faulty examples.

Faulty: False flattery is *when* you pay a lot of compliments that are not sincere.

My sailing trophy was *because* I won three races out of four.

Improved: False flattery is paying a lot of insincere compliments.

False flattery is the payment of a lot of compliments that are not sincere.

Winning three races out of four gained me the sailing trophy.

I earned the sailing trophy by winning three races out of four.

S5c. USE A NOUN CLAUSE, NOT A SENTENCE, AS THE SUBJECT OR COMPLEMENT OF *IS* AND *WAS*.

The use of a quoted sentence is generally accepted as a subject or complement:

"Because I could not stop for Death,/He kindly stopped for me" are two famous lines from a poem by Emily Dickinson.

In general, however, a sentence cannot be suitably used as a subject or complement of *is* and *was*. To correct the illogical construction, do one of the following: (1) change the sentence, or independent clause, into an adverbial clause; (2) reduce the independent clause to a phrase; (3) make the sentence into a dependent clause by using the proper subordinating conjunction, usually *that*.

Faulty: I had broken my leg was the reason I resigned from the team.

Bill's only virtue is he never is rude to his parents.

Improved: The reason that I resigned from the team was that I had broken my leg.

I resigned from the team because I had broken my leg.

Bill's only virtue is that he is never rude to his parents.

Bill has only one virtue: never being rude to his parents.

EXERCISE 9

Correct the following sentences:

1. Their home is where you can always have a pleasant visit.
2. A state of rebellion is when armed forces seize control of the government.
3. The reason the mower did not cut the grass was because its blades were dull.
4. I see in the paper where the weather has been unusually cold this winter.
5. The seat of the chair has been stood on so often by you children is the cause for its giving way under Mrs. Smith.
6. Only because they have formal clothes is why the dance is being held.
7. His definition of freedom is when you can look anyone squarely in the eye.
8. Perjury is where a person swears to tell the truth and then tells a lie.
9. Her father pointed out where she had been making the same mistakes for years.
10. The thing that upset our chickens was a skunk came into the henhouse looking for eggs.

S 5

EXERCISE 10

Follow the directions for Exercise 9.

1. The reason why students who drive a distance are late is because of mechanical trouble or road conditions.
2. Where a person takes and uses someone else's writing without giving proper credit is what is known as plagiarism.
3. When a girl can make her own decisions is when her parents feel she is maturing.
4. Whenever there are noises during study hours is the time Paula really gets angry.
5. Wherever large crowds gather is a sign of possible trouble.
6. In late May is when the peonies are in full bloom in this town.
7. If you work hard is one of the conditions of employment.
8. He had a fever is the reason he couldn't go to school.
9. Double-talk can be when you say one thing and mean another.
10. Jacques remembered where the announcer said the storm was over.

S6. Misplaced Modifiers

Relationships between words in an English sentence depend largely upon the *order* in which those words occur. Consider how the meaning of the following sentence changes as the position of the adjective is shifted:

> My *first* wife's job was in market research.
> My wife's *first* job was in market research.

Related words should be kept together so that their connection can be clearly seen. **Modifiers,** especially, should be placed close to the words or phrases they are intended to modify. (For a more detailed explanation of what the term *modify* means, see Section G4.)

S6a. AVOID A "SQUINTING" MODIFIER.

When a modifier is placed so that it could as readily modify the word or phrase preceding it as the word or phrase immediately following, it is said to "look two ways" or to be a **"squinting" modifier.** In the sentence "The boy who is delivering our mail *currently* needs a haircut," there is ambiguity. Is the boy who needs a haircut in current possession of the delivery chore, or is the official delivery boy in current tonsorial distress?

In speaking, there would be no problem. If you intended *currently* to modify, or go with, *delivering*, you would pause after saying it and before going on to *needs a haircut*. Or if you meant *currently* to modify *needs a haircut*, you would pause after *mail*. In speech, words have sound boundaries that show their relationship to other words. This aspect of spoken language is known as *juncture*, further defined in Section G10.

To clear up the confusion in writing such a sentence, you should revise. One way to do this is to add *certainly* after *currently*. In this way, you indicate that the adverb *currently* modifies *is delivering*, and the adverb *certainly* applies to *needs*. Another method is to move the modifier and include it with the material it modifies, i.e., transfer *currently* to a position between *who* and *is*, or (if such is the writer's intention), to a position following *hair-*

cut. If the resulting sentence is still awkward, rewrite it. Punctuation may also help in this instance, but it is not always a reliable guide.

S6b. PROPERLY POSITION SUCH WORDS AS *EVEN, HARDLY, NOT, ONLY, SCARCELY.*

These words (and similar ones like the correlative conjunctions —*both . . . and, either . . . or, not only . . . but also*) can cause confusion to the reader unless they are placed precisely.

Note how the position of *only* affects the following sentence in eight different ways:

> *Only* my sister asked me to lend her a few dollars.
> My *only* sister asked me to lend her a few dollars.
> My sister *only* asked me to lend her a few dollars.
> My sister asked *only* me to lend her a few dollars.
> My sister asked me *only* to lend her a few dollars.
> My sister asked me to lend *only* her a few dollars.
> My sister asked me to lend her *only* a few dollars.
> My sister asked me to lend her a few dollars *only.*

Such words as *only* are generally associated with the word or phrase immediately following or preceding. Thus:

> Ineffective: I *only* have one more lawn to mow.
> They *scarcely* have enough food to sustain them.
> More effective: I have *only* one more lawn to mow.
> They have *scarcely* enough food to sustain them.

S6c. PROPERLY POSITION PHRASES AND CLAUSES.

Modifying phrases and clauses, like modifying words, should be so placed that their meaning is entirely clear. Writers of the following could not have meant what their sentences say:

> We put the cake in the refrigerator, which we would eat the next day.
> I gave a jar of cucumbers to the teacher freshly pickled.
> WANTED: Asst. Supervisor for kindergarten children with college degree.

S
6

EXERCISE 11

Revise the following sentences by repositioning misplaced modifiers.

1. Fanta was singing as she walked home at the top of her voice.
2. Last summer Mrs. Wiggans almost killed thirty chickens a week.
3. We only bought small souvenirs to take home to our family and friends.
4. He first met the woman who was to become his wife on a crowded bus.
5. Shirley dumped the food right into the garbage can that she had on her tray.
6. A person who tries to show off frequently may be insecure.
7. Mario kept the skin of the tiger he had shot in his den.
8. Until recently, hay has either been taken from the field loose or in bales.
9. She asked him to meet her when night fell in front of the house.
10. At birth we all know that an infant is incapable of taking care of itself.
11. Ben was proud of the bookcase he had built from his own design in his bedroom.
12. My cousins John and Dan whom I visited recently went to Colorado for a vacation with their parents.

EXERCISE 12

Follow the directions for Exercise 11.

1. Unsatisfied creditors go away seldom happily.
2. Violet says that she remembers Christmases spent as a little girl well.
3. I hardly ever think that Jane and Joe go to the movies.
4. A coffee table stood before the fireplace with carved legs and a glass top.
5. The week Jerry made 20 dollars it almost seemed like a million.
6. We decided entirely to trust Danielle.
7. It was a beautiful sunny morning, such as you can only find in the North Woods.
8. Never give fruit to a baby that hasn't been strained.
9. The teacher picked up the essay Frances had written with a sigh.
10. The college Carla chose after deliberation rejected her application.

S7. Dangling Modifiers

A **dangling modifier** is a modifier that does not clearly and sensibly refer to some word in the sentence. Dangling modifiers are usually verbal phrases, including participial, infinitive, and gerund phrases. Sometimes they are elliptical clauses. Most often, dangling modifiers occur at the beginning of a sentence.

Dangling modifiers hang loosely in the sentence and produce confusion. Note the sentence below.

> Dangling: *Opening* the door, the odor of strong perfume struck me at once. (The subject of the clause is *odor*, but odor did not open the door.)

S7a. AVOID DANGLING VERBAL PHRASES.

Two methods can be used to correct sentences containing dangling verbal phrases: (1) making the verbal phrase an adverb clause; (2) adding the noun or pronoun (substantive) that the phrase sensibly modifies.

> Dangling: *Standing at the station*, the train hurtled by. (participial phrase)
> *To drive safely*, a good set of tires is needed. (infinitive phrase)
> *In typing a theme*, it is advisable to use wide margins. (gerund phrase)
>
> Improved: While I was standing at the station, the train hurtled by.
> Standing at the station, I saw the train hurtle by.
> To drive safely, you need a good set of tires.
> When you are typing a theme, it is advisable to use wide margins.

Participial phrases tacked on to the end of a statement with *thereby*, *thus*, and *therefore* are also dangling because they have no substantive to modify. Sentences containing such constructions can be corrected by rephrasing or by including the participle in a compound predicate.

> Dangling: I was taken aside by Della, thus causing me to lose my place in line.

S
7

Improved:	I was taken aside by Della and thus lost my place in line.
	Being taken aside by Della caused me to lose my place in line.

NOTE: When a verbal phrase is used to express a general action rather than a specific one, it is *not* held to be a dangling modifier:

> Generally speaking, tennis is a strenuous sport.

Words or phrases such as *according to, concerning, considering, owing to,* etc., are used prepositionally, not as verbals. "*Considering the circumstances,* he is not to be blamed" is a clear and proper sentence.

S7b. AVOID DANGLING ELLIPTICAL CLAUSES.

An **elliptical clause** is one from which the subject, verb, or both have been left out. Such a clause dangles unless the omitted subject or predicate, intended to be understood, is in fact the same as that of the main clause.

Dangling:	Though crying for attention, my aunt ignored the baby.
	When thirty-two, his third son was born.
	Before completely adjusted, you should not use this compass.

To correct such unclear sentences you should insert the needed subject and verb in the dependent clause or change the subject or subject and verb in the main clause.

Improved:	Though he was crying for attention, my aunt ignored the baby.
	Though crying for attention, the baby was ignored by my aunt.
	When he was thirty-two, his third son was born.
	When thirty-two, he rejoiced at the birth of his third son.
	Before it is completely adjusted, you should not use this compass.
	You should completely adjust this compass before you use it.

EXERCISE 13

Rewrite the following sentences so that they contain no dangling modifiers.

1. While lecturing to the class, a fly lit on the tip of Professor Moriarty's nose.
2. To understand the Middle Ages, Dante should be read with great care.
3. Being the oldest child of the family, Mother made an example of me in front of my brothers and sisters.
4. At the age of eleven, Wanda's father remarried.
5. If held correctly, one can get much pleasure from a kaleidoscope.
6. Looking over my right shoulder, Mount Mansfield was very impressive.
7. Stepping inside the huge building, a jet airplane is seen.
8. Being a small town in a farming community, the stores are open only on Saturday nights.
9. Just before slithering through a tiny hole in the wall, Morris caught the weasel.
10. Having never before been in Kansas, Wichita was a pleasant surprise.

S
7

EXERCISE 14

Follow the directions for Exercise 13.

1. A good dictionary should be at hand when writing themes.
2. Fish are easy to catch in these waters when using the right bait.
3. Falling softly past the window, we watched the first snow of the winter.
4. Having lost consciousness, the coach sent in a substitute for Sean.
5. Looking to the left and to the right, the water could be seen.
6. To punish me for misbehaving, I was forbidden use of the car for a full month.
7. Rose-colored glasses should always be worn when going on a blind date.
8. Not much interested in literature, especially poetry, *Hamlet* was lost on Cindy.
9. To make a good cake, fresh eggs are always required.
10. The napkin should always be kept in the lap when dining in a restaurant.

S8. Split Constructions

Nothing is actually incorrect about splitting, or separating, related elements in a sentence. However, in the interests of clarity, one should try to keep related materials as closely together as possible. Awkwardness often results from splitting such elements as verbs in a verb phrase, the parts of an infinitive, a preposition and its object, and other word combinations that logically belong together.

S8a. AVOID THE UNNECESSARY SEPARATION OF THE PARTS OF A VERB PHRASE.

Splitting an auxiliary verb and a main verb is rarely effective or natural. Consider the following sentences:

> The instructor *has*, although one would hardly believe it, *been* lecturing for over an hour.
> This was the recording we *had*, before we left Chicago, *heard* so often in discotheques.
> He *has*, to my great surprise, *sung* very well.

By bringing together the words in italics, the sentences become clearer and more direct:

> Although one would hardly believe it, the instructor *has been* lecturing for over an hour.
> This was the recording we *had heard* so often in discotheques before we left Chicago.
> To my great surprise, he *has sung* very well.

S8b. AVOID AWKWARD SPLITTING OF INFINITIVES.

A **split infinitive** occurs when words, phrases, or clauses are inserted between the infinitive sign *to* and the verb. Many good writers use and defend a split infinitive. It is true that in some constructions the split infinitive makes a smoother or more emphatic sentence, but it often makes an awkward sentence. Clearness and naturalness must be the test.

Permissible:	After we had caught a beautiful rainbow trout, we went home *to proudly display* our prize. (*Proudly to display* or *to display proudly* makes the sentence stiff.)
Unnecessary:	The radio announcer told the audience *to vigorously applaud* when he raised his hand.
Improved:	The radio announcer told the audience *to applaud vigorously* when he raised his hand.

S8c. AVOID THE UNNECESSARY SEPARATION OF SUBJECT AND VERB, PREPOSITION AND OBJECT, AND OTHER CLOSELY RELATED SENTENCE ELEMENTS.

On occasion, separation of such elements achieves special clarity. In general, however, the italicized elements in the sentences below should be written together:

> The king *summoned*, as soon as I had made my proposal, *his councillors*.
> *Gina*, upon hearing the remark, *reached for the telephone*.
> Billie walked *under*, although she was superstitious, *the ladder*.

S8d. PLACE COORDINATE ELEMENTS TOGETHER.

Two coordinate phrases or two coordinate dependent clauses should not be widely separated. Because of their approximately equal weight, they should be brought together and their relationship indicated by the appropriate coordinating conjunction:

Ineffective:	*Although he was conscientious on the job*, he could not win a promotion, *although he performed many extra duties*.
Effective:	*Although he was conscientious on the job* and *although he performed many extra duties*, he could not win a promotion.
Ineffective:	*Unless the blizzard lets up*, we cannot make it to the mountain lodge, *unless the roads are passable*.
Effective:	*Unless the blizzard lets up* and *unless the roads are passable*, we cannot make it to the mountain lodge.

EXERCISE 15

Find and correct all faulty split constructions in the following sentences.

1. Because it was raining, I did not want to go fishing, because the fish would not bite well.
2. I have found that it is sometimes possible to without much planning and with some haste in the writing compose a good essay.
3. If the coach gives us permission, we can play three sets of tennis today, if it does not rain.
4. I would like to merely and in simple words make a few statements about my trip to Mexico.
5. No one in my community has ever in all these years known such a dry spring.
6. We, during the last three years, have shared the rent.
7. Then the painstaking task of salvaging the rare books, which have been buried in mud, and the priceless paintings, which have been stained by the rising flood, begins.
8. During our visit to Mexico, we discovered that when the sun sets, people stroll around the town squares, when the evening breeze blows.
9. My sister, after a summer at camp, had, in many different ways, improved.
10. Martha did all she could to subtly and without showing any intention of doing so, thwart, harass, and disparage her rival for the starring role.

EXERCISE 16

Follow the directions for Exercise 15.

1. This landmark has, believe it or not, been here since 1874.
2. Marshall tried to gracefully reach the next step, but his foot slipped.
3. In spite of her interest in the game, Luella never broke a hundred for eighteen holes, in spite of her determination.
4. Our two dogs will soon, we hope, be adjusted to our new house.
5. We plan to eventually take a trip to Canada.
6. Otto, his eye on the clock and his hand on the ball, stalled until the game ended.
7. With bad weather, our picnic will be canceled, with lack of interest.
8. My father, after a long illness, had, in some way, lost interest in his business.

9. Terri, overcome by the presence of many friends at the cere-
   mony, wept happily.
10. With enough time, we should be able to master this course, with
    enough hard work.

S9. Faulty Coordination

The ideas expressed within a sentence have degrees of importance or rank. Elements of equal rank are **coordinate.** Those of
lesser importance are **subordinate** to first-rank thoughts.

   Careful writers will avoid too much coordination because it
is monotonous and frequently ineffective. Furthermore, they will
carefully distinguish between major or minor elements so as not
to convey hazy impressions or weaken the significance of the
main statement.

S9a. AVOID STRINGY, "RUN-ON" SENTENCES.

The compound sentence should not be overworked. Obviously, a
long series of short independent clauses joined by conjunctions
has the effect of running on and on, much as the strung-out speech
of a child: "We bought a beautiful car, and it has rubber wheels,
and it goes very fast, and we drive it every day." The best way to
correct such a sentence is to reduce predication. Change an
independent clause into a dependent one, a dependent clause into
a phrase, or a phrase into a single word.

> Ineffective: Yesterday it snowed, and we went sledding, and we
> went tobogganing, and we went skiing, but we
> didn't go skating and we didn't go iceboating.
> Improved: When it snowed yesterday, we went sledding,
> tobogganing, and skiing, but we didn't go skating
> or iceboating.
> Yesterday in the snow we went . . .

S9b. AVOID "SEESAW" SENTENCES.

Compound sentences containing two independent clauses of
nearly equal length can occasionally be effective. Such balanced

sentences, however, have a monotonous, seesaw quality when they appear in steady succession. The following would be improved by reducing predication:

> I did not have too good a time between the Fourth of July and Labor Day, but I managed to see a number of good friends during the summer. I met a nice girl named Sarajean at a beach picnic, and we went to a couple of movies together. She was quite interested in tennis and golf and active sports like that, but I never was too much of an athlete. Most of the gang liked her a lot, and they say they will miss her when she flies to Missouri next week. All in all, it was a pretty quiet two months, but I certainly shouldn't complain about the lack of excitement.

S9c. AVOID INACCURATE COORDINATION.

Two sentence elements should be related by the correct coordinating conjunction. Do not use *but* if *or* is the exact connective or use *and* for *but*, etc.

> I needed a haircut, *but* [not *and*] the barbershop was closed.
> Fran suffered a setback, *or* [not *but*] she would have finished first.

S9d. AVOID FALSE COORDINATION: DO NOT JOIN A RELATIVE CLAUSE TO ITS PRINCIPAL CLAUSE BY *AND*, *BUT*, OR *OR*.

Since *coordinate* signifies "of equal rank," a dependent clause can not be connected to an independent clause by a coordinating conjunction. This principle is most often violated by the so-called "and which" construction. Never use *and which, but which, and who, but who*, etc., unless this expression follows a coordinate *which* clause or *who* clause.

> She showed much enthusiasm at first, *but which* soon melted away.

This sentence can be corrected by omitting *but* and retaining the comma, since the clause is nonrestrictive. Another way is by providing a preceding *which* clause: *She at first showed much enthusiasm, which was praised by her teacher but which soon melted away.* Still another method is cutting away some of the deadwood: *Her great initial enthusiasm soon melted away.*

S9e. AVOID OVERUSING *SO* AS A CONJUNCTION.

So is correctly used as a conjunctive adverb following a semi-colon, and it is often used between independent clauses with only a comma before it. Nevertheless, there are three objections to *so* in such constructions: ineffectiveness through overuse, a juvenile effect in many instances, and a sense of inappropriateness in formal use. Overuse of *so* can be remedied by replacing that conjunction with *therefore, accordingly, thus, so that,* and similar expressions. Remember, however, to avoid the error of the comma splice (see Section S2).

Ineffective: He had to earn money for tuition, so he planned his leisure time carefully.
Twenty girls wanted to go, so we hired a bus.
Our school cafeteria has been completely redesigned so it can better accommodate the students.

Improved: He had to earn money for tuition; therefore, he planned his leisure time carefully.
Having to earn money for tuition, he planned his leisure time carefully.
Since twenty girls wanted to go, we hired a bus.
Our school cafeteria has been completely redesigned so that it can better accommodate the students.

EXERCISE 17

Rewrite the following sentences, eliminating improper coordination.

1. My brother and I have eye trouble, but we both wear glasses.
2. The train home was crowded, and we stood all the way.
3. There are many art courses offered so I shall have a wide choice.
4. I can be around a golf course and continue to play golf and there

will be many chances for me to go to different towns and states to play in tournaments.

5. They walked for miles and miles but finally they were arrested and Tess was taken to jail, and she was tried, and then she was finally sentenced.

6. We had a flat tire, but we should have been here an hour ago.

7. The students choose their own subjects, or they report on things they are interested in.

8. There was a good movie at one of the theaters so we decided to go.

9. In 1801 Springfield was planned, and in 1818 Clark County was created, and in 1827 Springfield was incorporated.

10. The clambake turned out to be a success even though it was undercooked a little, and the camping trip ended the day after the clambake.

11. We must learn to speak German fluently so we can transmit our ideas to business leaders in Berlin.

12. Mr. Harrison had been in the army and he sometimes addressed us as if he were still a top sergeant.

13. I went on a tour of the submarine base, and it proved to be very inspiring.

14. I have a sister who is 22 years old and she is in law school.

15. We told our camp leader that we did a passable job, but we were weary and our joints ached, and we told him we would turn in a full report tomorrow.

EXERCISE 18

Follow the directions for Exercise 17.

1. He didn't have a clean shirt, so he didn't go to the party.

2. This is a lovely room, and which we enjoy using it often.

3. Helga bought a new car, and it is light blue and has a stereo and a powerful engine.

4. Jacques dislikes sports, but he loves to read books. He enjoys visiting museums of all kinds. In addition, he likes to collect leaves and ferns.

5. I began to feel sleepy, stretched out on my bed, and so I took a good nap.

6. There is the harbor, but which we enjoy sailing boats in it.

7. The teacher lectured on atomic physics, and then answered our questions, gave the next assignment, and then dismissed the class.

8. My aunt read the advertisement in the newspaper but went out and bought the television set that same afternoon.
9. Our picnic was interrupted by a heavy storm, and we continued to enjoy ourselves just the same.
10. I had only a minor part in the play, and so I was through at the end of the second act.

S10. Faulty Subordination

Good writers recognize that not all ideas merit equal rank. They carefully select some ideas to be major ones and subordinate minor thoughts to these. As with proper and appropriate *coordination*, good **subordination** produces clear, effective, and mature writing.

S10a. AVOID PUTTING A COORDINATE IDEA IN A SUBORDINATE FORM.

S
10.

Ineffective: He was lean and energetic, *while* his brother was fat and lethargic.
Educated in Switzerland, she received her college degree in Canada.
I asked Nan to the game. *though* she was busy and couldn't go.

Improved: He was lean and energetic, *but* his brother was fat and lethargic.
He was lean and energetic, *whereas* his brother was fat and lethargic.
He was lean and energetic; his brother was fat and lethargic.

She was educated in Switzerland, *but* she received her college degree in Canada.
She was educated in Switzerland; *however,* she received her college degree in Canada.

I asked Nan to the game, *but* she was busy and couldn't go.
I asked Nan to the game; *however,* she was busy and couldn't go.

S10b. AVOID PUTTING THE MAIN IDEA OF A SENTENCE IN A SUBORDINATE FORM. CONVERSELY, AVOID PUTTING A SUBORDINATE IDEA IN A MAIN CLAUSE.

If an idea of less importance is put into an independent clause and an important idea is put in a dependent clause, the result, although grammatically correct, is an *upside-down subordination* of content. Determining the relative importance of ideas is sometimes difficult. Usually, however, the most dramatic incident and its effect comprise major elements. Preliminaries, such as time, place, and circumstances, usually form minor and subordinate elements.

Ineffective:	John was nearly out of breath when he spied a light in the distance.
	I was halfway across the field when the bull suddenly charged.
Improved:	When John was nearly out of breath, he spied a light in the distance.
	Just as (when) I was halfway across the field, the bull suddenly charged.

S10c. AVOID EXCESSIVE SUBORDINATION.

Subordinate statements that overlap each other in a mounting series are not effective. Clauses and phrases should be properly linked, but the finished structure should not resemble a staircase.

Ineffective:	These are lobsters which were caught off the coast of Maine, where the water is cold, and which were flown in today.
	I liked to watch the children who fed the elephants the peanuts that were peddled at the circus wagon that was near the main tent.
Improved:	These lobsters, caught off the Maine coast where the water is cold, were flown in today.
	These lobsters, caught off Maine's cold coastal waters, were flown in today.
	I liked to watch the children feeding peanuts to the elephants. The nuts were peddled at the circus wagon near the main tent.

EXERCISE 19

Rewrite the following sentences, correcting the faulty subordination.

1. As the lightning struck the house, Hilda was watching TV.
2. Easton is seven miles south of Bloomfield, having a population of 14,000.
3. One of my fondest memories is my first car, which I bought from the man who owns a delicatessen near Hague, where I took the train that took me to work.
4. Father had little resistance to disease, because when he contracted pneumonia, he spent over four weeks in the hospital.
5. I saw her frequently, when she looked at me queerly, and with her eyes blinking.
6. I was not driving fast through the intersection when a police officer shouted "Stop!"
7. During my year abroad I am living with a family that is headed by an elderly man whose sister was a college professor for some 50 years at l'Academie Industrielle, which is the other college in the city supported by public funds.
8. I was six years old when I was given my first pair of ice skates.
9. It was so noisy that I had to shut the door to hear the radio in the den that leads out to the terrace that is on the west side of the house that faces the pond that is covered with lily pads.
10. This unforgettable character was usually desperate, being out of work, and she had no money.

EXERCISE 20

Combine the sentences in each of the following groups. Use an appropriate subordinating conjunction to show the relationship between the subordinate clause and the main clause.

1. The sun came out. The storm passed by and headed southwest.
2. I shall wait here by the door. You sign slips for everyone who enters.
3. The coach claims his team will win. The offense and defense give 100 percent effort.
4. Susie will sing in the concert hall. She is reluctant to do so.
5. You must complete the credit application. We can make a decision about your loan.
6. She will buy you a new air conditioner. You want her to.
7. It always rains. I wash the family car.

8. I shall send you the minutes of the last club meeting. You can learn what happened.
9. I do not want to go to the Ricardos' party. I do not like them.
10. We were getting tired of hiking. We saw a bus approaching.

S11. Faulty Parallelism

In writing, **parallel** means "similar, having close resemblance." When two or more ideas in a sentence are alike in purpose, they should be expressed in the same grammatical form:

Words: Gene is *big* but *graceful.*
           Midge wants to *hop, skip,* and *jump.*
           His manner is *high, wide,* and *handsome.*

Phrases: *At work* and *at play,* Lisa always pushed herself hard.
           Over the river and *through the woods,* to Grandmother's house we go.

Clauses: My spirits rose *when I arrived in Puerto Rico* and *when I saw my roommate in the airport lobby.*
           I cannot drive in this state *until I am eighteen* and *until I pass my driver's test.*
           One of the tersest reports in American naval history is this: *"Sighted sub. Sank same."*

S11a. SENTENCE ELEMENTS THAT ARE COORDINATE IN RANK SHOULD BE PARALLEL IN STRUCTURE.

A prepositional phrase should be coordinate with a prepositional phrase, an infinitive phrase with an infinitive phrase, a dependent clause with a dependent clause, and so on.

Not parallel: This book is out of stock and not being printed.
               Our band plays at many school dances, town parades, and concert tours.
               My ambition is to win a Carver scholarship and that I might graduate from Cambridge.

Parallel: This book is out of stock and out of print.
               Our band plays at many school dances, marches in town parades, and makes several concert tours.

My ambition is to win a Carver scholarship and to graduate from Cambridge. (Or: I have two ambitions: to win a Carver scholarship and to graduate from Cambridge.)

Absolute parallelism is not always required. In the following sentences, the functions are parallel even though the form is not strictly so:

She dressed *flamboyantly* and *with a distinct flair.*
We saw *Carol, Helen,* and *a girl whom we did not recognize.*

S11b. AVOID MISLEADING PARALLELISM.

If ideas are arranged in parallel form but are neither parallel nor coordinate in content, they are only *apparently* parallel and will mislead the reader.

Ineffective: We bought that refrigerator from a discount store and with a four-year guarantee.

The chemist pointed out that nonsmokers have longer lives, enjoy better health, and can be more accurately tested in an experiment of this sort than smokers.

Improved: We bought that refrigerator from a discount store; it carries a four-year guarantee.

The chemist pointed out that nonsmokers have longer lives and enjoy better health than smokers; besides, they can be more accurately tested in an experiment of this sort.

A writer should be particularly cautious in handling a series of elements that, though appearing to modify the same element, are not actually parallel.

Ineffective: In your behalf in effect I will be bringing suit against the firm for $20,000.

Improved: In effect I will be bringing suit in your behalf against the firm for $20,000.

S11c. AVOID PARTIAL PARALLELISM.

In arranging a parallel series, make sure that each element is similar in form and structure to every other element in the series.

Not parallel: Corinne has served our local Red Cross as typist, ambulance driver, and has worked as an aide in the nursery room.

The movie is well directed, nicely choreographed, and the scoring is beautiful.

Parallel: Corinne has served our local Red Cross as typist, ambulance driver, and nursery-room aide.

The movie is well directed, nicely choreographed, and beautifully scored.

S11d. SENTENCE ELEMENTS FOLLOWING CORRELATIVE CONJUNCTIONS SHOULD BE PARALLEL IN FORM.

The four common pairs of *correlative conjunctions* are *both . . . and, either . . . or, neither . . . nor,* and *not only . . . but also.* Each part of the pair should be followed immediately by the same grammatical form, two similar words, two similar phrases, or two similar clauses.

Not parallel: You can *either* take the high road *or* the low road.

She *not only* is quite rich *but also* quite stingy.

The admissions director requests that you be *either* prepared to take the examination on Friday *or* that you submit another application in August.

Parallel: You can take *either* the high road *or* the low road.

She is *not only* quite rich *but also* quite stingy.

The admissions director requests *either* that you be prepared to take the examination on Friday *or* that you submit another application in August.

EXERCISE 21

Rewrite the following sentences, making the coordinate elements parallel in form.

1. Not only was she noisy and rude but also rather stupid.
2. André didn't like Democrats and especially to have one in the family.
3. I spend too much time both playing bridge and on bull sessions.
4. Jay is a man whom people respect but is not very approachable.

5. At about noon every day the siren blows and warning the residents of another big blast at the quarry.

6. The constant nibbling away of the rats and to hear them running across the foot of the bed undermined Craig's confidence.

7. Later that year, having lost his job and unable to find another, he had to sell his car.

8. My Uncle Julian wrote his autobiography but which was uninteresting because nothing had ever happened to him.

9. Students too often come to class with pencil and paper, carrying notebooks and texts, and a torpid mind.

10. The admiral was told he was either a liar or he was a fool.

EXERCISE 22

Follow the directions for Exercise 21.

1. It is well to invest in a variety of enterprises rather than putting all your eggs in one basket.

2. Professor Suarez assigned an article in Spanish and had to be read by Thursday.

3. Greta has a great sense of humor and who likes to play jokes on her friends.

4. What a joy it is to find an assistant who is conscientious, cheerful, and knows how to work independently!

5. The old house needed painting, to be papered, and a patch job.

6. To the yolks of three dozen eggs add a pint of goat's milk, three tablespoons of sunflower seeds, a head of lettuce, and then you should stir briskly for 45 minutes.

7. After you've been there awhile and beginning to know your way around, look up Charley.

8. My grandfather always voted Republican and being a conservative in every way.

9. Emma stumbled, fell, and the counselor reluctantly helped her to her feet.

10. Going rapidly and on only one water ski, Inger came to grief.

S 12

S12. Consistency

A good writer maintains a consistent point of view. The principle of *consistency* applies not only to a theme (see Section C8) but also to the construction of sentences. To be consistent, two or more elements in a sentence must agree and remain similar until a good reason exists for shifting them. Clear writing is consistent in verb tense, voice, mood, subject and verb agreement, pronoun reference, and figures of speech.

S12a. BE CONSISTENT IN THE USE OF SUBJECT AND VOICE IN A SENTENCE.

Voice is a term in grammar that indicates whether the subject is acting (*active voice*) or being acted upon (*passive voice*). In general, the active voice is more effective than the passive. However, the consistent use of either one removes a major cause of shifts in subject. Ordinarily, you should have a single subject in a sentence and should use only one voice.

Ineffective:	The diesel engine burns little kerosene, and Ed says it is completely reliable.
	As you sail across the harbor, channel markers can be seen.
Improved:	Ed says that the diesel engine burns little kerosene and is completely reliable.
	As you sail across the harbor, you can see channel markers.

S12b. BE CONSISTENT IN THE USE OF NUMBER.

Frequent mistakes in the use of *number* include switching carelessly from plural nouns to singular nouns or from singular to plural and failing to make pronouns agree in number with their antecedents.

Nonstandard:	I enjoy an ice-cream soda, but *they* tend to make me fat.
	If boys treated Grandmother with respect, she would surely respect *him*.
Standard:	I enjoy an ice-cream soda, but *it* tends to make me fat.
	If boys treated Grandmother with respect, she would surely respect *them*.

S12c. BE CONSISTENT IN THE USE OF TENSE.

Tense is the time of the verb (present, past, future, present perfect, etc.). Consistency in the use of tense may be a pitfall to writers of narrative, who often shift unnecessarily from present to past or from past to present or back and forth between the two. Note the switches in tense in the first example below.

> Nonstandard: Claire *was walking* briskly along the sidewalk when suddenly a riderless horse *came charging* around the corner. At a full gallop, it *races* down the middle of the street, then *veers* abruptly and *heads* directly for her. In panic, Claire *leaped* to the nearest doorway.

> Standard: Claire *was walking* briskly along the sidewalk when suddenly a riderless horse *came charging* around the corner. At a full gallop, it *raced* down the middle of the street, then *veered* abruptly and *headed* directly for her. In panic, Claire *leaped* to the nearest doorway.

S12d. BE CONSISTENT IN THE USE OF THE CLASS OR PERSON OF PRONOUNS.

Pronouns and antecedents should agree in person. Commonly, however, a careless writer will violate this principle by thoughtlessly shifting from the third person to the second:

> If *one* practices scales on the piano for one hour each day, *you* are bound to improve *your* finger dexterity.

S12e. BE CONSISTENT IN THE USE OF MOOD.

If you begin a sentence with the indicative mood, avoid switching to the subjunctive or imperative mood later in the same sentence. (The *indicative* mood is normally used for expressing a fact and making a statement; the *imperative* for issuing a command or making a request; the *subjunctive* for indicating a condition or probability or expressing doubt.) Occasionally it will be necessary to change the mood of the verbs in a sentence, but effective writers do not unnecessarily swing back and forth among the indicative, subjunctive, and imperative.

Ineffective: Last year at school I *would play* hockey on Thursday afternoons and *edited* the yearbook on Thursday evenings.

Improved: Last year at school I *would play* hockey on Thursday afternoons and *would edit* the yearbook on Thursday evenings.

Last year at school I *played* hockey on Thursday afternoons and *edited* the yearbook on Thursday evenings.

S12F. BE CONSISTENT IN THE USE OF FIGURES OF SPEECH.

Figures of speech are words used not in their literal sense but for the images they suggest.Used occasionally, they are effective and vivid. However, guard against sudden switches from literal to figurative speech and switches from one figure to another:

That supervisor is a cold fish who always has an axe to grind.

Before we pass judgment on the unfortunate supervisor, we must answer a question: What use has a fish for an axe? Perhaps this might be a clearer statement:

That disdainful supervisor always has a selfish motive.

EXERCISE 23

Improve the following sentences by eliminating the structural inconsistencies.

1. You can accomplish a great deal more in a day if one gets up early in the morning.
2. Whenever a paper is written, you should use good English.
3. Ms. Throop was idly watching the monkey when suddenly it jumps into her lap.
4. When tyranny threatens your country, a person should resist it, even though resistance means jail.
5. When you make sukiyaki, you must arrange the ingredients attractively, and it is cooked at the table.

6. My room at the dormitory has a large bookcase where you can keep your books.
7. Ingrid's father handed me my hat, and I was told by her mother not to return.
8. Just when Toro was on the ropes, Larkin's manager throws in the towel.
9. When my sister bought the *Encyclopaedia Britannica,* I was promised ten dollars by her for every volume I read.
10. One who travels abroad ought always to keep her passport where you can get to it easily.

EXERCISE 24

Follow the directions for Exercise 23.

1. The whole family was sitting around discussing their financial situation.
2. Cousin Milton was apprehended by the local police, and the F.B.I. seized Uncle Henry.
3. In strumming a guitar, you should not strike the strings vigorously, but they should be stroked with a sweeping motion.
4. What a nuisance a little brother can be when they are in a mischievous mood!
5. When one is tired and dispirited after a hard day at the office or in school, try a Whammo Atomic-Action Vitamin Capsule.
6. You kill the buffalo, David, and the lions will be taken care of by me.
7. My big sister came coasting down the hill on a bicycle and yells, "Look, Ma, no feet!"
8. Tourists can now cross the straits in a few minutes by bridge, whereas she often used to wait hours for a ferry.
9. By making that statement, Dolores really put her foot in her mouth, but there is no use in crying over spilled milk.
10. She bids a dramatic farewell to the world and its troubles and leaps into the river, only to discover that it had been dry since early June.

S
13

S13. Comparisons

The ability to make logical **comparisons** is often important in achieving clarity in writing. The rules that follow will help you to avoid making confusing or misleading comparisons.

S13a.   COMPARE ONLY THINGS OF A SIMILAR NATURE.

Illogical: Unlike most seaside places, the food here is very poor. (*Food* is compared to *seaside places*.)

Improved: Unlike most seaside places, this one does not serve very good food.

Illogical: In the new school, the teachers were more friendly than my old school.

Improved: The teachers in the new school were more friendly than those in the old school.

Illogical: I like William Wordsworth's poetry better than T. S. Eliot.

Improved: I like William Wordsworth's poetry better than T. S. Eliot's.

S13b.   INCLUDE THE WORD *OTHER* OR *ELSE* WHEN COMPARING ONE THING WITH A GROUP OF WHICH IT IS A PART.

Illogical: Henry is noisier than any boy in the bus.
Sharon has a higher scholastic average than any student in the junior class.
The Smiths have more cars than anyone on the block.

Improved: Henry is noisier than any *other* boy in the bus.
Sharon has a higher scholastic average than any *other* student in the junior class.
The Smiths have more cars than anyone *else* on the block.

S13c.   WITH THE SUPERLATIVE DEGREE, USE *ALL*. DO NOT USE *OTHER*, *ELSE*, OR *ANY*.

Illogical: Henry is the noisiest of all the *other* boys in the bus.
The Smiths have the most cars of anyone *else* on the block.
Biology is the most enjoyable of *any* of my courses.

Improved: Henry is the noisiest of *all* the boys in the bus.
The Smiths have the most cars of *all* the others on the block.
Biology is the most enjoyable of *all* my courses.

S13d. COMPLETE THE ELEMENTS OF ONE COMPARISON BEFORE ANOTHER IS INTRODUCED.

When a writer tries to include two comparisons in the same statement, a confused construction often results. A double comparison in the same sentence is acceptable, but only when the second is presented after the first has been completed.

Awkward: He is *as* sorry, if not sorrier, *than* Polly.
For a small man, Mike can wrestle *as* well, if not better, *than* Bob.

Improved: He is *as* sorry *as*, if not sorrier *than*, Polly.
For a small man, Mike can wrestle *as* well *as*, if not better *than*, Bob.

Preferable: He is *as* sorry *as* Polly, if not sorrier.
For a small man, Mike can wrestle *as* well *as* Bob, if not better.

Awkward: My sister is *one of the tallest, if not the tallest, woman* on the swim team.
The Lincoln-Douglas debate was *one of the greatest, if not the greatest, debate* in American history.

Preferable: My sister is *one of the tallest women on the swim team, if not the tallest.*
The Lincoln-Douglas debate was *one of the greatest debates in American history, if not the greatest.*

S13e. DO NOT OMIT WORDS NECESSARY TO MAKE A COMPARISON COMPLETE.

When a comparison is begun or implied, supply the words necessary to complete it and to make it clear. Never omit the standard of comparison.

Incomplete: He is so clever.
Improved: He is so clever that some of his disguises have never been penetrated.
He is really clever.

Incomplete: Your play has been the greatest triumph.
Improved: Your play has been the greatest triumph of any presented in this theater.
Your play has been a great triumph.

**S
13**

Incomplete: Science interested Ruth more than Sal.
Improved: Science interested Ruth more than it did Sal.
            Science interested Ruth more than Sal did.

EXERCISE 25

Correct errors in comparison in the following sentences.

1. Our school has one of the best gymnasiums.
2. Our region is rural, and the farmers, therefore, are more dependent upon one another.
3. Miriam is one of my favorite and definitely my most skillful cousin.
4. Jet planes in the future will be safer and more advanced in their performance and engineering.
5. The tourists cheer as loud, if not louder, than the rest of the bullfight aficionados.
6. This is one of the most, if not the most, important conferences of the fiscal year.
7. Mary Cassatt was the greatest influence on my painting than any other artist.
8. I enjoyed this kind of companionship with my white mice, and even wondered if they were more intelligent.
9. Our highways are very good in comparison with other countries.
10. He is one of the most talked about, but the average person knows less about, than anyone else.

EXERCISE 26

Follow the directions for Exercise 25.

1. My record is as good, if not better, than your record.
2. Strasiboski is older than anyone on the basketball team.
3. Her ambitions are bigger than any person I know.
4. Country life can be so peaceful and relaxed.
5. I can handle this car better than you.
6. Many villages and towns are plagued with as much or sometimes even more crime than the big cities.
7. I only hope that I am able to accomplish as much and more than I have planned.
8. I study my assignments more than most students.
9. Our factories produce the largest quantity of cheese than any other city in the state.

10. Scenes from nature that people take for granted are as beautiful, or more so, than anything that was ever put onto a painter's canvas.

S14. Conciseness

Concise means "brief and to the point." Although conciseness is primarily a concern of diction, it is also a problem in writing sentences.

A sentence may be fairly well constructed and still be ineffective because it is loaded with nonessential words. Furthermore, a sentence of a hundred words may be economical, whereas a sentence of twenty words may be verbose. The true test of conciseness in a sentence is effectiveness: are there so many superfluous words that the meaning is lost or so few words that the meaning is not fully conveyed?

For further discussion of wordiness, see the treatment of *conciseness* in Section D4 in the chapter dealing with diction.

S14a. REDUCE PREDICATION.

By reducing *predication,* you can make a sentence more concise. This method involves reducing the number of words used to make a statement—cutting out all unnecessary words by making one word serve the purpose of two or more. To reduce predication, you can use one or more of the following shortcuts.

1. Combine two short sentences into one.

Wordy: She was a buyer in a department store. She specialized in furniture and draperies.

Improved: She was a buyer in a department store, specializing in furniture and draperies.

2. Reduce a clause to a phrase.

Wordy: a fog that resembled the color of cotton
Improved: a fog the color of cotton

3. Reduce a phrase to a single word.

Wordy: a fog the color of cotton
Improved: a cotton-colored fog

4. Reduce several words to one or two words.

> Wordy: an officer on the police force
>
> Improved: a police officer

5. Reduce a compound or complex sentence to a simple sentence.

> Wordy: Apple pie for years has been a favorite American dessert, and there isn't anybody in the world who doesn't like apple pie.
> Everybody in the world likes apple pie, which for years has been a favorite American dessert.
>
> Improved: Everybody in the world likes apple pie, for years a favorite American dessert.

S14b.   AVOID WRITING SENTENCES CONTAINING UNNECESSARY DETAILS.

A sentence that contains an excess of details is ineffective because its longwindedness obscures the main idea.

> Wordy: Last winter the intramural squash tournament was won by Central High's Barry Stebbins with a racquet he had purchased two months before from a friend of his who had bought a new one made of catgut and who sold Barry his old one for $8.50.
>
> Improved: Last winter the intramural squash tournament was won by Central High's Barry Stebbins with a racquet he had bought from a friend for $8.50.
>
> Still better: Last winter Central High's Barry Stebbins won the intramural squash tournament with a secondhand racquet.

S14c.   AVOID THE USELESS REPETITION OF AN IDEA.

Useless repetition of an idea, or **tautology,** can weaken the impact of a sentence:

> Wordy: This entirely new and novel innovation in our program will delight our TV viewing audience; it has

just been introduced for the first time and will cause pleasure to many people who will be watching.

Improved: This innovation in our program will delight our TV audience.

EXERCISE 27

Improve the following sentences by eliminating superfluous words and phrases.

1. I have four good tires on my car, but in addition I always carry a spare tire besides.
2. Every student should know the correct procedure for successful theme writing in composition.
3. Since Jason was illiterate and couldn't read, he was generally pitied by most people.
4. The houses were mostly well built in construction, but the interior furnishings within the house left much to be desired.
5. I reflectively contemplated the fact that the machine was manually controlled and had to be operated by hand and not by another machine.
6. In the words of W. K., and I quote, "We're off to the drugstore to meet the kids."
7. On Christmas Eve in December last winter, Uncle Frank got stuck in the chimney.
8. Barbara knew only that Shakespeare was an ancient dramatist who wrote plays in the olden time.
9. Cora is an only child, as she has no brothers or sisters.
10. As a result of its feline nature, our cat Eric doesn't like to walk in the rain and get wet.

EXERCISE 28

Reduce predication in the following:

1. There are two basic forms of communication that we use. These two forms of communication are writing and speaking.
2. Las Vegas is a resort that is well known for gambling, and people who like to gamble often go to Las Vegas to pursue that activity.
3. In the distance we could see the peak of Mt. Shasta, which was covered by snow.

4. There, in the back hallway, I detected a smell that resembled the odor of gasoline.
5. Mr. Ames, an instructor in the department of Naval Science, gave a lecture on celestial navigation.

EXERCISE 29

Improve the following sentences by eliminating unnecessary details.

1. In reply to your letter of March 16, just a week ago, we are compelled to advise you that there has not yet been allowed to us a sufficient amount of time to prepare a compilation of the data that is to be encompassed by the Adams report.
2. Last summer a weekend journey was made to Paradise Lake, where the water is very cold, by five of us who were majoring in physics and who had borrowed a royal blue Packard from a car dealer in Buffalo, where these cars are no more common than elsewhere.
3. All that one needs to do in the process of boiling an egg is to lower a fresh egg, preferably a white one, into a pot containing water that has just begun to boil, and to keep the egg in the water for three minutes and then to lift it out gently with a spoon that is slotted.
4. A lot of time is required by many students in order to study the daily assignments in American history, which covers the entire period from the landing of the Pilgrims to the recent presidential election during which, as you know, a lot of fierce campaigning went on, including upright formal debating and downright mudslinging.

S15. Emphasis

Not all sentences are meant to be *emphatic,* nor should they be. A series of hard-hitting sentences will lose the reader's interest almost as quickly as a group of flabby, namby-pamby ones. Writers should learn to judge the tone of their composition and emphasize only the most important points. Minor thoughts should be arranged as background material.

The following paragraphs discuss various methods of securing *emphasis* in a sentence. Note that several of these methods depend on the positioning and arranging of words.

S15a. GAIN EMPHASIS BY PLACING STRONG AND RELATIVELY IMPORTANT WORDS AT THE BEGINNING OR END OF A SENTENCE.

First and last impressions are usually strongest. Thus, in sentences and in independent clauses, the beginning and end are the most emphatic and memorable parts. In these places the most important ideas should be put, so that they will claim attention where attention is sharpest.

Transitional words and phrases, though less vivid, are important and often deserve near-beginning positions. However, pure conjunctions, prepositions, and a number of other parenthetical expressions are usually not focal and normally should not start a sentence. Prepositions at the ends of sentences are neither grammatically incorrect nor unclear. They are merely ineffective — weak words that have been put in strong positions.

> Ineffective: This is the cafeteria that the students eat in.
> Mother is the only person I haven't yet written to.
> X-rays show that Martin suffered a broken neck.
> However, the boy will live, the doctor says.
>
> Improved: This is the cafeteria in which the students eat.
> The only person I haven't yet written to is Mother.
> The only person to whom I haven't yet written is Mother.
> X-rays show that Martin suffered a broken neck; however, the doctor says that the boy will live.

S 15

S15b. ARRANGE A SERIES OF IDEAS IN THE ORDER OF THEIR IMPORTANCE SO AS TO SECURE CLIMAX.

Within a sentence, a series of ideas should be arranged in *climactic* order. The initial idea in a given sentence would get the least of the reader's attention and the final idea the most.

> Ineffective: In this derailment, some died horrible deaths, some suffered serious injuries, and a few escaped with minor scratches.
>
> Improved: A few escaped from this derailment with minor scratches; but some suffered serious injuries; and some died horrible deaths.

Ineffective: Some of my instructors have been bad, some excellent, some indifferent, some fair.

Improved: Some of my instructors have been bad, some indifferent, some fair, and some excellent.

S15c. GAIN EMPHASIS BY USING THE ACTIVE VOICE.

Use of the *active* voice usually provides greater force than use of the *passive* for the simple reason that a subject being acted upon is rarely as effective as a subject acting. Your choice of active or passive voice depends upon context, upon the relative importance of the doer and the recipient of the action. Use the active voice whenever you want to state action, either mental or physical. Use the passive voice in impersonal writing and as little elsewhere as possible.

Your reader will react more strongly to "Buck *swept* Ninki into his arms" than to "Ninki *was swept* by Buck into his arms." Buck and Ninki probably do not care what voice you use and may be sorry you mentioned them at all. Also, it is possible that Ninki was as active in being swept as Buck was in sweeping. But your reader is your concern here, not the embracing lovers. Use the active voice.

S15d. USE PERIODIC SENTENCES OCCASIONALLY TO SECURE EMPHASIS.

Most of the sentences we speak and write are *loose* sentences. That is, they achieve some completeness of meaning before they reach their actual ends. An effective departure from this predominant pattern is the **periodic sentence,** one in which elements are transposed or inverted so that full meaning is not clear until the period is reached. When meaning is thus withheld, the reader continues in a state of suspense until the sentence ends.

Only if, which heaven forbid, we extend our present tribal conflicts to the other planets will the Moon become of military importance. (Arthur C. Clarke)

Tired, wet, and hunched against the cold, the passengers from the stalled bus stumbled the last hundred feet to the warm and brightly lit diner. At first slowly, then eagerly, then almost fiercely, each seized and drank a mugful of steaming coffee.

S15e. USE WORDS OUT OF THEIR NATURAL ORDER, ONCE IN A WHILE, AS A METHOD OF EMPHASIS.

The usual *word order* of most sentences is subject (and modifiers), predicate (and modifiers), and object or complement (and modifiers). This is the order readers expect to encounter. What they do *not* expect to encounter, therefore, is more likely to capture their attention. By putting the predicate or the object or the complement or an adverbial modifier first as an *occasional* change of pace, the writer will impart emphasis.

> Usual: The mighty and wicked are fallen.
> Seven little dwarfs lived here in the center of the dark forest.
> If any, speak; for I have offended him.
>
> Inverted and effective: Fallen are the mighty and wicked.
> Here, in the center of the dark forest, lived seven little dwarfs.
> If any, speak; for him I have offended. (Shakespeare, *Julius Caesar*)

S 15

S15f. OCCASIONALLY REPEAT IMPORTANT WORDS TO GAIN SENTENCE EMPHASIS.

Although faulty repetition should be avoided (see Section D4), you may heighten the effectiveness of your message by repeating key words in a series of sentences. All of us enjoy encountering the familiar; for example, much of our appreciation of music stems from our recognition of a repeated theme. When we come across certain words and phrases in a written passage or hear them in speech, we find that they have a special impressiveness and appeal. But repetition is a device, perhaps merely an artificial device, and should be used sparingly and only for a specific effect. It seems pleasing in the first of the illustrations that follow, but it may be grating in the second:

> *Give! Give* money when you see that men, women, and children are hungry. *Give* sympathy when you can cheer a beaten person. *Give* time to study conditions in your community. *Give* your whole self in an attempt to change and better the life of all humanity.

> *Do you want* luxury? *Buy* a home *in Oakdale. Do you want* good schools for your children? *Buy in Oakdale. Do you want* compatible neighbors? *Buy in Oakdale. Do you want* room and freedom to move around? *Buy in Oakdale. Oakdale* will satisfy every need and every *want* of every discriminating buyer.

S15g. USE BALANCED SENTENCES OCCASIONALLY FOR EMPHASIS.

A *balanced sentence* is one in which several parts are of similar length and structure. This type of sentence is particularly useful as a means of making contrast effective.

> Judith is fat; Marilyn is thin.
> Honesty recommends that I speak; self-interest demands that I remain silent.
> Severity breeds fear, but roughness breeds hate.

EXERCISE 30

Rewrite the following sentences, making them more emphatic.

1. Sven made a favorable impression upon Brigitte's father, although he was uneasy most of the time.
2. The talk by Ms. Golden on spinning reels was the high spot in some respects.
3. I could just grasp the furry body of a baby chinchilla by reaching down into the burrow to the point where it widened out into the nest.
4. After eating the spoiled custard, one child was rushed to the hospital and several were slightly ill.
5. Johnny will lose consciousness if the coach doesn't take him out of the game.

6. Erika's mountain-climbing companion fell and broke his leg because he wouldn't watch where he was going.
7. A battered old portable was the machine on which Janet Loo's early novels were written.
8. The misery of the stranded group reached a climax in some ways with the coming of the first freezing weather.
9. We thought more and more of Sue Jenkins as time went on.
10. Thousands of valuable trees throughout the state were uprooted by the savage hurricane.

EXERCISE 31

Follow the directions for Exercise 30.

1. In effect, what has been proposed by you will improve conditions in this school.
2. A preposition is a weak word to end a sentence with.
3. For years I looked forward to this day with fear, excitement, and interest.
4. The cold, wet, and weary climbers descended to the base camp carefully.
5. My first win came on my fourteenth birthday, as I recall.
6. Some exciting changes have occurred in international, cosmic, local, and national affairs.
7. This world needs more love: love of parents, love of God, love of all things good, love of animals, love of flowers and trees.
8. Your paper needs lots of work, to be frank with you.
9. Can spring be far behind, if winter comes?
10. Ms. Lopez is the only person whom we haven't as yet spoken to.

S
15

EXERCISE 32

Increase the effectiveness of the following sentences:

1. He started out to take a walk because he was desperate, unable to sleep, and tired of hearing the radio.
2. At first, she did not love him, but she came to like him as time went on.
3. This is not good soil to plant flowers in.
4. In short, both candidates promised to help the farmer out.
5. John's fender was bent when he did not have enough room to turn the station wagon around in.

6. You know that your bill will be paid by me as soon as I am able.
7. In order to accomplish this, you should be willing to give up honor, family, friends, and acquaintances, I think.
8. She became better liked as more people came to know her and gradually her circle of acquaintances widened.
9. The days when our hearts were young and gay are gone.
10. She came here to recuperate from a serious illness, play bridge, and have the sun brown her, I suppose.

S16. Transition

Transition means "passing from one state or position to another." In a sentence, some linking or bridging device is often needed to show the relationship of one part to another. Such devices are known as *transitional aids*.

S16a. USE TRANSITIONAL AIDS TO LINK PARTS OF SENTENCES.

Various pronouns and conjunctions should be used to show relationships between particular parts of sentences, as explained below:

1. Evidence of relationship between dependent and independent clauses may be shown by two different kinds of constructions.

   a. **subordinating conjunctions** such as:

although	in order that	until
as soon as	lest	when
because	since	where
if	unless	whereupon

   We decided not to go *because* the cost was too great.
   Keep away from that place *unless* you don't care what happens to you.
   I showed the officer my license, *whereupon* he gave me a ticket.

   b. **relative pronouns** such as:

   that, which   who, whom

Here is a book *that* I thought I had lost.
Marilyn is the student *who* led the class on that examination.

2. Evidence of relationship between independent clauses can be shown by five different kinds of constructions.

a. **Personal pronouns** such as:

I	you	she
my	your	her
me	he	they
we	his	their
our	him	them

b. **Demonstrative pronouns** such as:

this, that   these, those

c. **Simple conjunctions** such as:

and	or	neither
but	nor	yet

d. **Correlative conjunctions** such as:

either . . . or	neither . . . nor
not only . . . but also	both . . . and

e. **Conjunctive adverbs** such as:

besides	however	nevertheless
consequently	instead	still
hence	moreover	therefore

You may be right; *your* position is well stated.
This is my drink, *that* is yours.
I have to behave myself, *but* I don't want to.
Either you will pay now *or* you will pay later.
We thought we would win easily; *instead*, we were beaten badly.

S16b. AVOID INEXACT TRANSITION.

Because there are many transitional devices to choose from, it is not easy to select the expression that will most clearly and exactly show the relationship you have in mind.

Inexact: I cannot take time to buy a ticket, *but* I shall miss my train.
She wanted to go to Chicago, *and* her parents wanted her to come home to Cleveland.

S
16.

I know I forgot to pay the bill, *whereupon* I have the money in my purse.

Juan wants to invite Martha to the party, *and* he doesn't have the courage to do so.

Rosine had a sore throat *since* she couldn't sing her solo.

Exact: I cannot take time to buy a ticket *because* I shall miss my train.

She wanted to go to Chicago, *but* her parents wanted her to come home to Cleveland.

I know I forgot to pay the bill, *for* I *still* have the money in my purse.

Juan wants to invite Martha to the party, *but* he doesn't have the courage to do so.

Rosine had a sore throat; *consequently,* she couldn't sing her solo.

Important as transition is between the parts of a sentence, it is even more significant between sentences as they are used to form a paragraph. For further comment on transition, see Section P6.

EXERCISE 33

Use better connectives for the inexact ones in the following sentences.

1. Dinosaurs once roamed this area, because their bones are still to be found.
2. Carrie wonders if she should go to summer school this year or get a job.
3. I had a wonderful time at the county fair, but so did Liza, my favorite cousin.
4. Tommy likes to scale mountains, but Felipe prefers to scale fish.
5. We were all having a good time and didn't want to go home; nevertheless, the party lasted till dawn.
6. Wild strawberries grow on the island; on the other hand, blueberries are prolific, too.
7. Father lost his job in the fall of 1977; however, Mother was taken ill the same year.
8. Sylvia's great-aunt Margaret admires Mark, although he is fond of the elderly yet spry woman.
9. Jeremy and his aunts had barely got settled than the curtain rose.

10. As I was going to St. Ives anyway, I offered to take the things to the cleaner's.

EXERCISE 34

Transitions are needed between the short, choppy sentences and clauses in the following paragraph. Supply them.

> Baseball is said to be the national game. I do not like it. If it is the national game, millions must enjoy watching or playing it. I know people who do not ever attend a game. I know people who attend as many as fifty games a year. I should not make a dogmatic statement about the appeal of the game. I have never witnessed a game.

S17. Glossary of Sentence Errors

The following alphabetically arranged survey of errors that teachers and writers consider most important may serve you as a quick reference guide.

And which, but which, and who, but who. Joining relative clauses to independent clauses by using a conjunction (making dependent and independent clauses coordinate). Section S9d.

Climax, faulty. In a series of ideas, failure to arrange their order so that the weakest is put first, then the next stronger, etc. Section S15b.

Comma splice (comma fault). Using a comma between two independent clauses not joined by a conjunction (splicing two complete sentences with a comma if the second sentence does not begin with a conjunction). Section S2.

Comparisons, mixed. Using illogically the positive and comparative degree of adjectives or adverbs in one single statement. Also, including a member in a group and yet as a single member, or excluding a member from a group in which it belongs. Section S13.

Consistency, lack of. Unjustifiable shifting of tense, mood, voice, number, or the class or person of pronouns. Section S12.

Dangling elliptical clause. A dependent clause with its subject or predicate omitted, the omitted part not the same as that expressed in the independent clause. Section S7b.

Dangling verbal phrase. A phrase that should clearly modify a specific noun or pronoun but does not. Section S7a.

Dependent clauses, illogical. The use of noun or adverbial clauses to serve as parts of speech that they cannot correctly or effectively serve. Section S5.

Fused sentences. Two sentences in succession with no mark of punctuation between. Section S3.

Misplaced modifier. A word, phrase, or clause so placed that it modifies words other than those it should clearly modify. Section S6.

Parallelism, faulty. Not using the same grammatical constructions for sentence elements equal in rank. Section S11.

Rambling sentences. Sentences having grammatical completeness but violating unity. Section S4a.

Seesaw sentences. An ineffective series of compound sentences. Section S9b.

Separation of parts, needless. Unnecessary or ineffective separation of closely related sentence elements. Section S8.

"So" overused. Monotonous, overfrequent, and therefore ineffective joining of independent clauses with the conjunctive adverb *so*. Section S9e.

Split infinitive. Needlessly separating the sign of the infinitive *to* and the infinitive verb. Section S8b.

Squinting modifier. A word or word group that can look in two directions at once. Section S6a.

Stringy sentences. A series of short, independent clauses combined, or knotted, into a string. Section S9a.

Subordination, faulty. Confusing the structure of primary and subordinate ideas; employing excessive subordination. Section S10.

Transition, faulty, or lack of. Failure to make evident the relationship between clauses and sentences by means of transitional expressions. Section S16.

Unity, lack of. Inclusion of excessive detail or of unrelated ideas in the same sentence. Section S4.

Upside-down subordination. A structure in which the more important idea appears in a dependent clause or the less important in an independent clause. Section S10b.

Wordiness. Using too many or unnecessary words to express ideas; primarily, failure to reduce predication. Section S14.

REVIEW EXERCISE 1

The following sentences contain errors in sentence structure. Copy the sentences and correct the errors.

1. Assignments that are handed in later than Friday of this week, you might as well not hand it in at all.
2. We approached the city with great interest, it was not a small city with narrow streets, as we had expected, but a large city with towering skyscrapers.
3. Being only four years old, the nose specialist found it hard to examine Nicky.
4. Stooping to pick up a dime, Kenneth's suspenders broke.
5. Mamie thought that Lee was smart, bright, but was too eager for money and social position.
6. Because it was after midnight, we decided to excuse ourselves, because we were tired.
7. Although we have been able to invent such destructive forces as the atomic bomb, we have also found some new drugs that are very effective and some instruments that helped greatly in wartime to reduce the danger of death or disease from injuries or wounds received in wartime.
8. Marcella's assets were her ready wit, a fast talker, and seemed to inspire confidence in people.
9. Mike was approached by a couple with a baby daughter who were looking for an apartment.
10. My companions, who refused to stop talking, the people to the rear in back of them could not hear.

REVIEW EXERCISE 2

Follow the directions for Review Exercise 1.

1. I agree to drive with Rose to Maine and then that I should return alone by train.

2. His sources of income consist of the following: owner of a small vegetable market and for the past four years he has been manager of a produce department.
3. As she listened to the symphony, Luisa was suddenly conscious and disturbed by a certain giddiness among the first violins.
4. My next job was a bill collector for a doctor but which did not pay enough money.
5. If I have enough money left, I am going to fly there for Christmas, if my parents will let me.
6. When Esther returned home from camp, she finds a baby brother.
7. Because Sammy has reformed is why Pedro is so proud of him.
8. This teacher often quotes himself he thinks it adds flavor to his conversation.
9. The mechanic located the cause of our trouble in a flash.
10. At Central High they devote two weeks at the close of each semester to final examinations.

REVIEW EXERCISE 3

Follow the directions for Review Exercise 1.

1. The furniture was dusted and the ornaments washed in preparation for the party to be given tomorrow and which will celebrate the fiftieth wedding anniversary of my grandparents.
2. The salesclerk told Mr. Banks that the factory could not make the pair of shoes that he wanted and would he consider buying another type?
3. Instead of campaigns, bazaars, tag days, and other energy wasting drives that often did not produce even minimum funds for welfare work.
4. The hostile attitude of one of the adversaries who opposed us had in its character something that was rather belligerent in nature.
5. Todd had to see his dentist about a small cavity, which terrified him.
6. I can understand why Florida is a popular vacation spot: it has so many beautiful beaches.
7. It is my duty to clearly and emphatically say that football today is both war and sport.
8. Referring to the views of various experts, the fall was given by the majority as the best time for that kind of planting.
9. If one likes good French food, you should go to Paris or New Orleans.

10. Holly thinks that if one has a chance to get a job like Bernice's they should not let it slip.

REVIEW EXERCISE 4

For each sentence below, write a capital letter indicating that in order to correct the sentence you would:

A	insert a necessary word or take out a superfluous word
B	change the wording to correct an undesirable shift in point of view
C	rework the sentence to make the reference of a pronoun clear or correct
D	change the basic plan of the sentence so that its parts are logically united
E	*do nothing:* the sentence is acceptable as it stands

If so instructed, rewrite each faulty sentence on a separate sheet.

1. The reason why you are always slicing the ball is that you take too full of a backswing at the tee.
2. An intelligent Dalmatian is the kind of dog who can be trained easily.
3. It's true I don't care much for the food in the cafeteria, but at these prices I suppose you shouldn't complain.
4. I suppose I could select any of these magazines to read, but it must be illustrated.
5. My main objection to band practice was because we spent so much time walking around tracing out letters and diagrams on the field.
6. Although a telescope may increase the apparent size of distant objects, it invariably decreases their surface brightness — a fact that is something of a paradox.
7. Will Rogers said that if you encourage people to talk about themselves that you will hear nothing but good.
8. An ultimate limit to the population of the earth is set by its daily quota of solar energy, which cannot be altered by any change in the techniques of food production.
9. For Christmas my sister and I gave my grandparents two dozen damask dinner napkins, and they were also given a damask dinner tablecloth by my parents.
10. Because a small car uses less gasoline than a big car is a very good reason for buying one; the difference in the purchase price is also important.

REVIEW EXERCISE 5

Follow the directions for Review Exercise 4.

1. According to our teacher, the sonnets were usually directed to a person whom they were madly in love with.
2. I could never arrange an outing with Bert but what his kid brother wanted to tag along.
3. All four of the starters on our team have pitched remarkably well so far this season, which is why we are in the first division.
4. It may be the reason why cats and dogs dislike each other that from the evolutionary point of view they are closely related.
5. In contrast to the dark, indolent siren of popular supposition, the actual Cleopatra was probably blonde or red-headed, certainly commanded several armies in the field, bore three or four children, and reputedly mastered twelve languages.
6. This illustrated parts catalog, to which when answering inquiries you should refer to at need, is to be kept on your desk at all times.
7. The windmill first appeared in Europe shortly after the earliest crusade, and they were apparently among the useful inventions brought back from the Near East by returning French soldiers.
8. When Mother returned with Ellen, I could see that she was delighted with her performance.
9. The girl over there that you were just talking with, she seems to be very alert.
10. There are always new people with which to become acquainted.

The Paragraph

The *sentence* is the *unit of writing,* but the **paragraph** may be termed the *basic unit of thought.* The very heart of learning to write effectively lies in paragraph development. If the successful writer has a secret, it is the ability to form a thought—almost any thought—and then develop this idea, however vague and fragmentary it may be, so that it becomes clear and interesting to readers. Everyone has had the experience of writing a sentence or making a statement and then halting, aware that it needs expansion, certain that the idea standing alone seems bare and incomplete but unsure about how to "flesh it out."

The method of putting flesh on the bare bones, the skeleton of ideas, is known as *paragraph development.* That is, a paragraph is a group of statements, of sentences, developing an idea or topic. This idea may be independent or it may be one part of a larger topic. In other words, a paragraph may be part of a composition or a short composition in itself.

Single paragraphs appear frequently in print, such as, for example, short items in newspapers and magazines. Sometimes, when the occasion requires, a paragraph may consist of a single sentence.

Far more often, however, paragraphs depend for their development and meaning on their role as units of a larger topic. The wording of each paragraph is then dependent on the paragraph just before or after; it is not an independent unit but part of an organic whole.

Clear paragraphing is essential to both writer and reader. By properly separating sentences into groups, a writer controls subject and plots course. For the reader, clearly formed paragraphs are signposts by which to follow the path of the writer's

P
1

thought. By understanding the parts, the reader reaches an understanding of the whole.

P1. Topic Sentence

P1a. A PARAGRAPH IS A SERIES OF SENTENCES DEVELOPING A STATEMENT CALLED A TOPIC SENTENCE. THE TOPIC SENTENCE TELLS THE READER CLEARLY WHAT POINT WILL BE MADE IN THE PARAGRAPH.

The first requirement of a good paragraph is that it should have a definite point to make and should include nothing that does not contribute to that point. In other words, it should have *unity.* Think of the one point that you wish to make. Then list the ideas that you will use to develop that point. The sentence that tells the reader clearly what point will be made in a paragraph is called the **topic sentence.**

Generally, the topic sentence is the first sentence of the paragraph. Occasionally, it may appear somewhere toward the middle or at the end of the paragraph, depending upon content and the writer's method of organizing it. Sometimes the topic sentence is not expressed at all but is implied by the paragraph as a whole.

P1b. USE THE TOPIC SENTENCE AS A GUIDE FOR THE PARAGRAPH.

When you begin a paragraph with a topic sentence, you make a definite commitment to what you are about to discuss, and you arouse the reader's expectation. If your paragraph is successful, it will fulfill the promise in your initial sentence and satisfy the reader. Consider how the following paragraph achieves both objectives. The topic sentence is shown in bold print.

> **With his telescope Galileo made some important astronomical discoveries.** For instance, he discovered that there are satellites around the planet Jupiter. He saw that the moon was not flat, as people commonly believed, but that it had high and low areas,

and he even calculated the height of some of its mountains. The Milky Way revealed itself to him as a vast collection of stars, and by studying sunspots he reached the conclusion that the sun rotates.

P1c. VARY THE POSITION OF THE TOPIC SENTENCE.

The most common *position* of the topic sentence, as in the foregoing example, is at the beginning of the paragraph. In a short paper of three or four paragraphs, each could begin with a topic sentence. But in a longer paper of perhaps eight or more paragraphs, placing the topic sentence at the beginning of every paragraph might make the writing seem both mechanical and monotonous. It is then better to change the position of the topic sentence occasionally. It would not be difficult, for instance, to put the topic sentence about Galileo's telescope at the end of the paragraph:

> Galileo was the first man to discover that there are satellites around the planet Jupiter. He saw that the moon was not flat, as people commonly believed, but that it had high and low areas, and he even calculated the height of some of its mountains. He perceived the Milky Way as a vast collection of stars, and by studying sunspots he reached the conclusion that the sun rotates. **Thus with his telescope Galileo was able to make some important contributions to astronomy.**

Notice that here the topic sentence is used to sum up the paragraph instead of to introduce it.

When the topic sentence is placed within the paragraph, the sentence or sentences before it are usually introductory:

> Many people have heard about the famous Leaning Tower of Pisa, but few know that Pisa also has a university of ancient origin. In about the year 1580 its most illustrious student was a mathematical genius named Galileo Galilei, who was soon to invent the hydrostatic balance, a thermometer, and a proportional compass. **But Galileo's greatest invention was his telescope, which enabled him to make some significant contributions to astronomy.** It was this instrument that made it possible for Galileo to discover satellites around Jupiter, the unevenness of the moon's surface, and the fact that the Milky Way is a vast collection of stars. By studying sunspots, he was also able to infer the rotation of the sun.

Sometimes the topic sentence is not stated at all but is merely implied. Every good paragraph is so well knit that reasonably thoughtful readers can sum up the central thought of a paragraph in their own topic sentence. A paragraph of this kind, however, should focus on only one subject, like any other paragraph.

> Among the great geniuses of the Renaissance, many were artists, like Raphael, Titian, Michelangelo, Van Dyke, and Rembrandt. Others were poets, such as Spenser, Shakespeare, Tasso, and Ronsard. Still others were pioneers in science: Galileo and Kepler in astronomy, for instance, and Vesalius and Harvey in medicine.

The implied topic sentence here is, "The Renaissance produced many creative geniuses."

EXERCISE 1

Copy out the topic sentence in each paragraph below. If you think the topic sentence is merely implied, state what it would be.

1. Cowardice generally invites attacks. A dog may chase a girl who turns and runs, whereas if the girl holds her ground the dog will do her no harm and even let itself be patted. A boy who runs away at the first sight of a neighborhood gang will only attract pursuit. Had the boy just continued on his way, the gang might not have paid the least attention to him.

2. A robin or an oriole or any other bird will always build its nest in the same way. So will a beaver or a mole. Animals go by instinct. They have no need for invention. People, on the other hand, need to invent in order to adapt themselves to climatic or geographical conditions. In the Southwest, they build adobe houses; on the narrow island of Manhattan, they construct skyscrapers; in the far north, they fashion igloos.

3. One of Benjamin Franklin's rules was "Never ask another to do what you can do for yourself." It is a good rule. Students who depend on others to do their math problems or Spanish translations not only run the risk of getting the wrong answers but also are not acquiring self-reliance. There is no substitute for self-reliance. We cannot expect to go through life depending on others to do our thinking or to solve our personal problems.

EXERCISE 2

Write two paragraphs of between 75 and 100 words each, choosing any *one* of these topic sentences. In your first paragraph place the topic sentence at the beginning. In your second paragraph place it either toward the middle or at the end. Underline the topic sentence in each paragraph you write.

1. Practical jokes can be painful.
2. Going steady has its disadvantages (advantages).
3. Don't be a backseat driver.
4. Our student government could be improved.
5. Teenagers are seldom understood by their families.

P2. Substance

A composition may contain several good ideas as expressed in topic sentences but still be weakly written because its paragraphs are undeveloped or are padded with hazy generalizations. Such paragraphs are only the skeletons of what they should and could be.

"Everyone should learn to swim" is a good enough topic sentence, but if all you say about it is that the ability to swim may on some occasion save one from drowning, you have hardly begun. If you really start thinking your subject through, you can find some other things to say about it. For one thing, you might point out that swimming is a beneficial exercise. You might think of swimming at beaches and pools as a source of recreation. You could enumerate some enjoyable water sports for which knowing how to swim is necessary, such as skin diving, waterskiing, or surfing. And do not overlook your own experience as material, something relevant to swimming that you yourself have seen or learned or done.

P2a. DRAW ON YOUR OWN EXPERIENCE FOR MATERIAL.

Your own experience can often supply details you can use in developing your paragraphs. Your total experience lies not only in what you have done but also in what you have seen, heard, thought, felt, and learned. What you can find in your own experience, if only you look for it, will yield details that are alive and meaningful for the very reason that they are yours.

Such details are not the secondhand impressions and comments of someone else but are really a part of the essential you. Only you know precisely what you mean when you say, "Robin is fun loving and good-natured." Your observations of Robin in action, your thoughts about her, can and will help you develop this remark. For one example, you can relate how Robin revived a dull party that seemed to be dying, how through sheer good spirits she got everyone into a lively mood, ready and eager to enter into the spirit of a "fun" evening. Or you can contrast the good-natured reaction of Robin when made the butt of a practical joke with the sour or angry reaction of Dee in a similar situation. Or you can define what you mean by *fun loving* or *good-natured* or both, making specific references from your own experience of Robin's personality and mannerisms.

Let us suppose that you are writing about swimming. Presumably you know how to swim. How and when did you first learn? Have you or someone you know had any narrow escapes from drowning? Were you ever in a canoe or other craft that might easily have capsized? Where do you go swimming, and what gives you the most pleasure from this activity? If you really dig into your own experience, you might build your whole paragraph from it alone, as this beginning writer did:

> "Everyone should learn how to swim," my parents used to tell us. When I was seven and my sister Patty five, we lived not far from a small lake. Every Saturday afternoon that first summer my mother and father waded out with us, while they showed us the first stroke we were to use. After about the fourth time, my sister Patty could swim well enough to be allowed to go into water above her head, but try as I might, I could not get the hang of it. Whenever Mother took us out in the rowboat, it was I who had to wear a life preserver and endure the superior smirk of my little sister, who didn't have to wear one. But one weekday, when Father and Mother were away, I happened to go down to the lake with a couple of girls a year or two older than I was. They were soon in the water, swimming about and diving under and coming up sputtering and having a fine time, while I was watching on shore. Then, on a sudden impulse, I jumped in among them, and all at once, to my own amazement, I was

swimming! That evening at supper I turned to my parents. "Everybody should learn to swim," I said, "like me."

If you have not yet done so, consider starting to keep a journal or diary to record your experiences. Getting down on paper your feelings, the sights and incidents you see, and your daily thoughts about persons, places, and events will be of real help to you in developing paragraphs on a variety of topics.

P2b. DRAW UPON THE EXPERIENCES OF OTHERS FOR MATERIAL.

At times, you may be called upon to write about a topic that lies outside the range of your experience. Then your own thought and knowledge will not suffice; you will have to turn for material to the thoughts and experiences of others. You may get some material from conversations, but your chief sources will be books and works of reference, as well as newspapers and magazines. Television programs, even motion pictures, are other possibilities. Yet nothing you learn will become part of your knowledge unless you understand it well enough to put it in your own words.

P2c. AVOID ALREADY OBVIOUS STATEMENTS.

P
2

To tell your readers what they and everybody else already know will accomplish no more than boring them. One student, asked to write about the newspaper he read regularly, wrote this:

> The newspaper has several kinds of headlines. Among them are the main headings and subheads. The main headlines are found at the top of the page. . . .

Instead of interesting the class, he evoked yawns.

P2d. AVOID NEEDLESS REPETITION OF THE TOPIC SENTENCE.

Keep your topic sentence clearly in mind and use the remainder of the paragraph to develop the topic. Simply repeating what the topic sentence has already made plain is to mark time and get nowhere. Consider this example:

> I think a person makes a great mistake to drop out of school. Students should not leave school before they graduate. Those who stay long enough to get their diplomas get better jobs than the dropouts do.

EXERCISE 3

Point out the main weakness in each paragraph below. Tell how you might revise it to give the paragraph more substance and interest.

1. Fire fighters are brave men and women. They often risk their lives to save people from burning houses. They have to be ready to go out in all kinds of weather. At any time of year, even in zero weather, a fire fighter has to be prepared to answer an alarm.

2. Once I had a very embarrassing experience. My older sister was getting married, and I was to be an usher at the wedding. I had on a pair of new shoes, and all during the first part of the wedding my shoes squeaked. This was very embarrassing for me, and I guess for some of the other people too.

3. The government ought to help every person who wants to go to college and can't afford it. The government should give them money for tuition and books and also for board if they go to a college away from home. By helping them go through college, the government would benefit because it would have more educated people to run the government in the future. This is a great advantage. Therefore the government ought to help them get a college education.

4. Termites are small insects. They can do a great deal of damage. They damaged our house so badly that we had to call an exterminator, who did a lot of things around the house and charged a lot of money but did not get rid of all of the termites.

5. My favorite relative is my Aunt Winona. When she came on visits she always used to bring something for me. She also took me to a number of places of interest. Once she took me to a big-league ball game. No wonder she has always been my most favorite relative.

EXERCISE 4

Develop *one* of the following topic sentences into a substantial paragraph based wholly on your own experience. Supply specific details.

1. Once I scored a minor triumph.
2. Punishment is often deserved (unjust).
3. A little sister (brother) can be a nuisance.
4. Not only cats can be too curious.
5. Some people say that I am accident-prone.
6. My room is my castle.
7. Anyone can learn to dance.
8. Even two can sometimes be a crowd.
9. Some people think they are always right.
10. One can (cannot) always trust a friend.

P3. Methods of Development

Paragraphs can be developed in a number of ways. No one way is necessarily better than another. All can be said to have one purpose in common: to make the reader see exactly and fully the point specifically made in the topic sentence or implied by the paragraph as a whole. Often writers can achieve this purpose best by a combination of methods. When beginning a paragraph, they do not arbitrarily choose one method or another. Rather, they let the central idea determine the best way to make the reader visualize and understand it.

The only sure test of the worth of a paragraph is that of communication. Does it make the reader see, understand, and react to what you are writing? If you are developing an idea that might relate to your reader's experience and understanding, give *instances* and *examples* of what you have in mind. If the terms you need to use may not be clear to your reader, *define* them. On occasion, you can *compare* and *contrast* the idea contained in the topic sentence with something you feel certain your reader already comprehends.

These methods of developing paragraphs are explained and illustrated in the following pages. Most often, however, you will find it wise and even necessary to use a combination of methods.

P
3

P3a. DEVELOP A PARAGRAPH WITH PARTICULARS AND DETAILS.

Topic sentences can often be clarified and developed by the use of specific details and concrete particulars. This method involves expansion of the basic idea with separate items arranged in some logical order. It is illustrated by the following paragraphs, the first of which has only an implied topic sentence:

> The loft itself must have measured fifty feet, with dirty windows stretched along two sides; the floors were rotten, hairy as coconut shells, patched here and there with squares of tin. Half a dozen cumbersome etching presses with their great splaying wheels, shelves, benches cluttered with gear, and a flock of high stools left only narrow channels for locomotion. Half-way down the room stood the huge pot-bellied coal stove—red-hot this morning in early December—a stove that seemed to operate selfishly, refusing to communicate its warmth save to the big iron kettle whispering above. Beside the stove was an old-fashioned cane rocking chair with a greasy little cushion tied on its back. This was where Mr. Biggs always ate his lunch—in a picturesque oasis at the heart of the machine age.
>
> —From "Etcher's Heaven," by Peggy Bacon

> **There was quite a little ceremony connected with this part of the course.** Miss Folgil, and some lucky creature named as timekeeper and armed with a stop watch, rowed the prospective victim out to deep water. The pupil, dressed in high, laced tennis shoes, long stockings, heavy bloomers, and a middy blouse, then stood poised at the end of the boat. When the timekeeper yelled "Go!" the future boon to mankind dived into the water and, while holding her breath under the surface, unlaced her shoes and stripped down to her bathing suit. Miss Folgil never explained what connection, if any, this curious rite had with saving human lives.
>
> —From *My Sister Eileen*, by Ruth McKenney

P3b. DEVELOP A PARAGRAPH BY INSTANCES OR EXAMPLES.

This method of development uses a series of sentences that provide instances or examples of the more general statement in the topic sentence. The instance may be only partly specific, such as "Here is a woman who is overly ambitious." Or it may be more definite: "Consider Lady Macbeth, who was overly ambitious."

Following are paragraphs developed by instances or examples. In each, the topic statement is in bold print.

The story of the Arizona rancher who made out a $500 check on a six-by-three-foot cowhide recalls the **many curious surfaces on which checks have legally been written through the years:** in lipstick on handkerchiefs, on cigarette paper, on calling cards, fragile valentines, on whisky labels, Christmas cards, envelopes, newspapers, cigar-box tops, paper bags, laundry bills. A check written on a hard-boiled egg was cashed without trouble at the Victoria branch of the Canadian Bank of Commerce. A Midwestern lumberman made out so many checks on his own brand of shingle that his bank had to construct a special type of file cabinet for them. A contractor in Memphis once settled his weekly payroll by drawing on the bank with slabs of wood. A businessman eager to pay for a newly arrived television set recently pried off the side of the packing case and wrote his check on it.

—From "Topics," *The New York Times*

If we look at the world around us, we see that love has become a rare commodity, spontaneous warmth all but quenched, laughter is heard only through television tubes. We are bound together by our humanity yet dare not look one another in the eye for fear we will see some part of ourselves reflected there, some part in need that frightens and repels us. We give our help to the unemployed in the form of a check in the mails, our help to the sick aged in the form of drugs, our help to children in the form of gadgets, our help to one another in the form of alcohol, trinkets and gestures. Why is it that we can no longer be human and love and weep and laugh and relish making fools of ourselves? For we long to do these things, we long to be more human, to put more into life, get more out of life. It is as if we are going through life on tiptoe, never really experiencing it; life passes by like a painless and bland movie when we long to sink our teeth into its being. Why can't we? What has happened to us? What has been done to us?

—From *Love and Liberation*, by Lisa Hobbs

I was a slave to fashion—chopping off my hair one year to look like Twiggy, sweltering under a Dynel wig the year wigs were being worn, disappearing altogether for a while beneath an eye-obstructing curtain of bangs. Even when straight hair became fashionable, when girls slept on tin cans and ironed out their curls and when, presumably, I should have felt free to be myself, I felt, instead, the need to change my hair some other way—to alter the color or the length, to bleach a racing stripe down one side or tint it some other shade of brown, no better, maybe, but *different.* I grew up a believer in variety above all else, in quantity over quality, in "change of pace" (I heard that in a Lipton tea commercial and it stayed with me). No matter what you looked like, the way to improve your looks, I believed, was to change them. All through the sixties I fought nature, wore my face like a mask, my clothes like armor and my hair—that pinned, clipped, rolled, taped, teased, washed, set, sprayed mass, meant to hang straight forever—I wore it like a hat.

—From *Looking Back: A Chronicle of Growing Up
Old in the Sixties,* by Joyce Maynard

P3c. DEVELOP A PARAGRAPH BY COMPARISON OR CONTRAST.

A topic can be made clear by means of comparison or contrast or by the two methods either combined in one paragraph or in successive paragraphs. Comparison shows the likeness between the topic and something familiar to the reader; contrast reveals differences.

The oblique band of sunlight which followed her through the door became the young wife well. It illuminated her as her presence illuminated the heath. **In her movements, in her gaze, she reminded the beholder of the feathered creatures who lived around her home.** All similes and allegories concerning her began and ended with birds. There was as much variety in her motions as in their flight. When she was musing, she was a kestrel, which hangs in the air by an invisible motion of its wings. When she was in a high wind, her light body was blown against trees and banks like a heron's. When she was frightened, she darted noiselessly like a kingfisher. When she was serene, she skimmed like a swallow, and that is how she was moving now.

—From *The Return of the Native,* by Thomas Hardy

For many people moving is one kind of thing and travel is something very different. Travel means going away from home and staying away from home; it is an antidote to the humdrum activities of everyday life, a prelude to a holiday one is entitled to enjoy after months of dullness. Moving means breaking up a home, sadly or joyfully breaking with the past; a happy venture or a hardship, something to be endured with good or ill grace.

—From *Blackberry Winter*, by Margaret Mead

Taute people are very different from the Europeans they see in Lumi. They don't have radios or kerosene lamps, or nails, or any plastic or paper products whatsoever; very few have matches; and they don't have watches or clocks or the European concept of time. But it isn't simply the lack of material things that makes them different. For the Taute people, there is only one world. And in that world live human beings, animals, ghosts, and demons.

—From "Life and Birth in New Guinea," by Joyce S. Mitchell

P3d. DEVELOP A PARAGRAPH BY ANALYZING THE DIVISIONS SUGGESTED IN THE TOPIC SENTENCE.

Developing a topic by analyzing divisions means that a writer calls attention to two or more parts of a topic and discusses each briefly in the paragraph. For instance, if the topic sentence is "Three kinds of students are in my history class," the writer might identify each kind and briefly comment on it. The following paragraphs provide examples of this method of development:

There are two kinds of snobbishness. That of the man who has had a good many opportunities and looks down on those who lack them is recognized by all. The other kind of snobbishness is rarely understood, yet it is real. It is that of the self-made man who glories in his success in overcoming difficulties and admires greatly people who have achieved the things he considers of importance.

—From *This I Remember*, by Eleanor Roosevelt

The question—**"Which is the happiest season of life?"**—being referred to an aged man, he replied: "When spring comes, and in the soft air the buds are breaking on the trees and they are covered with blossoms, I think 'How beautiful is Spring!' And when the summer comes, and covers the trees with its heavy foliage, and singing birds are among the branches, I think 'How beautiful is Summer!' When autumn loads them with golden fruit, and their leaves bear the gorgeous tint of frost, I think 'How beautiful is Autumn!' And when it is sere winter, and there is neither foliage nor fruit, then I look up through the leafless branches, as I never could until now, and see the stars shine."

—From *Cheer*, April, 1960. Author unknown.

P
3

P3e. DEVELOP A PARAGRAPH BY DEFINITION.

This method of paragraph development involves answering the implied question of the reader, "What do you mean by this?" Sometimes, this method is called for when an unfamiliar term is used or when you employ a term in an unusual way. Ordinarily, this method involves the use of still other kinds of paragraph development, but here are two examples of straightforward definition:

> **Science is a method of knowledge** that arose and first proved its usefulness within the realms of mechanics, physics, and chemistry. In essence it is remarkably simple. The first step is to discover the pertinent facts. Next, you make a guess as to the law which accounts for these facts. And finally, you test the correctness of this guess by experiment. If your experiments do not verify the first guess, you admit that you were wrong, and make another guess. And so on, until you have found a piece of demonstrable knowledge, or demonstrated that the truth with regard to that particular matter is so far unknown.
>
> —From "The Pretensions of Science," by Hugh Stevenson Tigner

> **Let me define my terms.** By social ethic I mean that contemporary body of thought which makes morally legitimate the pressures of society against the individual. Its major propositions are three: a belief in the group as the source of creativity; a belief in "belongingness" as the ultimate need of the individual; and a belief in the application of science to achieve the belongingness.
>
> —From *The Organization Man,* by William H. Whyte

P3f. DEVELOP A PARAGRAPH BY REASONS OR INFERENCES.

When the topic sentence states a general opinion, especially a debatable one, the point of view expressed must be supported. The writer can do so either (1) by giving reasons for the assertion or (2) by drawing inferences from certain facts that are presented.

> **Our citizens will have to learn at least one foreign language.** The reason is not so they can sell things to the Brazilians, or study German medical books, or appreciate those beauties of

Homer which are lost in translation. Nor is it because they will gain satisfaction in recognizing the Latin roots of the word *satisfaction*. It is not even because grubbing for roots is good discipline. It is because they cannot understand their own language unless they have studied another. The native of any country is immersed in his own language and never sees it as a linguistic structure. He cannot learn what he ought to know about language from talking about his own.

—From "Education and Freedom,"
by Robert Maynard Hutchins

Sexual stereotypes are not to be identified with sexual or innate differences, for we know nothing about these matters. John Stuart Mill was the first man (since Plato) to affirm that we could know nothing about innate sexual differences, since we have never known of a society in which either men or women lived wholly separately. Therefore, he reasoned, we can't "know" what the pure "nature" of either sex might be: What we see as female behavior, he maintained, is the result of what he called the education of "willing slaves." There is still no "hard" scientific evidence of innate sexual differences, though there are new experiments in progress on male hormones of mice and monkeys. Other hormonal experiments, especially those using adrenaline, have indicated that, for human beings at least, social factors and pressures are more important than physiological ones.

—From "Sexual Stereotypes Start Early," by Florence Howe

P
3

P3g. DEVELOP A PARAGRAPH BY CAUSE OR EFFECT.

In this type of paragraph development, the topic sentence provides a conclusion (effect) drawn from data. The data make up the supporting material of the paragraph, the cause or reasons. Or, conversely, the supporting material might describe various results or effects of a particular cause stated in the topic sentence.

The birth of a volcanic island is an event marked by prolonged and violent travail: the forces of the earth striving to create, and all the forces of the sea opposing. The sea floor, where an island begins, is probably nowhere more than fifty miles thick — a thin covering over the vast bulk of the earth. In it are deep cracks and fissures, the results of unequal cooling and shrinkage in past ages. Along such lines of weakness the molten lava from the earth's interior presses up and finally bursts forth into the sea. But a submarine volcano is different from a terrestrial eruption, where the lava, molten rocks, gases, and other ejecta are hurled into the air through an open crater. Here on the bottom of the ocean the volcano has resisting it all the weight of the ocean water above it. Despite the immense pressure of, it may be, two or three miles of sea water, the new volcanic cone builds upward toward the surface, in flow after flow of lava. Once within reach of the waves, its soft ash and tuff are violently attacked, and for a long period the potential island may remain a shoal, unable to emerge. But, eventually, in new eruptions, the cone is pushed up into the air and a rampart against the attacks of the waves is built of hardened lava.

— From *The Sea Around Us,* by Rachel Carson

There are few scientific explanations for male fragility. The cardiovascular disorders, like coronary disease, have a much higher incidence in men even in early youth. Part of the problem may be the environmental stresses imposed on men by society — to compete, to produce, to succeed. Part of the problem may be hormonal. Dr. Hamilton's findings suggest that the male hormone testosterone induces a slightly higher metabolic rate in most tissues and that the male thus "burns out" faster. Other research indicates that the female's estrogen hormones may help retard the aging of blood vessels — something testosterone does not do. To be sure, testosterone is a delightful hormone, as hormones go, but I must say the estrogens seem to be much more helpful physiologically.

—From "A Remarkable and Marvelous Sex," by Dr. Estelle Ramey

P3h. DEVELOP A PARAGRAPH BY A COMBINATION OF METHODS.

Each of the methods so far explained is useful, and examples of several of them can be found in every published essay or article. Many paragraphs, however, do not follow a single method but use a combination of methods. The following is one example of methods in combination. For the sake of reference, a number is assigned to each sentence: (1) topic sentence; (2) amplification by contrasting statement; (3) cause; (4) effect, again contrasting statement; (5) illustration. As a whole, the paragraph supplies reasons to support the topic statement, but, as you can see below it does so in more than one way.

> (1) The people have no tradition of outsiders and no procedures for handling them. (2) They are not hostile, but they are suspicious and afraid of them. (3) History has proved that to talk to strangers sooner or later leads to trouble or ends up costing money, and so history has rendered them incapable of telling truths to outsiders. (4) They don't lie, but they never of their own will provide the truth. (5) There are people in Santa Vittoria who are capable of denying knowledge of the town fountain when it can be heard bubbling behind their backs.
>
> —From *The Secret of Santa Vittoria,* by Robert Crichton

A final illustration: Some time ago, a student was reading about attempts of scientists to launch persons into interstellar travel. Plans and preliminary steps to this end were being ridiculed by the author of the article, and the student had the thought that throughout history, daring thinkers and discoverers had been laughed at. He also recalled that many of those who have been ridiculed have later come to be accepted as great persons because of their eventual success. Such reflection helped him come up with this topic sentence: "Shortsighted people ridicule what they cannot understand." After further thought and much reading, he developed the following paragraph. Notice that it uses several methods of development.

> **History follows a pattern of first denouncing great discoveries only to honor them after the discoverers themselves are destroyed or ridiculed by their detractors.** For centuries, we have honored the teachings of Socrates as preserved in the *Dialogues* of Plato, but the man himself was condemned to death for corrupting youth with his novel ideas. Lee de Forest was prosecuted for using the mails to defraud because he wrote that his vacuum tube "would transmit the human voice across the Atlantic." And this was as recently as 1913! Daguerre, the creator of photography, was committed to an insane asylum for insisting that he could transfer a likeness to a tin plate. The automobile was opposed because agriculture was felt to be doomed by a vehicle that ate neither oats nor hay. Stephenson's locomotive was denounced on the grounds that its speed would shatter both minds and bodies. The eminent Sir Walter Scott called William Murdoch mad for proposing to light the streets of London with coal gas, and the great Emperor Napoleon laughed off the idea as

a "crazy notion." Some churchgoers argued against the plan as being blasphemous, since God had divided the light from the darkness. And some physicians insisted coal-gas lights would induce people to stay out late and catch cold. Who are the heretics and mad people of our time who will be honored and acclaimed a decade or century from now?

EXERCISE 5

By means of one of the eight methods of paragraph development discussed and illustrated in Section P3, develop one or more of the following topic sentences (as your teacher suggests).

1. Sending people to the moon is (is not) lunacy.
2. Movies are (are not) better than ever.
3. Here is one way to win friends and influence people.
4. A boring job is like a _____.
5. Yes, there is a Santa Claus.

EXERCISE 6

Follow the instructions for Exercise 5.

1. My favorite spectator sport is _____.
2. What is a good student?
3. The greatest need of this town is _____.
4. Atomic energy is changing our lives in many ways.
5. School is a poor place in which to get an education.

EXERCISE 7

The following paragraph, from "The Reading Machine," by Morris Bishop, is developed by an example (Section P3b).

"Think of the efficiency of the thing!" Professor Entwhistle was really warming up. "Think of the time saved! You assign a student a bibliography of fifty books. He runs them through the machine comfortably in a weekend. And on Monday morning he turns in a certificate from the machine. Everything has been conscientiously read!"

Write a paragraph developing Bishop's idea with a different method (or combination of methods).

EXERCISE 8

The following paragraph, from "Such, Such Were the Joys . . ." by George Orwell, is developed by cause or effect (Section P3g).

> But this sense of guilt and inevitable failure was balanced by something else: that is, the instinct to survive. Even a creature that is weak, ugly, cowardly, smelly, and in no way justifiable still wants to stay alive and be happy after its own fashion. I could not invert the existing scale of values, or turn myself into a success, but I could accept my failure and make the best of it. I could resign myself to being what I was, and then endeavour to survive on those terms.

Write a paragraph developing Orwell's thought with a different method.

P4. Unity

No matter by which method or combination of methods a paragraph is constructed, every sentence should contribute to the central thought. In other words, a paragraph should have **unity**, or oneness, a singleness of focus.

The key to paragraph unity is the topic sentence. Therefore, when you develop a paragraph, concentrate on the topic in hand and do not let it slip away. However enticing a momentary thought may seem, if it leads you into any sentence, even so much as a phrase, that has nothing directly to do with your topic, put it out of mind or save it for a different paragraph.

P4a. OMIT MATERIAL UNRELATED TO THE MAIN THOUGHT OF THE PARAGRAPH.

Lack of unity is ineffective. A reader who has been following you down one line of thought would not only be puzzled but understandably annoyed to come abruptly upon a statement that has no relation to what the paragraph has thus far been treating. Here are two sound tests for unity, whether the writing be a composition, a paragraph, or even just a sentence: (1) *omit* all material that is not an essential, logical part; (2) *include* all material that is an essential, logical part and do not place it in another sentence or paragraph where it does not belong.

The italicized sentences and parts of sentences that violate unity are shown in italics in the following paragraph:

> Tennis has certain other advantages over golf. It is a less time-consuming activity. In most communities tennis courts are more easily accessible than golf courses. *In my town, real estate taxes are high, and housing developments are springing up all over nowadays.* A pair of tennis players will often be on their second or third set while the golfing twosome is still on its way to the course or waiting for its turn to tee off. In a couple of hours or so, the tennis pair will have had its fill of fun and exercise, while the golfers will take the better part of a day to play their eighteen holes, *although less enthusiastic players, like my sister and brother, play only nine holes.*

By mentioning real estate, the writer veers away from the topic. Since the comparison has been between tennis players and golfers in general, the remarks about less enthusiastic players are irrelevant. Omitting both comments would have ensured a unified paragraph.

EXERCISE 9

Point out the lack of unity in each of the following paragraphs.

1. Lake-of-the-Woods is an excellent place for the sports enthusiast to spend the summer. If you like to fish, there are all kinds of freshwater fish to be found, the most common of which is the pike. A few miles away, up in the mountains, the streams are filled with brook trout. For people who like to winter fish, there is ice fishing nearly every day. People who are fishing there for the first time can obtain guides, leaving the town early in the morning before the weather gets hot and returning in the cool of the evening.

2. Thanksgiving is always a happy time at my home. This is the time of the year to be thankful for all the things we have in this country. Thanksgiving was first started by the Pilgrims during the time of the foundation of our country. The Pilgrims left England in September, 1620, and arrived at Plymouth in November. They had a long, hard winter; many died. But the fol-

lowing year was prosperous, and in gratitude to God they celebrated the first Thanksgiving with prayers and a bountiful feast. They invited many Indians to the feast. At Thanksgiving our family is always together for at least one time during the year. Sometimes we have friends in for dinner; at other times we have a large family reunion. When all of the relatives are present, everyone has a wonderful time.

3. There are many superstitions all over the world. In some foreign countries like New Guinea, superstitions have more meaning to the people than they do here in the United States. Many people believe in superstitions to the extent that they would stake their lives on them. However, the other group of people disbelieve in superstitions. I am one of these people who disbelieve them, and I am proceeding to tell why I do.

P5. Order

A paragraph can have fully developed, interesting, and unified content and still be unsuccessful unless its sentences are correctly and logically arranged. If a book you were reading began with chapter 5, followed by chapters 2, 4, 1, and 3, you would be confused and impatient with the author. So would the reader of a paragraph in which the sentences follow one another in helter-skelter fashion because the writer has not kept related parts of the topic together, has shuttled back and forth between ideas, or has set down afterthoughts that should have been stated earlier.

P
5

P5a. ARRANGE SENTENCES IN A CLEAR, ORDERLY SEQUENCE.

The sentences in a paragraph, like the chapters of a book, should show clear progress or readily understandable forward movement. But since the ideas that pop into our minds do not automatically shape themselves into paragraphs, we first have to arrange them properly. Anyone who has tried to tell a story or who has heard one told knows how easy it is to present ideas in the wrong order.

Several kinds of arrangement can be used. Which of these is

best depends upon the subject matter of the paragraph and the effect desired. All arrangements, however, have one end in view: the thought in the paragraph must move forward in some way, must *progress*. The three principal types of arrangement are these:

1. **Arrangement by chronology (progress through time).** Sentences follow one another in the order of the events narrated, the steps of a process, or the description of something that involves passage of time, as, for example, a sunrise or the approach of a storm.

   For instance, if you are writing a paper about your activities on a typical day, you might begin with what you do upon arising and then proceed with an account of eating breakfast, going to school, and attending classes. This activity would be followed by mention of lunch, afternoon classes and sports, return home, an evening meal, and what you did during evening hours before bedtime.

2. **Arrangement by physical point of view (progress through space).** Details are arranged from near to far, left to right, inside to outside, top to bottom, etc., or the reverse, as in describing a landscape, a building, a painting, and countless other objects.

   If, for example, you are describing a building, you should not shift carelessly and without warning from the back to the front of it, or from the outside to the inside, or from one floor to another. Your readers will be confused if they think you are writing about the outside of a building and suddenly, without proper transitional aids, you begin to comment on a picture in one of the rooms or the furnace in the basement.

3. **Arrangement by logical reasoning (mental progress).** The writer makes a general statement and follows it with details, or states an effect and then cites causes, or names a term and then explains it.

   Notice that each of the illustrative paragraphs in Section P3 follows a logical plan of development: a *cause* followed by an *effect*, a *general statement* followed by *details*, an *inference* made after *reasons* are developed, and so on.

In addition to doing the following exercises, turn to Section C8 for further comment on the ordering of paragraphs within a composition.

EXERCISE 10

Rearrange the sentences of these paragraphs in an orderly sequence. Write the numbers of the sentences in the order in which you feel they should appear.

(1) The view at Lookout Point was spectacular. (2) As far as one could see were mountains. (3) Closer by, off to our right, rose enormous cliffs, from one of which cascaded a waterfall that disappeared into the chasm below. (4) It was amazing to think that we had driven up so high along that winding road. (5) It was so quiet that we could hear the roar of the water. (6) To our left was a deep, wooded gorge. (7) Way down below we could see the roof of the hotel we had left that morning. (8) As it was midsummer, I was surprised to see there was still snow on some of the highest peaks.

(1) Parson's Creek is a very small village in western Ohio. (2) A few years ago my parents and I visited my grandfather, who has lived there ever since he was born. (3) It has a population of only 127. (4) In such a small place there wasn't much for me to do but swing in the hammock or go fishing and swimming in the creek. (5) People have to go six miles to Harbury to shop. (6) Parson's Creek has a small church but no post office or general store. (7) Once I rode a borrowed bicycle all the way to Harbury just for an ice-cream soda.

P6. Transition

P 6

A well-written paragraph depends not only on a writer's control of what is said but also on the ease and smoothness with which thought moves from sentence to sentence. Ease of movement between sentences is aided by a skillful use of *transitional devices.* Lack of them, or of effective use of them, often accounts for awkwardness in writing. It is important to know what different kinds of transitional devices are available and to what uses you can put them.

Transition means "passage or change from one position or stage to another." In writing, transition involves *showing* evidence of the links between related units (sentences and paragraphs).

Even though a paragraph contains ample substance, with its sentences logically and clearly arranged, it will not make sense to a reader if the sentences appear to be loosely joined or even disconnected. Our own processes of thought are so familiar to us that we are likely to forget that our readers do not understand the relationships between our ideas unless we show them what that relationship is. To show the relationship of one sentence to another in a paragraph often *requires* the use of transitional words. Have you ever noticed that some teacher or other speaker is particularly easy to understand because he or she constantly relates one thought to another by using such transitional devices as *however, on the other hand, for example, similarly, conversely,* and the like?

Transitions resemble highway signs: "Detour: 100 Yards"; "Slow Down: End of Pavement"; "Form Single Lane"; "End of Construction." Such signs prepare a motorist for changing conditions. Transitional expressions have precisely the same effect upon the reader. For example, when you complete a paragraph, you can then let the reader know what is coming next. When you finish a group of paragraphs dealing with one phase of a topic, you can let the reader know that another topic is being taken up. Sometimes, you can sum up what has been written; more often you may point out the road ahead, a continuation in the same direction.

P6a. USE TRANSITIONAL EXPRESSIONS WITHIN THE SENTENCE, BETWEEN SENTENCES, AND BETWEEN PARAGRAPHS.

The transitional expressions listed below are all useful, but be sparing in employing them. Transitions should be unobtrusive and not weigh down the paragraph. Rarely if ever use the same transitional expression more than once in the same paragraph.

To add an idea:	besides, also, moreover, in addition, another way, a second method, furthermore, similarly
To contrast ideas:	but, yet, nevertheless, still, however, in contrast, on the contrary, instead, otherwise, on the other hand, whereas, unlike
To compare ideas:	like, similarly, equally, correspondingly, in like manner

To show result:	therefore, thus, consequently, as a result, hence
To show time:	then, afterward, later, meanwhile, now, earlier, immediately, henceforth, before
To show frequency:	often, frequently, sometimes, now and then

P6b. REPEAT A KEY WORD OR A VARIATION OF A KEY WORD.

Simple repetition of a key word in successive sentences, sometimes even in the same sentence, is frequently effective for emphasis. When emphasis is not a primary consideration, a more subtle transitional device is using a different form of the same word the second time.

> One of the greatest disappointments of *childhood* is a *broken* promise. An adult who *breaks* a pledge never fully regains a *child's* confidence.

> They knew it would take a long time for the *dust* to settle out of the air. In the morning the *dust* hung like fog, and the sun was as red as ripe new blood. All the day the *dust sifted down* from the sky, and the next day it *sifted down*.
>
> —From *The Grapes of Wrath*, by John Steinbeck

P 6

P6c. USE DEMONSTRATIVE ADJECTIVES (*THIS* AND *THAT*) AND PRONOUNS AS TRANSITIONAL AIDS.

The demonstratives *this* and *that* are effective transitional words but *should not be used to excess*. Be especially careful in your use of *this*, and do not use it by itself to refer to a general statement. It should refer to a specific noun, and then only if the reference is entirely clear.

> A rumor was recently circulated that Easter vacation would be shortened to three days. *This* rumor is false.

Pronouns are common transitional aids. No narrative could dispense with them, and they occur frequently in all other types of writing.

Live oaks are so called because *they* do not lose *their* leaves. *They* also differ from other oaks in that *they* have relatively short trunks out of which spring heavy curved or crooked limbs. Because of *their* shape and because *their* wood is tough and durable, *they* were once much sought after by shipbuilders. Today, in certain areas, many of *them* are being killed by infestations of Spanish moss.

P6d. AVOID LABORED AND ARTIFICIAL TRANSITIONS.

Be sure to make your transitions smooth and inconspicuous.

Inadequate
transition: Television viewing is said to be the national pastime; I do not like it. If it is the national pastime, hundreds of thousands must enjoy it constantly or occasionally. I know people who do not ever watch a TV show; I know people who view 25 shows over a weekend. I should not make a dogmatic statement about the appeal of the activity; I have never owned a set.

Clumsy
transition: Television viewing is said to be the national pastime; *however*, I do not like it. *Yet* if it is the national pastime, hundreds of thousands must enjoy it constantly or occasionally. *To be sure*, I know people who do not ever watch a TV show; *on the other hand*, I know people who view 25 shows over a weekend. *Perhaps* I should not make a dogmatic statement about the appeal of the activity; *you see*, I have never owned a set.

Smoother
transition: *Although* television viewing is said to be America's national pastime, I do not like *it*. *Yet* if *it* is the *national pastime*, hundreds of thousands must enjoy *it* constantly, and millions more must enjoy *it* occasionally. I know people who do not ever watch a TV *show* and *couldn't* be persuaded to see *one;* on the other hand, I know people who view 25 *shows* in the course of a weekend and *couldn't* be dragged away from *them*. *Perhaps* it is all a matter of taste, *and perhaps* I shouldn't make a dogmatic statement about the appeal of television viewing. *You see*, I have never owned a set.

EXERCISE 11

Supply correct transitional words and phrases where they are needed within and between the sentences in the following paragraph.

It seems to be a cold day; the temperature was only 30°. I had risen early; my alarm clock went off too soon. Connie was still asleep. I shook and shook her; she did not move. I left her behind, hurried to Janet's house. She was asleep. She got up, dressed herself; we set out on our long-anticipated hike. Both Janet and I like to walk; we had a good time. The winter day was too short; we had to return in a few hours. Connie had stayed indoors all day.

EXERCISE 12

Each of the two original paragraphs below contains seven incomplete sentences. The sentence subjects (topics) are numbered in proper order. Reconstruct each paragraph, making each statement into a sentence and supplying whatever transitions you consider necessary.

(1) Little security for musicians, even if famous. (2) Uncertain today whether job tomorrow. (3) Most well paid, seldom save money, travel town to town expensive. (4) Leader of orchestra paid much more, works harder for money. (5) Many responsibilities, orchestra successful, leader's name famous. (6) Always in music feeling of beauty, makes people happy. (7) Musician's life rough, many compensations.

(1) Fire wardens hard work. (2) Area to patrol, no fires except at designated camp grounds. (3) Visit lumber camps, no smoking permitted. (4) Much walking, patrolling of lakes in outboard boat. (5) If fire, must organize fire fighters. (6) Observe game laws, help game wardens. (7) Cooperate together in searching lost persons.

EXERCISE 13

The following underdeveloped paragraphs lack proper transitional aids. Rewrite each.

1. "Never cross a bridge till you come to it" is a wise saying. Many

people worry too much. W. H. Auden said we live in an "age of anxiety."

2. In most European countries students are taught to speak English the way it is pronounced in England. I know someone from Australia whose speech is hard to tell from American.

3. Many girls use too much makeup. Some girls use too much eye shadow. There are many rinses on the market that a girl can use to make her hair any color she likes.

P7. Length

The **length** of a paragraph depends on the weight and value of its controlling idea in relation to other paragraphs in the same paper. No definite rule for paragraph length can be given. About the *average* length, however, something can be said. This varies with an author's subject and the demands made upon the readers. If the subject is analytical, philosophical, or scientific — one demanding full concentration from readers — the paragraphs will tend to be longer than those in a popular magazine designed to be read rapidly. In the former, the average length of paragraphs might be 400 words; in the latter, the longest would rarely exceed 150 words.

P7a. AVOID SHORT, UNDERDEVELOPED PARAGRAPHS.

Although an occasional short paragraph is effective for emphasis and variety, especially in a long paper, it must always be a complete unit of thought. If it is short simply because the writer has not thought out the topic, it will leave readers stranded, for they have been led to expect something that the topic statement indicates but never supplies. In the following examples, in which the key statements are italicized, the writer was evidently careless and too easily satisfied.

As an attendant at a filling station last summer, *I met some strange people.* One car even had an Alaska license plate.

What about those "strange people" the writer was to tell about?

> *An interesting program of arts and crafts* has been started at our civic center. Wood carving was canceled, though, because there wasn't enough interest.

Specifically, why was the program interesting? Was wood carving canceled because it was an uninteresting course or because not enough people registered for it?

P7b. AVOID OVERLY LONG, RAMBLING PARAGRAPHS.

Overly long paragraphs make it difficult for a reader to follow the main idea. They are also tiring to read, since breaks in thought are infrequent.

Actually, a very long paragraph is probably a poorly conceived one. The chances are that its main idea is too broad to be developed in just one paragraph. In such a case, the material should be reworked into two or more new paragraphs.

Although every paragraph should be adequately developed, the length of paragraphs usually depends upon their use in a composition of several paragraphs. For this reason, turn to Section C6 for further comment on the matters of length and proportion.

P
7

EXERCISE 14

Count the number of words in five consecutive paragraphs of some essay in an anthology or magazine. How many words does the longest contain? The shortest? What is the average? Repeat this exercise for another article by another writer on a different subject. Make a comparison of the two.

EXERCISE 15

Compare the average length of paragraphs in an article in *The Atlantic* or *Harper's Magazine* with the average length of an article in *Time, People, Newsweek,* or *Reader's Digest.*

P8. Variety

There are many different kinds of sentences, each of which may be good in itself. But, a series of similarly constructed sentences quickly becomes monotonous and ineffective.

No definite rule can be set down about how much **variety** sentences should have. Indeed, good professional writers neither count the number of words in their sentences nor consciously intersperse simple and compound sentences with complex. But they do achieve variety in sentence structure. They vary length and, occasionally, word order. They use declarative, imperative, interrogative, and exclamatory sentences. They refresh a series of simple sentences by using various kinds of words, phrases, and clauses as beginnings or endings.

Sentences also involve sound and rhythm. Make a practice of reading your paragraphs aloud to yourself. Often the ear will detect what the eye has passed over. How do your sentences *sound?* If some of them seem halting and jerky, perhaps you have broken your thought into several short sentences that need revising or combining. On the other hand, if the pace seems slow and lumbering, you may have combined ideas that should be expressed in shorter sentences. Your ear may also detect awkward or jarring sound combinations that the eye has failed to observe.

P8a. AVOID USING TOO MANY SHORT SENTENCES IN SUCCESSION.

In the paragraph below, the first two brief sentences are effective because they engage our attention at once. But thereafter, short sentences that lack variety beat upon us like hailstones, the monotony of which is not relieved even by transitional devices.

> An exciting thing has happened in our town. A circus has set up winter quarters. Animals are being trained for the spring shows. The circus owners also saw a chance to make some extra money. They put some of their animals on television. A young girl put the elephants through their paces. She is said to be the youngest elephant trainer in the world. After the TV program, many people rushed to the winter quarters. Again the owners made extra money. They charged 25 cents admission. So far I have gone three times. Each performance was different. At the first,

they were training seals. At the second, the bareback riders were practicing. The third, however, was best. A panther was being taught to roll over and to jump through a hoop. I will be sorry to see the circus leave.

This paragraph has other flaws (improper order of sentences and lack of unity), but its greatest fault is lack of sentence variety.

P8b. AVOID USING TOO MANY LENGTHY SENTENCES IN SUCCESSION.

A sequence of overloaded sentences makes heavy reading. Besides crowding together unrelated ideas, prolonged sentences tend to be pompous. If the following paragraph were read aloud, some of the sentences would require several intakes of breath.

Because little of note ever happens in our town, considerable excitement was generated when a circus established its winter quarters in our midst. During the winter, circus people occupy themselves primarily with rehearsing and improving their acts and training animals for performances to be given in the spring. The circus owners, seizing the opportunity to earn some extra money, exhibited some of their animals on a television program, which also showed a young girl, said to be the youngest elephant trainer in the world, putting the pachyderms through various stunts. As a result of this publicity, many people hastened to the winter quarters, where the shrewd owners again netted a profit, this time by charging an admission fee of 25 cents, which, however, was well worth paying, for each performance was different from the one before. I first witnessed the training of seals, next some bareback riders practicing, and last, the best exhibition thus far, a panther being taught to lie down and turn over and also to jump through a hoop. I doubt whether anyone will be more regretful than I to see the circus depart.

P8c. DO NOT BEGIN SUCCESSIVE SENTENCES WITH THE SAME WORD OR PHRASE OR DEPENDENT CLAUSE.

Avoid beginning a sentence with the same words that end the sentence before it. Also, avoid sentences that begin with such shopworn words and phrases as *there is, there are, there was, it was, it, this, that, I, we, she,* and *these.*

> Awkward: Celestial navigation is very confusing. Celestial navigation involves many facts and figures that one must look up. Celestial navigation encompasses many different fields of science, requiring knowledge of astronomy, mathematics, physics, and electronics.

> Improved: Celestial navigation is confusing to the beginning student, involving as it does many facts and figures that must be looked up. The study, which encompasses many different fields, requires some knowledge of astronomy, mathematics, physics, and electronics.

> Awkward: There was a house at the top of the hill. There was a sinister look about the house because there was a tree in front of it covered with Spanish moss. There was a pair of tombstones close beside the tree, and to add to the gloomy effect there was a black cat sitting on what looked like a new grave.

> Improved: There was a house at the top of the hill. A tree in front of it, covered with Spanish moss, gave the surroundings a sinister look. A pair of tombstones close beside it, and a black cat sitting on what appeared to be a new grave, added to the gloomy effect.

Avoid beginning every sentence with a phrase and avoid overusing the same kind of phrases (participial, prepositional, prepositional-gerund, absolute, adverbial) as a beginning. Consider the monotony of the following paragraph:

> Having decided to take a summer job, I wrote to various firms about available jobs. Receiving several replies, I gave them careful study. Deciding that a job in an oyster hatchery would be most interesting, I made an appointment to meet with the manager of the Pine Island Marine Station. Being hired, I made plans to start work on June 29. Having carried out these plans, I am now here, starting a new page in my personal journal.

Avoid, too, beginning every sentence with a dependent clause, and especially avoid beginning a series of dependent clauses with the same subordinating conjunction.

P8d. DO NOT PLACE THE SUBJECT AT THE BEGINNING OF EVERY SENTENCE.

In ordinary speech, it is natural to start sentences with the subject. In writing, a series of subject + verb + complement structures is monotonous. Occasional deviation from this order is refreshing.

Usual order: I met those singers when I was in San Francisco.
A person who can sing with an octet is fortunate.
Varied: Those singers I met when I was in San Francisco.
Fortunate is a person who can sing with an octet.

EXERCISE 16

Rewrite the following, eliminating whatever is monotonous. Rephrase and add words if necessary, but preserve the original meaning.

1. My buddy and I once went on a camping trip through the state parks. First we visited the Dunes, on Lake Michigan. Then we drove south to Turkey Run. Then we went to McCormick's Creek. Then we went to Spring Mill, where an old pioneer village has been restored. Next we went to Clifty Falls on the Ohio River, and finally to Brown County.
2. Jensen was forty-two years old. But he had never learned to read. He was very industrious, and his intelligence was only a little below average. But educational opportunities had never come his way. He had left school at an early age.
3. After the ingredients required for making bread have been combined, the resulting dough should be kneaded. After it has been kneaded, it should be put in a warm place to rise. When it has doubled its size, it should be kneaded again, shaped into loaves, and allowed to rise a second time. When it has once more doubled in bulk, it is ready to bake.
4. I was born on a farm, and I have lived on farms all my life. I like country life — the clean air, the animals, even the work, though I admit I sometimes wish I didn't have to do quite so much work. I should also like it if I weren't quite so far away from town and social life.
5. Jay wants to go to New York City for his vacation, but Rose wants to visit her cousin in Iowa. His idea of a good time is to hear topflight jazz bands, but she prefers to visit with relatives and old friends. My guess is that they will go to New York.

P
8

EXERCISE 17

Rewrite each of the following paragraphs so that the sentences will exhibit greater variety in structure and length.

1. Thanksgiving originated in New England. The first one was in 1623. There had been a bad drought. The colonists had a day for fasting and prayer. While they were praying, rain began to fall. The prayer was changed to giving thanks. For years Thanksgiving was a harvest celebration. Finally President Lincoln made it a national holiday. He set it as the last Thursday in November. He did that in 1864.

2. When my parents bought the encyclopedia set and the bookcase to hold it, I was disappointed because it meant that I would not get the new bicycle I wanted. When I first showed my parents the picture of the bicycle in the mail-order catalog, they said I could have it, as my old one, which I had bought secondhand, had a wobbly front wheel, rusty handlebars, and most of the paint chipped off the frame, but after they paid for the encyclopedia they said they couldn't afford to buy me a new bicycle. When I saw my mother and my older sister taking volumes of the encyclopedia out of the bookcase and looking up different things in them, I was still annoyed about the bicycle, but after a while my curiosity got the best of me and I began to look up some things I'd wanted to know, like where Guadalcanal is and how General Custer made his last stand. When I later got my newspaper route, I saved up enough money to buy the new bicycle anyway, and I was never sorry again that we had a good encyclopedia, because I get a lot of use out of it.

3. Having received a stiff lecture from their coach, the team, promising to do its best, went out for the second half. Receiving the kickoff, Jim Matthews, dodging the first two tacklers, carried the ball to the 35-yard line, before being downed. Making three first-downs in succession, the team reached the opponents' 30. Fading back, Dave Prokowski heaved a pass to Stan Graminian in the end zone. Matthews' kick, sailing neatly between the crossbars, brought loud cheering from our side in the stands, the score now being in our favor 7 to 6.

EXERCISE 18

Copy a paragraph from a book or magazine that seems to contain especially good sentence variety. Write a brief analysis of the length and structure of the sentences.

P9. Mechanics

The few rules for *mechanical correctness* in paragraphs are easy to learn. The following are the principal ones.

P9a. INDENT THE FIRST LINE OF EVERY PARAGRAPH.

The break of distinct paragraph indentation is a clear and effective help to both writer and reader in recognizing the divisions of thought within a composition. When you are writing in longhand, *indent* (set in) the first line of each paragraph about three-quarters of an inch. Keep your indentations the same throughout so that they line up neatly and evenly. If you typewrite, indent five spaces each time. (Business letters are sometimes typed without indentations. Also, some book designs leave certain paragraphs without indentations, as is done in this book.)

P9b. DO NOT LEAVE PART OF A LINE BLANK WITHIN A PARAGRAPH.

It is difficult in writing or typing to keep right-hand margins even, but try to keep them as even as you can. Gaps at the end of lines not only produce a jagged appearance but also are a hindrance to the reader, who is accustomed to seeing spaces at the ends of paragraphs and whose eye must make constant readjustments when the spaces occur earlier.

P9c. WHEN WRITING DIALOGUE, USE A NEW PARAGRAPH FOR EACH NEW SPEAKER.

In recording conversation and writing dialogue, use a separate paragraph for each speaker's words. Most of these paragraphs will be short, sometimes very short, but starting a new paragraph for each change of speaker enables the reader to keep track of who is talking to whom. When only two persons are speaking, the routine speaker-identifications, such as *James said, Joan asked, Bill replied,* etc., can also be reduced to a minimum.

Mr. Stilby had always had us recite in alphabetical order. He had called on me yesterday, as I had known he would, and I had taken care to be prepared. As my name was next to last in Mr. Stilby's roll book and there were twenty-two names ahead of mine, I hadn't done today's reading assignment. At the moment, I was pondering the problem of which of several boys to invite on the soccer team I was forming, and the teacher's voice seemed only a sort of background static. Suddenly I had the strange notion that someone was calling me by name. Then I heard it again. It was really a voice — the voice of Mr. Stilby. I rose to my feet.

"Yates!"

"Sir?" My heart was pounding like a pile driver.

"I assume you have normal hearing, Yates?"

"Yes, sir." What did he want of me? Today wasn't my turn.

"Then how do you explain that I had to call your name *three* times?"

An explanation would have been complicated. Besides, I didn't think it would interest Mr. Stilby very much. All I could do was to say I was sorry, and I did.

"Very well. But don't let it happen again, Yates. Now suppose you tell the class why knocking on the gate in *Macbeth* is so dramatically effective."

"I don't know, sir." I remembered that we were supposed to have read some essay about that. I was going to read it, too, sometime.

"Oh, you don't know, sir." He was mimicking me. Someone snickered. I knew it was Luke Chapman. "Then sit down, Yates!"

I knew Mr. Stilby was putting a neat zero in his roll book, but I didn't care. All I cared about just then was crossing Luke's name off my list.

REVIEW EXERCISE 1

Locate the topic sentence in each of the following paragraphs. Then indicate (1) the *kind* and (2) the *order* of development used in each selection.

(1) Like any other modern literary type, the novel evolved from various unsettled forms that preceded it. The professional teller of tales was an important figure for centuries before the invention of printing and still retains prominence in places where

reading is not widespread. In ancient Egypt, in India, and in Greece and Rome, fables of beasts, fairy tales, and stories of adventure thrived. Italy and France produced many narrative writers, and for three centuries the medieval romance flourished in England. In Elizabethan England people began to turn to fiction as well as to drama for entertainment.

Order: (1) chronological; (2) physical point of view; (3) logical reasoning

Development: (1) definition; (2) cause and effect; (3) examples or instances; (4) contrast

(2) From a large picture window in the living room of our present home I can see a quiet, dreaming old millpond surrounded by weeping willows and waving marsh grass. As I turn to glance inside, I am again struck by the centuries-old beams and planking that were a part of this structure when it was a gristmill. As a reminder of bygone days, an ancient piece of mill gear, now a hat rack, hangs from steps leading up to the second floor. For more than a century the grinding of wheels and pouring of water have been stilled; the house is now as silent and calm as the old pond outside. I find it difficult either to understand or appreciate this quiet repose, because only two months ago we were living in a modern apartment on a traffic-laden street in a large city. There we looked out upon straining trucks, hooting taxis, and hurrying pedestrians. Our living room was as advanced as tomorrow with its mirrored walls, blue-and-gold color scheme, and wall-to-wall carpeting. Not even in the normally still watches of the night did street noises ever cease. Nothing about our former home suggested age or tranquillity; everything reminded of the bustling present.

Order: (1) chronological; (2) physical point of view; (3) logical reasoning

Development: (1) definition; (2) cause and effect; (3) examples or instances; (4) contrast

(3) Exposition is that type of writing that defines, explains, and interprets. Put another way, to distinguish it from the other traditional forms of discourse, exposition is all writing that does not primarily describe an object, tell a story, or maintain a position. It includes by far the greatest part of what we write and read: themes, textbooks, magazine articles, newspaper editorials, and all criticism of books, plays, motion pictures, television and radio programs, and musical compositions. Further-

more, it appears in most other forms of discourse and mediums of presentation: most novels, for example, explain and interpret; so do many motion pictures, radio speeches, and picture magazines.

Order: (1) chronological; (2) physical point of view; (3) logical reasoning

Development: (1) definition; (2) cause and effect; (3) examples or instances; (4) contrast

REVIEW EXERCISE 2

Using *definition* as your method, develop one of the following topic sentences in a paragraph of 100 to 150 words.

A fashion is usually a fad.
This is what I mean when I refer to a "successful person."
What is meant by the phrase "inner city"?
This school is fully equipped to provide a good education to those who want one.
Ms. Santiago is my idea of a dedicated teacher.

REVIEW EXERCISE 3

By means of *illustration* (examples and instances) develop one of these topic sentences in a paragraph of 100 to 150 words.

Sunday afternoon is the best time of the week.
Television commercials are often too frequent and too insistent.
This school's greatest need is ____.
Public opinion polls are often misleading.
First impressions are frequently wrong.

REVIEW EXERCISE 4

Using *contrast* as a method, develop in 100 to 150 words one of the following sentences.

Let me tell you why I like summer better than winter.
Before I moved here I lived far out in the country.
My parents and I have different ideas about ____.
What's the difference between PG and R movies?

REVIEW EXERCISE 5

Select one of the following adages and develop a paragraph of 100 to 150 words by any method you choose.

Still waters run deep.
Love makes the world go 'round.
Two's company, three's a crowd.
The love of money is the root of all evil.

REVIEW EXERCISE 6

Using two or more methods of development, write a paragraph of 100 to 150 words on one of these sentences.

I don't see what's so funny about comic strips.
A part-time job can be both a help and a hindrance.
When I get what I want I don't want it.
Gambling is a serious disease.
My best friend is a practical joker.

REVIEW EXERCISE 7

Study the following paragraph. Does it lack *unity?* If so, what sentences should be deleted?

P
R

The island of Malta lies almost in the middle of the Mediterranean Sea — 55 miles from Sicily and about 150 miles from Africa. Its area is less than 100 square miles. The island was originally all rock, no soil whatever. Legend has it that all the soil was shipped in from Sicily years ago. The island was under the control of the British for many years. The highest point on the island is the small town of Rabat, 700 feet above sea level. Malta's strategic location made possible raids on Italian and German shipping to Africa, when General Rommel's German forces were in Egypt and Tunisia. This was during World War II. The population is mainly Italian. They remained loyal to the British during the war. The poet Samuel Taylor Coleridge was for a time the Secretary to the Governor of Malta. He wrote the famous poem, "The Rime of the Ancient Mariner," about how a sailor was accursed because he killed an albatross. Coleridge planned to come to America and establish a happy colony on the banks of the Susquehanna River. He died in 1834.

REVIEW EXERCISE 8

The *order* of sentences in the following paragraph is neither clear nor effective. Why? Be specific.

Since the topic assigned concerned dictionaries, I have looked up a great mass of material on dictionaries and their background. The first dictionary aiming to give a complete collection of English words was published in 1721 by Nathan Bailey, and was called *The Universal Etymological English Dictionary*. This book was also the first in English to trace the derivation of words and to mark the accents as an aid to pronunciation. The greatest American lexicographer was Noah Webster. His dictionary was published in 1828 and has been repeatedly revised. It provided features such as illustrations, synonyms, abbreviations, and other helpful additions. The earliest Greek and Latin dictionaries did not contain all of the words of the language, but instead contained the more difficult words and phrases. Samuel Johnson published a dictionary in London in 1755; he had married a woman some twenty years older than he was. A pronouncing dictionary was prepared by Thomas Sheridan; he was the father of Richard Brinsley Sheridan, who wrote a number of plays and gave some speeches in Parliament. The earliest dictionary was written in the seventh century B.C. and was printed on clay tablets. The dates and specific information about these dictionaries were taken from a reference book I have.

The Composition

If you think of writing a composition as a single operation, or process, it will seem like an overwhelming task. But writing is not a single process. It is an operation consisting of three parts. Each of these parts, or steps, is dependent upon the others. And yet the act of writing is considerably less involved and more manageable if it is broken into its three phases and handled separately.

These three parts are (1) planning, (2) writing, and (3) revising.

Planning

If you could sit down to *write what you have thought* and not sit down to *think what you will write*, the difficulties in actually putting words on paper would lessen. You can do so if you approach writing gradually by planning ahead, or *prewriting.*

Prewriting has been called "writing on the hoof." By this is meant "writing" all the time as you go about your daily activities. Whether you realize it or not, you are constantly tossing about ideas while walking, eating, talking, taking a bath, working, reading, and even sleeping. If you can pull together these ideas for your writing, you will be doing what most professional writers do. The successful novelist Somerset Maugham once remarked that he wrote "all day long." He went on to say that authors write at their desks, while thinking, while reading, and while experiencing and that everything they see and feel is significant. The late James Thurber once remarked that he never quite knew when he was not writing.

In one sense, you have been engaged in a form of prewriting since your first-grade days. Have you uttered any remarks to yourself before saying them aloud? Have you thought through any letters or papers before writing them down? This kind of thinking ahead is not often considered writing, but it is. In fact, it is an essential part of writing.

Form the habit of jotting down in a notebook or diary some of the thoughts and impressions that come to you each day. If you do this, you may find that you have a great deal of material that you can use in your papers.

Planning involves selecting something to write about and narrowing that subject into one segment, which becomes a manageable *topic*. Next comes consideration of whom you intend to write for and what purpose you hope to achieve. Also part of the before-actual-writing stage is gathering material to develop your topic. This material may come from varied sources, yourself not least important among them. The final step in prewriting is shaping (that is, outlining) the material you have assembled. Sections C1, C2, and C3 that follow deal with these steps involved in planning.

Writing

When the basic decisions involved in planning are completed, you can then concentrate on the actual writing, putting words on paper. The act of writing consists of carrying out preplanned decisions through a draft that may or may not be complete and that will certainly require revision.

Sections C4–C10 discuss such matters as beginning and ending papers, proportioning the length of paragraphs and arranging their position, ensuring that the paper deals with one topic and only one, and phrasing a title for the paper. Above all, these sections deal with *coherence* and *consistency*, factors essential if writing is to be a medium of clear communication.

Revising

When your first draft is completed, you are ready for the third, and final, step. This involves revision and usually considerable actual rewriting.

In everything anyone writes, errors of some sort are inevitable. Not even a skilled professional writer can preplan, write, revise, and proofread all at one time. Especially not skilled writers—they know from experience that first drafts are rarely satisfactory.

Unless a paper has been thoroughly preplanned and "written in your head" many times, it is likely to contain errors in thinking, in organization, in logical development, and in sentence and paragraph structure. Even if your paper contains no such flaws, it is almost certain to reveal errors in punctuation, spelling, and mechanics.

Sections C11–C14 deal with specific items that usually require careful inspection and substantial revision.

C1. Choosing a Topic

When your teacher leaves the choice of a theme topic to you, and you can think of nothing much, refer to the sources mentioned for paragraph substance (Section P2). Consider the following paragraphs before you finally decide on your subject.

C1a. CHOOSE A TOPIC OF INTEREST TO YOURSELF.

First, you should have a genuine interest in the subject. If you choose it largely because you are expected to write a certain number of words, you will probably produce a piece of writing that is padded with generalities and dull. Your writing has a chance to be lively and sincere if you can show some enthusiasm for your topic.

You could give a more interesting account, for example, of how to build a tree house you once constructed yourself than you could of one you saw in a Tarzan film. Or again, you may never have given any particular thought to labor relations. But if someone in your family or in that of a close friend joined a picket line or became a victim of an unjust strike, labor relations might come alive as a potential subject for writing.

Sometimes, your instructor may assign topics that seem to leave no room for originality. Keep turning the subject over and over in your mind until you hit upon some phase or angle that directly appeals to you. Almost always, you will be able to write with confidence and vitality when your interest is immediately involved. When it is not, it is almost a waste of your time and that of your readers to bother writing at all.

C
1

C1b. CHOOSE A TOPIC OF INTEREST TO YOUR READERS.

When you decide upon your subject and begin examining its possibilities, you must consider the reader you intend to address. Your potential readers fall into two groups. In the first are your actual readers: your instructor, your classmates, someone in your family, a friend, or anyone else to whom you may show your paper.

Also, you will be writing for readers in another category, readers who you imagine would be interested in your theme if they saw it in print. Suppose, for instance, you had chosen as your subject hitchhiking, a means of travel in which you have had considerable experience. If your intention is to provide helpful pointers on how to get lifts from passing motorists, your imagined readers would be those who had never thumbed a ride or who had gone about it in the wrong way. If one point you are making suggests an amusing hitchhiking incident you want to tell about, you would be writing for all readers in both categories who relish a funny story.

The following list suggests topics that would interest most readers:

1. **The readers themselves:** as readers, we are all interested in material that will benefit us in some way, whether it be educational, entertaining, or practical.

2. **Other people:** unique, prominent, well-known, unforgettable.

3. **Personal reminiscences:** especially recollections told in the form of dialogue, incident, or anecdote (that is, in story form) and making a point with which the reader can easily identify.

4. **Places:** historical, scenic, unusual (or uncommon features of common places, unfamiliar features of familiar places) that the reader would like to visit or that can be visualized or recollected.

5. **Life, property, welfare:** important matters involving other people that have direct relationship to the reader's own welfare and ideas, such as money, health, self-improvement, etc.

6. **Conflict:** contests between people, between people and nature, within the individual. (Conflict is the basis of all narrative writing: plays, short stories, narrative poems, and novels.)

7. **Amusements, hobbies, recreation:** television, movies, radio, recordings; spectator and participation sports; development of, interest in, and profit from, hobbies.

Other topics are the varied ways in which people earn their living (occupations), religion (both formal and informal) and the lack of it, relationships between the sexes, nature, and dozens of other topics.

C1c. CHOOSE A TOPIC ABOUT WHICH YOU KNOW SOMETHING.

Most magazine articles and nearly all books are based on many months or years of direct observation, study, and personal familiarity with the subject involved. Good writers go to their own experiences—to those things they know or have thought or seen or heard. But good writers also remember that their experiences are quickly exhausted as writing materials unless they develop from them some new insights. Any one of your well-recollected experiences will become boring to your reader unless you use it to develop some new relationship or idea that has a meaning to the reader above and beyond the experience itself.

Some topics you can develop by relying entirely on what you already know. But some topics will send you on a search for information. For example, if you need to know whether the Monroe Doctrine applies to Cuba, you should spend some time in the library (see Section LR2). It would be foolish for you to write on such a topic without exact information secured from sources other than yourself. In getting to know your subject intimately, you are merely doing what good writers take for granted as a necessary task. Besides, learning about a subject that really interests you can be rewarding and fun.

C 1

C1d. NARROW A TOPIC TO ONE THAT YOU CAN TREAT ADEQUATELY.

In selecting a topic, keep in mind the approximate length of the paper you plan to write. It is impossible to write an adequate theme of 500 words on a subject that would require 5000. The shorter a composition is, the more limited its subject should be. A thorough discussion of social injustice would require a book or a number of books. But limiting your subject to a case of social injustice that you have observed in your own neighborhood or by which you yourself have been affected could be treated in a short theme. The American Automobile Association has discussed safe driving in a series of pamphlets, but you can write a short theme on an error in driving or on elementary courtesy for drivers.

The word **theme** implies a single, well-defined *phase* of a subject. Consequently, you must limit a broad subject so that your composition can deal with it with reasonable thoroughness. A short composition on a large and lengthy subject will be fragmentary and generally ineffective. When you restrict a subject, you narrow the range of investigation and thus increase your chances of finding out what it is you really want to say to your reader. Your success with a pinpointed topic is much more likely than with a broad subject, no matter how great your interest in it or that of your reader.

EXERCISE 1

List five incidents in your life that you think might be developed into compositions interesting to other members of your class. Include an explanatory (topic) sentence for each incident.

EXERCISE 2

From the following general subjects, select four about which you have information perhaps not shared by possible readers: *animals, athletics, childhood, dancing, food, friends, illness, memories, movies, music, reading, recreation, relatives, sorrow, sports, success, superstition, vacations, wearing apparel.* Restrict each of these four chosen subjects to a *specific, limited topic* that you think might interest a particular type of reader, which you should also specify.

EXERCISE 3

From the following list of American holidays and special occasions, select four about which you have or can find detailed information probably not shared by your classmates or other readers *whom you specify.* For each of the four selected holidays or special events, write two limited topics that interest you and possibly will appeal to designated readers: *New Year's Eve, New Year's Day, Martin Luther King Day, Lincoln's Birthday, Washington's Birthday, International Women's Day, April Fool's Day, Memorial Day, Fourth of July, Labor Day, Halloween, Armed Services Day, Christmas Eve, Christmas Day, my birthday, a family anniversary.* For each of the limited topics (eight in all) write an explanatory (topic) sentence.

EXERCISE 4

Apply the four tests (Sections C1a, b, c, d) to the following suggestions for compositions and suggest what readers you have in mind.

1. The greatest personal disaster I can imagine.
2. Favorite TV programs.
3. My criticism of a motion picture recently seen.
4. The school cafeteria at lunch hour.
5. Our family doctor.
6. Dating customs now and 50 years ago.
7. Fighting the school bully.
8. My ideas about friendship.
9. Why I can't understand people over thirty.
10. My greatest fault.

C2. Analyzing and Developing a Topic

C 2

Assume that you have chosen or been assigned a subject and have limited it in accordance with the approximate length of the paper you plan to write. What you should do next is analyze the topic carefully so that you will fully understand what it involves and how you can most effectively develop it.

Begin by asking yourself these basic questions:

1. For what *purpose* am I writing? What is it I wish to communicate about my topic?
2. For what specific *reader* or group of readers am I writing?

3. Can I phrase a *core sentence* for my paper?
4. Can I make a *list of points* that will be useful in developing my paper?
5. What *tone* should I give my paper, and can I be consistent in its use?
6. In developing my paper, can I get enough *material* to develop it without plagiarizing someone else's work?

C2a. HAVE A CENTRAL PURPOSE CLEARLY IN MIND.

If you have thought out your subject so that you know what you intend to do with it, you ought to be able to state the central purpose of your theme. To illustrate, suppose your first general idea for a subject is summer jobs for students, too broad for a 600-word paper you intend to write. It needs limiting. Suppose further that you have held two summer jobs: one as a file clerk and one waiting tables in a summer resort. You choose the second as more interesting. You might then jot down the following items on a work sheet:

Limited subject:	My experiences as a summer waiter.
Possible title:	"Tips on Summer Tables"
Reader:	Student contemplating a job for his or her next summer vacation.
Short summary:	Waiting on tables in a summer resort, you can make a sizable sum in tips by giving good service and learning the individual preferences of finicky guests. You will also have enough leisure time for an afternoon dip in the pool and for evening entertainments and dances.
Probable method:	Mostly explanation, with some narrative and descriptive details.

C2b. SELECT MATERIAL WITH A SPECIFIC READER, OR READERS, IN MIND.

Usually, your readers will be your teacher and classmates, but on occasion you may wish, or be asked, to write for others. Whoever your readers may be, remember that they are limited to the written word and cannot ask questions of a writer who is normally not present. How much do they already know about the topic? What do you think readers may not know that will be interesting to them and will coincide with your underlying purpose in writing? What background information should you supply? What terms need defining? What kinds of examples, illustrations, and descriptive details will make the topic as clear and interesting to your readers as it is to you? Consider readers objectively. Do not write down to readers; unneeded definitions and explanations are irksome and insulting. Never underestimate the intelligence of your readers. However, never overestimate their information.

C2c. START WITH A CORE SENTENCE.

As repeatedly mentioned in this book, you should *never*, repeat *never*, start writing a composition of any length without taking an essential first step: state in a single sentence your central purpose, the dominating idea of what you propose to say. To play on words, what is the *theme* of your theme? A **thesis statement,** a summarizing, guiding, or topic sentence, will define your purpose and help you gather supporting material that bears directly on the topic in hand.

Assume, for example, that you have recently visited a planetarium and had an exciting glimpse into the heavens. You have never been particularly interested in any science—certainly not astronomy—but, to your amazement, what began as a project to kill a few hours turned into a fascinating experience. You believe that certain of your classmates might enjoy a planetarium visit if only you can convince them that the trip will be both educational and exciting. So you phrase a title "I Saw Stars!" and a thesis sentence: "A trip to a planetarium can be an informative, thrilling, and humbling experience."

With this general plan in mind, you list several items that might be usable. Some of these will come from your own experience; some will require the knowledge of others, to be secured from conversation and reading. Such a list might begin like this:

1. What a planetarium is
2. What one looks like
3. History of the planetarium I visited

C
2

4. My talk with a planetarium guide
5. Location
6. Cost of operation
7. Special exhibits
8. Special lectures
9. Mechanics of the projecting machine
10. My recommendations and suggestions about a planetarium visit
11. Best days to go to avoid crowds and admission fees
12. My outstanding experiences there

Each of these items is generally applicable to your topic, but in view of the core (or thesis) sentence, several should be eliminated and others added. A summary sentence will save you time and effort in gathering material. In addition, it will force you to stick to one central purpose and thus have a more forceful appeal to your readers.

C2d. MAKE A LIST OF POINTS TO BE INCLUDED.

To clarify your purpose further, make a list of details that might be covered. Jot them down on a work sheet as they spring to mind; you can rearrange them later. You may then want to eliminate some of them in view of the limited length of your theme, or you may discover a few points about which you need to know more.

For the sample paper on waiting tables discussed earlier, a list of points to be included might be as follows:

1. Experience unnecessary
2. Neat appearance essential
3. Apply early in spring

   Query: I used Carter's Employment Agency. Do some of the other agencies also list resort jobs? Will check by telephone.
4. Instructions from headwaiter
5. Annoyances: cranky and fussy guests; children spilling milk
6. Clothes to bring: two pairs of dark slacks to wear with uniform jacket or two dark skirts to wear with uniform apron
7. Early rising (6 A.M.)

8. Hours for work, for recreation
9. Be pleasant, cheerful; sometimes hard to do
10. Cooks: irritable when diners send back overdone eggs or meat
11. Tips: good if you're attentive
12. Allowed to mingle with guests in off-hours and evenings

    Query: Is my experience typical of what one would encounter at most resorts? Check with Jim Gaines and Rhoda McKay on their experiences. Also, find out how they applied for and got jobs.

Now review your summarizing sentence and rearrange your list to place items in the order in which you want to treat them. Should any be omitted? What should be added? Which points need the fullest development? Which should be mentioned only briefly?

Arranging the items to be finally included in the form of an outline will provide you a clearer view of how to proceed. (See Section C3.)

C2e. MAINTAIN A CONSISTENT TONE.

When you have worked out the central purpose of your theme and how you propose to develop it, consider what *feeling* you have toward the material and your prospective reader. In other words, in what **tone** are you going to write? A paper about waiting on tables at a resort might adopt an informal, even intimate, approach. You might choose to be candid about the advantages and disadvantages of such a job, with perhaps an occasional touch of humor from your own encounters with eccentric guests or irate cooks. Your purpose here would be to let your readers know what situations they might encounter, both favorable and unfavorable.

On the other hand, if you were attempting to persuade readers in general to accept your point of view for or against a more serious subject, such as, for example, capital punishment, your tone should be formal and serious, since any humor would be decidedly out of place. You might, however, use an ironical or satirical tone in writing about some aspect of society that strikes you as absurd and which you want to persuade your readers to

C
2

view in the same light. But whatever tone you adopt in a composition, make sure it is appropriate to your purpose, your material, and your reader.

You should choose and maintain a consistent tone. When you have finished writing, check to see that you have not, for example, used a light, bantering tone in one paragraph and a solemn, dignified approach in the next. Every good theme possesses unity of tone and purpose.

C2f. BE HONEST ABOUT THE MATERIAL YOU GATHER.

Taking the ideas and words of another and stating them as your own is **plagiarism.** In a short, ugly word, it is *stealing*.

When you use an idea new to you, whether you express it in your own or in quoted words, state your indebtedness. Sometimes you can acknowledge a source with a mere phrase: "as Salinger suggests in *The Catcher in the Rye*," or "These writers, Joseph Warren Beach says in *American Fiction*, were influenced by social conditions." Occasionally, you will need to make fuller acknowledgment in a footnote (see Section SC2f).

In general, it is permissible and even necessary to borrow, but always indicate who the lender is. In gathering material from others, think about it, try to absorb it, and attempt to state in your own words what you learned, unless you are quoting directly. But whether quoting or paraphrasing, do not attempt to pass off as your own what you have taken from others.

EXERCISE 5

Examine the following possible audiences of papers written for English classes. Which seem appropriate or inappropriate? Which seem too general? Too specific?

1. Anyone who has a younger brother or sister
2. Anyone not from the state of Colorado
3. My best friend
4. People who live in large cities
5. Everyone who hates to eat breakfast

EXERCISE 6

For *one* of the following broad subjects, list ten to fifteen points or items that might be used in its development.

1. School politics
2. Socialism in America—past and present
3. Dating customs in this town
4. Weekend fun
5. State parks
6. Vocational experiences my friends have had
7. Driver education
8. My philosophy of life
9. Peaceful uses of atomic energy
10. The value of a time budget

EXERCISE 7

Consider each of the following as a core (thesis) sentence. Select one of them. With a specific, named reader in mind, list five items from your own experience (observation, imagination, reflection) that could be used as developing material for a composition of 300–400 words.

1. Movies are (or are not) better than ever.
2. Television programming does (does not) accurately reflect our cultural tastes and levels.
3. All forms of dancing are (are not) a waste of time.
4. Beauty is (is not) in the eyes of the beholder.
5. Interscholastic sports should (should not) be abolished.

C
2

EXERCISE 8

For the topic selected in Exercise 7, indicate how items of developing material would differ for each of the following imagined readers.

1. My English teacher
2. My best friend
3. My parents
4. A pen pal in some named country
5. My aunt

EXERCISE 9

For three of the subjects listed in Exercise 7, briefly discuss two or more tones (attitudes) that might be used in the development of each.

EXERCISE 10

Follow directions given for Exercise 7, except for item sources. For *one* of the five topics listed, write five sentences indicating material to be based on resources other than your own.

C3. Outlining

After you have analyzed a topic and jotted down the points you want to make, you must then determine in what order to present them. If you have only two or three points to cover for a short paper of 200 or 300 words, your problem is rather simple. But if you have several or a dozen ideas to arrange for a longer theme, putting them in effective order amounts to making an *outline*. For that is what **outlining** really is—arranging groups of related ideas in a sequence that will efficiently carry out the purpose of a composition as expressed in a summarizing sentence.

An outline need not be complicated, nor need it be followed exactly. You can revise it, if need be, as you proceed with writing. An outline is not a strait jacket. It is a guide of one's own choosing.

Frequently, teachers, who have had to read many poorly organized papers, will ask students to submit outlines before beginning to write. Students have been known to argue that an outline hampers their spontaneity and that they can write better without one. Sometimes they confess privately to having written their compositions first and their outlines afterward. This is a topsy-turvy procedure, for the purpose of an outline is to help with the writing.

When time is short, as in writing an impromptu theme in class or answering a discussion question on an examination, a very brief "scratch" outline, consisting of jotted down ideas, will serve the purpose. More detailed, and far more efficient, outlines are of three types: the topic outline, the sentence outline, and the paragraph outline. Your teacher will usually state a preference for one type. Sometimes the choice may be left to you. You should therefore be familiar with all three forms discussed and illustrated in the following sections.

C3a. FOLLOW A SUMMARIZING SENTENCE IN CONSTRUCTING AN OUTLINE.

As pointed out in Section C2c, a summarizing sentence suggests the material to be developed. It will not include everything you may wish to cover, but it should serve as advance notice of what is to come. The clearer a summarizing sentence is, the easier the preparation of an outline will be. A summarizing sentence serves as a check against the unity and coherence of an outline and the theme written from it.

C3b. USE A TOPIC OUTLINE TO MAKE CLEAR THE ARRANGEMENT OF IDEAS.

A **topic outline** uses words and phrases but no complete sentences. It may be quite simple:

Tips on Summer Tables

I. How to apply
I. Learning the job
III. Problems with people
IV. Monetary rewards
V. Leisure-time activities

This is basically a **sketch outline** suggesting only major divisions of a proposed theme. It can be made more elaborate by listing some of the details you intend to discuss under the major headings above, as in the following example:

Tips on Summer Tables

I. How to apply
 A. At employment agencies
 B. By writing to resorts

C
3

II. Learning the job
    A. Mechanical aspects
        1. Setting tables
        2. Taking diners' orders
        3. Carrying trays
    B. Problems with people
        1. Dealing with fussy guests
        2. Soothing irate cooks
III. Monetary rewards
    A. Free room and board
    B. Substantial tips
IV. Leisure
    A. Short periods between meals
        1. For letter writing
        2. For swimming
        3. For walks
    B. Evenings
        1. Public (guest) entertainments
        2. Dances
        3. Trips to nearby town
        4. Dates

C3c. USE A SENTENCE OUTLINE TO MAKE CLEAR TO YOURSELF OR OTHERS THE ARRANGEMENT OF IDEAS.

As the term implies, a **sentence outline** consists of complete sentences for main divisions and all subordinate sections. Since the items in a sentence outline are fully stated, they are likely to be both clearer to the writer than a topic outline and more informative to a teacher or other reader who may wish to offer helpful suggestions.

Tips on Summer Tables

  I. Summer jobs of waiting on tables are not hard to obtain.
    A. Some agencies list such openings.
    B. Application can be made direct to resorts.

II. You will learn the mechanics of the job from the headwaiter.
   A. You must know how to set a table and clear away.
   B. You must master the art of balancing loaded trays.
   C. You must learn how to remember what each guest orders.
III. You will learn a lot about human nature, including your own.
   A. You must not show annoyance at difficult guests.
   B. You must be patient with undisciplined children.
   C. You must be diplomatic in dealing with temperamental chefs.
IV. If you are good at your job, your rewards can be high.
   A. You will have only minor expenses.
   B. You will take home a substantial sum from tips.
   C. You will be asked to come back next summer if you wish.
V. Your job will not be all work.
   A. You will have some leisure hours between serving meals.
   B. Your evenings will be free for entertainments, dances, and dates.

C3d. USE A PARAGRAPH OUTLINE MAINLY FOR SUMMARIZING THE WORK OF OTHERS.

A paragraph outline is composed of a series of sentences, each of which gives the gist of an entire paragraph. Sometimes the topic sentence of a paragraph will serve the purpose. The sentences of a paragraph outline are numbered in the order in which the paragraphs themselves follow one another.

This method can be helpful in planning the successive paragraphs of your own theme, but it is especially useful as a means of taking notes on the content of paragraphs in a selection to be studied. Efficiently summarizing successive paragraphs in an essay or a chapter of a book involves reading them with attention and understanding.

For example, assume that each of the thirteen subheads in the sentence outline shown in Section C3c is to be developed in a paragraph. The first five items in a paragraph outline based on this topic might be as follows:

1. Numerous employment agencies list summer job openings and welcome applications from interested and qualified persons.

2. If you wish, you can bypass employment agencies and write directly to resort hotels and restaurants you know or have seen advertised.

3. The headwaiter or an assistant will provide thorough training in place and table settings and in the removal of silver, cutlery, china, and glassware.

4. You will need instruction and practice in the difficult art of loading trays fully and balancing them comfortably and safely.

5. Learning to remember which guest ordered what is a fundamental requirement when waiting tables.

And here is how a paragraph outline might be prepared from (and for) a chapter in a book:

The First Railroads

1. Neither roads nor canals provided a fully satisfactory method for transporting individual goods.

2. The first roadbeds, built in Germany in the fifteenth century, were tramways made by laying heavy timbers in parallel rows to bear the wheels of heavy wagons drawn by horses or oxen.

3. Tramways later introduced into England were made of iron, were either privately owned by miners, manufacturers, and merchants or were open to the public at a toll charge.

4. The modern railroad was at first little more than an attempt to substitute the steam engine for the horse.

5. When in 1825 England built the first railroad, trains were run at a speed of 10 to 15 miles per hour.

6. The early English railroads, like the turnpikes and tramways, were rented to any person who wished to pay the tolls, but this process grew so complicated that commercial companies took them over.

7. American engineers made many improvements in order for trains to make the steeper grades and longer distances in North America.

8. Americans also found a way of getting around sharp curves by putting swivel axles on the cars and built more flexible

roadbeds than the British, whose tracks were rigidly mounted on piles driven into the ground.

9. Most English railroad lines were short, averaging only 14 miles.
10. The need for government regulation of the railroads in England gradually grew, and in 1893 the maximum rates they could charge were fixed by statute.
11. England's experiments with railroads showed the way to the rest of Europe with respect to engineering and social problems.

—From *The History of Western Civilization,* by Harry Elmer Barnes

C3e. MAKE OUTLINES CORRECT IN FORM.

If you prepare an outline only for personal use, the main require-ment is a logical arrangement of major and minor divisions so that the theme will be sensibly constructed. But an outline to be submitted to your teacher should also conform to certain conven-tions of long standing that you should fully understand.

When constructing a *topic outline,* follow these suggestions:

1. For major divisions, use Roman numerals I, II, III, IV, etc., placing them flush with the margin.
2. For subdividing major divisions, use the capital letters A, B, C, etc., indenting them evenly.
3. Indent again if you have a subdivision under any of these letters and use the Arabic numerals 1, 2, 3, etc.
4. In the event that you want to subdivide still more, use an-other indentation and the lowercase letters a, b, c, etc.
5. Follow each number or letter with a period. The use of a period after each topic is optional, but be consistent in whichever practice you follow.

When constructing a *sentence outline,* follow the same pro-cedure as for the topic outline, with one exception: place an end stop—a period, question mark, or exclamation point—after each sentence.

C
3

The following skeleton indicates correct form for either a topic or a sentence outline:

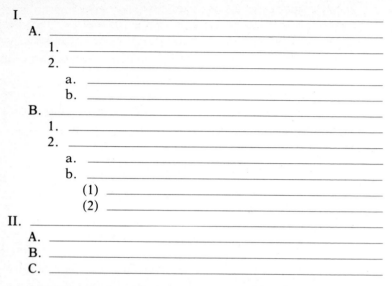

I. _____
  A. _____
    1. _____
    2. _____
      a. _____
      b. _____
  B. _____
    1. _____
    2. _____
      a. _____
      b. _____
        (1) _____
        (2) _____
II. _____
  A. _____
  B. _____
  C. _____

In a *paragraph outline* the sentences are indicated by Arabic numerals and must also have end stops. As in the other outlines, a period follows each number. The beginning of each sentence may be flush with the margin and the runover sentences indented, or the beginnings may be indented with the runover sentences coming out flush with the numbers.

Any outline that clearly reveals the structure of a theme is effective. Correctness in form is more often a matter of convention and practice than of logic. Writers, however, have tended to follow certain conventions with which you should be familiar:

1. Outlining is division; subdivision means division into at least two parts. If a single minor topic (subhead) must be mentioned, express it in its major heading or add another subhead.
2. Use parallel phrasing. Do not use a word or phrase for one topic, a sentence for another. Topic, sentence, and paragraph outlines should be consistent in structure throughout.
3. Avoid meaningless headings such as *Introduction, Conclusion, Reasons,* and *Effects.* If you feel they must appear, add specific explanatory subheads.

4. The first main heading of the outline should not repeat the title of the theme. If the idea expressed in the title logically should appear in the outline, at least rephrase it.
5. Avoid putting into a subhead any matter that should appear in a large division; even more importantly, do not list in a main heading material belonging in a subdivision.

EXERCISE 11

Revise the following outline so that items will follow a correct form:

How Drivers Cause Accidents

    I. By violating traffic regulations
        A. Passing a halted school bus
        B. Going through a stoplight
        C. Turning a corner without flashing a signal
   II. By being selfish
        A. Not moving over for a passing car
        B. Blocking another car when parking
        C. Failing to dim lights when meeting another car
  III. By being unfit to drive
        A. Driving while intoxicated
        B. Driving in wrong direction on one-way street
        C. Being too young or too old to drive
        D. Having poor vision
        E. Driving an unreliable car

EXERCISE 12

Make the following into a consistent topic or sentence outline:

My First Day at Work

    I. Prework jitters
        A. The night before
           1. I set the alarm for 6 A.M.
           2. I could not sleep
           3. Fear of failing
        B. The next morning at home
           1. Dressed hurriedly
           2. Bolted my breakfast

C
3

II. The Workday
  A. My first hour
    1. I meet the supervisor
    2. Friendliness of other workers
    3. My tension gradually eases
  B. How the day went
    1. Slow passage of time
    2. Lunch hour
    3. Afternoon weariness
    4. Quitting time
    5. I feel satisfied and ready for tomorrow
      a. I get to sleep quickly, tired but relaxed

EXERCISE 13

Criticize these outlines. State how each could be improved.

(1.) Meet My Best Friend

  I. Physical appearance
    A. Height and weight
    B. Complexion
  II. Chief character trait
    A. Good-natured

(2.) My Favorite Restaurant

  I. It serves two kinds of food
  II. It serves Italian dishes
  III. It serves American dishes
  IV. Its service is excellent
    A. The waiters are courteous
    B. They are also very efficient

EXERCISE 14

Rewrite the following outlines, eliminating all errors.

(1.) Why Accidents Happen

  I. Major reason for accidents
    A. Drivers at fault
  II. Minor reasons for accidents
    A. Roads and highways at fault
  III. Proposed solution
    A. Better driver training

(2.) Three 4-H Activities
  I Junior leadership
    a) age
    b) experience
    C) projects
  II Clothing
    a) Age
    B) experience
    C) Time
    D) Cost
  III Freezing
    a) where purchased
    B) Cost

C4. The First Paragraph

Having completed the planning stages of your theme, you must now start to write it. Although the *body*, or middle, will naturally be the main part, both the beginning and ending are important because they are the first and last impressions your reader will have of your paper. They should be written with care and forethought. Neither should be abrupt nor mechanical; neither should be so lengthy as to throw your theme out of proportion.

Because the beginning of a paper is so important, you will probably wish to revise it several times as you work on the composition. It may be that you will wish to rewrite the first paragraph after the entire paper has been completed.

C4a. AVOID HAVING AN OPENING SENTENCE DEPEND ON THE TITLE FOR ITS MEANING.

Title and theme are independent. A first sentence should be self-explanatory without indirect or vague reference to the title. Avoid reference words like *this*, *that*, or *such* in beginning sentences.

Ineffective beginnings:
1. Someday I hope to follow my mother's footsteps in this profession.
2. Raising these has fascinated me since childhood.
3. I once endured the discipline of such an academy for a year.

Improved beginnings: 1. Someday I hope to follow my mother's footsteps in the practice of law.
2. Raising tropical fish has fascinated me since childhood.
3. I once endured the discipline of a military academy for a year.

C4b. AVOID UNNECESSARY FORMAL INTRODUCTIONS.

Write an introduction only if your theme needs one. Introductions are usually needed only in long papers that begin with a definition of terms, a history of the subject, or an explanation of reasons for the study of a problem. The shorter your composition is, the shorter your introduction should be.

C4c. AVOID WORDY BEGINNINGS.

Students frequently use up space in preliminary sparring with a subject before facing up to it. Examine your second and third paragraphs. If your theme really begins there, throw away everything preceding it. Otherwise, you are writing a theme that will be mostly beginning, with little between it and the ending.

Unless you are dealing with a controversial subject, avoid beginning with expressions such as "I think," "In my opinion," "It seems to me." Since you are the person writing the paper, it can be taken for granted that the thoughts and opinions are yours unless you state otherwise.

C4d. AVOID BEGINNINGS THAT ARE ABRUPT.

Instead of starting a theme with "The first step in building a bookcase is . . ." or "We must have better laboratory equipment because . . .," the writer should begin with at least a brief paragraph to prepare the reader for the process or argument to follow.

An abrupt opening with a quotation, however, can sometimes be effective. Such a device should be used sparingly and with skill. It should also be followed immediately by an explanatory passage to make the situation clear to the reader, as in this example:

> "Hey you, Slim!"
> The boss at the cement plant, where I worked last summer, had given me the nickname my first day on the job. Now he was calling me to drive a truckload of bags to the freight yard.

C4e. MAKE THE FIRST PARAGRAPH CLEAR AND PURPOSEFUL.

A firmly composed beginning that leads directly toward the topic will engage the reader's attention and cause him or her to read on. Many types of openings are available to you. Here are a few examples of effective beginnings:

1. Beginning by repeating or paraphrasing the title.

> This is a song of the once open road. Is there as much as five miles of highway left in the United States today without ten filling stations and at least one farmhouse called "Ye Willowe Inne"?
> —From "The Once Open Road," by Charles Merz

> I stand here ironing, and what you asked me moves tormented back and forth with the iron.
> —From "I Stand Here Ironing," by Tillie Olsen

2. Beginning with a question.

> What is this democracy for which we fight?
> —From "The Citizen's Charter," by Geoffrey Crowther

> What is success? And how is it gained?
> —From "Vocabulary and Success," by Johnson O'Connor

3. Beginning with an exclamation.

> Something is wrong somewhere! That is the obvious thing to say about poetry in America today.
> —From "Outline for a Defense of Poetry," by Earl Daniels

4. Beginning with a quotation.

> "None can love freedom heartily but good men; the rest love

C
4

not freedom, but license." That was Milton's opinion, and he had thought much about freedom and goodness.

> —From "Of Goodness," by Elizabeth Jackson

" 'That woman Estelle,' " the note reads, " 'is partly the reason that George Sharp and I are separated today'. "

> —From "Slouching Toward Bethlehem," by Joan Didion

5. Beginning by showing the divisions of the topic to be discussed.

Two things become increasingly evident as the sickness of our American democracy approaches its inevitable crisis: one is the surpassing genius of the founders of this Republic; the other is the transience of even the greatest of political resolutions.

> —From "Loyalty and Freedom," by Archibald MacLeish

6. Beginning with a framework or setting for the topic.

Suppose there were no critics to tell us how to react to a picture, a play, or a new composition of music.

> —From "How Do You Know It's Good?" by Marya Mannes

Knowing that Mrs. Mallard was afflicted with a heart trouble, great care was taken to break to her as gently as possible the news of her husband's death.

> —From "The Story of an Hour," by Kate Chopin

7. Beginning with a general misconception that the writer intends to correct.

Science is often defined inadequately as "an organized body of knowledge." This would make cookbooks, Sears, Roebuck catalogues, and telephone books science, which they are not.

> —From "The Nature of Science," by Ralph Ross
> and Ernest Van den Haag

Many people, if not most, look on literary taste as an elegant accomplishment, by acquiring which they will complete themselves, and make themselves finally fit members of a correct society.

> —From "Literary Taste: How to Form It," by Arnold Bennett

8. Beginning by directly addressing the reader.

If you are an average reader you can read an average book at the rate of 300 words a minute. You cannot maintain that average, however, unless you read regularly every day. Nor can you attain that speed with hard books in science, mathematics, agriculture, business, or any subject that is new and unfamiliar to you.

—From "How to Find Time to Read," by Louis Shores

As we enter the new year, it is time to take stock of the fact that we are living through the greatest revolution in the history of mankind.

—From "A Vision of the Year 2000," by Clare Boothe Luce

EXERCISE

For exercises, see the end of Section C5.

C5. The Final Paragraph

To come to a sudden stop because you have reached your quota of words is not to end a paper but to abandon it. Obviously, a theme must have an ending as well as a beginning. A proper ending gives the reader a sense of completeness. You should foresee your ending by the time you begin developing the last item in your outline, if not before. A good ending should emerge naturally from what precedes and not be tacked on as an afterthought.

C5a. USE A SHORT, COMPACT ENDING.

What has been said about avoiding abruptness, wordiness, and formality in beginnings applies equally to endings. An abrupt ending brings readers up short; a rambling one strains their patience. An effective ending is a happy medium between these extremes.

In a theme of normal length, the ending should be compact. As a general rule, you should manage it in no more than two or three sentences. Often a single sentence that summarizes or rounds off the content is sufficient. You may make your ending the closing words of your last paragraph or, if you wish to give it more emphasis, set it apart.

In ending, avoid expressions such as "thus we see," "to sum up my conclusions," "in closing, let me state," etc. Even in argu-

C
5

mentative writing, where there is some excuse for them, such phrases are overworked.

C5b. USE AN APPROPRIATE ENDING.

Various types of endings can be used, but it is important that you write one that fits your composition. If, for instance, your paper contains a number of debatable statements, the ending might summarize them and give the gist of their contents. If your paper has described and characterized an individual, the final paragraph could fittingly state your dominant impression of that person. If you have been explaining how to learn some activity, the last paragraph might list the necessary steps in order.

Numerous other methods of concluding a composition are available, including these:

1. Ending with a question.

> Or shall we really get down to the roots of good and evil and wrestle with our theories until we bring them into some kind of working conformity, not only with one another but with fact?
>
> —From "Of Goodness," by Elizabeth Jackson

> The miracle is that what he did in the little space of seventy years could have been done at all, even by a great genius. Is it any wonder that he had no time to be a man?
>
> —From "The Monster" (Richard Wagner), by Deems Taylor

> Aren't there any flesh-and-blood women to be proud of anymore?
>
> —From "What Are You Supposed to Do If You Like Children?"
> by Anne Bernays

2. Ending with an exclamation.

> If present-day Louisiana has any claim to individuality, a color, a note of her own, it is lodged unmistakably in this sport-loving, sun-loving, unquenchable spirit which was and is New Orleans, Mistress of chivalry, cuisine, and the dance; cosmopolis of legend, caprice, and motley; the Columbine of the cities — New Orleans!
>
> —From "Louisiana," by Basil Thompson

3. Ending with a direct or indirect quotation.

> But if he does remember poems pleasantly, no matter how few; even if there be only one, among those quoted here, which

he has in the slightest degree liked, he is invited to continue in our common adventure after the peculiar pleasure of poetry, assured, in advance, of fun, and, I hope, of discovering in his experience

> life and food
> For future years.

—From "Outline for a Defense of Poetry," by Earl Daniels

The elder Dumas enunciated a great principle when he said that to make a drama, a man needed one passion, and four walls.

—From "The Novel Démeublé," by Willa Cather

4. Ending by bringing up and stressing a final important point.

I will close with one last point. Science is fun, even for the amateur. Every scientist is himself an amateur in another field of science which is not his specialty, but the spirit is the same. Science is a game that is inspiring and refreshing. The playing field is the universe itself. The stakes are high because you must put down all your preconceived ideas and habits of thought. The rewards are great because you find a home in the world, a home you have made for yourself.

—From "Faith in Science," by I. I. Rabi

Finally, it is a spirit of leadership seeking both courage and tolerance: the courage to search for truth and speak it even when, especially when, it pains; and the tolerance to understand that good and evil in human relationships, from the personal to the international, are not absolutes.

—From "Lo, the Old College Spirit," by G. Gaddis Smith

5. Ending by summarizing the central thought or point of the theme or essay.

Thus it is no mere transcript of life at a certain time and place that Hardy has given us. It is a vision of the world and of man's lot as they revealed themselves to a powerful imagination, a profound and poetic genius, a gentle and humane soul.

—From "The Novels of Thomas Hardy," by Virginia Woolf

To assign unanswered letters their proper weight, to free us from the expectations of others, to give us back to ourselves — there lies the great, the singular power of self-respect. Without it, one eventually discovers the final turn of the screw: one runs away to find oneself and finds no one at home.

—From "On Self-Respect," by Joan Didion

C
5

It is no longer good enough to blame man for keeping woman ignorant. For man himself is ignorant and in the sum total no more capable or enlightened than woman.

—From "Love and Liberation," by Lisa Hobbs

6. Ending with a prediction or a warning.

A less commercial, more responsible America, perhaps a less prosperous and more spiritual America, will hold fast to its sentiment, but be weaned from its sentimentality.

—From "Sentimental America," by H. S. Canby

Comfort is a means to an end. The modern world seems to regard it as an end in itself, an absolute good. One day, perhaps, the earth will have been turned into one vast feather-bed, with man's body dozing on top of it and his mind underneath, like Desdemona, smothered.

—From "Comfort," by Aldous Huxley

If women's lib wins, perhaps we all do.

—From "What It Would Be Like If Women Win,"
by Gloria Steinem

The important thing to remember in ending themes is this: When you have said all you intended to say, *stop*. Do you remember the story of the guest who lingered at the door mumbling, "There was something else I wanted to say"? To this the hostess made a wise response, "Perhaps it was *good-bye*."

EXERCISE 15

Choose five articles or essays from your literature anthology and study their beginnings and endings. Is each effective and appropriate? Does any one of them seem unnecessary or unnecessarily long?

EXERCISE 16

Apply the directions given in Exercise 15 to five articles selected from one issue of a magazine such as *The Atlantic, Holiday, Esquire, National Geographic, Scientific American.*

EXERCISE 17

Which of the following beginnings are clear and effective and which are not? State reasons for your answers.

1. Have you ever thought what life was like 5 million years ago?
2. The title of this theme suggests a number of important questions.
3. Three important steps toward effective studying are selecting a definite place to study, planning ahead, and concentrating.
4. A space station orbiting the earth was a dream of yesterday, it is a possibility today, and it will be a reality tomorrow.
5. I think this is the most important question a high school student can ask. (Theme title: "Am I Going to Be Ready for the Future?")

EXERCISE 18

Which of the following endings are clear and effective and which are not? State reasons for your answers.

1. These facilities and many more like them make Oakdale a wonderful place in which to live.
2. Experiments in teaching tricks to animals are enjoyable for me. Why don't you try them? You might enjoy them, too.
3. Then the band began to play the recessional and the line of graduates began to move. I smiled as we walked forward to meet tomorrow. (Theme title: "Graduation Day at Junior High")
4. From recent experiments in rocketry, we realize that a dream of yesterday is a possibility of today and will be a reality of tomorrow.
5. I have known her for only three weeks, but I wish I had never met her at all.

C
6

C6. Proportion

Proportion requires that you develop each section of your theme according to its relative importance. For instance, you may have disposed of an introduction in a short paragraph, then devoted a longer paragraph to the next item (not one of major import), developed the most important item in three paragraphs, given two paragraphs to the next (of secondary importance), and used a brief paragraph for the ending. This could represent a well-proportioned theme.

In determining what to expand and what to contract in writing a theme, keep in mind not only the subject you are writing about, but also your purpose and your reader. Also, use a well-planned outline (Section C3). It helps in proportioning.

C6a. GIVE ADEQUATE ATTENTION TO THE CENTRAL THOUGHT OF YOUR THEME.

Avoid elaborating minor details either in the beginning or later in your theme. Doing so may throw your theme out of proportion, obscure main points, and distract the reader.

For example, your purpose in writing a theme may be to persuade fellow students to support the debating team. Your reasons are that debating is a more important activity than they believe, that debating deals with significant issues of the day, and that debating is better preparation for adult life than are team sports. Proceed quickly to the heart of your argument. You need no long introduction about famous debates of the past, such as Lincoln versus Douglas or Darrow versus Bryan. Nor need you provide a long list of issues that might be worth debating; two or three good examples will suffice.

C6b. AVOID DEVELOPING DETAILS FAMILIAR TO YOUR READERS.

Do not waste time and space defining common terms or describing objects that you can presume your readers know as well as you do.

Suppose your hobby is photography and that your purpose is to tell your readers how to enlarge snapshots for framing. Your topic presupposes that you are addressing yourself to readers who own cameras of one kind or another. You would be wasting their time and your own by explaining the difference between a positive print and a negative, by describing a flashbulb, and by defining time exposure. You can safely assume that your readers know such facts. What they do want to learn from your theme is how to use an enlarger, how much one costs, whether it is timesaving and money saving to do one's own enlargements or advantageous to have them done commercially. Proceed to these points immediately and stress them throughout your paper.

C6c. MAKE SURE THAT YOUR PARAGRAPHS ARE CORRECTLY PROPORTIONED.

Proportioning paragraphs depends upon analysis and judgment of the ideas used in developing a theme. That is, you should plan and outline a paper in advance and then, after it is completed, carefully weigh the separate paragraphs to make certain that each contributes its share, and no more than its share, to the development of the paper as a whole. These suggestions may help you proportion your paragraphs effectively.

1. Consider the whole subject before you start to write. What is your central purpose? What effect upon the reader are you aiming for?

2. Always keep your reader in mind. Does each paragraph have a central idea worth communicating? What, to your reader, is the value, the weight, of each paragraph?

3. If your assignment calls for a certain number of words, make a tentative allotment for each paragraph before you begin to write. Alter this plan if you need to.

4. Shorten any paragraph that does not carry its weight, even though you like its details and must sacrifice valued wordage in cutting it down.

5. Lengthen a paragraph if its central topic seems to deserve further development by detail, illustration, definition, or any other means necessary to communicate to a reader.

EXERCISE 19

Count the number of words in each paragraph of *two* of your most recent compositions. Write a paragraph commenting on the proportion used, giving consideration to the topic, your reader(s), and your purpose.

EXERCISE 20

Study one of the essays in an anthology or a magazine. Does each paragraph seem to make a point the relative importance of which is proportionate to its length?

EXERCISE 21

Indicate the number of words proportionately correct for each paragraph of a 400-word composition devoted to the explanation of a process: learning to dance, or playing bridge, or giving a party, or playing tennis, or some comparable activity, sport, or recreation. Select *one* subject and adapt or alter the following plan, as necessary:

Learning to Swim

A. Correct mental attitude for the beginner
B. Correct body position
C. How to breathe
D. How to handle the arms
E. How to handle the feet and legs
F. Fears to overcome
G. Errors to be avoided
H. Summary

In a 400-word paper, is each of the 8 paragraphs worth exactly 50 words? Why? Why not? (Your answer will depend more upon the needs and attitudes of your readers than upon your particular interests, knowledge, or enthusiasms.)

C7. Unity

Unity means "oneness, singleness of purpose." The principle of unity applies to the whole composition, to the sentence (Section S4), and to the paragraph (Section P4).

A theme is a short paper dealing with a single phase of a subject. Constantly keep in mind "the *theme* within the *theme*." If every paragraph bears upon this phase or develops it in some way, the entire paper has unity. But if even so much as one sentence introduces an unrelated detail, the unity of the theme is impaired.

C7a. DEVELOP IN A THEME ONLY ONE PHASE OF A SUBJECT.

Beginning writers frequently assume that certain details are pertinent to the topic they are discussing when in fact these are irrelevant or, at best, only loosely connected with it. Several misjudgments are responsible for such assumptions:

1. Not being thoughtful or self-critical enough to eliminate irrelevant items from a guiding outline or having prepared no outline at all.

2. Tacking on useless preliminary matter to a beginning or ending in order to pad out a theme to the required number of words. An example would be beginning a book review by stating the facts of the author's life or ending a theme on target shooting with comment on the history of the rifle since the flintlock.

3. Including material that has some possible relation to the central idea but that makes no real connection to the purpose of the theme. For instance, if your purpose is to give an account of an original experiment in chemistry, it would break the unity of the theme to describe the supply room or cabinet from which you selected chemicals.

C7b. GIVE YOUR THEME UNITY OF TONE.

Whether your purpose is to inform, to persuade, to satirize, to ridicule, or whatever, be consistent. The tendency of basketball coaches to give preference to candidates according to height could be treated seriously as a questionable trend, or it could be treated humorously by speculating how some major schools might compete for a player who happened to be seven feet three inches tall. But to mix the two in the same theme would be equivalent to offering your reader oatmeal and dill pickles in the same dish.

In short, avoid mixing comedy and tragedy, satire and pathos, humor and stateliness, reverence and irreverence, absurdity and dignity in the same composition. A solemn paper on the assassination of President Lincoln should not refer to humorous anecdotes of which Lincoln was fond — even though one such anecdote might have a general bearing on the subject and would enable you to fill out the word quota needed. For another illustration, it would be difficult to maintain unity of tone in a serious paper on international relations if you decided to add a comical or satirical anecdote.

EXERCISE 22

Discuss violations of unity in the following plan (sketch outline) for a theme:

My Best Friend's Father

   I. My friend's father is an excellent lawyer.

  II. He studied hard when he was in college and law school and received many honors.

 III. His parents died during his last year at law school.

 IV. My friend is not a good student; he is more interested in dancing, girls, and sports cars than he is in school subjects.

  V. After he was graduated, my friend's father had a financial struggle for ten years.

 VI. He now has a large practice and substantial income.

VII. He is getting older, is in poor health, and has hired a young lawyer as an assistant.

VIII. My friend and his father have many personality traits in common.

EXERCISE 23

Indicate how the following composition lacks unity. If your teacher requests, rewrite the paper by removing irrelevant ideas and adding material that seems appropriate.

The Inventor of the Automobile

Credit is usually given to a group of men who were said to have invented the automobile. These fifteen or twenty inventors each contributed something toward the invention of the automobile. The period of years for the contributions of these inventors fell between the years of 1880 and 1903. These inventors gained significance by the invention of a horseless carriage or a motor-driven vehicle. However, the latest facts prove that a man named Siegfried Marcus should receive full credit for the invention. In 1861, the first automobile chugged down the street in a small town in Germany. This information has been presented quite recently, and has startled many automobile fans.

In the first years of automobiles, people were decidedly against them. Automobiles were declared a menace to humanity. Farmers were constantly suing drivers for scaring their chickens and horses. A few states tried to obtain laws against automobiles but did not succeed.

As time went by, the public was gradually realizing that automobiles were becoming more useful. Roads and other conditions were now in favor of the automobile instead of against it.

C8. Consistency

To be *consistent*, a theme must maintain a uniform point of view, mood, and tone. *Unity* is primarily concerned with content, **consistency** with the writer's point of view and feeling toward subject matter.

Point of view has several different meanings. *Physical* point of view has to do with the position in time and space from which one approaches or views material. *Personal* point of view concerns the relationship through which you narrate or discuss a subject, whether first, second, or third person. *Mental* point of view involves attitude and feeling toward a subject.

C8a. BE CONSISTENT IN THE PHYSICAL POINT OF VIEW.

C
8

Whenever you write a paper involving physical point of view, choose some point in space or time from which to consider your subject. If you wish to describe a lake, for instance, choose a particular season of the year (obviously this makes considerable difference) and a specific spot from which you view it. Then use a consistent method of depicting scenic details. You could proceed clockwise or counterclockwise around the lake, from the nearby to the distant, or the reverse. Always let your readers know if and when you shift your point of view. They will be confused if you veer suddenly from the far shore of the lake to comment on the dock upon which you stand.

Unless you know your material firsthand, your account of it may exhibit inconsistency in facts, such as describing a garden with lilacs and roses in full bloom at the same time.

Aimless or abrupt shifts in time are also bewildering. Do not jump suddenly from one period in history to another or give the impression that it is morning and then unaccountably mention that it is evening.

Both space and time were ignored in the following; a thousand miles disappeared between the two sentences:

> Not long after dawn the four survivors were picked up by a French naval ship some thousand miles off shore. To their surprise, they were immediately seized by port authorities and clapped in jail.

C8b. BE CONSISTENT IN THE PERSONAL POINT OF VIEW.

In most themes, you will choose one of four personal points of view. Which choice you make depends on your subject, your reader, and appropriateness in general. In relating a firsthand experience or in taking the reader into your confidence in a discussion, use the *first person: I, my, mine, me, we, our, ours, us.* In addressing the reader directly, use the *second person: you, your, yours.* When speaking about someone or about some group, use the *third person: she, her, hers, he, his, him, they, their, theirs, them.* In writing explanatory or argumentative papers, you may have occasion to use the *impersonal: one, anyone, everybody,* etc., or nouns such as *a person, a student, a writer,* etc.

Combinations of personal points of view (*I* and *you, we* and *they*) are frequently used by writers. But do not carelessly shift the point of view from *I* to *we* or *you* to *one* or from any one of these to another. If such a shift is necessary, as may happen, make sure that the reader will be prepared for the shift and will readily understand what you are doing.

C8c. BE CONSISTENT IN THE MENTAL POINT OF VIEW.

Mental point of view may be considered in two ways. The first is the *objective attitude* taken in discussing or arguing an issue. You may weigh pros and cons, but it should be clear that you are consistently upholding a position, not changing it in midtheme or being so ambiguous that the reader is confused about where you stand. For example, much can be said in favor of learning about science in a laboratory and learning about it in a general science course. You could be consistent in pointing out the merits of each, or you could argue in favor of one or the other, but you should make clear to the reader at the outset what your point of view is, and you should uphold it throughout.

Another aspect of the mental point of view is the *subjective response* to writing, the frame of mind or mood in which a writer approaches a given subject. Going fishing on a fresh spring morning might bring forth a lighthearted mood. An expected failure on an upcoming examination might make you feel pessimistic. But if you merely told your reader "I felt lighthearted," or "I was deeply pessimistic," you would be making an observation, not creating a mood. Establishing a mood requires choosing details consistent with it. Observe how the italicized words in the following example build up a dreary and solemn scene.

> In outward appearance, the whole of the courtroom scene was *drab, ordinary.* There was the *stuffy* rectangle of a room, *half dark* in the *January dusk.* The electric lights glowed with *meager* incandescence. There was the judge, in his *robe,* at the desk of the court. There were the jurors, *solemn* as in church. There were the reporters from the daily journals, more *aloof,* more *judicial* than the judge. There were the police officers and court attendants, relaxed of body, concentrated of eye, jealous of the dignity of the court as a house dog of its master's room. Through the windows could be seen the *bulk of the Tombs, heavy, hopeless, horrible* as the things whence it takes its *chilly* name.

C
8

C8d. MAKE YOUR WRITING CONSISTENT IN PHYSICAL IMPRESSION.

In addition to maintaining a unified point of view, you may wish to create for your reader a distinct *physical impression,* a sense of being on the spot, present where the action is. To do so, try appealing to one or more of the senses: sight, sound, smell, touch, taste. The impression you create may be favorable, positive, and pleasant, or it may be unfavorable, negative, and unpleasant. Whatever it is, the impression should be consistently developed.

In the following paragraph, the dominant physical impression is one of *smell*. Notice that the italicized words consistently appeal to that sense:

> Of all hours of the day there is none like the early morning for *downright good odours*—the morning before eating. Fresh from sleep and unclogged with food a man's senses cut like knives. The whole world comes in upon him. A still morning is best, for the *mists* and the *moisture* seem to retain the *odours* which they have distilled through the night. Upon a *breezy* morning one is likely to get a *single predominant odour* as of *clover* when the wind blows across a *hay field* or of *apple blossoms* when the wind comes through the orchard, but upon a perfectly still morning, it is wonderful how the *odours* arrange themselves in upright strata, so that one walking passes through them as from room to room in a *marvellous temple of fragrance*. (I should have said, I think, if I had not been on my way to dig a ditch, that it was like turning the leaves of some *delicate* volume of lyrics!)
> —From *Adventures in Contentment*, by David Grayson

EXERCISE 24

What is the *physical* point of view (place, time) of some short story or other narrative that you have read? Does this point of view shift?

EXERCISE 25

What is the *personal* point of view in one of the essays or short stories in your literature anthology?

EXERCISE 26

What is the *mental* point of view in one of the essays in your literature anthology?

EXERCISE 27

What is the *physical impression* created in one or more pieces of description that you have read?

EXERCISE 28

The Declaration of Independence is an outstanding example of effective, consistent prose. Below are reprinted the closing paragraph of the original and a version written by H. L. Mencken in what he called "American." Discuss the difference in tone between the two versions. Is each thoroughly consistent in its style and development?

> We, therefore, the representatives of the United States of America, in general Congress assembled, appealing to the Supreme Judge of the world for the rectitude of our intentions, do, in the name and by the authority of the good people of these colonies, solemnly publish and declare that these united colonies are, and of right ought to be, free and independent states; that they are absolved from all allegiance to the British crown, and that all political connection between them and the State of Great Britain is, and ought to be, totally dissolved; and that, as free and independent states, they have full power to levy war, conclude peace, contract alliances, establish commerce, and to do all other acts and things which independent states may of right do. And for the support of this declaration, with a firm reliance on the protection of Divine Providence, we mutually pledge to each other our lives, our fortunes and our sacred honor.
>
> —From "The Declaration of Independence"

> Therefore be it resolved, That we, the representatives of the people of the United States of America, in Congress assembled, hereby declare as follows: That the United States, which was the United Colonies in former times, is now a free country, and ought to be; that we have throwed out the English King and don't want to have nothing to do with him no more, and are not taking no more English orders no more; and that, being as we are now a free country, we can do anything that free countries can do, especially declare war, make peace, sign treaties, go into

C 8

business, etc. And we swear on the Bible on this proposition, one
and all, and agree to stick to it no matter what happens, whether
we win or we lose, and whether we get away with it or get the
worst of it, no matter whether we lose all our property by it or
even get hung for it.

—From *A Mencken Chrestomathy*, by H. L. Mencken

C9.   Coherence and Transition

Coherence as applied to themes means a "holding together" of
parts so that the relationship of ideas is immediately clear to the
reader. In writing a theme, you are actually trying to *transfer*
thoughts from your own mind to the reader's mind and at the
same time trying to show clear and orderly progress from start to
finish. In a coherent composition, each paragraph grows out of
the preceding one and each group of paragraphs dealing with one
section of a theme is closely related to other paragraph groups. A
composition is coherent when its parts have been so carefully
woven together that the reader is never confused about the
relationships of ideas.

C9a. LEAVE NO MISSING LINKS IN THOUGHT.

Connections between ideas that seem sufficiently clear to you do
not always strike the reader the same way. The fault may be that
you have used an ambiguous reference word (*it* or *they*, for
instance) that has one meaning to you, a different one for the
reader. Or perhaps you have confused the reader by omitting an
important connective detail.

For example, in one paragraph you write that you are at an
airport intending to fly to Chicago, but fog has grounded all
planes. In the next paragraph you describe having dinner at a
Chicago restaurant with a friend. "How did you get there?" your
reader wants to know. "Did the fog lift? Did you hitchhike? Go by
train?" Only *you* know the answer, and it could have been easily
supplied in a single sentence: "There was nothing to do but wait

for the fog to lift (or resign myself to going by train, or undertake the hazards and uncertainties of getting a lift in such weather)."

C9b. ATTAIN COHERENCE BY USING TRANSITION.

Transition, by providing links between ideas, is an important means of achieving coherence in a theme. A writer who builds transitional bridges between paragraphs is likely to see and to correct any missing thoughts.

Each new paragraph indentation is a signal to the reader to expect a changeover, a movement of some kind, in the writer's thought. The opening sentence of the paragraph must make this movement clear by transition—by the use of a transitional word, phrase, dependent clause, or sentence. Transitional expressions and devices are discussed in some detail in Section P6.

Here is an example showing the opening sentences of five successive paragraphs concerning the early history of science, with transitions italicized:

1. There is no doubt whatever that our earliest scientific knowledge is of Oriental origin.
2. *For example,* as early as the middle of the fourth millenium, the Egyptians were already acquainted with a decimal system of numbers. (The writer then gives some additional examples.)
3. *These examples* will convince you that a considerable body of systematized knowledge was far anterior to Greek science.
4. *At any rate,* in the present state of our knowledge there is a gap of more than a thousand years between the golden age of Egyptian science and the golden age of Greek science.
5. *The spirit of Greek science,* which accomplished such wonders within a period of five centuries, was essentially the Western spirit, whose triumphs are the boast of modern scientists.

C
9

EXERCISE 29

In your literature anthology or in a current magazine, select an essay and study its transitional devices. Limit your study to transitions between paragraphs. Prepare for class a brief discussion of your findings.

EXERCISE 30

For another selected essay, list the transitional devices mentioned in Section P6 that occur both within and between paragraphs.

C10. Choosing a Title

A good **title** for a composition usually can be chosen only after the paper is completed. However, a tentative title should be selected in advance to help keep the subject in focus. In addition to its unifying effect, a title can secure the attention of a reader. Giving a composition a good title is an important step in making an entire paper effective.

C10a. DISTINGUISH BETWEEN A SUBJECT AND A TITLE.

The term *subject* is broader and more inclusive than the word *title*. If your teacher suggests a composition on eating habits, you have a subject but neither a specific *topic* nor a title. But if a limited topic or actual title is assigned, then you must find out what subject is referred to. The most effective titles of papers indicate not a general subject but a specific topic with a stated *theme*.

For example, if you are writing a paper on the general subject of school athletics, you can phrase a more effective title for it than "Athletics in This School." Perhaps one of the following would be more exact and interesting: "School Is for Students, Not Jocks" or "Athletes Aren't Human" or "Sports Build Character, Books Don't" or "Sexism on the Playing Fields" or "Why I Hate (or Love) Sports." In the next section you will find several examples of titles that show the difference between a subject and a specific topic.

C10b. WORD THE TITLE CLEARLY AND EFFECTIVELY.

A title cannot mention everything a composition contains, but it should provide at least a hint of the contents. Most effective titles provide a clear suggestion of what is to follow and are also catchy. If you cannot phrase a title that is both descriptive and arresting, settle for the former quality. These titles are effective, even though not unusually imaginative or intriguing: "Why a Classic Is a Classic," "How to Find Time to Read," "The Case for Greater Clarity in Writing," "What Happens in College," "College Athletics: Education or Show Business?" "A Windstorm in the Forest," "An Apology for Idlers," "How Americans Choose Their Heroes." As a working title for your first draft, try to come up with something accurate and clear; later you may be able to add appeal.

Here are three simple suggestions for phrasing effective titles:

1. **Avoid long titles.** The most memorable titles usually do not exceed six to eight words. "My Interview with Mr. Bixler" is not as attention-getting as "The Time My Teacher in Seventh Grade Sent Me to the Principal's Office," but it is preferable because of its comparative brevity.

2. **Avoid misleading or confusing titles.** A title such as "Watch the Birdie" might refer to a paper on photography or bird-watching or golf or badminton. Examine a title from a reader's viewpoint. Will it mean to the reader what it does to you?

3. **Avoid vague and commonplace titles.** Many a good composition has gotten off to a poor start because of an unclear or dull title. A trite title such as "An Embarrassing Experience" can be altered to "My Face Was Red"; "A Trip to Washington" can be called "A Capital Journey"; "How to Paint a Room" might become "Good-bye, Old Paint"; "My Operation" is duller than "Proudly I Wear a Scar."

C 10

C10c. PLACE AND PUNCTUATE THE TITLE CORRECTLY.

A title should be centered on the page, on the first line of ruled paper or two inches from the top of unruled paper. Leave a space between the title and the first line of the theme.

Capitalize important words (see Section PM12). Do not underline (italicize) a title or enclose it in quotation marks unless it is itself a quotation or unless you quote it in the theme. If the title is a question or exclamation, use a question mark or exclamation point, but never place a period at the end.

EXERCISE 31

Consult three or four copies of widely circulated magazines such as *Time, People, Newsweek, Reader's Digest.* Examine the titles of articles; then skim the articles to decide whether the titles are (1) both descriptive and arresting, (2) neither of these, (3) one of these, (4) too novel or contrived.

EXERCISE 32

Apply the directions for Exercise 31 to the titles of five essays or articles in your literature anthology.

EXERCISE 33

One of the most famous articles ever written was a study of automobile accidents and fatalities. It was called "— And Sudden Death." Can you phrase more effective titles for articles on the following subjects?

1. Why an airplane flies
2. Advertisements designed to appeal to children
3. A study of American cowhands
4. A criticism of American sports
5. How statistics can tell lies
6. Why money isn't everything in life
7. The story of Gettysburg National Cemetery
8. The fun of being lazy
9. The best way to get good marks in school
10. How to train a dog

EXERCISE 34

What title (or titles) would you suggest to writers of papers on these topics?

1. Whether a boy wants to grow a beard and wear his hair long is his own business and should not be regulated by school authorities.
2. Young people are disillusioned about politics and politicians, and only a few of them want to make a career in government.

C11. Writing and Thinking

Two basic problems are involved in whatever kind of writing you do: (1) formulating ideas, and (2) communicating your thoughts to the reader. The first of these steps is *thinking*. The second is *writing*. The two are inseparably linked. No one can think without using language. No one should try to write without genuine thought.

And yet many persons do attempt to write without adequate thought. They tend to start writing without preplanning what they are going to put on paper. While writing, they are so intent upon getting words on paper that they do not consider what they are actually saying. Finally, as they read what they have written, they are only too likely to ignore the possibility that what they have accomplished is filled with errors in logic, organization, and the mechanics of writing.

You may be excused for errors in thinking while you are preplanning a paper. You may also be forgiven for flaws in thinking while you are putting words on paper. But no one can overlook your failure to revise and rewrite after you have completed the draft of your paper and before you turn it in for someone else to read and evaluate.

Specific steps to take in revising a paper are outlined in the next sections. But learning something about the process of thinking as it applies to writing will make your tasks of revision much easier and will help you to plan and organize the material you wish to communicate with far greater clarity and appeal.

C11a. INDUCTION AND DEDUCTION

C
11

Two common methods of thinking are *induction* and *deduction*. **Induction** seeks to establish a general truth or conclusion. The inductive process begins by using observation or specific facts. It classifies these facts, looks for similarities among them, and from a sufficient number of these facts draws a conclusion. Movement of thought is always from the particular to the general.

Deduction begins by taking a general conclusion, which is then used to establish a specific fact. Movement of thought is from the general to the particular.

In other words, induction is the process of thinking by which one generalizes from particulars. Deduction is that form of reasoning wherein we infer particulars from a general statement.

Processes of thought such as these may seem different from any thinking you consider yourself capable of doing, but look at this example. Early in history, people became convinced that no one lives forever, that sooner or later we all die. Through inductive thinking, a general conclusion was arrived at: All people are mortal. A generalization as well established as this, one that needs neither reexamination nor further testing, can be used as a starting point, that is, a *premise* in deductive thinking. In the light of the general truth that all persons are mortal, we examine the future of a person named George White. In the form of a **syllogism** (a three-part form for stating a deductive argument), this deductive process can be expressed as follows:

> Major premise: All persons are mortal.
> Minor premise: George White is a person.
> Conclusion: George White is mortal.

Although we do not formally arrange our thoughts in syllogisms such as the one just illustrated, we nevertheless reason in much the same way. For example, we assume that events encountered in the future will be like those met in the past. What, indeed, is the real meaning of the saying, "A burnt child dreads the fire"?

In induction, the possibility of exceptions always exists, but those general conclusions reached by inductive processes are usually acceptable. When you write, "Most honor graduates of high school do well in college," you cannot be absolutely certain because you cannot possibly have examined all records of past and present students, nor can you be positive about the future. But the statement is sufficiently probable. So is the inductive conclusion that no two people have identical fingerprints, although this statement, too, is only theoretically capable of being proved.

It is through inductive reasoning that the *laws* (that is, the generalized and descriptive statements) of any science (such as biology, chemistry, and physics) have been arrived at. Through deductive reasoning, they are applied in particular situations: the launching of a space rocket, the manufacture of a computer, the development of a vaccine. In pure and applied science, such reasoning is virtually foolproof. But loopholes do occur where human beings and human behavior are directly concerned.

It is impossible to write a paper without making use of induction or deduction or both. An important part of reviewing and revising what you write is checking again and again to make certain that it contains no obvious flaws in its deductive and inductive processes.

C11b. LOGICAL LOOPHOLES

No matter how carefully you plan a paper, you are apt to commit some flaws in reasoning. The best time to probe for such errors is while you are looking over your completed draft.

The paragraphs that follow comment briefly on the most common everyday offenses against straight and clear thinking. One or more of these errors is likely to appear in every paper you write, talk you make, or conversation you engage in.

Hasty Generalization

The most common error in inductive reasoning is observing only a few instances and then jumping to an unwarranted conclusion. For instance, you know a few athletes whom you consider stupid; does it follow that all, or even most, athletes are mentally deficient? What is the inductive evidence for labeling certain groups "teenage gangsters," "irresponsible women drivers," "absentminded professors"? What is the evidence for "Every schoolchild knows . . ." or "All good Americans realize . . ." or "Statistics show . . ."? Fundamental honesty and your own personal responsibility should prevent loose and unwarranted conclusions.

C 11

Non Sequitur

The major error in deductive thinking, *non sequitur,* is an inference or conclusion that does not proceed from the premises upon which it is apparently based. This fallacy can be caused by a false major premise and by a minor premise that is only apparently related to the major premise. For example, some good professional writers admit to being poor spellers. Are you justified in concluding that you, too, also a poor speller, are destined to be a good professional writer? These syllogisms illustrate the *non sequitur* flaw in thinking:

All members of X club are conceited.
Frances is not a member of X club.
Therefore, Frances is not conceited.

Some members of X club are conceited.
Frances is a member of X club.
Therefore, Frances is conceited.

Post Hoc, Ergo Propter Hoc

This Latin term, a name applied to a variation of hasty generalization, means in English "after this, therefore on account of this." It is a mistake in thinking caused by assuming that, when one event follows another, the latter event is the result of the first. "I have a cold today because I got my feet wet yesterday." "No wonder I had bad luck today; I walked under a ladder yesterday." "The Roman Empire fell after the birth and spread of Christianity." Would anyone seriously argue that Christianity *alone* directly *caused* the fall of Rome? Those who do—and many have—make the *post hoc, ergo propter hoc* error in reasoning.

Biased or Suppressed Evidence

Facts that furnish grounds for belief and help prove an assumption constitute evidence. An obvious and serious flaw in reasoning (and in basic honesty) is selecting evidence from questionable sources or omitting evidence that runs contrary to the point you wish to make. The testimony of dedicated club members is in itself not sufficient to prove that club membership promotes good scholarship or a happy social life. What do non-club members think? What do teachers think? Other school authorities? Parents?

Figures and statistics themselves can be made to lie if evidence is biased or suppressed. Many of the so-called truths we hear and read have been prepared by paid propagandists and directly interested individuals or groups. Biased and suppressed evidence has caused everyone to recognize that "figures don't lie, but liars figure."

Distinguishing Fact from Opinion

A *fact* is based on actuality of some sort, a verifiable event or statement, whereas *opinion* is an inference that may be mingled with a supposed fact. That William Faulkner was an American writer is a statement based on actuality that can be positively proved. That Faulkner was the greatest American novelist of the twentieth century is only an opinion of those who hold it. That Thomas Jefferson was President from 1801 until the inauguration of James Madison in 1809 is a fact; that Jefferson was our greatest President is a matter of opinion. A favorite device of many writers and speakers is to mingle opinions with facts and thus obscure the difference between them.

Begging the Question

This flaw in thinking consists of taking a conclusion for granted before it is proved. A question such as "Should a vicious man like C. Melvin Jones be allowed to hold office?" is "loaded" because it assumes what needs to be proved.

Common forms of begging the question are *slanting, name calling,* and *shifting the meaning of a word.*

Using unfairly suggestive words to create an emotional attitude (as in the application of *vicious* to C. Melvin Jones, above) is a form of **slanting.** It is also a form of *argumentum ad hominem,* a Latin phrase meaning "argument against the person." That is, it is an argument against the person who may hold an opinion rather than against the opinion itself: "Only an idiot would believe that."

Guard against using or fully believing such suggestive words and phrases as "bigoted," "saintly," "progressive," "reactionary," "undemocratic ideas," "dangerous proposal." Use them if you have supporting evidence; accept them if the proof offered seems valid and thorough. Otherwise, avoid slanting in writing and be on your guard for it when reading and listening.

Name-calling is closely allied to slanting. It appeals to prejudice and emotion rather than to the intellect. It employs "good" words to approve and accept, "bad" words to condemn and reject. In writing and reading, be cautious in using such terms as "wolf in sheep's clothing," "angel in disguise," or "rabble rouser."

Shifting the meaning of a word consists of using the same word several times with a shift in meaning designed to confuse the reader or listener. A *conservative* disposed to preserve existing conditions and to agree with gradual rather than abrupt changes is one thing; a *conservative* against all progress, a thorough reactionary, is another. *Student unions* are one thing; *labor*

C
11

unions are another. Should every citizen vote the *Republican* ticket because ours is a great *republic* or vote the *Democratic* ticket because this is a great *democracy?*

Evading the Issue

This error in logic is common everywhere but most of all in heated arguments. It consists of ignoring the point under discussion and making a statement that really has no bearing on the argument. If you tell a friend that she drives too fast, and she responds that you are a poor driver yourself, she has evaded the issue. She may be right, but she has neither met your objection nor won the argument.(Actually, she has employed the *ad hominem* argument mentioned above.) Such argument is especially common in political campaigns, both those in school and out. It is only too easy to sidestep an issue and launch a counterattack.

Faulty Analogy

Because two objects or ideas are alike in one or more respects, they are not necessarily similar in some further way. *Analogy* (partial similarity) can be both accurate and effective; otherwise we could not employ either similes or metaphors. But when we use a figurative language analogy, we do not expect such a figure of speech to *prove* anything. In much of our own writing, we *are* trying to be clear and trying either to develop an idea or defend a position.

In the kind of writing most of us do most of the time, an analogy is chiefly useful as an illustration. In many analogies, differences outweigh similarities. "Why do we need social security? Do we help trees when they lose their leaves in autumn winds? Do we provide assistance to dogs and horses in their old age? Don't some tribes kill people when they are too old to be useful?" Such false analogy as this is obviously absurd, but even more literal analogies than this can be ridiculous. You may, for example, reason that since the honor system has worked well in several small schools you have attended, it will work equally well in the high school in which you are now a student. Are the similarities between the schools either superficial or less important than the differences? The whipping post was a deterrent to crime in seventeenth-century New England. Is it false analogy to suggest that similar punishment should be inflicted on twentieth-century criminals?

Testimonials

Citing statements from historical personages or well-known contemporaries is not necessarily straight thinking. In an attempt to bolster an argument, we are quick to employ such phrases as "authorities have concluded," "science proves," "doctors say," "laboratory tests reveal." George Washington, Thomas Jefferson, and Abraham Lincoln—justly renowned as they are—might have held economic, social, and political views not necessarily valid in the twentieth century. Douglas MacArthur was a great military strategist, but something he said about combustion engines may be less convincing than the words of a good local mechanic.

Is an authority in one field an oracle of wisdom about any subject outside that field? As a witness for or against an important interscholastic policy, how effective would an eminent surgeon be? A football hero? A TV personality? If you were writing an attack on vaccination, would you reasonably expect the cited opposition of George Bernard Shaw to outweigh the pronouncements of the entire medical profession? Thomas A. Edison was a great inventor, but you would be ill-advised to cite his odd notions about gravity. Henry Ford would not be a wise choice for you to quote in some argument about history.

But even where there is little question of the validity of authority, be careful, as has been suggested, to see that neither bias nor the time element weakens your presentation. Some business and labor leaders are experts on economic problems, but their particular interests might prevent their having the impartiality of a disinterested observer, such as a professor of economics. And even a professor might be biased in favor of some specific school of economic thought.

As for timing, remember that, in many fields of human activity and knowledge, authorities soon become obsolete. Charles Darwin no longer has the last word on evolution; Sigmund Freud is not universally considered the final authority in psychoanalysis.

In conclusion, **logic** may be called the rule by which we evaluate the statements and arguments of others, particularly when our skeptical minds and common sense have already made us suspicious. It should also be the rule by which we measure our own thinking in order that it will produce the effects we wish.

In school, no greater opportunity exists for checking on your thinking than the papers you write. Look them over carefully.

Apply to them the lessons learned in this section. Also, keep in mind the necessity for straight thinking as you take the specific steps suggested in the next section.

EXERCISE 35

In your own compositions, those of your classmates, and newspaper articles, try to locate statements that can be criticized according to the following list of suggestions prepared by Professor Macklin Thomas, formerly of Chicago State College.

1. The statement needs qualification; it is too sweeping or dogmatic.
2. The facts cited are not such as are likely to be accepted on the writer's bare assertion. Some authority, occupational experience, or other support should be cited.
3. The writer's argument is good so far as it goes, but it is unconvincing because it has failed to dispose of some obvious and overriding argument that can be made on the other side.
4. The evidence supplied is pertinent but falls far short of proof. One good reason does not build a case.
5. There is such a thing as being too specific if the writer does not make clear what generalization is supported by the instances given. A well-developed train of thought works back and forth between the general and the specific, showing the connections and applications intended at each point.
6. The writer's treatment here is obviously marked by particular bias and prior emotional commitment. This does not necessarily make the conclusions false, but it does make them all suspect.
7. The writer's approach here is essentially moralistic and directive rather than analytical. No law exists against preaching, but one should distinguish preaching from investigation, analysis, and reasoning.
8. Here the writer is exploring religious or philosophical questions that have been discussed for thousands of years by serious thinkers without being brought to a conclusion.

EXERCISE 36

On a separate sheet of paper, identify the logical fallacy in each of the following statements, using these letters: (A) hasty generalization; (*B*) *non sequitur;* (*C*) *post hoc, ergo propter hoc;* (*D*) biased or suppressed evidence; (*E*) fact from opinion; (*F*) begging the question; (*G*) evading the issue; (*H*) faulty analogy; (*I*) testimonial.

1. In reply to Ms. Marsh's claim that her administration is prepared to help the poor, I wish to point out that she has never been hungry in her entire life, that she has inherited a vast fortune, and that her children attend exclusive private schools.

2. Courses in marriage and the family cannot prepare young adults for marriage. To try to educate them for marriage is like trying to teach them to swim without letting them go into the water. It just can't be done!

3. "Carol Cole—star of stage, screen, and television—says 'I smoke New Way cigarettes. They contain a balanced mixture of carbon and hydrosyntheme'."

4. Oliver Wendell Holmes, Jr., the Supreme Court Justice, was a greater American than his father, the poet, essayist, and doctor.

5. Ladies and gentlemen of the jury, the prosecution is prepared to prove to you that this wretched murderer who sits before you is guilty as charged.

6. There are three Norwegians in my math class. They invariably get the highest scores on exams. Obviously, Norwegians are mathematically inclined.

7. Lazy students often flunk out of school. My neighbor is one of the laziest students I have ever met. Therefore, he is flunking because of his laziness.

8. Aunt Greta suffered from rheumatism all last summer. Her illness disappeared, however, when she began drinking German beer. Therefore, we are all convinced that German beer is a remedy for rheumatism.

9. Dissecting animals is an evil, wicked practice. How would you like it if someone snipped off your arm, leg, or finger?

10. I refuse to vote for a divorced man, for how could John Wilbur, a home wrecker, be trusted to lead this nation?

C
11

EXERCISE 37

In a biography entitled *Napoleon,* Emil Ludwig shows how Paris newspapers changed their tunes from the time the deposed emperor escaped from the island of Elba on March 1, 1815, until he arrived in Paris three weeks later. Write a composition of 300–

400 words as a commentary on this kind of name-calling and on the weaknesses of human nature thus exhibited.

> —The monster has escaped from his place of exile.
> —The Corsican werewolf has landed at Cannes.
> —The tiger appeared at Gap, troops were sent against him, the wretched adventurer ended his career in the mountains.
> —The fiend has actually, thanks to treachery, been able to get as far as Grenoble.
> —The tyrant has reached Lyons, where horror paralyzed all attempts at resistance.
> —The usurper has dared to advance within 150 miles of the capital.
> —Bonaparte moves northward with rapid strides, but he will never reach Paris.
> —Tomorrow Napoleon will be at our gates.
> —His Majesty is at Fontainebleau.
> —The Emperor has reassumed his imperial duties in Paris.

EXERCISE 38

Without paying much attention to exact names for the flaws in thinking involved, comment on and explain errors in the following sentences.

1. Today's society has changed considerably in the past century.
2. Good students are always working ahead to prepare themselves in advance.
3. The interior of the car showed that it had been driven many miles.
4. Teaching me good English makes about as much sense as teaching a cat to fight an elephant.
5. In commenting on the fire, the chief explained that Mr. Smithers, in whose apartment the blaze had started, had a habit of smoking in bed.
6. The folder mentions how many people this medicine has helped. I am going to get some.
7. He is an attractive person and has many friends; therefore, he deserves your vote as class president.
8. Because some people choose to read obscene books and go to sexy movies, all books and movies should be censored to protect the public.
9. The way to prevent war is to be fully prepared for war.

10. Students who do more work than is assigned make it hard for the rest of us to get good grades. If it weren't for such people, I'd be getting an A instead of a D.

C12. Revising

"There is no such thing as good writing; there is only good rewriting." Many students have objected to this statement. Yet good writers know that it is true.

When asked about revising, short-story writer Frank O'Connor replied that he did so "endlessly, endlessly, endlessly." Then he added, "And I keep on rewriting after something is published."

Alberto Moravia, a widely respected and popular writer, once commented, "I like to compare my method of writing with that of painters centuries ago, proceeding from layer to layer. The first draft is quite crude, by no means finished. After that, I rewrite it many times—apply as many layers—as I feel to be necessary."

Such remarks make writing seem like hard work. Well, it often is. But those unwilling to revise and rewrite are skipping an important step toward becoming better writers. If this recommendation seems grim, then relax over this amusing comment by the English poet Jonathan Swift:

> Blot out, correct, insert, refine,
> Enlarge, diminish, interline;
> Be mindful, when invention fails,
> To scratch your head and bite your nails.

C
12

C12a. CAREFULLY REVISE EVERY COMPOSITION.

Four kinds of alterations are possible when you rework a paper. You can *add* material, *delete* material, *substitute*, and *rearrange*. One or more of these types of revision may be necessary to ensure that your paper is as effective as you can make it.

You might, for example, add a bit of dialogue to increase the appeal of your paper or add an example to reinforce your argument. On the other hand, you might remove a section that seems dull or repetitious. Eliminating words that were hard to come by and now seem precious is probably the most difficult and most important phase of the entire rewriting process.

Revision Checklists

When revising a paper you should review its *purpose, organization, development, sentence structure, diction, grammar, usage,* and *mechanics.* The following checklists should serve as helpful guides to these matters.

Purpose

1. Does the paper have a clear, definite theme, a central point? Is it built around a stated or clearly implied *thesis sentence?*
2. Does it keep in mind the reader or readers for whom it is intended? Is the *tone* appropriate to the audience?

Organization

1. Does the plan of the paper follow a clear method of organization? For example, does it begin with a cause and proceed to an effect or begin with an effect and then develop the causes for that effect? Or if the order is based on time, does the paper begin at the beginning and proceed to later stages?
2. Are the paragraphs arranged in logical order, one paragraph naturally following another?

Development

1. Is each paragraph adequate in material, unified in substance, and correctly proportioned in relation to other paragraphs in the paper?
2. Does the sum of the paragraphs reveal enough material to convince readers of the point you are making? Conversely, have you included unnecessary or irrelevant material?
3. Are there adequate and clear transitions between paragraphs and between ideas?
4. Does the paper contain any *logical loopholes,* or flaws in reasoning, that will weaken your argument?

Sentence Structure

1. Does the paper contain any fused sentences? Any comma faults? Any unjustified sentence fragments?
2. Are there any dangling modifiers? Any misplaced modifiers? Any awkward split constructions?
3. Does the paper contain any sentences that reveal faulty parallelism, faulty coordination or subordination, and illogical constructions?
4. Does the paper have any inconsistencies in tense, tone, or mood?

Diction, Grammar, and Usage

1. Is each word in the paper as suitable and effective as possible? Does the paper contain stale expressions, unnecessary words, and inappropriate examples of jargon and slang?
2. Does the paper contain any glaring errors in grammar and usage—incorrect reference of pronouns, faulty agreement, incorrect verb forms, mistakes in the case of pronouns?

Mechanics

1. Does the paper contain any words misspelled because of ignorance or carelessness?
2. Is all of the punctuation in the paper logical, necessary, and a clear aid to communication?
3. Is the paper neat in appearance, and has it been prepared in accordance with prescribed form? (See Section C14.)
4. Has the complete paper been carefully proofread to eliminate careless errors of any kind? (See Section C13.)

C 12

EXERCISE 39

Make an honest analysis of the time spent on three of your compositions written outside class. Estimate the amount of time spent on preparation for writing, actual time spent in writing, and the time spent revising and proofreading.

EXERCISE 40

Rewrite a paper that you have turned in and gotten back. Submit both papers either to your instructor or to another student for comments on the two versions.

C13. Proofreading

When you read, you comprehend words and even groups of words at a glance. But this is not the kind of reading designed to spot errors in the papers you write.

In **proofreading** you narrow the range of your vision, looking closely at individual words and letters. No matter how carefully you have prepared a paper, it may still contain errors in spelling, capitalization, punctuation, and the like. These errors can be spotted only by careful proofreading.

It is best to put your paper aside for at least an hour before you reread it for the last time. If you read it over immediately after you have written it, your mind will still be so full of what you intended to say that you may not notice your errors. Even professional writers have to check their final drafts for oversights.

EXERCISE 41

Following the suggestions in this section, carefully proofread a paper that you are ready to hand in. How many mistakes did you find that needed correcting? Make a list of them and write a short paper about your findings.

EXERCISE 42

Write a paragraph with this topic sentence: "Careless errors in writing hinder communication as much as any kind of static hinders conversation."

C14. Manuscript Form

As interesting and well planned as your paper may be, it is unlikely to win approval if it is untidy and illegible. Try to give your ideas the outward appearance that will guarantee ready communication.

C14a. CONFORM TO STANDARDS IN PREPARING MANUSCRIPT.

If your class has been given instructions for preparing manuscript, follow those directions. If not, use the following suggestions as a guide.

1. **Paper.** Use prescribed paper or standard-sized sheets, 8½ by 11 inches, with lines of handwriting or typing ⅓ to ½ inch apart. Write on only one side of the sheet.

2. **Ink.** Use black or blue-black ink. Ball-point pens should be of good quality to write legibly and without smears.

3. **Typing.** Use black ribbon and be certain that the type is clean. Submit typewritten compositions only if you typewrite them yourself.

4. **Margins.** Leave a frame of white space all *around* each page—about 1½ inches at top and left, 1 inch at right and bottom.

5. **Indentation.** Indent each paragraph equally, almost 1 inch in longhand, five spaces when typewriting.

6. **Paging.** Mark each page after the first by placing an Arabic numeral in the upper right-hand corner. Arrange the pages in proper order.

7. **Title.** Center the title about 2 inches from the top of the page.

8. **Insertions.** Use a caret (∧) when inserting something omitted. Preferably, recopy the page.

9. **Cancellation.** Draw a neat line through material you wish to omit. Do not use brackets or parentheses. Preferably, recopy the entire page.

C14b. AVOID NUMEROUS CORRECTIONS IN YOUR FINAL DRAFT.

We are all prone to make errors even in the final drafts of our writing. Sometimes the errors are few and can be corrected without numerous erasures and canceled words. It is better, however, to rewrite a whole page than to submit a manuscript with several erasures, blurs, and canceled or inserted words.

C14c. MAKE YOUR HANDWRITING LEGIBLE.

1. Use a good pen with black or blue-black ink.
2. Do not crowd your writing by running words together; do not write consecutive lines too closely together; leave ample margins.
3. The consecutive letters in a word should be joined.
4. Take your time.

C14d. IF POSSIBLE, TYPE YOUR THEMES AND OTHER WRITTEN WORK.

Typescript is more legible than handwriting. In addition, you can detect mistakes in typescript more easily than in handwriting. If you do not know how to type, learning might be an excellent investment of time and money. If you do type, be certain to double-space all lines; quotations of more than four lines, however, should be single-spaced.

EXERCISE 43

Find a paper that you wrote earlier in the year and recopy or retype it so that it conforms to proper manuscript form.

The Special Composition

The following sections deal with the *report*, the *research paper*, the *précis*, the *paraphrase*, and *letters*. Each of these types of writing has a distinct purpose and is appropriate for special writing tasks. You will probably need to use each kind of *special composition* studied in this unit some time in your school or working career.

SC1. The Report

A **report** is a piece of writing based on an experiment or an investigation that results in either a summary of information or a series of recommendations. For example, class activities in most schools require reports from class officers.

Report writing may involve two or three pages of expository writing or, possibly, many pages bound in a folder containing pictures, diagrams, and charts. Regardless of length or form, report writing and letter writing are likely to be the two forms most frequently used and most important to your success in adult life.

SC1a. PLAN AND OUTLINE THE REPORT CAREFULLY.

A good report is one that contains enough accurate and pertinent information to accomplish the job designed—and not one bit more. In order to ensure adequate but not excess coverage, *outline* the report before you begin or frame an outline as you proceed (Section C3). No satisfactory report was ever written without an outline prepared in advance or developed as the writing progressed.

Such a plan for an informal report might cover these questions:

1. Who asked you to study the problem? When? Why?
2. Precisely what is the subject to be reported on?
3. How was the investigation made? (Authorities consulted, people interviewed, places visited, tests made, reading done.)
4. What are the specific results or recommendations?

A list of topics on club conditions in your school might resemble this:

1. Summary
2. Members of the investigating committee
3. Methods of conducting the survey
4. Number and kinds of clubs investigated
5. Means of selecting club members
6. Activities of the clubs involved in this study
7. Club contributions to the school
8. Clubs and school elections
9. Clubs and the community
10. Effects of clubs on the student body

SC1b. BEGIN THE REPORT WITH A SUMMARY STATEMENT.

A formal or lengthy report usually begins with a *summary* of methods used to obtain information and of results or recommendations. This summary is followed by the main body of the report, which discusses these summary points in detail.

The plan of an effective report is usually dictated by the opening summary, an illustration of which follows:

> The purpose of this report is to determine (1) whether the program designed to give new employees an understanding of the products and social significance of the company has actually justified its cost in time and money; and (2) whether changes are needed to improve the program if it is retained.
>
> The investigation has been based on four sources of information: (1) interviews with employees who have completed the program; (2) interviews with supervisory personnel; (3) statistical

comparisons of work efficiency between those who have and have not taken the program; (4) published reports on related programs at four other industrial centers.

The report establishes the value of the program and recommends its continuation. Suggestions for improvement: (1) top-level executives should contribute more actively to the program through individual interviews with employees and by lectures to groups; (2) greater use of visual-aid material is needed to explain certain complex company operations; (3) the orientation course should be extended by two weeks.

SC1c. THE REPORT SHOULD BE SELECTIVE BUT COMPREHENSIVE.

No report reveals everything known about any subject. A good report writer must be selective in deciding which details to include and which to omit. Nevertheless, no competent reporter regrets collecting more material than will eventually be used.

SC1d. A REPORT SHOULD BE OBJECTIVE.

An investigator who knows in advance what answers are desired and who uses data to support a predetermined point of view is neither a competent nor fair reporter. A report should be approached without personal prejudice. Results and recommendations should be based on materials collected and assembled with an open mind. An effective report contains no exaggerations and few superlatives. The reliable report writer presents facts as clearly as possible and phrases recommendations without resort to argument and appeals to emotion.

SC1e. A REPORT SHOULD BE DIRECT.

SC 1

Each paragraph in a report should begin with a topic sentence. A reader who wishes to examine in detail a particular part of the report should be able to locate that part at once by glancing at topic sentences only. The writer of a good report comes to each point at once and adds no unnecessary details.

EXERCISE 1

As your teacher directs, prepare an informal or formal report on one of the following topics:

1. Student control in study halls
2. Furnishing a recreation room
3. How cafeteria officers are chosen
4. Safety programs in this school
5. Student transportation to school

EXERCISE 2

Follow the directions for Exercise 1.

1. A plan for handling school social functions
2. Treatment of athletes injured in school games
3. School-sponsored community activities
4. Discipline in this school
5. Curricula offered in this school

SC2. The Research Paper

Research can be defined as "intensive search with the purpose of becoming certain." Actually, the essentials of research procedure are almost as natural as eating and sleeping. On your own, you have gone from one store to another to locate the suit or dress or jeans that best became both your appearance and your pocket-book. You have tried out various restaurants, diners, soft drinks, and amusement places in what are actually research projects. What, actually, is the activity of dating but a problem in research?

After you have had some practice in theme writing, you may be assigned a **research paper** (also called a *term paper*, *library paper*, or *investigative theme*). This will be somewhere between 1500 and 6000 words, depending on the subject and the limit set by your teacher. Your purpose should be to make a careful search for information about a particular subject and then to present and interpret what you have found out. A research paper should not be a mere reading report or a hodgepodge of quotations and summaries. An effective paper is an orderly, systematic study undertaken for a specific purpose.

To turn out a good investigative theme takes time. It constitutes a task you cannot do hastily or postpone until the last moment. It means choosing a suitable subject and knowing how and where to inform yourself about it. It means knowing how to take efficient notes on your reading and having a clear conception of what is relevant to your subject and what is not. Further, preparing a good paper requires knowing the mechanics of research and having the patience and will to write and rewrite.

As overwhelming as this task may appear to you, your labors will seem less burdensome if you have a genuine interest in your subject and the curiosity to get at the facts behind it. You will not be the first to discover that researching a subject and coming upon a missing fact for which you have been hunting has the fascination of detective work. Students who approach a research assignment with reluctance often become engrossed in their subject once they begin gathering information.

An increasing number of students enter colleges where professors take for granted that term papers will be the result of original research and will be correctly written and documented. Even in business and community life, the writing of reports and preparation of speeches involve basic principles of gathering information and presenting it.

SC2a. SELECT AND ANALYZE YOUR SUBJECT CAREFULLY.

1. Choose a subject that already interests you or conceivably can engage your interest. But avoid selecting one that is overly technical or too specialized to be of interest to your readers.

2. Choose a subject that you can treat adequately in the space assigned. A topic suitable for a paper of 1000 words could be spun out to 5000 only by padding and repetition.

3. Select a subject about which enough has been written for you to obtain pertinent information. Consider the resources of the library where you intend to do your investigating.

4. Have a clear purpose in view as you start gathering material. Form an idea of what you plan to demonstrate or prove by investigating your subject—what conclusions you expect to draw from it. (See Section C2.)

SC 2

SC2b. BE THOROUGH IN INVESTIGATING YOUR SUBJECT.

Many scholars, as well as authors of historical novels, often spend months and even years in the world's greatest libraries. You have only a matter of days or weeks to gather your material. No one expects you to learn *all* about a subject in so brief a time. You should, however, learn how to make efficient use of books of reference, periodical indexes, and the general card catalog.

From these, make out a preliminary list of books and articles that seem *likely* to contribute to your subject. Write each item on a 3 × 5 inch card. Be careful to put down *full* information. This will save you time in two ways: (1) you will have detailed facts should you need the information for the bibliography of your paper; (2) you need not repeat these facts on note cards. How a bibliography card can be made is shown on page 450. Observe that the material is arranged as it will appear in the bibliography, except that you may not need to include the publisher's name. Note also that the card lists a library call number. This number can also save time if you have to put in a second request for the book to check it again, as happens even to experienced researchers.

The number shown for the biographies of Conrad illustrates a common way of cataloging biographies. Many biographies have call numbers that consist of: (1) the letter *B* (for *biography*); (2) the first letter of the person's last name (in this case, *C*); (3) a special number representing the person (in this case *754* represents Conrad, so that all biographies with *C 754* are biographies of Conrad); (4) the first letter of the author's first name (in this case, *J*). The card for Conrad's novel *The Shadow Line* illustrates a common way of cataloging fiction: *F* stands for fiction and *C* for the author—in this case, Conrad. A novel by Emily Brontë would be cataloged *FB;* one by Katherine Mansfield, *FM*.

Having filled out bibliography cards for as many books and articles as you believe you will need, begin examining the items themselves. Keep those that contain information pertinent to the phase of the subject you are concerned with and reject those that do not. You can reach this decision by glancing through articles and studying the prefaces, tables of contents, and indexes of books. When you are fairly certain which of this material you will need for your paper, you are ready to start taking notes.

SC2c. TAKE CAREFUL NOTES FROM YOUR READING.

The most efficient way to take **notes** is on 4 × 6 inch cards, one note to each card. Note cards should be larger than bibliography cards because they will need to hold more information. Sheets of paper of about this size, or larger, or pages from a loose-leaf notebook will also answer your purpose, but cards seem preferable because they are easier to sort and rearrange, an important step preparatory to writing your paper.

Before you take notes on a book, examine the preface and table of contents to learn the scope and purpose of the book. If the volume has an index, save time by looking there for your particular subject or material related to it.

Keep your notes compact. You will only waste time by taking down whole pages. You can often condense a paragraph, sometimes even a page, to a single summarizing sentence.

Unless you are quoting exactly, always take notes *in your own words.* You can then use material from your note cards when you are writing the paper without having to reword it. You are entitled to borrow information from an author and are required to acknowledge your debt in a footnote. You are *not* entitled to use an author's sentences except as direct and acknowledged quotation. When you find something you wish to quote in your paper, copy it carefully and accurately and surround it with quotation marks for later use.

Also, try to judge the reliability of your sources. If the material is controversial, consider the possible bias of an author. If your subject is largely factual, how recently was a particular item of information published? Is there a later book on the subject that is more accurate and up to date?

For an efficient method of note-taking, examine the sample note cards shown on pages 450–451. Note the bibliographical information, with the author's name in its normal order as it would be given in a footnote. (This information need appear only on the first note card on each book or article. Thereafter you can use abbreviations for the same source.)

As your notes accumulate, regroup them so that those dealing with the same aspect of your subject are together. In this way you can more readily see which topics you have dealt with sufficiently and which require more information. This grouping will also help shape a preliminary outline for your paper.

Jean-Aubry, Georges.

Joseph <u>Conrad</u>: <u>Life</u> and <u>Letters</u>.

2 vols. New York: Doubleday,
Page and Company, 1927.

B
C 754 J

<u>Otago</u>   (Joseph Conrad)

   Conrad outwardly calm on appointment
to command, which is an abstract idea
to him. He suddenly realizes it involves
the concrete existence of a ship.
   "A ship! My ship! It was mine, more
absolutely mine for possession and
care than anything in the world; an
object of responsibility and devotion."
p. 40
Joseph Conrad, <u>The</u> <u>Shadow</u> <u>Line</u>, (New
York: Doubleday, Page and Company, 1926).

F
C

Small 3 × 5 inch cards are useful for bibliographical information. Larger cards, 4 × 6 inch preferably, are more useful for extended note-taking. An explanation of the call numbers (*FC* and *B*/*C 754 J*) is given on page 448.

Citizen and Master

August 19, 1886, Joseph Conrad Korzeniowski, "subject of the Russian Empire, of the age of twenty-nine years, mariner, unmarried," was given a certificate of British naturalization.

November 11, 1886, awarded "Certificate of Competency as Master." p. 111.

Georges Jean-Aubry, *The Sea Dreamer: a Definitive Biography of Joseph Conrad*, (New York, 1926, 1957).

B
C 754 J

SC
2

SC2d. PREPARE AN ADEQUATE OUTLINE FOR YOUR PAPER.

While taking notes, presumably you had in mind a controlling purpose (Section SC2a). You should therefore be able to arrange your grouped notes to form a tentative sentence or topic **outline** for your paper (Section C3). You will, however, probably want to make changes before deciding on a final outline. For example, you may want to shift a note or group of notes to achieve a more effective beginning or ending.

A tentative outline, suitable for some subjects, might cover these major points:

I. Purpose of the paper
II. Value of the subject (importance, significance)
III. Background or history of the subject
IV. Nature of the investigation (its substance)
V. Conclusions (generalized statements based on the investigation.

Do not begin writing your paper until you have worked out an outline in its final form. This is essential to assure a well-structured whole. A meandering discussion unfortunately implies that the writer's research was equally haphazard.

SC2e. WRITE A FIRST DRAFT OF YOUR RESEARCH PAPER.

Your paper is the end result of all your reading and note-taking. If the final outline is well designed and sufficiently detailed and if your notes are arranged to follow its divisions, you should be able to write the paper with only normal difficulty.

You should, however, write a **first draft** as a working copy to get material down on paper to see how it looks and sounds. Leave one or two spaces between the lines for revisions. You can then make changes in sequence, strengthen your beginning, eliminate overlapping details, or make your discussion more effective in any other needed way. Determine which facts require acknowledgment and write out proper footnotes for them. Prepare your bibliography from your 3 × 5 inch cards, putting them in alphabetical order according to the authors' names. In short, the greater likeness of first draft to final one, the easier the last stage of your writing will be.

A research paper is an objective presentation of the facts about a subject. Its point of view is *impersonal*. Ordinarily, do not refer to yourself as "I" or to the reader as "you." If you refer to either—and you should rarely do so—speak of "the present writer" and "the reader."

Write in as clear and straightforward a manner as you can. A research paper need not be stiff, overformal, or pedantic. It can be enlivened by touches of irony, humor, or a well-turned phrase. Most research papers are duller than they need be. A good research paper is a living, tangible accomplishment. You may be delightfully surprised at your success in mastering one phase of a subject and communicating it with clarity, vigor, and appeal.

SC2f. USE FOOTNOTES TO INDICATE SOURCES OF INFORMATION.

In addition to writing as clearly and correctly as possible, you must also document the borrowed materials you use. Documentation involves the use of both **footnotes** and a *bibliography*.

The purpose of a footnote is either to mention the authority for some fact stated or to develop some point referred to in the body of a paper.

Commonly known facts or quotations do not require footnotes, but you must avoid *plagiarism*. Unless the idea and the phrasing are your own, refer the reader to some source for your statement. To be completely honest, acknowledge every source of indebtedness, even when no direct quotation is used.

Occasionally you may wish to develop, interpret, or refute some idea but not want an extended comment to clutter up the body of your paper. Use a footnote.

How many footnotes should appear in a research paper? One investigation may call for twice the number of entries as another. Some pages of your paper may call for a half dozen or more footnotes. Others may need only one or two or none at all. Acknowledge credit where it is due and provide discussion footnotes where they are required for understanding.

Systems of footnoting are numerous, but whatever method you choose should be used consistently throughout your paper and be immediately clear to any intelligent reader.

SC
2

For books, standard usage favors this form: (1) author's first name or initials followed by surname; (2) title of book (in italics) and number of edition; (3) place of publication; (4) name of publisher (optional); (5) date of publication; (6) volume and page reference.

In listing information about periodical material, place the title of the article or story after the author's name and before the name of the periodical. The title is put in quotation marks, the name of the magazine is italicized (underlined). Place the volume number, in Roman numerals, immediately after the name of the magazine or journal. By using Roman numerals for the volume number and Arabic numerals for the page numbers, you avoid the necessity for volume and page abbreviations. Examine the correct forms for entering the following kinds of information.

Footnote Form for Books

[1] Mary Cogan Bromage, *Writing for Business*, (Ann Arbor, Michigan, 1965), 152.

[1] Barbara Ward, *The Rich Nations and the Poor Nations*, (New York, 1962), 107.

[1] Charles Neider, ed., *The Great West*, (New York, 1958), 168.

[1] Marcel Proust, *Remembrance of Things Past*, trans. C. K. Scott Moncrieff (New York, 1935), I, 31.

Footnote Form for Articles (Essays, Stories)

[1] Foster Nostrand, "Out of a Clear Blue Sky," *Yachting*, CXXII (October 1967), 42.

[1] Alice Alldredge, "Appendicularians," *Scientific American*, vol. 235, no. 1 (July 1976), 98.

[1] Edith Wharton "Xingu," *Short Stories*, ed. Edwin H. Sauer and Howard Mumford Jones (New York: Holt, Rinehart and Winston, 1963), 204.

In documenting your research paper, you may be urged by your teacher to use abbreviations wherever possible for increased efficiency. The forms shown above may well be used less often than shortcut versions. For example:

ibid. The same. If a footnote refers to the same source as the one referred to in the footnote *immediately* preceding, the abbreviation *ibid.* (from the Latin *ibidem*, meaning "in the same place") can be used. If the volume, page, title, and author are the same, use *ibid.* alone. If the volume and page differ, use, for example, "*Ibid.*, III, 206." *Ibid.* usually comes at the beginning of a footnote and is capitalized for that reason only.

op. cit. The work cited. After the first full reference to a given work, provided no other work by the same author is mentioned in the paper, succeeding references may be indicated by the author's surname followed by *op. cit.* (from the Latin *opere citato*, meaning "in the work cited") and the volume and page:

> Corwin, *op. cit.*, V, 41.
> Parsons, *op. cit.*, p. 12.

However, *op. cit.* does no real work and its use is being abandoned in favor of an entry containing only the author's last name and the page number involved: "Smith, p. 320."

passim. Everywhere, throughout. It is used when no specific page reference can be given.

loc. cit. The place cited. If the reference is to the exact passage covered by an earlier, but not immediately preceding, reference, use *loc. cit.* (from the Latin *loco citato*, meaning "in the place cited"). Like *op. cit.*, *loc. cit.* seems wordy and is gradually being discarded in research writing. Actually, *ibid.* can do anything *loc. cit.* can.

p. (*plural,* **pp.**). Page (pages).

l. (*plural,* **ll.**). Line (lines).

vol. Volume.

chap. (*plural,* **chaps.**). Chapter (chapters).

ff. Following (e.g., pages 424 ff.).

v. Verse.

ante. Before.

art. Article.

sec. (*plural,* **secs.**). Section (sections).

n. (*plural,* **nn.**) Note (notes).

SC 2

A footnote is indicated by an Arabic numeral placed above and to the right of the word requiring comment. If the reference is to a quotation, place the numeral at the end of the passage. In front of the actual footnote at the bottom of the page, repeat the number used in the text. Asterisks or other symbols should not be used in place of Arabic numerals.

Footnotes may be numbered consecutively throughout the manuscript or separately for each page. Follow the directions given by your teacher.

Footnotes may appear at the bottoms of pages, between lines in the text proper, or all together at the end of the manuscript. Most teachers prefer the first of these methods. If footnotes are to be placed at the bottom of the page, care should be taken not to crowd them. Always leave a clearly defined space between the text and the footnotes.

SC2g. USE A BIBLIOGRAPHY TO DOCUMENT YOUR RESEARCH PAPER.

In a research paper, a **bibliography** is an alphabetical list containing the names of all works quoted from or generally used in the preparation of the paper. Every formally prepared research paper should include a bibliography begun on a separate page and placed at the end of the paper.

Bibliographical items should be arranged correctly and consistently. Usage may vary, but unless your teacher rules otherwise, follow these suggestions:

1. Arrange items alphabetically by last names of the authors. Each surname is followed by a comma, then by the author's given name(s) or initials.
2. If the author's name is not given and not known, list the item by the first word (except *a, an, the*) in the title. List titles by the same author alphabetically, using a blank line about three-fourths of an inch long in place of the author's name after its first appearance.
3. The author's complete name is followed by a period.
4. A period follows the title of a book. Citing the publisher's name is optional.
5. Place and date of publication are separated by a comma and are not put in parentheses.

The following are examples of citations of books and of articles from periodicals.

Bibliography Form for Books

Dee, P. Christopher. *The Togetherness of Words: Composition in the Classroom.* New York: Harper & Row, 1970.

Hull, Helen Rose. *The Writer's Book.* New York: Barnes and Noble, 1956.

Montgomery, Lucy Maud. *The Road to Yesterday.* Toronto: McGraw-Hill, 1974.

Newman, Dorothy M. *Canadian Business Handbook.* New York: McGraw-Hill, 1964.

Spectorsky, A. C., ed. *The Book of the Sea.* New York: Grosset & Dunlap, 1954, 124-126.

Bibliography Form for Articles

Alpert, Hollis. "How Useful Are Film Festivals?" *Saturday Review* (July 8, 1967), 56-58.

Bolling, Richard. "What the New Congress Needs Most," *Harper's Magazine,* CCXXXIV (January 1967), 79-81.

Cipnic, Monica. "Magic with Masking," *Popular Photography,* vol. 79, no. 6 (December 1976), 102-105.

Pryor, Karen. "Orchestra Conductors Would Make Good Porpoise Trainers," *Psychology Today,* vol. 10, no. 9 (February 1977), 61-64.

Silberman, Arlene. "A Matter of Life or Death," *Reader's Digest* (March 1977), 185-189.

SC2h. MAKE YOUR FINAL DRAFT CORRECT AND ACCURATE.

SC 2

The *final version* of your paper must be carefully prepared. Except for minor changes, it will be essentially a transcription of your last previous draft. It should be as nearly letter-perfect as possible. To make sure of this, first read slowly through the text with an eye to spelling and punctuation. Corrections in these can usually be made without blemishing your manuscript. Larger errors involving revision of a sentence or the addition of one should necessitate rewriting a whole page.

Next, check your footnotes. Are they correct in form and complete in detail? Last, ask yourself the same questions about the bibliography. Then lay the paper aside, preferably for several days but at least for one day. When you look at it again, you can view it with a fresher eye. If you discover no other lapses, you have probably done the best you can. No one can ask more than that.

Sample Manuscript Pages

JOSEPH CONRAD AS A COMMANDER

For fourteen months of his twenty years as a mariner, Joseph Conrad Korzeniowski, as he was then known, held command of a ship, the 350-ton barque <u>Otago</u>, owned by an Australian company.[1] The command ended with his abrupt resignation. What kind of master did he prove to be? What were his strengths and his shortcomings? We have no profile on him in this capacity. If no

[1]Georges Jean-Aubry, <u>The Sea Dreamer: A Definitive Biography of Joseph Conrad</u> (New York, 1957), p. 132.

complete one is possible, some of the lineaments may be sketched in from evidences in Conrad's own writings, the recollections of persons who knew him at this time, and the accounts of his biographers.

In 1886, First Officer Korzeniowski was awarded two certificates in London. The first granted his British citizenship, the second qualified him as Master.[2] Since there were no vacancies for captains, and he had to support himself, he had to be content to serve under other commanders. When two years later he obtained a ship of his own, it was through pure coincidence.

Conrad himself tells us about it.[3] Having left his last ship at Singapore, he was staying

[2]Ibid., p. 111.

[3]In The Shadow Line (New York: Doubleday, Page & Company, 1926). The book is a reminiscence of Conrad's first command for the first two months. The account begins with his arrival at Singapore and ends with his return on the Otago.

SC
2

at the Sailors Home waiting for passage to Europe, when he was summoned by the harbor master and offered command of the <u>Otago</u>. The barque was currently at Bangkok, her former master having died near that port. Outwardly calm, the newly appointed captain was understandably elated:

> A ship! My ship! She was mine, more absolutely mine for possession and care than anything in the world; an object of responsibility and devotion.[4]

Before he was long aboard the <u>Otago</u>, his responsibilities grew to staggering proportions and his devotion underwent a serious test. Mr. Burns, the mate, several years the captain's senior, was resentful and taciturn. Having been acting commander after the death of the former master, he had expected to be named as successor. The new captain met the issue head-on:

> "Look here, Mr. Burns," I began, very firmly. "You may as well understand that I did not run after this command. It was pushed my way. I am here to take the ship

[4]<u>Ibid.</u>, p. 40.

home, and you may be sure that I shall see
to it that every one of you on board here
does his duty to that end. That is all I
have to say at present."[5]

But at present few of the men were able to do

their duty. All were feverish and weak to the

point of helplessness. The steward was taken

ashore, where he died. A Chinese, hired to re-

place him, stayed aboard just long enough to run

off with the captain's hard-earned savings of

thirty-three gold sovereigns.[6] Mr. Burns, a vic-

tim of the contagion, was carried off, delirious,

on a stretcher.

The captain was beginning to discover that

"even the command of a nice little barque may be

a delusion and a snare for the unwary spirit of

---

[5]Ibid., pp. 63-64. Actually, in real life
the acting commander was named Born as is pointed
out in Jocelyn Baines, Joseph Conrad: A Critical
Biography (New York, 1960), p. 93.

[6]Jean-Aubry, The Sea Dreamer, p. 133. In his
earlier book, Life and Letters, Jean-Aubry gives
the sum as "thirty-two pounds."

SC
2

pride in men."[7] He needed Mr. Burns. The mate knew the ship and the adjacent waters. The enforced delay had already lasted two weeks. But he would not leave port without his first officer. Captain Korzeniowski's orders were to bring his ship to her home port as soon as possible, and he would brook no further delay.

Feverish and raving as he still was, Burns was brought aboard at the captain's orders and put to bed. Ransome, the cook, already doubling as steward and suffering from a heart ailment, also now served as nurse. Only he and the captain escaped contagion.

[7]Joseph Conrad, <u>Falk</u>, <u>A</u> <u>Reminiscence</u> (New York: Doubleday, Page & Company, 1920), p. 20.

SC3. The Précis

A **précis** (pronounced "pray-see"; the form is both singular and plural) is a short summary of the essential ideas of a long composition. In a précis, the basic thought of a passage is reproduced in miniature, retaining the mood and tone of the original. No interpretation or comment should be interjected. It is the author's exact meaning which should be scaled down, without omitting any important details.

The material to be reduced must be carefully chosen. Some choices readily lend themselves to condensation, but others are so compactly written that further reduction is almost impossible. Loosely knit selections such as most novels, stories, speeches, and essays are suitable for the making of précis, whereas very taut material such as some poems, prayers, and inscriptions are not. Avoid writings that have already been summarized, abridged, or edited; the essential thought of the original becomes distorted through constant "boiling down."

SC3a. READ THE SELECTION CAREFULLY.

Since a précis must be brief, clear, but, above all, faithful to the original, you must read through the chosen material analytically and reflectively. After reading the whole selection to determine its central ideas, reread it paragraph by paragraph, noting as you do the topic of each one and searching for key expressions you can use to project the flavor of the original. See how the author has organized the material, what literary devices are used, and what kinds of illustrations support the thesis.

SC3b. USE YOUR OWN WORDS.

Though you must master and present the major thought of the selection, the précis itself should be your own composition. Some quoting of sentences from the original may be appropriate, but by and large the author's phrasing cannot readily be used. Furthermore, quoting sentences, perhaps topic sentences, from each paragraph will produce a sentence outline, not a précis. The author's wording and order may serve as a guide, but the summary statement produced must be yours.

SC3c. SET LIMITS TO THE NUMBER OF WORDS YOU USE.

Précis are condensations, and although their length cannot be arbitrarily set, they can be used to reduce most prose by two-

SC 3

thirds to three-quarters. Some poetry is so tightly written that reduction is virtually impossible; other verse can be pared even more than prose. Leave out nothing of importance, but *limit* your summary to one-fourth or one-third of the original.

SC3d. FOLLOW THE PLAN OF THE ORIGINAL.

In order to be faithful to your selection, you must preserve its *proportion*. Changing the author's logical plan would distort its essence. Refrain from rearranging facts and thoughts, and try to preserve the original mood and tone.

A précis is not likely to be so well written as the selection itself, but it must possess clear diction and effective sentence construction. Its unity and coherence should be emphasized through smooth transitions. Remember, your summary must be understandable to a reader who has not seen the original.

EXERCISE 3

In the light of the comments above, analyze each of the following student précis. What suggestions can you make to improve each one? Write your own précis of either the excerpt from Robinson or that from Steinem.

A. ORIGINAL

A third kind of thinking is stimulated when anyone questions our beliefs and opinions. We sometimes find ourselves changing our minds without any resistance or heavy emotion, but if we are told that we are wrong we resent the imputation and harden our hearts. We are incredibly heedless in the formation of our beliefs, but find ourselves filled with an illicit passion for them when anyone proposes to rob us of their companionship. It is obviously not the ideas themselves that are dear to us, but our self-esteem, which is threatened. We are by nature stubbornly pledged to defend our own from attack, whether it be our person, our family, our property, or our opinion. A United States Senator once remarked to a friend of mine that God Almighty could not make him change his mind on our Latin-American policy. We may surrender, but rarely confess ourselves vanquished. In the intellectual world at least, peace is without victory.

Few of us take the pains to study the origin of our cherished convictions; indeed, we have a natural repugnance to so doing. We like to continue to believe what we have been accustomed to accept as true, and the resentment aroused when doubt is cast upon any of our assumptions leads us to seek every manner of excuse for clinging to them. *The result is that most of our so-called reasoning consists in finding arguments for going on believing as we already do.* [242 words]

—From "On Various Kinds of Thinking," by
James Harvey Robinson

PRÉCIS

A third kind of thinking occurs when we are told that our beliefs and opinions are wrong. We may have been heedless in their formation, but our self-esteem will not permit us to change. We may have to give up, but we are not convinced. We do not study the origin of our beliefs; we believe as we have been accustomed to believe, and we seek arguments for continuing to believe as we already do. [75 words]

B. ORIGINAL

Men now suffer from more diseases due to stress, heart attacks, ulcers, a higher suicide rate, greater difficulty living alone, less adaptability to change and, in general, a shorter life span than women. There is some scientific evidence that what produces physical problems is not work itself, but the inability to choose which work, and how much. With women bearing half the financial responsibility, and with the idea of "masculine" jobs gone, men might well feel freer and live longer. [80 words]

—From "What It Would Be Like If Women Win,"
by Gloria Steinem

PRÉCIS

For varied reasons, men live more unhealthy and shorter lives than women. This condition may change when the sexes share financial responsibilities and common jobs. [25 words]

SC 3

EXERCISE 4

Write several précis of selections from your literature anthology. Choose not more than three paragraphs from an essay or article. Or perhaps your teacher will prefer to make a uniform assignment.

EXERCISE 5

Choose an article in a current magazine and condense it as you think *Reader's Digest* would.

SC4. The Paraphrase

Much of what we learn in school comes from writings that contain timeless ideas and concepts expressed in unique ways. Moreover, the process of learning demands that at least temporarily we make the ideas of these writers *our* ideas, their statements *our* statements, their thoughts *our* thoughts. Restating the sense of a passage through the use of our own words is called **paraphrasing.**

SC4a. PARAPHRASING AND CLARIFYING

Frequently we come across writing that is difficult to comprehend. Before a passage can fully "come through" to us, we must put the sense of it into words of our own. Our aim should not be to compress the author's statements (as is done when making a précis) but rather to rephrase those statements in their full proportion. We may agree or disagree with that message, accept or reject it. Either way, the author's thinking has been translated into our own thought processes.

A paraphrase of a good poem or essay cannot rival the original. It should, however, be a faithful rewording of all that the original contains in its meaning, organization, details, proportion, and even tone. Achieving a successful paraphrase calls for careful reading and reflection, for disciplined interpretation, for precise writing. Consider the following suggestions:

1. **Read and reread the original carefully until its full meaning is clear.** Sometimes a statement will have exact and implied meanings; both must be understood. Determine the central idea and study its method of presentation, how subordinate thoughts are arranged, what purposes they serve. Weigh individual words and phrases and consider the author's reasons for selecting them.

2. **Using your own words, reshape phrases in familiar terms.** If an original word or phrase is exact and understandable, do not change it. On the other hand, *do* change words and phrases that are unfamiliar so that their meaning will be clear.

3. **Restate the entire passage in its original proportion.** You must be objective in order to paraphrase well. Subtracting part of a passage because you think it is extraneous or do not agree with it will upset the balance that the author set. Adding interpretations or personal ideas will do the same. A paraphraser's thinking should be directed solely toward a faithful recreation of the author's statement.

4. **Preserve the tone and form of the original.** The qualities in a great poem or a speech such as the Gettysburg Address are unique, and their duplication in a paraphrase is impossible. However, try to retain as much of the tone and form of the original as clarity permits.

5. **Use good English.** Restatement of an original passage deserves and demands the best writing of which the paraphraser is capable. Careful and sensitive reading, constructive thought, and precise interpretation will result in paraphrasing that most nearly matches the original.

EXERCISE 6

From your book of readings, select five short poems or five paragraphs from an essay. With the advice of your teacher, select *one* of these poems or paragraphs and write a paraphrase of it.

EXERCISE 7

Criticize the following student paraphrases in the light of suggestions given in Section SC4.

SC 4

A. ORIGINAL

Let me not to the marriage of true minds
Admit impediments. Love is not love
Which alters when it alteration finds,
Or bends with the remover to remove:

O, no! it is an ever-fixed mark
That looks on tempests and is never shaken;
It is the star to every wandering bark,
Whose worth's unknown, although his height be taken.
Love's not Time's fool, though rosy lips and cheeks
Within his bending sickle's compass come;
Love alters not with his brief hours and weeks,
But bears it out even to the edge of doom.
    If this be error and upon me proved,
    I never writ, nor no man ever loved.

—William Shakespeare

PARAPHRASE

I do not acknowledge any real obstacles to true love. Love is counterfeit when it changes because of problems or wavers if one of the lovers tries to alter the relationship. On the contrary, true love is steadfast. Just as we cannot know what a star's true value is, although we can measure its altitude and navigate by it, just so we cannot know what love is really worth despite its guidance. Love is no jesting servant of Time, even though lovers do wither and die; true love lasts to the brink of eternity. If what I say is wrong, and can be proved wrong, then I have never made a valid statement, and no one has ever loved.

B. ORIGINAL

What has happened is simply that our society has become one giant rational construct. It is an intellectual abstraction and no longer relates to the warm, groping, shabby and sometimes hilarious realities of our human nature. These concepts under which we live, which force us forever to compete, to play sexually stereotyped roles, to marry as we do, raise children as we do, make war as we do, make love as we do, work as we do and relate as we do—these concepts have polluted our souls.

—From *Love and Liberation*, by Lisa Hobbs

PARAPHRASE

What has come about is that our society has turned into a complex and unrealistic structure built from simpler ideas and images. It is composed of a set of mistaken notions that no longer reflect real human nature. These false ideas require us to struggle against each other constantly, to play fixed sexual roles, and to marry, rear children, make love and war, and work with each other in ways that corrupt and distort our true nature.

SC5. The Letter

In social, business, and professional life no form of written communication is as widely used as the **letter.** Letters are, and should be, a reflection of their writer. Just as a speaker's facial expressions, gestures, and voice project personality and attitude, so do the message in a letter, the quality of paper that bears it, the typing or penmanship producing it, even the way it is folded and sealed. Furthermore, the message of a letter is, in effect, a *theme*, and as such it must be governed by the requirements of good theme writing: clarity, force, correctness, and appropriateness.

Two main kinds of letters are *informal* (or friendly) and *business* letters. A third category, *formal* letters, includes elaborate invitations and their replies, the patterns for which are standardized and may be found in a reference book on etiquette.

SC5a. INFORMAL LETTERS

We should try to cultivate in our **letters** the art of communicating friendship. This obligation requires thoughtfulness and takes time, but the result will be worth the price paid. Here are some suggestions that will improve your technique in friendly letter writing.

1. **Write legibly.** A letter must be capable of being deciphered. Moreover, the appearance of your writing or typing must convey respect for your reader, no matter how close a friend. Letters that by general sloppiness or careless scrawl proclaim, "I haven't the time or inclination to take pains, you can take this or leave it" are neither courteous nor effective. A friendly letter is, and should be, more personal and intimate than a business letter, but informality is no excuse for inconsiderateness.

2. **Think about your reader, not only about yourself.** Your correspondent will, of course, be interested in your activities and affairs, and one of your purposes in writing is to report on them. However, no one should risk boring a reader with an excessive number of *I*'s, *me*'s, and *myself*'s. Show sincere interest in your reader's concerns and activities and offer,

SC 5

too, accounts of other events, persons, and places in which you are not necessarily the sole actor.

3. **Take your time.** Many friendships are kept alive through the medium of letter writing, but *all* letters to friends should suggest that the writing of them is a pleasurable and rewarding undertaking. Five or six letters dashed off in 30 minutes, each beginning with "I'm in a hurry," or signed "Yours on the run," merely imply that the writer finds the task tiresome and the friends not worth much trouble. A good correspondent makes mental or written notes about people, ideas, and events that will interest readers and then sits down to describe them with thoughtfulness and liveliness. A good informal letter takes more time than a 10-minute note, but it is an investment in friendship that possibly you cannot afford to overlook. It is time well spent.

4. **Give details.** A clear, detailed description of one event will likely be more interesting to read than a series of random and terse notes on several incidents. Disjointed notes are really topic sentences only, each of which needs enlargement. A good letter expresses or implies a central theme inspired by one primary incident, conversation, description of a person or place, or expression of thought. Such a letter may contain more than one topic, but all topics should be clearly related and adequately developed.

5. **Make your letters appropriate.** The activities and tastes of individual friends differ and so should the individual letters you devote to them. Identical birthday gifts would not suit all recipients. Similarly, an account of an incident written for one friend might not particularly interest another. Always tailor the content of a letter to the specific interests of the person you write to. Your nine-year-old nephew and your forty-year-old aunt would not find the same things interesting.

In addition to long letters that give information, we must often write *brief notes* in certain special circumstances. Thanks for hospitality (sometimes known as a bread-and-butter letter) or for a gift, appreciation of a favor, a bon-voyage message, or written congratulations are examples of such notes. These are so personalized and varied that no one suggestion can cover them all. Here is an example of a short bread-and-butter letter:

Natick Academy
Sinclair, Indiana
December 16, 19--

Dear Mrs. Curtis:

Friday evening was clear and crisp. I was
enjoying a delicious supper, and I was with old
friends who are dear to me. Tonight it is raining; we have just finished some tasteless stew,
and I am alone in my room except for a buzzing
insect that may be old but certainly is not
dear. I wish that favorite and well-remembered
evenings were like lucky pennies, to spend at
will and find again in our pockets.

The Swiss have really made a happening of
cheese fondue. Amy has often spoken about her
mother's favorite recipe, but I was unprepared
for the delicious meal you served. The ritual
of eating was fun, too--spearing cubes of bread
with a fork and swirling them in bubbling
cheese, trying to be careful not to lose a
cube in the fondue lest we "owe the master a
glass of wine."

SC
5

Now it's back to the books for me. We will
see you again soon, because our families will be
together on New Year's Day. And don't forget
that you and Mr. Curtis are invited to our school
performance of Macbeth on February 10. Remember,
I am to be "a most believably hideous witch."

    Thank you again for a most delightful
evening.

                              Affectionately,

                              Sue

SC5b. BUSINESS LETTERS

The purpose of a **business letter** is largely utilitarian: to convey a message clearly. Your primary concern as a writer of business letters is with *presentation* and *content*, that is, with the order and expression of your material and with the subject matter itself. There are many kinds of business letters, the most common of which are order letters, inquiries, sales letters, adjustment letters, credit letters, collection letters, letters of recommendation, and letters of application. All of these kinds of business letters are written to a form now standardized in six parts.

1. **The heading.** This contains the sender's *full* address and the date, usually placed in the upper right-hand corner of the sheet, an inch or more below the top edge and flush with the right margin, and typed or written single-space. On stationery with a letterhead, only the date is entered, either flush with the right-hand margin or centered under the letterhead.

2. **The inside address.** The name, preceded by a proper title, and the address of the person or company written to should appear flush with the left-hand margin of the paper. It is usually placed two or four spaces below the heading but sometimes farther, depending upon the length of the letter. If only the last name of the person written to is known, the letter is directed to the firm and an attention line, consisting of *Attention: Ms.—* or *Attention of Mr.—*, is inserted two lines below the address and two lines above the greeting. It has no bearing on the greeting, which is indicated by the first line of the inside address.

3. **The greeting or salutation.** This comes two spaces below the inside address, is flush with the left-hand margin, and is usually punctuated with a colon only. It should be in harmony with the first line of the inside address and the general tone of the letter. For example, correct forms would be *Dear Sir*; *My dear Ms.—*; or, preferably, *Dear Ms.—*.

4. **The body.** The body, beginning two spaces below the greeting, is the message of the letter. It is commonly single-spaced and has two spaces between paragraphs, which may be in block form or indented. Long messages are never continued on the back of a sheet but are carried over to a second sheet. The second sheet should contain at least two lines in addition to the complimentary close and signature, and it should carry in a top line some sort of identification such as the addressee's initials, the page number, and the date.

5. **The complimentary close.** Usually placed at the middle or slightly to the right of the middle of the page, two or three lines below the last line of the letter's body, the close harmonizes with the formality or semi-formality of the greeting. Correct forms, capitalized in the first word only and usually followed by a comma, include *Yours truly, Very truly yours, Your sincerely, Cordially yours, Cordially,* etc. (*Cordially yours* is often used among business friends and by older people writing to younger.) Independent of the last paragraph, the close should not be linked to it by participial phrases such as "Thanking you in advance, I am," etc.

6. **The signature.** Unless a letter is mimeographed or is plainly a circular, it should have a handwritten signature placed directly below the complimentary close. If the name is typed

ın, four spaces should be allowed for signature. A business title is usually typed on the line below the typed name.

A good business letter, correct and attractive in form, reflects a courteous attitude toward the reader. Unruled, white paper of good quality and standard size (8½ x 11 inches) or half size (8½ x 5½ inches) contributes to this impression of courtesy, as does neat typing or legible longhand. The layout of the letter should be balanced on the page, with margins at least 1 inch wide and with the right-hand margin as even as possible.

In writing a business letter, you may arrange the lines of the heading and of the inside address according to the *full block* or the *modified block* system. In the full block form, all the parts of the letter, including the heading, complimentary close, and signature, begin at the left-hand margin. In the modified block form, the heading, complimentary close, and signature are in their conventional place, on the right side of the letter.

Finally, as a business correspondent you should observe convention in folding the letter and inserting it in its envelope. For the standard large envelope, fold the lower third of the letter over the message and fold the top third to within a half-inch of the creased edge. For the standard small envelope, fold the lower part of the page to within a half-inch of the upper edge; then fold from the right slightly more than one third so that the left folded portion will come slightly short of the right creased edge. Attention to such details may seem tedious, but it has a valid purpose. It makes opening and reading your letter as easy as possible, so that your reader can focus on what you have to say.

You should apply to a business letter the general rules of effective writing. The first paragraph should state your subject or purpose and should include any pertinent background information. After making your purpose evident, your letter should reveal your thoughts in logical, easily followed units, with short, separate paragraphs for separate ideas. The letter should close strongly and effectively with a complete sentence—a direct question, an invitation, a restatement of the subject, or an important comment.

A cogent business letter contains no hackneyed, worn-out "business" expressions such as these, sometimes referred to as "letter killers": *am pleased to advise, beg to acknowledge, contents noted, enclosed please find, in receipt of, thank you in advance, under separate cover, wish to advise,* and many others. Instead, it is written in an informal style, using much the same language that is used in a business conversation over the telephone.

In composing a business letter, whether your subject is a one-sentence request, a multiple-item order, a detailed inquiry, or a job application with a request for an interview, you should be brief, clear, and exact. Here is an example of a letter of application. Note how the writer comes to the point as quickly as possible and how she then proceeds without delay to describe herself and her qualifications.

```
                                    135 Summerville Road

                                    Maple Ridge, Maryland

                                    February 15, 19--
```

```
Mr. Ralph Knox, President

Knox Sporting Equipment, Inc.

1403 Sullivan Avenue

Concord, New Jersey   08555
```

```
Dear Mr. Knox:
```

```
    Ms. Carol Foster, coach of the Arcadia High

School girls' basketball team, has informed me

that your firm intends to open a branch store in

Baltimore late this coming spring and that you
```

SC
5

will need an additional salesclerk during the summer. I should like to apply for that position.

A resident of suburban Baltimore, I am a junior at Arcadia High, where I have been a member of the girls' basketball, swimming, and volleyball teams. In addition, I have had five years of tennis instruction and competition under the joint auspices of the Arcadia Field Club and our local YWCA.

My age is 17. I am in excellent health, am 5'7" tall, and weigh 125 lbs. I have maintained a B-plus average in grades in high school.

We shall have our midwinter recess during the week of February 27. I shall be staying with my aunt in nearby Trenton and can drive to Concord for an interview at any time convenient to you. What day and hour would be most agreeable?

Very truly yours,

Karen Hughes

Karen Hughes

Note how the above applicant has presented her case effectively, briefly, and precisely. She has also suggested an interview in a way that would be hard to turn down. She will probably get her interview—and perhaps the job.

Here are examples of an *order* letter and of one requesting an *adjustment*. Both of these letters are brief, precise, and to the point. And both will probably get prompt attention.

240 Mill Road

Maryton, Colorado   80305

May   6, 19--

Black Department Store

8765 Third Avenue

Denver, Colorado   80203

To the Mail Order Department:

Please send me, by return parcel post, four

photograph albums, size 9 x 12 inches, spiral-

bound, with self-stick pages.   In payment, I en-

close a money order for twelve dollars ($12.00).

Yours very truly,

Brian Manning

Brian Manning

SC
5

240 Mill Road

Maryton, Colorado 80305

July 5, 19--

Black Department Store

8765 Third Avenue

Denver, Colorado 80203

To the Mail Order Department:

On May 6, I ordered from you four photograph albums, size 9 x 12 inches, spiral-bound, with self-stick pages, total price $12.00.

The albums arrived on July 3, too late for me to give them as a high school graduation present, as planned. In addition, the albums were size 4 x 10 inches and required additional sticking tabs.

Since it is too late to have the order corrected, I am returning the albums by parcel post and am asking that you return to me the purchase money of $12.00. Thank you for your prompt atten-

tion to this refund.

Yours very truly,

Brian Manning

Brian Manning

EXERCISE 8

Answer the following want ad: WANTED: Counselors and aides for boys' and girls' camps, June through August. Children are from 8 to 13. Give full details concerning qualifications. Apex Summer Camps, Lake Ormandy, Vermont.

EXERCISE 9

Answer the following want ad: WANTED: Student to wait tables and serve as cashier in local tea room. Hours 3 to 6. Time for study during work. Give age, references, and previous experience, if any. Dept. S-7, *Courier*, New Bedford, Mass.

EXERCISE 10

Write an intormal invitation asking a friend to join you and your family on a week's camping trip.

SC
5

EXERCISE 11

Write a letter to a friend who is in the hospital for a long stay following a serious operation.

EXERCISE 12

Collect and bring to class at least eight examples of business letters. (Perhaps a relative or business acquaintance may lend you some letters.) Study the letterheads used. Note especially both the usual and unusual features about the six parts of the letters (heading, inside address, greeting, body, complimentary close, signature). Notice the quality of paper used, the spacing and length of the paragraphs, the tone of the letters.

EXERCISE 13

Write a bread-and-butter note to a friend who has given you a surprise birthday party.

EXERCISE 14

Write a letter of sympathy to a friend who has just lost a close relative due to an automobile accident.

EXERCISE 15

Write a letter of inquiry to your state historical society concerning some old industries in your town.

EXERCISE 16

Write a request for a refund on an unused bus ticket.

EXERCISE 17

From a magazine advertisement, write a letter ordering the item or items advertised.

Language Resources

The six sections that follow conclude this handbook. They appear last for two reasons. Their prominent closing position is an indication of their importance. In addition, they treat subjects that apply as much to other subjects you may be studying as to English itself.

No matter what subjects you are now taking and no matter what you do after you complete your schooling, you should be aware of the language resources discussed in these sections. A substantial part of your time in later years will be spent in listening to others, in talking, in reading, and in taking tests of one sort or another.

Finally, no mastery of any activity or study in school will pay greater dividends now and in later life than learning how to use a dictionary and a library. The sensible and constant use of a reliable dictionary and the knowledge and skills to be gained from familiarity with an adequate library will vastly improve your performance in any school subject and will enrich your growth as a responsible individual throughout your life.

LR1. Using a Dictionary

To speak and write competently, everyone needs as a guide a reliable **dictionary.** No speaker or writer of English knows all the words in the language. Occasionally, if not often, every user of language needs help with the meaning, spelling, pronunciation, and specific use of a particular word.

If you have not done so yet, make the acquaintance of your dictionary *now.* Better still, make it your friend and constant companion.

The following dictionaries are recommended:

The American College Dictionary (*A.C.D.*) (New York: Random House)

The American Heritage Dictionary of the English Language (*A.H.D.*) (New York: American Heritage)

Funk & Wagnall's Standard College Dictionary (*S.C.D.*) (New York: Funk & Wagnalls)

The Random House Dictionary of the English Language, College Edition (*R.H.D.*) (New York: Random House)

Thorndike-Barnhart Comprehensive Dictionary (*C.D.*) (Chicago: Scott, Foresman)

Webster's New World Dictionary of the American Language (*N.W.D.*) (New York: World)

Webster's New Collegiate Dictionary (*N.C.D.*) (Springfield, Mass.: Merriam)

Any one of these dictionaries would represent an excellent investment in a practical, constantly useful, and reliable aid in speaking and writing.

Excellent larger dictionaries are available also. Each of them contains at least three times as much information as those listed above. Entries are not only more numerous but are frequently more detailed and often provide finer shades of meaning. Such dictionaries are called "unabridged" versions. However, unabridged dictionaries are more expensive than the works suggested above, are usually more awkward to handle, and are difficult to carry around. Such sizable and valuable dictionaries are often placed in classrooms, in school libraries, and in teacher's offices and staff rooms. The best known and most available of the unabridged dictionaries are

Funk & Wagnalls New Standard Dictionary of the English Language (New York: Funk & Wagnalls)

New English (Oxford) Dictionary (New York: Oxford; *The Shorter Oxford Dictionary* appears in both one- and two-volume editions; the larger work is in twelve volumes and a supplement)

The Random House Dictionary of the English Language (New York: Random House)

Webster's Third New International Dictionary (Springfield, Mass.: Merriam)

LR1a. LEARN HOW TO USE AND INTERPRET A DICTIONARY.

Many persons consult a dictionary to find the spelling or meaning or pronunciation of a word, or all three of these bits of information. However, using it for no more than this ignores many other kinds of valuable and useful material that it provides.

Dictionaries differ somewhat in their presentation of material. If you have never done so before, examine your dictionary carefully and critically. Read its table of contents. Examine the material given on the inside of front and back covers. Read, or at least skim, some of the prefatory pages as well as supplementary material at the back. After you have done this, you should read carefully and attentively articles headed "General Introduction," "Guide to the Use of This Dictionary," "Guide to Pronunciation," "Etymology Key," "Explanatory Notes," "Symbols and Abbreviations Used." Your dictionary may not have sections entitled precisely thus, but it will contain equivalent material. You really cannot use your dictionary with full effectiveness until you are acquainted with its plan and method of presentation.

Although dictionaries differ in methods of listing entries and citing information, all reliable dictionaries have a common purpose: they report on the way language currently is used and, occasionally, on how it has been used in the past.

The skilled persons who make dictionaries, called *lexicographers,* do not themselves decide what words mean or even how they should be spelled and pronounced. A good dictionary is the product of careful study and research, a report on what is known as *standard English,* that is, the English of most educated speakers and users of the language.

A dictionary is not an "authority" in any exact meaning of the word. Nor does it even pretend to be. It does not dictate or prescribe except in the sense that it records and usually interprets the status of English words and phrases. It indicates what is general language practice; only in this way can it be said to constitute authority. When you have a specific problem about usage, apply in your own writing and speaking the information recorded and interpreted in your dictionary. But do not think of your dictionary as a final arbiter of what is right and what is wrong. To do so is to act as illogically as to say, "That must be right; I saw it in print."

LR1b. MASTER THE VARIETY OF INFORMATION GIVEN FOR WORD ENTRIES.

As an attentive reader, writer, and speaker you should actually *study* each word you look up. Time spent in learning words thoroughly will save time, errors, and annoyance later.

For any word listed in an adequate dictionary, each of the first five of the following items is given. For many words, some of the last five kinds of information are provided:

1. Spelling
2. Syllabication
3. Pronunciation
4. Part(s) of speech
5. Meaning(s)

6. Level(s) of meaning
7. Derivation (origin)
8. Synonyms
9. Antonyms
10. Other information

> **abridge** \ə-'brij \ *vt* **abridged; abridg·ing** [ME *abregen*, fr. MF *abregier*, fr. LL *abbreviare*, fr. L *ad–* + *brevis* short—more at BRIEF] **1 a** *archaic* : DEPRIVE **b** : to reduce in scope : DIMINISH <attempts to ~ the right of free speech **2** : to shorten in duration or extent <modern transportation that ~*s* distance> **3** : to shorten by omission of words without sacrifice of sense : CONDENSE *syn* see SHORTEN *ant* expand, extend— **abridg·er** *n*
>
> **abridg·ment** *or* **abridge·ment** \ə-'brij-mənt\ *n* **1** : the action of abridging : the state of being abridged **2** : a shortened form of a work retaining the general sense and unity of the original *syn* ABRIDGMENT, ABSTRACT, SYNOPSIS, CONSPECTUS, EPITOME, *shared meaning element* : a shorter version of a larger work or treatment *ant* expansion

Spelling

The basic, or "entry," word is ordinarily given in black (boldface) type. Associated with the main entry may be other words in black type indicating run-on entries. (Endings such as *–er, –like* may be added—*begin, beginner; clerk, clerklike*—and alternative entries of variant forms—*Bern, Berne; diagram, –gramed, –graming* or *–grammed, –gramming*.) Note especially the following:

1. The plurals of nouns are given if a noun forms its plural other than by adding *–s* or *–es*.
2. The comparative and superlative degrees of adjectives and adverbs are given if a spelling change is made in the addition of *–er, –est*.
3. The past tense, past participle, and present participle of verbs are given if these forms differ from the present-tense form or if the spelling changes in the addition of an ending.
4. Many compound words spelled with a hyphen or as one word or as two words are so indicated.

When a word has two or more spellings, the preferred spelling form is usually given first. Sometimes the variant spelling is also placed separately as a vocabulary entry.

The spelling of proper names (people, places, etc.) is given either in the regular place in the alphabetical listing or in a special section or sections at the back of the dictionary, depending upon the dictionary.

Syllabication

Learn to distinguish between the light mark, or dot (·), used to separate syllables (ri · dic · u · lous) and the hyphen (-) used to show that the word is a compound (*hard-hitting*). All reliable dictionaries use the dot system of indicating syllabication. Some substitute for the dot in the vocabulary entry an accent mark after the stressed syllable.

Knowledge of syllabication is important in two ways. First, it helps in the pronunciation of words, which in turn helps in correct spelling. Second, it shows where to divide words between syllables, if division is necessary at ends of lines (Section PM8).

Pronunciation

Pronunciation is based upon accent or emphasized syllables and upon the sound given to letters or letter combinations.

Both accent marks and syllabication dots are included in the entry word by some dictionaries. Other dictionaries carry only

LR 1

the syllabication dots in the entry word and include the accent marks in the "pronunciation" word.

Learn to distinguish the accent marks. Primary, or heavy, stress is shown by a heavy mark (′) and secondary, or less heavy, stress by a light (′) or double (″) mark: *com′ pass′, com′ pass″, dif′ fer′, dif′ fer″, spell′ ing′, spell′ ing″, pro′ nounce′, pro″ nounce′.*

Pronunciation of sounds is more complicated than accent. The fact that 26 alphabetical letters are used in 250 common spellings of sounds is evidence that you need considerable help. Linguists have successfully developed systems whereby 40 to 60 symbols, depending upon the dictionary, are adequate to solve most pronunciation problems. The common method is the use of a "pronunciation" word that is usually found in parentheses just after the entry word. It is a respelling of the word, giving the sounds of vowels and consonants by syllables and according to the pronouncing key that the dictionary has adopted. Familiarize yourself with this pronouncing key in your dictionary. It may be included at the bottom of each page or alternate pages, or it may be inside the front or back cover or both.

Learn to interpret diacritical marks. These marks (¨) placed over the second of two consecutive vowels are used when each vowel is pronounced separately. As a variant method, hyphens may be used instead. Examples: *naïve, reënforce* or *re-enforce, preëminence* or *pre-eminence.* As such words become common, diacritical marks or the hyphen may be left out, as in *preeminence.*

For foreign words or those newly adopted from a foreign language, your dictionary may include a separate "foreign sounds" key.

Generally, when two or more pronunciations of a word are included, the one more commonly used is given first. A variant pronunciation may occasionally be labeled *British* or *Chiefly British* (*Brit.* or *Chiefly Brit.*), to show that this pronunciation is the common one in Great Britain.

Part(s) of Speech

Since all English words are parts of speech, the part of speech of every entry is generally given. If the word is used as more than one part of speech, such information is provided, with the particular meaning or meanings under each explained. Also shown are the singular or plural forms of many nouns, the comparative and superlative degrees of many adjectives and adverbs, and the correct use of verbs as transitive, or intransitive, or both.

Study the following excerpt:

> **sweet** (swēt) *adj.* **sweeter, sweetest. 1. a.** Having a sugary taste. **b.** Containing or derived from a sugar. **2.** Pleasing to the senses, feelings, or the mind; gratifying: *"Sin was yet very sweet to my flesh, and I was loath to leave it"* (Bunyan). **3.** Having a pleasing disposition; lovable: *a sweet child.* **4.** Not saline; fresh: *sweet water.* **5.** Not spoiled, sour, or decaying; fresh: *This milk is still sweet.* **6.** Free of acid. **7.** *Music.* **a.** Designating jazz character-ized by adherence to a melodic line and to a time signature. **b.** Performing jazz in this way: *a sweet combo.* —*n.* **1.** The quality of being sweet; sweetness. **2.** Something that is sweet or contains sugar. **3.** *Usually plural.* Candy, preserves, or con-fections. **4.** *British.* Anything relatively sweet served as a dessert. **5.** A dear or beloved person. [Middle English *swe(e)te,* Old English *swēte.* See **swād-** in appendix.*] —**sweetly** *adv.* —**sweet′ ness** *n.*
>
> **Sweet** (swēt), **Henry.** 1845–1912. British philologist and phone-tician.
>
> **sweet alyssum.** A widely cultivated plant, *Lobularia maritima,* native to the Mediterranean region, having clusters of small, fragrant white or purplish flowers.
>
> **sweet basil.** A species of **basil** *(see).*
>
> **sweet bay.** A small tree, *Magnolia virginiana,* of the southeastern United States, having large, fragrant white flowers.
>
> **sweet birch.** A tree, the **black birch** *(see).*
>
> **sweet·bread** (swēt′brĕd) *n.* The thymus gland of an animal used for food [SWEET + BREAD (euphemism for the food).]
>
> **sweet·bri·er** (swēt′brī′ər) *n.* Also **sweet·bri·ar.** A rose, *Rosa eglanteria,* native to Europe, having prickly stems, fragrant leaves, and pink flowers. Also called "eglantine."

By permission. From *The American Heritage Dictionary of the English Language,* copyright © 1969, 1970, 1971, 1973, 1975, 1976, Houghton Mifflin Company.

This reprint from *The American Heritage Dictionary* provides substantial information about *sweet* as an adjective, adverb, and noun. Additional entries reveal how the word *sweet* appears in other words and word combinations. If you were to keep reading, you would come across entries for *sweet cherry, sweet cicely, sweet cider, sweet clover, sweet corn, sweeten, sweetening, sweet fern,*

LR

1

sweet flag, sweet gale, sweet gum, sweetheart, sweetie, sweeting, sweet marjoram, sweetmeat, sweet pea, sweet pepper, sweet pepperbush, sweet potato, sweetsop, sweet sultan, sweet tooth and *sweet William.* Such a collection of word entries should indicate the vast amount of information that a good dictionary provides not only about parts of speech but on other important matters as well.

Teach yourself the more common abbreviations from the table of abbreviations or elsewhere in your dictionary. The following is a partial list of abbreviations commonly used:

act. for active	*p.p.* for past participle
adj. for adjective	*pred.* for predicate
adv. for adverb	*prep.* for preposition
auxil. for auxiliary	*pres.* for present
conj. for conjunction	*prin. pts.* for principal parts
fut. for future	*pron.* for pronoun
n. for noun	*sing.* for singular
part. for participle	*subj.* for subjunctive
perf. for perfect	*v.* for verb
pl. for plural	*v.i.* for verb intransitive
poss. for possessive	*v.t.* for verb transitive

This list is a reminder that knowledge of grammar and grammatical terms is necessary for intelligent and successful use of the dictionary (see sections on grammar, especially Section G10).

Meanings

Words may have one or more of the following meanings: a traditional meaning, a historical meaning, a figurative meaning, a special meaning, a new meaning. Note the various definitions giving both usual and specialized meanings. Learn the method used in the order of definitions—for example, by parts of speech, by historical development of meanings, by frequency of occurrence, or by general to specialized meanings. Master, too, the significance of definitions preceded by Arabic numbers (1, 2, 3, etc.) or by letters of the alphabet (a, b, c, etc.). Note the method of entry for capitalized and small-letter words, for words known as homographs and homonyms, and for words having a superficial resemblance. Although all these may have similar spellings or pronunciations, their meanings are quite different. Place the meaning of the word into the context of your encounter with it in reading and listening.

Hyphenated words and two or more words forming phrases that have idiomatic, specialized, or figurative meaning are explained in the regular alphabetical listing, and either entered separately or put under the main word. Abbreviations and foreign words or phrases are, in most dictionaries, included in their alphabetical position.

Level(s) of Meaning

Entry in a dictionary is not a guarantee that a word is in good use or that its special meanings are suitable in current English. Your dictionary enables you to weigh the appropriateness of a word by the absence or presence of a restrictive label. Some words have no labels, and others have labels for certain meanings or for use as a certain part of speech. Any word not given a restrictive label is acceptable in formal and informal English. Any word labeled *colloquial* is usually suitable in *all* informal speech and writing. All other labels are guides to special appropriateness of word use.

Four classifications of restrictive labels are common.

Geographical, indicating a country or region of a country where the word is in general use: *Chiefly U.S., British, Scotch, New England, Western U.S., dialect,* etc. The necessity for geographical labels is not surprising in view of the fact that 300,000,000 people in various parts of the world share English as their native language and an even larger number use it as a second language.

Time, indicating that the word is no longer used, is disappearing from use, or is still used but has a quaint form or meaning: *obsolete, obsolescent, archaic.* However, words with these labels are no longer common, and when words are no longer used, dictionaries seldom record them. Words having no time label are in current use.

Subject, showing that a specialized word or word meaning belongs to a limited area of knowledge such as science, technology, craft, and sport. As many as a hundred of these labels are used, including astronomy, biology, electrical engineering, architecture, dentistry, painting, football.

Cultural, indicating whether the word or a special meaning is substandard or suitable as informal English: *illiterate, slang, dialect* (which may be geographical also), *colloquial,*

LR
1

poetic, literary. Absence of any such label signifies that the word is acceptable in formal and informal writing and speaking.

NOTE: There is no Supreme Court for the English language to which a final appeal can be made. Lexicographers can only use their best judgment in collecting and interpreting data on language. Dictionaries may therefore differ in the labels they give to certain words or certain meanings. For example, the same word in several dictionaries may carry the label *obsolete* or *archaic* or *dialect* or even no qualifying label whatever.

Some dictionaries carry comments on levels of meaning and the usage problems involved. Here, for example, is such an entry:

> *Usage: Like*, as a conjunction, is not appropriate to formal usage, especially written usage, except in certain constructions noted below. On other levels it occurs frequently, especially in casual speech and in writing representing speech. In formal usage the conjunctive *like* is most acceptable when it introduces an elliptical clause in which a verb is not expressed: *He took to politics like a fish to water. The dress looked like new.* Both examples, which are acceptable on a formal level to 76 per cent of the Usage Panel, employ such elliptical, or shortened, expressions following *like.* If they were recast to include full clauses containing verbs, *like* would preferably be replaced, in formal usage, by *as, as if,* or *as though: took to politics as a fish takes to water; dress looked as if it were new.* The examples that follow illustrate the difference. All employ *like* to introduce full clauses containing verbs; all are termed unacceptable by more than 75 per cent of the Usage Panel, and in every case a more desirable construction is indicated: *He manipulates an audience like* (preferably *as*) *a virtuoso commands a musical instrument. The engine responds now like* (preferably *as*) *good machinery should. It looks like* (preferably *as if*) *they will be finished earlier than usual. He had no authority, but he always acted like* (preferably *as if*) *he did.* The restriction on *like* as a conjunction does not affect its other uses. Fear of misusing *like* often causes writers to use *as* in its place in constructions where *like* is not only acceptable but clearly called for. It is always used acceptably when it functions prepositionally, followed by a noun or pronoun as object: *works like a charm; sings like an angel; looking for a girl like me* (not *I*); *spoke like one who had authority* (but not *like he had authority*). Used prepositionally, *like* indicates comparison; in modern usage *as*, in place of *like*, would imply the assumption of another role: *He behaved like* (not *as*) *a*

child. She treated him like (not *as*) *a fool. John like* (not *as*) *his grandfather earlier, chose to ignore politics.*

By permission. From *The American Heritage Dictionary of the English Language,* copyright © 1969, 1970, 1971, 1973, 1975, 1976, Houghton Mifflin Company.

Origin

The origin of a word—in linguistics, its **etymology**—may be two-fold: (1) less commonly, a narrative account of how a word was formed or was given its meaning (see in your dictionary, for example, *derrick, burke, macadam, radar*) or (2) whenever known, the ancestral or foreign languages through or from which the word evolved to its English form. Old English, Latin, Greek, German, and French have heavily contributed, but several other languages have had a part: Italian, Spanish, Scandinavian, etc.

Such derivations, generally entered between brackets, may come near the beginning or at the end of the vocabulary entry. They help fix the meaning and spelling of words in your mind. Learn the more common abbreviations with which your dictionary indicates them: *OE (Old English), L. (Latin), Gk. (Greek), Sp. (Spanish),* etc. Learn also the space-saving shortcuts: *b. (blended of); f. (formed from); t. (taken from); < (derived from);* etc. A table or tables of such abbreviations is contained in every dictionary.

Synonyms

Words that in one or more of their definitions have the same or similar meanings as other words are called **synonyms.** Make a study of synonyms; often these approximate equivalents have significant differences in meaning that enable you to choose exact and emphatic words (see Section D5). So important is this study that whole books have been compiled for the benefit of writers and speakers, such as *Webster's Dictionary of Synonyms, Crabb's English Synonyms,* and *Roget's International Thesaurus of English Words.*

Dictionaries include the listings and often brief discussions of hundreds of synonyms, indicating differences in meaning of apparently similar words and signifying by a number which usage is part of synonymous meaning.

LR
1

Antonyms

Antonyms are pairs of words that have opposite or negative meanings: *man—woman, man—boy, human—beast, mortal—God, holy—unholy*, etc. These opposite meanings are not all-inclusive: a word may be an antonym of another only in a certain restricted meaning. For example, one antonym of *man* concerns sex; another, age. Dictionaries suggest antonyms for many words.

Other Information

Other information that may be carried as part of an entry or as separate entries in the main part of your dictionary includes abbreviations; biographical names; capitalized words and words spelled with both capitals and small letters; cross-references to words listed elsewhere; examples of word use in phrases and sentences; foreign words and phrases (usually labeled as such or given a special symbol); geographical names; homographs and homonyms (the former, words spelled alike but having different meanings, and the latter, words spelled differently but pronounced alike); meaning of idiomatic phrases; prefixes, suffixes, and other combining word elements; and, for some words, graphic or pictorial illustrations.

As an instance of the wealth of material contained in every good dictionary, assume that you need to refer to the entry for the word *look*. Having mastered the main entry, let your eye wander on; here is some, and only some, of what you might find later along:

> —**It looks like 1.** it seems that there will be **2.** [Colloq.] it seems as if —**look after** to take care of; watch over —**look alive** (or **sharp**) [Colloq.] to be alert; act or move quickly: usually in the imperative —**look back** to recall the past; recollect —**look down on** (or **upon**) **1.** to regard as an inferior **2.** to regard with contempt; despise —**look for 1.** to search or hunt for **2.** to expect; anticipate —**look forward to** to anticipate, esp. eagerly —**look in** (**on**) to pay a brief visit (to) —**look into** to examine carefully; investigate —**look on 1.** to be an observer or spectator **2.** to consider; regard —**look (like) oneself** to appear to be in normal health, spirits, etc. —**look out** to be on the watch; be careful —**look out for 1.** to be wary about **2.** to take care of —**look over** to examine; inspect —**look to 1.** to take care of; give attention to

2. to rely upon; resort to **3.** to look forward to; expect **—look up 1.** to search for in a book of reference, etc. **2.** [Colloq.] to pay a visit to; call on **3.** [Colloq.] to get better; improve **—look up and down 1.** to search everywhere **2.** to examine with an appraising eye; scrutinize **—look up to** to regard with great respect

SYN.—look is the general term meaning to direct the eyes in order to see [don't *look* now]; **gaze** implies a looking intently and steadily, as in wonder, delight, or interest [to *gaze* at the stars]; to **stare** is to look fixedly with wide-open eyes, as in surprise, curiosity, abstraction, etc. [it is rude to *stare* at people]; to **gape** is to stare with the mouth open in ignorant or naive wonder or curiosity [the child stood *gaping* at the elephant]; to **glare** is to stare fiercely or angrily [he *glared* at her for talking]; to **peek** is to take a quick furtive look, as through a hole or from behind a barrier, at something not supposed to be seen; to **peer** is to look searchingly with the eyes narrowed [she *peered* down the well] See also APPEARANCE

In addition to the wealth of information included under each vocabulary entry, good dictionaries offer other materials in the front or back pages. Familiarize yourself with this material. Besides a discussion of spelling (orthography), pronunciation, usage levels, etc., sections may give guidance on punctuation, grammar, letter writing, proofreading, and rhyming; a list of American colleges and universities; and other helpful and interesting information.

LR1c. USE A DICTIONARY TO IMPROVE AND INCREASE YOUR VOCABULARY.

The kind and number of English words you know and are able to use and understand will be important throughout your life. As is pointed out in Section D2, building and using a vocabulary is a lengthy process that requires years and, indeed, is never completed. But you can make genuine and even rapid progress in vocabulary growth through intelligent use of a good dictionary. Study of this never-failing companion and tool can help supplement your vocabulary.

LR

1

EXERCISE 1

Read carefully every word on *one* page of your dictionary. Write a paper of 300–400 words mentioning and developing three or four of the interesting items you have found.

EXERCISE 2

What restrictive label, if any, is attached in your dictionary to each of the following words?

> baloney, benison, boughten, caboose, cocky, colleen, dight, disremember, dogie, eld, jiffy, larrup, lulu, mavourneen, nohow, nubbin, pectin, pesky, renege, sashay

EXERCISE 3

What is the total number of meanings listed in your dictionary for each of the following words?

> about, appeal, belt, direct, field, fix, free, give, go, it, place, play, point, protest, set, spring, stay, strike, walk, work

Prepare for class an oral or written discussion of *one* of these words; develop your report around these questions: Which meanings are the most common? Which meanings seem most unusual? What idiomatic phrases does the word appear in? To how many parts of speech does it belong?

EXERCISE 4

Give the derivation (origin) of these words:

> agnostic, agriculture, April, bazooka, biped, boondoggle, cape, Christian, football, magenta, marathon, meander, microscope, nicotine, pastor, police, professor, sadism, Thursday, traitor

EXERCISE 5

With the aid of your dictionary, list three or more synonyms for each of the following:

> bad, building, defend, enthusiasm, faithful, greedy, heavy, play, strength

(If your dictionary does not carry a list of synonyms for each of these words, ask your teacher about other source books you can use.)

EXERCISE 6

List one or more antonyms for each of the following:

chaotic, fabulous, fair, free, huge, lean, obscure, pleasant, refined, slow

(See the note in Exercise 5 about consulting your teacher.)

EXERCISE 7

When the following words begin with a capital letter, they mean one thing. When they begin with a small letter, they mean another. For each of the following, distinguish both meanings:

chinook, derby, husky, polish, revere, sac, scotch, seine, utopia, warren

EXERCISE 8

With the aid of your dictionary, answer the following questions:

1. *Bomb* may be used as what parts of speech?
2. What is the meaning of *S.P.Q.R.?*
3. Can *cabbage* be used as a verb?
4. What is the meaning of the phrase *in status quo?*
5. What was O. Henry's real name?
6. Can *how* be a noun?
7. Can *dieing* ever be a correct spelling?
8. Where was ancient Ilium?
9. What is minestrone?
10. What is the meaning of the mathematical symbol $<$?

LR2. Using a Library

If you are a normally alert and curious person who wishes to become better informed about one or a thousand different subjects, the library should be the first stop in your quest for knowledge. It may not be the last or only stop, but millions of library users and book lovers insist that no other source can provide greater riches. Learning to use a library intelligently can lead to a less monotonous, more exciting, far richer life for everyone.

One primary reason for attending school, according to many students, is to make friends. If you will learn to use them sensibly and resourcefully, the best and longest-lasting friends you or anyone else is ever likely to make in school are the library and a good dictionary. (See Section LR1.)

But the resources and genuine pleasures of neither a library nor a dictionary can be yours until you learn how to use them intelligently and without waste of time and motion. Libraries differ greatly in actual content and physical arrangement, yet the basic principles that determine library organization are sufficiently standardized to enable you to use *any* library, provided you understand the following:

1. The physical arrangement of a library
2. The card catalog and its uses
3. The uses of periodical indexes
4. Reference books and their resources

LR2a. PHYSICAL ARRANGEMENT

Before losing time through a trial-and-error method of discovering the resources of the school or public library you use, devote a free hour (or several of them) to a tour of its physical arrangement. Your use of a library, any library, will be far more efficient if you know the location of the main items you may wish to use.

Examine the main reading room, reserved-book room, study alcoves, reference section, and periodical room. Your particular library may not be arranged to include such divisions, but it will have an equivalent organization, on either a smaller or larger scale. You should find out where the loan desk and card catalog are located and where current magazines and newspapers are filed. Books of fiction (novels and stories) are arranged in most libraries in sections by themselves, shelved alphabetically by authors. Stroll in the room or section where reference books are located and discover the kind and location of books there. In short, "case the joint" thoroughly. Doing so will save time, trouble, annoyance, and disappointment for you, your teacher, and the library staff.

A large school or public library may have available a handbook that explains the organization of the library and sets forth regulations for its use. If so, examine this publication carefully. In addition, both your teacher and librarian will be eager to answer any reasonable questions you may have about the physical arrangements of the library and the most efficient means of using its resources.

LR2b. THE CARD CATALOG

A large library contains a vast amount of material of varied kinds. Even a small library has a wealth of resources that will bewilder one unaccustomed to them. The key that will open this treasure (or at least its collection of books and bound magazines) is the card catalog.

This index to a library consists of 3 × 5 inch cards filed alphabetically in long trays or drawers and located in a series of filing cabinets. Book information may be found in a card catalog in three ways: (1) by author, (2) by title, (3) by subject.

In most libraries, every nonfiction book is represented by at least three cards. If you know the author or the title of a book, you will most easily get needed information from an author or title card. If you know the name of neither, consult the subject cards for books dealing with the subject about which you are seeking information.

In addition to unlocking the resources of a library, the card catalog provides the call number by means of which each book is located on the shelves. Many libraries are arranged so that all books are placed on open shelves easily accessible to readers. If this is the system used in your library, then the call number will help you quickly locate the volume you are seeking. In other libraries, the main collection of books is shelved in closed stacks. In order to get a book, you must fill out a call slip furnished by the library and present it at the circulation or loan desk. A copy of the book you wish will be located by a library worker, through the use of its call number, and then made available to you.

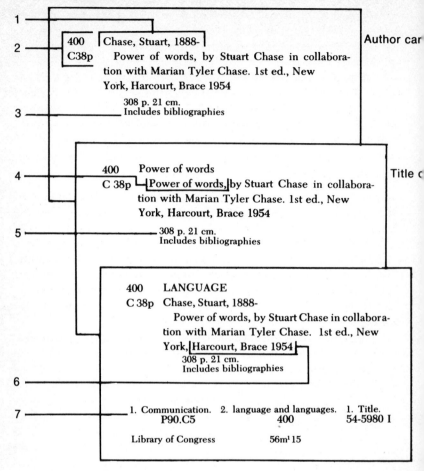

1. Author and date of birth
2. Call number
3. A bibliography is included
4. Title
5. Number of pages
6. Publisher and date of publication
7. Other headings under which the book is listed

In every library, books are arranged according to a definite system, the notational expression of which is the first part of the call number. The two classification systems most commonly used in the United States are the Dewey decimal classification and the Library of Congress classification. The former, named for its developer (Melvil Dewey, an American librarian), is more often found in high school libraries than the latter, but some knowledge of each is helpful because you may find occasion to study in different libraries at different times.

Dewey Decimal System

In the Dewey decimal system, fields of knowledge are arranged in ten groups, including one group for reference or general books. Each major class and each subclass is represented by a three-digit number. Further subdivisions are indicated by numbers actually following a decimal point. On a separate line beneath the Dewey number will be found the author and book number. Books are classified in the Dewey decimal system as follows:

Dewey Decimal System	
000–099	General works (encyclopedias, periodicals, etc.)
100–199	Philosophy (psychology, etc.)
200–299	Religion (mythology)
300–399	Social sciences (economics, government, etc.)
400–499	Language (linguistics, dictionaries, etc.)
500–599	Pure science (mathematics, chemistry, etc.)
600–699	Applied science (engineering, aviation, etc.)
700–799	Arts and recreation (painting, music, etc.)
800–899	Literature (poetry, plays, etc.)
900–999	History (travel, 910–919; biography, 920–929)

In the Dewey decimal system, every book has its individual call number. An illustration: American literature has the subclassification 810–819. An edition of Longfellow's *Evangeline* has the call number 811 and beneath this the author and book number, L86e. The *811* is the Dewey decimal classification. The *L86e* is the author and book number: *L* is the first letter of the author's name, *86* the book number, and *e* the first letter of the title. With this explanation in mind, you can see now why the Stuart Chase title noted on p. 498 has the call number it does.

Library of Congress Classification

The Library of Congress classification uses letters of the alphabet followed by other letters or by Arabic numerals. Its main classes are as follows:

Library of Congress Classification	
A. General works	K. Law
B. Philosophy, religion	L. Education
	M. Music
C. History, auxiliary sciences	N. Fine arts
	P. Language and literature
D. History, topography (except American)	Q. Science
	R. Medicine
E,F. American history	S. Agriculture, husbandry
G. Geography, anthropology	T. Technology
	U. Military science
H. Social sciences	V. Naval science
J. Political science	Z. Bibliography, library science

In this system, PS 303–324 is devoted to American poetry; PS 700 on, to individual authors; PS 2250–2298, to Henry W. Longfellow. Longfellow's *Evangeline* has the call number PS 2263.

Those confused and bewildered by innumerable trays of cards filed in the card catalog see no sense in the filing system. Some libraries use a strictly alphabetical order, but most of them follow the rules outlined below.

All libraries file by entry, that is, according to what appears first on the card, whether author, subject, or title. Articles (*a, an, the*) that comprise the first word of a title are ignored. Most libraries file letter by letter, including spaces, to the end of the word. This means that the title card *The American Way* would be filed in front of the subject card AMERICANISMS just as all cards beginning with "New York" would be filed in front of the cards with "Newark" as the entry word. Libraries that use a system of strictly alphabetical order would, of course, file *–isms* before *way* and *–ark* before *York*. It may be noted that encyclopedias, as well as library catalogs, differ in this fundamental rule.

Books that are *about* an author (considered subject entries and typed in red or in black capitals) are filed after books that are *by* that author.

Author cards having the same surname as the entry word are filed according to the given name. Always note carefully the first name, or at least the initials, of an author and the *exact* title of the book you wish.

Abbreviations and numerals are filed just as they would be if the words they represent were spelled out.

When an entry name is the same, all authors by that name precede all subjects, and all subjects come before all titles. Hence, Washington, George (books by); WASHINGTON, GEORGE (books about); *Washington Merry-go-round* (title) are filed in that order.

LR2c. PERIODICAL INDEXES

Most libraries display current, and sometimes recent, issues of magazines on racks or in a special periodical room. Older issues of many magazines and of some newspapers are bound in book form or are recorded on microfilm. You will find what you need from back issues by consulting **periodical indexes.** These are helpful guides to articles and other material that might lie buried except for the ready aid provided by indexes.

When you consult a periodical index, turn first to the front. Here you will find full, helpful instructions for use of the volume and also a list of the periodicals indexed.

For example, here are two entries from *Readers' Guide to Periodical Literature* and their meanings.

Author entry:

MANCHESTER, Harland
What you should know about flammable fabrics. Read Digest
90:37-8+ My '67

This entry means that Harland Manchester wrote an article entitled "What You Should Know About Flammable Fabrics" that was published in *Reader's Digest* in May, 1967. The volume number is 90. The article begins on page 37 and continues on page 38 and later pages.

Subject entry:

WOMEN athletes
Giving Girls a Sporting Chance? il Sr Schol 107:18+ S 23 '75

LR
2

An article on the subject women athletes entitled "Giving Girls a Sporting Chance?" will be found in the September 23, 1975, issue of *Senior Scholastic*. The volume is 107; the page is 18.

Indexes are of two kinds. *General indexes* list the contents of magazines and a few newspapers of widespread circulation and interest. Unless you are working on some highly specialized and rather unusual subject, a general index, such as *Readers' Guide to Periodical Literature, Facts on File, The New York Times Index,* or *Social Sciences and Humanities Index,* will probably meet your needs. *Special indexes,* occasionally more helpful than general ones, restrict themselves to coverage of one particular area. *Agricultural Index, Applied Science and Technology Index, Art Index, Chemical Abstracts, Engineering Index,* and *Pyschological Abstracts* are examples of special indexes.

Here is brief comment on the ten periodical indexes likely to be of most use to you:

1. *Annual Magazine Subject-Index,* 1907–1949.

    A subject index, until discontinued, to a selected list—dealing mainly with history, travel, and art—of American and British periodicals and professional or cultural society publications.

2. *Bibliographic Index: A Cumulative Bibliography of Bibliographies,* 1937–.

    A subject index to separately published bibliographies and to bibliographies included each year in several hundred books and approximately 1500 periodicals.

3. *Public Affairs Information Service Bulletin,* 1915–.

    A cumulative subject index to current books, pamphlets, periodicals, government documents, and other library material in the fields of economics and public affairs.

4. *Facts on File,* 1940–.

    A weekly world news digest with cumulative index, including world, national, and foreign affairs, Latin America, finance and economics, art and science, education and religion, sports, obituaries, and other miscellany.

5. *Index to Legal Periodicals,* 1908–.

    A cumulative subject and author index to articles in law journals.

6. *Social Sciences and Humanities Index,* formerly the *International Index to Periodicals,* 1907–.

A cumulative author and subject index to articles in domestic and foreign periodicals dealing with literature, history, social science, religion, drama, and pure science. It is a supplement to *Readers' Guide*, below.

7. *The New York Times Index*, 1913–.
   A cumulative guide to events of national importance by reference to day, page, and column of *The New York Times*. Material is entered by subjects, persons, and organizations. The only index to an American newspaper, it is an indirect guide to events in other newspapers.

8. *Nineteenth Century Readers' Guide to Periodical Literature*, 1890–1899, with supplementary indexing, 1900–1922, 2 vols.

9. *Poole's Index to Periodical Literature*, 1802–1906.
   An index of articles, by subject only, in American and British periodicals, 7 vols.

10. *Readers' Guide to Periodical Literature*, 1900–.
    A cumulative index, most useful to the general reader, to over 100 popular and semipopular magazines. Entries are according to author, subject, and fiction title.

LR2d. REFERENCE BOOKS

Any book can be used for reference, but those that really merit the name are condensed, authoritative, conveniently arranged, and up to date. (You should remember, however, that because the preparation of a genuine reference book is expensive in time, money, and effort, it cannot be revised and reprinted very often.)

In many libraries, reference books are available on shelves open to students or on tables in a special reference section. Your teacher or the school or reference librarian can tell you which of the scores of reference books at hand are likely to be most helpful with a particular subject. In addition, if your library has a copy of any of the following titles, examine it carefully for useful, time-saving hints on using reference books:

General Reference Guides

Barton, Mary Neill. *Reference Books: A Brief Guide for Students and Other Users of the Library*, 7th ed. Baltimore: Enoch Pratt Free Library, 1970.

LR
2

Murphey, Robert W. *How and Where to Look It Up*. New York: McGraw-Hill, 1958.

Prakken, Sarah L. *Reader's Adviser: Layman's Guide to Literature*, 12th ed. New York: R. R. Bowker, 1974.

Sheehy, Eugene P. *Guide to Reference Books*, 9th ed. Chicago: American Library Association, 1976.

Wynar, Bohdan S., ed. *Reference Books in Paperback: An Annotated Guide*, 2d ed. Littleton: Libraries Unlimited, 1976.

Reference works are so numerous and so varied in content and quality that no fully adequate discussion can be provided here. But you should become acquainted with at least such important works as these:

General Encyclopedias

Collier's Encyclopedia. 24 vols. (Kept up to date with an annual volume, *Collier's Year Book Covering National and International Events.*)

Columbia Encyclopedia, 3d ed.

Columbia-Viking Desk Encyclopedia, 2d ed.

Encyclopaedia Britannica. 30 vols. (Kept up to date with an annual volume, *Britannica Book of the Year: A Record of the March of Events.*)

Encyclopedia Americana. 30 vols. (Kept up to date with an annual volume, *The Americana Annual: An Encyclopedia of Current Events.*)

Lincoln Library of Essential Information.

New International Encyclopaedia. 25 vols. (Kept up to date with an annual volume, *New International Year Book: A Compendium of the World's Progress.*)

Seligman, Edwin R. A. and Alvin Johnson, eds. *Encyclopaedia of the Social Sciences* (commonly known as *E.S.S.*). 15 vols. (Less comprehensive than the other volumes listed, it deals with many subjects directly and indirectly related to the social sciences.)

World Book Encyclopedia. 22 vols. (Kept up to date with an annual volume, *World Book Year Book: An Annual Supplement.*)

General Dictionaries

(See Section LR1.)

Funk and Wagnalls New Standard Dictionary of the English Language.

Murray, Sir James A. H., and others, eds. *A New English Dictionary on Historical Principles*, reissued as *The Oxford English Dictionary.* 13 vols. (Commonly referred to as the *NED*, *N.E.D.*, *OED*, or *O.E.D.*)

The Random House Dictionary of the English Language.

Webster's New International Dictionary of the English Language.

Yearbooks

In addition to the annual yearbooks of the various encyclopedias (see above).

Annual Register: A Review of Public Events at Home and Abroad (British).

Europa Yearbook. 2 vols. (Vol. I, Europe; Vol. II, Africa, The Americas, Asia, Australasia.)

Information Please Almanac. (Miscellaneous information in compact form.)

International Yearbook and Statesmen's Who's Who. (Data on countries and political leaders.)

Statesman's Year-book: Statistical and Historical Annual of the States of the World. (Over 100 annual volumes have been published.)

United Nations Yearbook.

World Almanac and Book of Facts. (Miscellaneous information.)

In addition, your library probably has many other encyclopedias, handbooks, and dictionaries. Special reference works are available dealing with subjects such as biography, business and economics, education, drama and the theater, history, language, literature, music and dance, painting and architecture, philosophy and psychology, religion, and science. Some of these special-subject reference books will be useful and helpful. Once again, a good reference book is the place where you should start—but only *start*—any research project you have.

EXERCISE 9

After you have become familiar with your library, choose three of the following sentences. Use each as the first (topic) sentence for a paragraph. Develop each idea into a paragraph of about 100–150 words.

1. Several things impressed me about our library.
2. The ___ room in the library is an interesting place.
3. Here are directions for borrowing books from the library.
4. The library has a ___ room.
5. The library is a busy place.

EXERCISE 10

Make a floor plan of the main reading room of your school library, showing the location of shelves, tables, and any special sections devoted to particular kinds of books or periodicals.

EXERCISE 11

In your library, what is the (1) most recent book by Margaret Mead, (2) most recent book about Mead, (3) most recent magazine story or article by Mead, (4) most recent article about Mead, (5) most recent review of a book by Mead?

EXERCISE 12

How many books does your library have about Queen Elizabeth II, Langston Hughes, Eleanor Roosevelt, Winston Churchill? Copy the title and author of one book about each person named.

EXERCISE 13

Who are the authors of the following works?

1. *An American Tragedy*
2. *Wuthering Heights*
3. *Dombey and Son*
4. *Henry Esmond*
5. *Ship of Fools*
6. *A Raisin in the Sun*
7. *Robinson Crusoe*
8. *Madame Bovary*
9. *War and Peace*
10. *My Antonia*

EXERCISE 14

Who were the following? What did they do? When did they live? When did they die? (1) Thomas à Becket; (2) Thomas Aquinas (3) Thomas Hardy; (4) Thomas Henry Huxley; (5) Thomas Woodrow Wilson; (6) Thomas Carlyle; (7) Thomas A. Edison; (8) Thomas Jefferson.

EXERCISE 15

List sources in which you could best find the following:

1. A brief biography of one of your two United States senators
2. A quotation from Shakespeare when you remember only one key word
3. The total number of baseball records broken in the 1966 world series
4. A synopsis and analysis of Arthur Miller's play, *Death of a Salesman*
5. A recent biographical sketch of choreographer Twyla Tharp
6. A list of essays and articles about Sylvia Plath that have appeared in books and magazines
7. The origin of the English word *barrister*
8. Whether the Garrick Club was an organization, a golf club, or a weapon
9. A good general discussion of American jazz
10. A recent magazine article on inheritance taxes

LR
2

EXERCISE 16

What references would you consult in order to locate the following:

1. An account of the origins and customs of St. Valentine's Day
2. A summary of the history of the Negro in American theater
3. An evaluation of the work of the German composer, Ludwig van Beethoven
4. A report of recent developments in undersea exploration
5. A brief discussion of the career of Cyrus Vance that would include his present position
6. Information about religion, culture, and racial distribution of Hawaii
7. A scholarly discussion of lobbying followed by a bibliography
8. A list of magazine articles concerning the relationship of smoking to cancer
9. The date of the birth and death of the American poet Emily Dickinson—without using a book
10. The source of the following quotation: "To the victor belong the spoils."

LR3. Speaking

This handbook emphasizes *writing,* an important and involved series of processes that requires close attention and intelligent, hard work. And yet it is obvious that we *speak* a thousand words for every one that we write. It is also true that writing and speaking share one common goal: *communication.* Consequently, some consideration of speaking should shed light on the aims and purposes of communicating orally as well as in writing.

LR3a. DIFFERENCES BETWEEN ORAL AND WRITTEN COMPOSITION

We are normally more relaxed in speaking than writing, less concerned with rules and errors. But just because speaking comes more naturally to us than writing, this does not mean that speech has no requirements, no aims, no goals. In fact, the circumstances of speaking impose conditions that are sometimes more difficult than those of writing.

For example, a spoken message usually has only one hearing. The speaker who does not immediately gain the attention and interest of listeners has lost them forever; a reader can always go back and reread. Again, one's hearer cannot usually meditate upon something a speaker has said without losing what follows. For these two reasons, oral style markedly differs from written style.

As a speaker, your sentences are properly shorter than most of those you use in writing. Language is usually more direct and simpler in speech than in writing. A reader and writer are normally separated, but in most instances a speaker and listener are thrown into close association. The reader is usually alone or in a quiet room free from distractions. The listener, conversely, is normally surrounded by others and is sometimes distracted by them. Even when following a speech over TV or the radio, a listener's mind may wander, and what is lost cannot be recaptured. Finally, the speaker's voice and gestures are important considerations that influence oral communication but have no exact counterparts in writing. In short, speaking is more widespread than writing can ever be, is faced with more problems of delivery, and needs to be worked at to be genuinely effective. A speech has been called "an essay on its hind legs," but all speeches and all speaking are much more than just that.

There is a final critical difference between writing and speaking. You can rewrite until your thoughts are clear, well organized, and effective. But you usually cannot "retalk."

LR3b. CONVERSATION

Conversation is a universal form of social activity and our most important means of communicating with others. The good conversationalist—one who listens courteously and attentively to others and also has something interesting to say—is welcomed everywhere. A lack of opportunities for exchange of talk can produce irritation, boredom, and even serious mental disorders. One of the most severe of all prison punishments is solitary confinement.

LR 3

Good conversation—a genuine meeting of minds—has nothing to do with mere talkativeness, such as chatter about dates, games, clothes, food, and the weather. Conversation is a stimulating pastime when it represents an honest interchange of facts and opinions. Superficiality may save one the trouble of clarifying or defending a position in a conversation, but it actually wastes the time of both speaker and listener.

How can one become a good conversationalist? Here are a few suggestions:

1. Be sincere but also tactful and friendly. A spirited discussion may be argumentative—a group of people will seldom agree about any matter of real consequence—but one can state opinions firmly and frankly without hurting the feelings of others, without being rude and brusque.

2. Try to find out as much as you tactfully can about the person to whom you are talking. For example, if you are left with the guest of honor at a reception, a stranger at a party, or a teacher at a school function, do not talk about yourself but try to draw the other person out. You probably will learn some highly interesting facts. Even if you don't, your listener will not fail to be flattered by your interest and will consider you an excellent conversationalist. A good conversationalist, as a matter of fact, is a good listener.

3. Study every conversation you have an opportunity to overhear or engage in. Analysis of such conversations will indicate that the best talkers are those with the largest fund of interesting experiences or, better yet, the most familiarity with subjects of greatest interest to the people in the circle. You will also observe that the best conversationalists do not talk constantly and are fully capable of quiet listening.

4. Try to get, and keep, informed about subjects of timely interest: current events, political affairs, personalities in the limelight, music, sports, art, and literature. Read as much as you can: books, worthwhile magazines, a daily newspaper. Try to remember good stories you hear or read, funny or interesting incidents that happen to you or your friends, amusing or significant happenings you see or read about.

5. Practice conversation. Join in good talk whenever you can. Listen in on good conversations when you have the opportunity to do so without being a pest or an eavesdropper.

LR3c. GROUP DISCUSSION

Various types of public discussion are in general use today, but all have basically the same purpose: to pool the information of a group and try to find a satisfactory approach to the problem under discussion. Hundreds of thousands of people have had an opportunity to speak in public through discussion groups; millions have heard group discussions on TV and radio programs.

1. The single-leader type

This kind of program often follows a speech and provides an open-forum period during which members of the audience may address questions or remarks to the speaker. The speaker may preside, or someone may act as moderator and direct questions to the speaker. If no formal speech is involved, a leader may recognize speakers from the audience, guide the discussion, and summarize remarks at the end of the session. Most assemblies and parliamentary bodies follow a system of this type and are governed by specific rules of conduct and order.

2. The panel, or round table, type

A group of experts or well-informed people, literally sitting around a table, discusses various aspects of a selected topic. The discussion, usually informal, resembles a spirited conversation. The function of the moderator is to keep the talk going, to sift out agreements where possible, to summarize the argument for the audience at the end. Panel discussions occur frequently on TV and radio programs.

3. The town meeting type

A group of experts—usually four—discusses opposing attitudes toward some important public question. Each speaker is given at least one opportunity to reply to another's argument. The audience is provided chances to enter the discussion and to ask questions of the speakers. A moderator presides over the meeting, introduces the speakers, and controls audience participation.

4. The debate

Formal debate has characteristics in common with more informal discussions, but it is closely controlled by rules. This

LR
3

form of intellectual sport is far less popular now than in previous years, but it continues to crop up in political campaigns and is still encouraged by debating coaches at numerous schools and colleges. In formal debates, the proposition to be argued is carefully formulated so as to avoid ambiguity and ensure direct clash of opinion. Opposing members are organized into teams, each with a captain. Each speaker is usually allowed to speak twice in a prescribed order; a rigid time limit is imposed. A judge, or a board of judges, awards a decision to the team that has played this intellectual game more skillfully.

EXERCISE 17

Write a 300-word description of the best conversationalist you know.

EXERCISE 18

Listen to what you consider a typical conversation between two friends or schoolmates. Summarize it for the class, using direct quotations if you can. Criticize the conversation from the point of view of Section LR3b.

EXERCISE 19

Find an example of an interesting conversation in one short story from your book of readings. Read it to the class and tell why you think it is interesting and effective.

EXERCISE 20

Listen to a television or radio speaker who interests you. Prepare a report, oral or written as your teacher directs, that analyzes this speaker's performance in the light of comments made in Section LR3.

EXERCISE 21

Find an interesting modern speech in a collection or in an issue of *Vital Speeches*. Prepare a detailed outline of it, including purposes and central theme, and list the rhetorical devices the speaker used.

EXERCISE 22

Prepare a three-minute speech to be delivered to the class on a subject you have previously used for a composition. In advance, hand in an outline of the speech and a summary of the differences between the speech and the composition.

LR4. Listening

You do a lot of reading and writing in school, but you *listen* much more often than you do either. It may be fair to say that school essentially provides an opportunity to listen. Certainly, much of what we know—including the prime ability to speak our language—has come through our ears.

Listening is a learning tool, perhaps the most significant one available to us whether in school or out. When we understand this fact, we discover that nearly everyone within hearing distance becomes a potential source of information. A good listener is in a position to learn far more than the person who pays little attention or who talks incessantly.

LR4a. BEING A GOOD LISTENER

Ability to listen is directly related to how much opportunity we have to learn by ear. A person talking to you is usually affected by how you listen. If you are attentive, you help the speaker. Inattentiveness acts as a brake on the person speaking, who will sometimes falter, stop, or lose interest in continuing. (Ask any teacher why she or he feels more effective in certain classes than in others.)

Try an experiment. In an empty room, talk out loud to yourself about some simple fact or happening. Your words may not flow smoothly; you may become confused, bored, or listless. Ask someone into the room and explain the fact or happening again. Probably you will find doing so far less difficult. We all *need* listeners, good listeners; without them, we are mentally lost as we talk. Consequently, when we are on the receiving end of oral information, we have an obligation to help produce effective communication by being attentive and receptive. And remember that good listening is not easily faked. Facial expressions, body posture, eye movements, and gestures betray the poor listener and support the good one.

LR4b. TAKING NOTES ON LECTURES

Some students fail to take good lecture notes because of inattentiveness, but perhaps even more fail because they attempt to write down too much of what is being said. Many students feel that they should transcribe as many of the lecturer's words as possible. Actually, efficient note-takers spend most of their time listening and a minor amount writing. They listen carefully and *think* about what they are hearing, with comparatively little emphasis on the mechanical process of writing. They know that neither food nor ideas can be nourishing unless they are digested.

Properly proportioning time between listening and writing is found in the *précis* system of note-taking (see Section SC3). That is, you listen for the period of time it takes a speaker to make a point, and then you write down that point in a one-sentence summary. A classroom talk, for example, is usually organized so that the teacher makes a series of points (comparable to the topic sentences of written paragraphs; see Section P1) that support a main idea. Catch these points and summarize them.

This kind of note-taking requires practice, but actually the amount of time you need to listen and to write will become more obvious as you gather experience in learning how talks, lectures, sermons, and so forth are organized. When you become more skilled at précis writing, you will find your notes more useful. For one reason, they will contain central ideas. Also, they will help you remember the facts that should be in your mind because you were listening and not writing constantly during the lectures.

Here are two worthwhile suggestions: (1) Leave ample space around each sentence that you write in your notebook; (2) As soon as possible after a talk, review your précis notes and, where possible, expand them with whatever they bring to mind about the lecture. In this way you will produce a more effective set of notes depending less on memory, yet your note-taking will not have interfered with attentive and creative listening.

LR4c. LEARNING TO LISTEN WHILE LISTENING TO LEARN

Compared to reading, listening is sometimes a faster and more efficient means of gathering information. If you need to learn something about a subject quickly, you can often find an authority who is likely to speak in terms you can understand. Depending upon your interest and attentiveness, this expert may select and consolidate information to give you an accurate view of the subject, a view that might require many hours of reading to acquire. Furthermore, if you do not understand something, you can ask a question and get immediate clarification. Listening is no substitute for reading but on occasion is surely a complementary learning tool.

Also, writing that may seem difficult and even dull can often be understood and appreciated when it is listened to. The plays of Shakespeare are a good example. They were written to be heard and are at some disadvantage when presented simply as words on a page. However, if you first hear one of the plays and then read it carefully, the visual experience is increased and your chances of really appreciating Shakespeare are greatly enhanced. It is rarely difficult to find a friend who will join you in reading aloud. Also, if you have access to a record player, investigate the spoken-word records now produced in quantity and available in many school and public libraries. On such records accomplished speakers and actors read classical literature and famous authors read their own writings. They truly bring alive our literary heritage.

Finally, good listening is one of the best-known ways for improving language facility. This fact probably stems from early childhood, when we learned to talk by listening to and imitating our elders. The principle remains at work regardless of how old we are. Otherwise, how can one explain the large amounts of time and money wisely expended, for example, on language laboratories? In school, you have many opportunities to listen to accomplished speakers in public-speaking situations, in classrooms, and in conversation. Use them.

LR4d. LISTENING OUTSIDE OF SCHOOL

When you leave school, your ability to listen may become more important than ever. Adults spend at least half their communication time in listening. That poor listeners are expensive and expendable employees is being increasingly recognized in the business world. Indeed, many of our most important affairs depend on listening. What does a jury do? It listens, sometimes to millions of words of testimony, and then decides about the case on trial. The way one votes in an election depends to a large extent upon one's ability to listen. Listening situations and opportunities confront us many times every day. What else can and should one expect in a nation that has millions of television sets, more radios than bathtubs, and several million *new* telephone installations every year?

EXERCISE 23

You may have acquired some bad listening habits that thwart your attempts in learning to listen while listening to learn. These habits will be less difficult to overcome if you are aware of them. Honestly consider the following faulty listening habits. Do you recognize any of them in yourself?

Write a paragraph analyzing your problems with *one* of these patterns of listening:

1. **Supersensitive listening.** Some persons refuse to listen to anything that does not agree with their own private thoughts. Hearing statements that they do not like, they immediately plan a rebuttal and stop listening to what the speaker has to say. Perhaps they should make it a policy to hear the speaker out before making a final judgment.

2. **Avoiding difficult explanations.** If something is difficult to understand, many listeners tend to give up too easily. They blame the speaker for not being clearer. The remedy: go out of your way to listen to material that is hard to grasp. Stick with the subject from beginning to end and make a concerted effort to force yourself to listen. Listening requires practice, just as writing does.

3. **Premature dismissal of a subject as uninteresting.** If a speaker's material seems dry, some of us use that impression as a rationalization for not listening. We feel that if a speaker's material is not stimulating, it is not worth hearing. Such an opinion is not always correct. Someone once remarked that there are no uninteresting subjects, only uninterested people. When you form the habit of listening attentively, many previously dull subjects seem to take on new life. Have you never become friends with, or even fallen in love with, someone whom you used to consider dull and uninteresting?

4. **Finding fault with a speaker's delivery or appearance.** Sometimes we become so deeply involved in a speaker's delivery or appearance that we cannot concentrate on what is being said. If the speaker's manner or appearance creates an unfavorable impression, we lose interest. Conversely, a speaker's looks or manner may cause romantic or other dreams that distract us with equal loss of comprehension. The most important task in listening is to learn what the speaker says, not the way it is said or how the speaker looks when saying it.

LR5. Reading

Writing and **reading** are two closely linked parts of one process: the communication of moods, thoughts, and emotions. When you write effectively, you convey ideas and feelings to others; when you read well, you receive from others their ideas and feelings. Learning to improve your writing will help also to improve your reading.

It has not been fully proved that all good writers have been efficient readers, but generations of high school students and their teachers have discovered a striking parallel between efficient reading and effective writing. The powerful influence of television, radio, motion pictures, and varied audiovisual devices may eventually alter the situation, but at least for now a good general education cannot be acquired by anyone who cannot read both accurately and thoughtfully.

LR5a. READING TO COMPREHEND

Much of our reading is neither accurate nor thoughtful. When we read a newspaper, a light short story, a mystery, or a comic book, we are usually seeking relaxation, and we naturally skip and skim. Ordinarily, such reading fare as this neither deserves nor receives careful attention. But all too often we attempt to read meaty fiction and drama, closely reasoned essays, carefully wrought poems, and fact-packed textbooks in the same way. When we do, we receive all too little of the meaning intended and thus grow bored or discouraged. Reading to understand does not necessarily mean reading with speed and never involves reading with inattention and lack of concentration. The reading of genuinely important material must be painstakingly careful.

Reading for comprehension means reading for the following:

1. To gain and understand accurate information and ideas
2. To recognize organization and style
3. To interpret what is read in terms of personal experience
4. To analyze and evaluate

LR5b. SPEED IN READING

Reading effectively is reading with *both* comprehension and speed. Through a conspiracy of silence in high schools, until recently little attention was given to rapid reading. But the necessity for reading with reasonable rapidity has finally been recognized, and numerous steps have been taken to achieve this end. The necessity for learning to skip and scan certain kinds of material is now considered as important as learning to read other kinds of material with care and concentration.

An efficient reader reads thought units, not word by word. The technique involved is connected with the number of fixations the eyes make as they move across a page. Our aim should be to reduce the number of fixations, to lengthen the span of our eye movements. Our reading rate will increase as we learn to do this efficiently and so will our comprehension. A skillful reader does not work with isolated units but with context—what precedes and follows the particular material being looked at. A good reader rarely loses time by having to refer to the beginning of a sentence or paragraph. Rather, the thought will have been carried through in one series of lengthened glances.

The best advice for learning to read with speed as well as comprehension is to "read with your head, not with your eyes." Doing this will enlarge comprehension by reducing the number of fixations and increasing concentration. Practice finding main thoughts in a passage and separating them from subordinate thoughts. Learn to find key words and key sentences and to distinguish them from purely illustrative material. These steps will greatly increase reading speed without reducing the even more important matter of comprehension. Your school may maintain a special reading class or laboratory designed solely for the purpose of helping you learn to read with greater speed and understanding; if so, consult your teacher about it.

The reading rate of the general literate population of this country is about 250 words a minute with an attained comprehension of about 70 per cent. This may seem a rapid rate, but actually it is about the sixth-grade level. As a high school student, you should be able to read much more rapidly than this, although one must never forget that different kinds of material require different reading speeds.

LR5c. READING AS A READER

When you read as a *reader*, your purposes should be to acquire information, to form opinions, to draw conclusions. You try to stock your mind with ideas for use in thinking, discussion, and writing. You consider new problems, answers to questions, visual details that widen your experience and understanding. Careful reading of any selection should lead to an understanding of the central theme and purpose as well as the organization of main divisions and supporting material. Efficient reading of a selection will also enable you to answer these questions:

What is the author attempting to do?
How well does she or he succeed in this attempt?
What value has the attempt?
Has the author affected me personally?

LR5d. READING AS A WRITER

When you read as a *writer*, you should focus not only on the approaches mentioned above but also upon the author's technique. It should become habitual for you to study a writer's choice and use of words, sentence and paragraph development and structure, and even such relatively minor matters as punctuation and mechanics. Look deliberately and carefully for the methods by which an author secures interest and attention: humor, irony, anecdote, reports of conversation, appeals to emotions, and the like. Reading as a writer involves reading thoroughly, imaginatively, creatively. It implies consideration of subject matter, style (the imprint of an author's personality on subject matter), and technique.

LR6. Taking Tests

Tests have become a part of your life. There is no escaping them. As a student, you face a test of one sort or another nearly all the time, whether it be ten brief questions intended to check on a reading assignment or a two-hour essay examination designed to evaluate a semester's work. But tests are not confined to course work. Some of you, for example, will take college entrance examinations. The results of these tests will be used to determine readiness for college, admission to the school of your choice. scholarship eligibility, and advanced standing. Others will take tests used by employers to evaluate skills necessary for various types of jobs. Most of you, no matter what you do, will continue to take tests for a long time to come.

It is obvious that *study* is the best preparation for most tests. Tests used for college admission and for employment evaluation, however, attempt mainly to determine general knowledge and ability. Detailed study of specific subject matter is impossible. But you can prepare for these tests by acquainting yourself with the kinds of questions that are asked. This section explains the kinds of language questions that frequently appear on various tests of general knowledge. It also contains advice on approaching tests of several other types. The accompanying exercises are designed to give you practice in answering the kinds of questions you frequently encounter.

LR6a. VOCABULARY QUESTIONS

As a general rule, the larger an individual's **vocabulary,** the greater his or her knowledge. There is a direct relationship between the size of your vocabulary and the amount of knowledge you possess. Consequently, questions dealing with **vocabulary** are commonly used on tests of general ability.

Matching Words with Definitions

In this type of question, a column of *definitions* is presented opposite a column of words to be defined. You are asked to match each word with its definition.

The best way to answer such a question is to consider, one at a time, the words to be defined. Search the opposite column for the definition that seems best. If more than one definition seems possible, go on to the next word. Narrow the field of choices by first selecting only those you are sure of.

EXERCISE 24

Number your paper from 1 to 20. Write opposite each number the letter of the group of words in the second column that best defines it.

1. **Penury**	a. marked by shrewdness		
2. **Deter**	b. express indirectly		
3. **Anticipate**	c. utter and total confusion		
4. **Proficient**	d. open to view		
5. **Instigate**	e. extreme poverty		
6. **Rebate**	f. take away		
7. **Composite**	g. a return of a portion of a payment		
8. **Wrath**	h. prevent from acting		
9. **Dire**	i. noisy in an offensive manner		
10. **Jocular**	j. urge forward		
11. **Adroit**	k. showing reverence or devotion		
12. **Imply**	l. deserving imitation		
13. **Vulnerable**	m. violent anger		
14. **Exemplary**	n. given to jesting		
15. **Pious**	o. a false idea		
16. **Blatant**	p. foresee		
17. **Rescind**	q. made up of distinct parts		
18. **Overt**	r. desperately urgent		
19. **Chaos**	s. open to attack		
20. **Fallacy**	t. well advanced in an art or occupation		

**LR
6**

Choosing from Several Definitions

In this type of question, a word to be defined is followed by four or five definitions. You are asked to select the one that offers the *best* definition. Often, more than one definition may seem to fit. You must then pick the one that fits *best*. The usual procedure is to place the letter preceding your choice in the space provided on the answer sheet or to blacken the area corresponding to the letter on a specially prepared answer sheet.

EXERCISE 25

On your paper write the number of each sentence. Next to each number, write the letter corresponding to the *best* definition.

> Example: *Sinister* means most nearly (a) serious (b) threatening evil (c) gloomy (d) sorrowful (e) difficult.
> Answer: b

1. **Tepid** means most nearly (a) foreign (b) precise (c) moderately warm (d) intensely interesting (e) hopeless.
2. **Profane** means most nearly (a) skillful (b) irreverent (c) competent (d) profound (e) pleasant.
3. **Relinquish** means most nearly (a) abandon (b) remain (c) control (d) construct (e) modify.
4. **Contrite** means most nearly (a) opposed (b) foolish (c) furious (d) decisive (e) sorry.
5. **Hypothesis** means most nearly (a) complexity (b) theory (c) feeling (d) fascination (e) indication.
6. **Garnish** means most nearly (a) direct (b) cover (c) frequent (d) embellish (e) complete.
7. **Garrulous** means most nearly (a) dangerous (b) angry (c) talkative (d) loud (e) persistent.
8. **Patent** means most nearly (a) defective (b) exact (c) quiet (d) careful (e) obvious.
9. **Impeccable** means most nearly (a) flawless (b) imperfect (c) inconsiderate (d) competent (e) workable.
10. **Fallacious** means most nearly (a) incomplete (b) faltering (c) deceptive (d) resolute (e) aggravating.
11. **Nurture** means most nearly (a) object (b) confess (c) foster (d) separate (e) fail.

12. **Repugnant** means most nearly (a) acceptable (b) modern (c) adequate (d) dreary (e) repellent.

13. **Replica** means most nearly (a) substitute (b) reproduction (c) remembrance (d) movement (e) strategy.

14. **Contrived** means most nearly (a) controlled (b) destroyed (c) artificial (d) incomplete (e) convincing.

15. **Remunerate** means most nearly (a) pay (b) enumerate (c) repair (d) rebuild (e) copy.

16. **Germane** means most nearly (a) fertile (b) pertinent (c) possible (d) sufficient (e) desirable.

17. **Subterfuge** means most nearly (a) deception (b) alliance (c) scandal (d) plan (e) escape.

18. **Dire** means most nearly (a) enough (b) pleasant (c) formidable (d) significant (e) extreme.

19. **Diminutive** means most nearly (a) positive (b) intelligent (c) small (d) direct (e) helpful.

20. **Arcane** means most nearly (a) distant (b) usual (c) conceited (d) mysterious (e) comprehensive.

Choosing Synonyms

The English language is rich in vocabulary. The richness is due in part to the fact that many words have a number of *synonyms*, words that have basically—but not exactly—the same meanings. Questions that require you to identify a word's synonym appear frequently on tests of general ability. Such questions effectively measure your ability to exploit the resources of language to the fullest.

EXERCISE 26

On your paper write the number of each item. From the choice given, select the word or group of words that most nearly means the same as the bold-faced word. Write the letter of your choice next to the appropriate number.

1. **Sanguine** (a) thorough (b) special (c) optimistic (d) particular (e) bright

2. **Precarious** (a) dangerous (b) stable (c) preventable (d) helpful (e) satisfying

LR
6

3. **Intermittent** (a) frequent (b) regular (c) unusual (d) creative (e) periodic
4. **Appease** (a) create (b) decorate (c) calm (d) distribute (e) repeat
5. **Maelstrom** (a) congregation (b) turmoil (c) thunder (d) miracle (e) steadiness
6. **Mercurial** (a) changeable (b) balanced (c) inquiring (d) new (e) daily
7. **Dissipate** (a) disperse (b) brusque (c) happy (d) organized (e) beautiful
8. **Curt** (a) talented (b) brusque (c) happy (d) organized (e) courteous
9. **Interdict** (a) please (b) intertwine (c) remove (d) frequent (e) prohibit
10. **Indigent** (a) poor (b) indecent (c) dependent (d) unhappy (e) composed
11. **Altercation** (a) movement (b) perfection (c) beginning (d) quarrel (e) reparation
12. **Proffer** (a) offer (b) exit (c) return (d) proceed (e) spread
13. **Transient** (a) perpetual (b) changeable (c) short-lived (d) different (e) automatic.
14. **Incessant** (a) irritating (b) secret (c) scarce (d) doubtful (e) unceasing
15. **Dogmatic** (a) animal-like (b) dictatorial (c) automatic (d) religious (e) efficient
16. **Obtuse** (a) dull (b) characteristic (c) fortunate (d) trustworthy (e) enthusiastic
17. **Stoic** (a) experienced (b) excited (c) average (d) impassive (e) perfect
18. **Vivid** (a) muddled (b) comparative (c) graphic (d) ancient (e) intelligent
19. **Voluble** (a) expectant (b) glib (c) domestic (d) enlightened (e) unstable
20. **Prosaic** (a) unimaginative (b) tragic (c) devoted (d) possible (e) ineffective

Choosing Antonyms

An *antonym* is a word of opposite meaning. You will frequently encounter questions that require you to choose the antonym of a given word. A word is followed by several choices, one of which is its opposite. At the outset, it is a good practice to search the choices for synonyms, which are commonly included among the choices. The immediate elimination of synonyms enables you to focus your attention upon the remaining choices.

EXERCISE 27

Each of the words given below is followed by five lettered choices. Number your paper from 1 to 20. Choose the lettered word that is most nearly *opposite* in meaning to the bold-faced word. Write the letter representing your choice next to the appropriate number.

1. **Punctual** (a) precise (b) dilatory (c) rare (d) concise (e) succinct
2. **Subsequent** (a) eventual (b) comparative (c) prior (d) subservient (e) succeeding
3. **Apropos** (a) pertinent (b) contrite (c) sensible (d) ancient (e) irrelevant
4. **Infringe** (a) respect (b) perceive (c) bestow (d) encircle (e) violate
5. **Succor** (a) neglect (b) arrange (c) administer (d) fragment (e) help
6. **Transitory** (a) temporary (b) bearable (c) permanent (d) troublesome (e) numerous
7. **Culpable** (a) responsible (b) obedient (c) innocent (d) immoral (e) anticipated
8. **Dogmatic** (a) reasonable (b) militant (c) expectant (d) rigorous (e) constrained
9. **Intrinsic** (a) necessary (b) basic (c) extraneous (d) magnificent (e) furtive
10. **Clandestine** (a) overt (b) secret (c) shadowy (d) brilliant (e) mellow
11. **Abridge** (a) offset (b) build (c) condense (d) discard (e) expand
12. **Restive** (a) simple (b) comfortable (c) reticent (d) hardy (e) patient
13. **Voluble** (a) large (b) fluent (c) reticent (d) complete (e) vexing
14. **Lachrymose** (a) happy (b) tearful (c) laden (d) brown (e) latent
15. **Migratory** (a) moveable (b) subversive (c) subtle (d) satisfied (e) stationary
16. **Orthodox** (a) sound (b) plentiful (c) usual (d) heretical (e) reactionary
17. **Prodigious** (a) abundant (b) minute (c) slow (d) deadly (e) amateurish
18. **Ingenuous** (a) real (b) rustic (c) everlasting (d) clever (e) flexible
19. **Capricious** (a) entertaining (b) steady (c) erratic (d) splendid (e) jovial
20. **Obfuscate** (a) aver (b) estrange (c) clarify (d) confuse (e) assemble

Choosing Words in Context

Words do not appear in a vacuum. They appear in *context*, surrounded by other words. Words typically have more than one meaning. Context determines the particular meaning a word has.

Your ability to use a word in context indicates your control over the various meanings of words.

In tests designed to evaluate your ability to use a word in context, blank spaces are usually provided in sentences. From a number of choices given, you are to select the one word that best fits the context.

EXERCISE 28

Each of the following sentences contains a blank space where a word has been omitted. From the choices following each sentence, select the one word that best fits the context. Number your paper from 1 to 10 and write the letters corresponding to your choices next to the appropriate numbers. (All of the sentences in this exercise are taken from the works of practiced writers.)

1. They (the Custodians of Language) hold that there is a right and a wrong way of expressing yourself, and that the right way should be ____ by works of a certain description, chief among them the dictionaries of the language. (Mario Pei)
   (a) suggested (b) prescribed (c) counterbalanced (d) eradicated (e) replaced

2. The first of all the challengers, in point of time, bulk of literature and noise, number and ingenuity of supporters, is Francis Bacon, whose claim, first advanced in 1785, rests fundamentally on the assumptions that the author of the plays was ____ and that Bacon not only knew everything but had practically a monopoly on information. (Bergen Evans)
   (a) daring (b) omnipotent (c) academic (d) omniscient (e) attentive

3. In the middle of 1964—a year otherwise marked in Russia by attempts to ____ the ordinary citizens—the Soviet Government announced a new drive to wipe out religious influences among its people. (Barbara Ward)
   (a) conciliate (b) arouse (c) insult (d) aggravate (e) compromise

4. He knew only that his clouded heart was oddly ____ with the sunny, candid autumn day. (Carson McCullers)
   (a) analogous (b) dissonant (c) different (d) temperate (e) similar

5. In Europe the frontier is stationary and presumably permanent; in America it was ____ and temporal. (Walter Prescott Webb)
   (a) ugly (b) primitive (c) transient (d) routine (e) false

6. In both cases, there was at first a ____ courtship, whose significance it was necessary to conceal from outside observers. (Mary McCarthy)
   (a) whirlwind (b) subterranean (c) desperate (d) dolorous (e) prolonged

7. Every spring in the wet meadows and ditches I hear a little shrilling chorus which sounds for all the world like an endlessly ____ "We're here, we're here, we're here." (Loren Eiseley)
   (a) confused (b) stubborn (c) reiterated (d) remote (e) disguised

8. He hadn't the remotest notion in those days that she really hated that inconvenient little house, that she thought the fat Nanny was ruining the babies, that she was desperately lonely, ____ for new people and new music and pictures and so on. (Katherine Mansfield)
   (a) pining (b) averse (c) lilting (d) reacting (e) oblivious

9. In the opening scene of the movie *Scarface,* we are shown a successful man; we know he is successful because he has just given a party of ____ proportions and because he is called Big Louie. (Robert Warshow)
   (a) clever (b) opulent (c) standard (d) satisfactory (e) lasting

10. It is curious that fire, the most impermanent of all phenomena, is precisely that which (like the sea) shows no change, but is itself an endless thread of ____ through the years. (John Lafarge)
    (a) continuity (b) amusement (c) absurdity (d) performance (e) courtesy

Completing Analogies

Verbal analogies appear frequently on tests of general knowledge. In a verbal analogy, you select, from a number of choices, the one pair of words that is related to each other in the same way as a given pair of words. Since such a question demands that you be able to analyze and identify basic relationships, it is thought to provide a good measurement of mental ability.

Every analogy begins with a pair of words written as follows: BASKET : STRAW. The symbol (:) stands for *is related to* or simply *is to*. The base pair is followed by several choices, and the whole question is written as follows: BASKET : STRAW: :(a) dress : stitch (b) house : room (c) table : leg (d) desk : write (e) blanket : wool. The symbol (::) stands for *in the same way as* or simply *as*.

LR
6

In working out an analogy, you must begin by determining the nature of the relationship that exists between the two words in the base pair. In our example, analysis indicates that *straw* is a material from which a *basket* might be made.

The next step is to study the relationships existing between the words in the pairs that make up the choices. In our example, a study of the first pair indicates that a *stitch* is that which holds the parts of a *dress* together. But a dress is not made of a stitch. In the second choice, *room* is related to *house* in that a room is a part of a house. A room, however, is not the material from which a house is made. Similarly, a *leg* is a part of a *table* in the third choice, but the basic material of a table is not a leg. In the fourth choice, *write* refers to the type of activity that often takes place at a *desk*. In the final pair, *wool* is a type of material from which a *blanket* might be made. Of all the choices given, the words in the final pair match most closely with the relationship expressed in the base pair. Consequently, choice *e* provides the best answer.

In working out analogies, you should keep in mind that the pair of words that comprises the correct answer must match the base pair in *form* as well as relationship. If, for example, the base pair illustrates a relationship between two nouns, the correct answer will also consist of two nouns. If, moreover, the base pair is made up of two plurals, the correct answer will be made up of two plurals. Sometimes even a quick examination of the choices will enable you to reject immediately choices that do not have the same form as the base pair. In the example you have just studied, choice *d* could be eliminated immediately because it is made up of a noun and a verb, whereas the base pair consists of two nouns.

Verbal analogies frequently illustrate common relationships. The following are worth noting:

1. **A part is to a whole.** *County: State*
2. **A member is to a class.** *Gold: Metal*
3. **Synonyms.** *Hard: Difficult*
4. **Antonyms.** *Simple: Complicated*
5. **A quality is to a possessor.** *Bravery: Soldier*
6. **A person is to an activity.** *Pilot: Fly*

There are, of course, other types of relationships that can best be understood through close study of the base pair.

EXERCISE 29

Each of the following questions consists of two capitalized words that have a certain relationship to each other, followed by five lettered pairs of related words. Select the lettered pair of words related to each other in the *same* way as the original words are related to each other. Number your paper from 1 to 25. Write the letters corresponding to your choices next to the appropriate numbers.

1. COW: MILK : : (a) bird: nest (b) tree: sap (c) street: curb (d) water: river (e) plum: tree.
2. TRANSPARENT: TRANSLUCENT : : (a) clear: foggy (b) night: day (c) black: white (d) frog: water (e) intelligent: dull.
3. SAKI: JAPAN : : (a) grain: Iowa (b) water: ocean (c) politics: Washington (d) Chianti: Italy (e) beer: Milwaukee.
4. CONTEMPLATION: MONK : : (a) quiet: noise (b) desk: chair (c) model: beauty (d) activity: salesperson (e) reader: magazine.
5. SAND: BEACH : : (a) paint: wall (b) water: ocean (c) farm: soil (d) gems: bracelet (e) salt: pepper.
6. MUNIFICENT: PHILANTHROPIST : : (a) inventive: scientist (b) searching: astronomer (c) competent: doctor (d) parsimonious: miser (e) circumspect: race car driver.
7. HAM: EGGS : : (a) blue: turquoise (b) meatball: spaghetti (c) wheel: rim (d) cloud: sky (e) bacon: bread.
8. ABHOR: LOVE : : (a) hope: despair (b) happiness: sorrow (c) like: enjoy (d) hate: disgust (e) fear: terror.
9. HOMER: GREECE : : (a) Frost: America (b) Naples: Italy (c) Virgil: Rome (d) Poland: Russia (e) Wordsworth: England.
10. ELEGY: POETRY : : (a) sing: bird (b) wheat: harvest (c) bread: flour (d) corn: grain (e) tractor: farm.
11. VACCINATION: SMALLPOX : : (a) doctor: disease (b) antibiotic: flu (c) caution: carelessness (d) activity: fatigue (e) condition: accident.
12. FRATERNITY: BOY : : (a) congress: representative (b) sorority: girl (c) voter: electorate (d) light: electricity (e) class: student.
13. NOCTURNAL: DIURNAL : : (a) annual: perennial (b) dark: light (c) pope: church (d) outside: inside (e) midnight: noon.
14. GRASS: SEED : : (a) map: territory (b) idea: invention (c) plant: flower (d) wall: room (e) book: reader.
15. OBESE: EMACIATED : : (a) thin: slender (b) cavity: tooth (c) obsolete: new (d) lead: silver (e) twenty dollars: fifty dollars.
16. SHE: HER : : (a) man: men (b) boy: boy's (c) yours: ours (d) boy: boys' (e) theirs: they.

LR
6

17. LIGHTHOUSE: DANGER : : (a) cold: snow (b) foundation: house (c) symptom: disease (d) deadline: work (e) ship: channel.

18. GOLD: ORE : : (a) dear: cheap (b) iron: steel (c) pearls: oysters (d) steel: iron (e) intelligence: astuteness.

19. STEAK: STEER : : (a) boat: sail (b) grass: green (c) flour: wheat (d) street: curb (e) wool: sheep.

20. SHIP: HARBOR : : (a) mountain: rock (b) house: roof (c) chrome: bumper (d) sole: shoe (e) car: garage.

21. BRAKE: AUTOMOBILE: : (a) stop: red (b) conscience: person (c) current: canoe (d) saw: tree (e) thinking: doing.

22. ALPS: EUROPE : : (a) Pyrenees: France (b) Mt. McKinley: Alaska (c) Rockies: United States (d) Andes: South America (e) Sierras: California.

23. CAREFULNESS: SAFETY : : (a) tires: automobile (b) siren: police car (c) frugality: security (d) binding: book (e) planning: success.

24. B: TWO : : (a) C: six (b) F: nine (c) X: fourteen (d) A: ten (e) M: thirteen.

25. AVIARY: PEACOCK : : (a) kennel: dog (b) fish: aquarium (c) warren: rabbit (d) covey: quail (e) cage: parrot.

LR6b. READING COMPREHENSION

Numerous quizzes, tests, and examinations are designed to find out how well and how rapidly you can read. Such tests usually seek to discover whether you can understand what you read, whether you can draw conclusions from your reading—that is, make judgments and inferences—and whether you can do all of this within specified and reasonable time limits. Here is an example of such a test of **reading comprehension,** based on a selection by Thomas Henry Huxley that is not light or easy reading. Concentrate as you read.

Those who take honors in Nature's university, who learn the laws which govern men and things and obey them, are the really great and successful men in this world. The great mass of mankind are the "Poll" [mob], who pick up just enough to get through without much discredit. Those who won't learn at all are plucked [dropped]; and then you can't come up again. Nature's pluck means extermination.

Thus the question of compulsory education is settled so far as Nature is concerned. Her bill on that question was framed and passed long ago. But, like all compulsory legislation, that of Nature is harsh and wasteful in its operation. Ignorance is visited as sharply as willful disobedience—incapacity meets with the same punishment as crime. Nature's discipline is not even a word and a blow, and the blow first; but the blow without the word. It is left to you to find out why your ears are boxed.

The object of what we commonly call education—that education in which man intervenes and which I shall distinguish as artificial education—is to make good these defects in Nature's methods, to prepare the child to receive Nature's education, neither incapably nor ignorantly, nor with willful disobedience; and to understand the preliminary symptoms of her pleasure, without waiting for the box on the ear. In short, all artificial education ought to be an anticipation of natural education. And a liberal education is an artificial education which has not only prepared a man to escape the great evils of disobedience to natural laws, but has trained him to appreciate and to seize upon the rewards, which Nature scatters with as free a hand as her penalties.

That man, I think, has had a liberal education who has been so trained in youth that his body is the ready servant of his will, and does with ease and pleasure all the work that, as a mechanism, it is capable of; whose intellect is a clear, cold, logic engine, with all its parts of equal strength, and in smooth working order; ready, like a steam engine, to be turned to any kind of work, and spin the gossamers as well as forge the anchors of the mind; whose mind is stored with a knowledge of the great and fundamental truths of Nature and of the laws of her operations; one who, no stunted ascetic, is full of life and fire, but whose passions are trained to come to heel by a vigorous will, the servant of a tender conscience, who has learned to love all beauty, whether of Nature or of art, to hate all vileness, and to respect others as himself.

—From "A Liberal Education," by Thomas Henry Huxley

EXERCISE 30

Answer the following questions, which are based on the selection you just read.

1. Distinguish between "Nature's university" and "artificial education."
2. What is the primary object of artificial education?
3. A liberal education has what effects upon the body?

LR
6

4. A liberal education has what effects upon the intellect?
5. A liberal education has what effects upon the mind?
6. A liberal education has what effects upon moral and social conduct?
7. Your evaluation: What do you think is meant by "Nature's discipline"?
8. Your evaluation: Can one attain the liberal education described here or is this a "counsel of perfection" and therefore impossible to achieve?

LR6c. ESSAY QUESTIONS

Probably no type of test question frightens students so much as an **essay question.** Most students would rather submit to objective tests than be faced with questions that demand somewhat lengthy answers in intelligible prose.

Essay questions, however, are necessary because they test for the type of information that objective questions tend to ignore. An essay question enables the tester to determine a student's ability to put facts into perspective, to generalize from the data assembled, and to draw subjective conclusions. The essay question can also be used to measure how well a student is able to communicate in writing.

You should approach an essay question with the same care as you would any formal written assignment. A careful reading of the question is indispensable. You must determine exactly what it is the question seeks to discover. It is also good practice to sketch out an outline before you begin to write. The preliminary steps in answering an essay question are as important as they are in planning a formal composition.

Perhaps the most difficult step in an essay answer is the framing of the first sentence of the first paragraph. It is frequently possible to restate the central part of the question as the opening sentence. Note the followng question:

> In a famous definition, Aristotle pointed out that the tragic hero was someone who was not preeminently virtuous or just, but one who came to a tragic end through some error of judgment, rather than through some essential lack of goodness. How well do you feel that Macbeth measures up or fails to measure up to Aristotle's definition? Use incidents from the play to support your judgment.

Depending upon your judgment, the central part of the question might be expressed in the first sentence of your answer as follows: "Macbeth fits (or does not fit) perfectly Aristotle's definition of the tragic hero."

Some essay questions merely require you to provide factual data. Most, however, demand that you come to a conclusion or formulate a judgment based upon your study. You must see to it that your conclusions are concretely supported by pertinent facts and examples. Moreover, the relationship between your supporting facts and your conclusion must be evident. Note that the sample question above directs students to support their answers by citing incidents from *Macbeth*.

For example, you may write that Macbeth's judgment was affected by his impatience and rashness. In an essay answer, such a statement should be supported by mention of Macbeth's determined disregard of consequences in seeing the witches again. On the other hand, if you feel that his judgment was distorted more by his fear than his rashness, you might refer to the stark terror and sense of guilt that overcame his momentary desire to spare Macduff's life. Again, you may wish to write that Macbeth's judgment was affected by weakness or his sense of pity for others; if so, you should refer to the conflict by which he is torn between a need to rely on his wife, Lady Macbeth, and his own protective love of her. Whatever your approach, your answer should consist of a conclusion or series of conclusions based on specific examples that exactly set forth what you are trying to communicate.

The body of an essay answer should illustrate the same attention to the techniques, conventions, and mechanics of writing as a formal composition assignment. Paragraphs should be unified, coherent, and amply developed. Care should be taken in spelling and punctuation. If time permits, it is a good idea to set down a rough draft before writing your final copy.

There is very little correlation between length and impressiveness. Common sense indicates that there is merit in brevity. Many students have a tendency to expand their essay answers, believing that those who evaluate them will be favorably disposed toward bulk. On the contrary, those who must read essay answers are much more impressed by pertinent material economically expressed.

EXERCISE 31

The following essay questions are representative of the type that you might encounter on semester or year-end examinations. Choose one and answer it as best you can, paying particular attention to the structure of your answer. Keep in mind that you would be graded for both content and quality of the writing.

1. Plot has been defined as a series of causally related events working up to a conclusion. A distinction can then be drawn between story and plot. Events that are chronologically related to each other comprise what we call "story." "The king died and then the queen died" constitutes the essentials of story. "The king died and then the queen died because of grief" constitutes plot. By referring to a short story or novel that you have read recently, isolate at least five events that constitute plot, indicating how each is causally related. Explain each relationship in some detail.

2. Many literary works express a theme that the author wishes the reader to understand. Identify the theme presented in a recent work that you have read. Support your judgment by referring to specific incidents in the work.

3. Relate the following quotation to one of the works you have read recently.

   Every age has its arbiters who do not grow with their times, who cannot tell evolution from revolution or the difference between frivolous faddism, amateurish experimentation, and profound and necessary change.

   —Marya Mannes

LR6d. THE COLLEGE ENTRANCE EXAMINATION

If you plan to go to college, you will probably have to take the entrance examination developed and administered by the College Entrance Examination Board. This examination, called the Scholastic Aptitude Test (SAT), is required for admission by a great number of American colleges and universities.

The SAT examination is a three-hour test designed to measure your ability to handle college-level work. It is a test of general ability, consisting of both verbal and mathematical questions. The verbal questions are, for the most part, of the type presented in this section. Questions that measure reading comprehension are also included. The mathematical section tests your ability to understand number concepts. Your score on this test is forwarded to the college that you specify when you take the test.

The SAT is a test of general ability. Consequently, it is impossible to prepare for it by mastering specific material. Familiarizing yourself with the type of questions presented in this section and in the "bulletin of information" published by the College Entrance Examination Board will provide the best preparation. You might also wish to obtain one of the many review books available that provide additional exercises of the type presented here.

It is also a good idea to take the Preliminary Scholastic Aptitude Test, which is given in October of each year. Since this test consists of questions identical to the type presented on the SAT, it provides an excellent indication of how well you might do. Your score on this test is reported only to you.

The College Examination Board also provides achievement tests in specific subject areas that are required by some colleges. These tests are offered in English, social studies, mathematics, German, Latin, Spanish, French, biology, chemistry, physics, Hebrew, and Russian. Each test is an hour long. These tests are sometimes used by colleges to verify the student's high school record.

Since 1960, some colleges have required a writing sample of all applicants. An essay of between 350 and 450 words must be written in one hour. The College Examination Board does not grade this writing sample. It merely forwards it to the college of your choice.

A bulletin of information concerning the Scholastic Aptitude Test, the achievements tests, and the writing sample is available upon request from the College Entrance Examination Board, P.O. Box 592, Princeton, New Jersey 08540.

LR 6

Index

Editor: *Laura Mongello*
Editing Supervisor: *Linda Richmond*
Design Supervisor: *Joe Nicholosi*
Production Supervisor: *Ellen Leventhal*
Permissions: *Caroline Levine*

Text Design: *Wladislaw Finne*
Cover Design: *Aspen Hollow Artservice*